The Emerging Markets Investor's Guide to Country Risk

"There has been an elephant in the room that impact investors operating in the EMDEs have been consistently ignoring. It is this elephant—the foundational and institutional playing field—that then is the cause for surprise when investments do not pan out as expected. What then transpires is investment periods are always longer, actual returns are always significantly less (if at all), and yet the market rinses and repeats. Now we finally have a book that addresses this elephant in investment assessment, adding value to the more standard approach when assessing investment risk. I look forward to this being a widely adopted tool."

—Njeri Mungai Ngaruiya, Investment Director, *Impact Fund Denmark*

"*The Emerging Markets Investor's Guide to Country Risk* stands out for its intellectual depth and practical clarity by offering a rigorous and structured synthesis of macroeconomic fundamentals, institutional quality, financial system dynamics, structural global shifts, climate exposure, and technological change shaping developing economies. Richard and Philipp are not treating Risk as a static checklist. They move beyond the traditional sovereign risk metrics to provide a dynamic framework—the "Investor's Rutter"—that resonates with real-world investment practice and equips investors and decision-makers with a disciplined methodology to interpret evolving risk signals and translate them into investment decisions. This book is a timely, analytically robust, practical, and indispensable guide for professionals navigating capital allocation in increasingly complex investment environments in the Emerging Markets. Thank you to Richard and Philipp."

—Félix Bikpo, Chairman of the Board, *The African Guarantee Fund*

"This book provides practitioners with an "Investor's Rutter" for navigating the high seas of EMDE investing. Like seafarers' rutters of old, it is painstakingly drawn from decades of the authors' experience on the frontlines. It does not offer a map in the conventional sense, nor a formula to be applied mechanically. Instead, it offers something far more valuable—a practical framework that captures the dynamic interplay of forces shaping country risk and investment outcomes. At the same time, the book is refreshingly contemporary. It recognizes that geopolitics, climate change, and AI are no longer peripheral considerations, but central factors in how we assess and price risk in EMDEs today. A highly recommended read for investors who seek not merely to better understand emerging markets, but to navigate them with greater clarity, discipline, and judgement."

—Shuyin Tang, Co-founder and CEO, *Beacon Fund*

"This is an insightful book by two seasoned emerging markets investment experts, Richard Marney and Philipp Waeber. They propose a new approach in analyzing "country risk", an essential part in the investment process in emerging markets, as such macroeconomic risks often endanger the success on the microeconomic level. With their "Investor's Rutter" they present an all-encompassing tool integrating country and macroeconomic risk analysis into the micro-analysis throughout the investment lifecycle from origination to divestment. The authors go much deeper than the usual macro-analysis. Their approach starts with assessing country and market fundamentals and emphasizes then the institutional framework in emerging markets like the rule of law or sound fiscal or monetary policies very often decisive for the long-term outcome of investments. Richard and Philipp also consider in their risk analysis the changing geopolitical landscape after the peak of globalization now followed by a US-led Western bloc and an emerging China-centered bloc. Demography, artificial intelligence, and, last but not least, climate change are also covered as macro-risks. Four case studies demonstrate the practical value of the "Investor's Rutter" which could well prove to be a very useful tool for better investment decisions in emerging markets. Overall, this is a solidly researched book deeply rooted in decades of investment experience of the two authors. Well written, well structured, with sound arguments. Highly recommended as essential reading!"

—Markus Schladt, Principal—*Equity Financing Sub-Saharan Africa, KfW*

"Marney and Waeber offer a rigorous and intellectually engaging examination of the identification and assessment of country risk drivers. They translate complex and interrelated concepts—such as institutional development and policy effectiveness—into structured, decision-oriented frameworks, most notably the Investment Climate Roadmap and the book's introduction of the "Investor's Rutter". Particularly compelling is their treatment of convergence as a dynamic and evolving process, which broadens the relevance of their framework beyond emerging markets to developed economies as well. The book successfully bridges conceptual analysis and practical application. It is an indispensable resource for investment practitioners seeking to deepen and systematize their country risk assessment and investment processes. A highly recommended contribution to the field."

—Alberto Alonzo, Co-founder and Partner, *Sustainable Food Strategies*

"Richard Marney and Philipp Waeber's *The Emerging Markets Investor's Guide to Country Risk* offers a timely and perceptive framework for professionals engaged in investment across EMDEs. The authors effectively reorient the discussion from static evaluations to a more dynamic analytical framework, introducing the "Investor's Rutter" as a rigorous instrument for interpreting evolving political, economic, and institutional signals. I appreciated how the book moves from foundational themes like macroeconomics and institutions in Part I to broader global shifts such as geopolitics and climate in Part II, with the Part IV case studies—like Tomorrow's Energy and Enterprise Bank—bringing these concepts to life through real-world application.

The structured approach and the key learnings in the closing chapters make it invaluable for investors seeking to anticipate risks rather than simply react to them. Overall, it is an essential read for those seeking to construct resilient EM portfolios in an increasingly uncertain global environment."

—Kewal Shah, Investment Officer, *responsAbility Investments AG*

"One of the finest investment books on EMDEs (Emerging Markets and Developing Economies) that I have encountered in over two decades of investing in these markets. Investing in EMDEs is inherently complex and often unstructured. Navigating them in today's already intricate global environment requires not only decades of EMDEs deal making experience but also the ability to interpret macroeconomic signals and discern patterns—not from isolated events, but from sequences of events that reveal deeper trends. Richard and Philipp have illuminated the associated risks and introduced a powerful, dynamic framework—the Investor's Rutter—to steer through uncharted waters. This invaluable tool reflects the authors' decades of hard-earned experience. Their case studies equip readers with the ability to keep an ear to the ground and act decisively before the drumbeat of change becomes unmistakably loud."

—Chris Teoh, Investment Director, *M&G Investments*

"Richard Marney & Philipp Waeber's book skillfully integrates the key factors in analyzing country risk in Emerging Markets and Developing Economies into a framework entitled "The Investor's Rutter", which is then applied in a broad range of case studies. The case studies, in addition to be varied in terms of their range of industries and scenarios, also include debriefs analyzing the cases' particulars and providing commentary based on the authors' deep experience in country risk and international portfolio management. In terms of visual appeal, Mr. Marney's watercolors of scenes from EMDEs are a colorful addition to the work. This book is even well recommended for Junior to Mid-level investment professionals with a moderate understanding of Economics. As such, it makes a valuable contribution in bridging academia with the needs of practitioners charged with managing investments in the EMDEs."

—Lynn Exton, Managing Partner-Exton & Partners Risk, *Governance & Analytics.*

"Richard and Philipp have written an essential guide for financiers and professionals in emerging markets. Their clear, practical framework for understanding EMDE systemic country risk is brought to life by rich historical and geographic context, incisive analysis, decades of in-country experience, and engaging writing. Readers will find this modern-day "investor's rutter" (or *routier*) an invaluable resource for navigating the (often) treacherous shoals, currents, and tempests of EMDE risk."

—Timothy Stubbs, Partner, *Dentons Europe*

Richard Marney • Philipp Waeber

The Emerging Markets Investor's Guide to Country Risk

Systematic Risks and the Threats to Investment Performance

palgrave
macmillan

Richard Marney
Risk Management (Senior Advisor)
responsAbility Investments
Penang, Pulau Pinang, Malaysia

Philipp Waeber
Credit Analysis & Portfolio Management
responsAbility Investments
Zurich, Switzerland

ISBN 978-3-032-26823-5 ISBN 978-3-032-26824-2 (eBook)
https://doi.org/10.1007/978-3-032-26824-2

Cover Image Credit: Greg Pease via Getty Images

This Palgrave Macmillan imprint is published by the registered company Springer Nature Switzerland AG.
The registered company address is: Gewerbestrasse 11, 6330 Cham, Switzerland

To our families and all those close to us,
for their love, companionship, and support.

Foreword

For those of us working in the development finance industry, country risk is a daily reality, not just a concept. It shapes where capital flows, how resilient investments are, and whether financing actually reaches the businesses it is meant to support.

The African Guarantee Fund (AGF) has learned from working in African countries that we need to look beyond sovereign ratings and macro indicators to fully understand country risk. These indicators matter, but they do not tell the full story. To truly assess risk, one must appreciate how institutions function, how financial systems channel capital to the real economy, and how political and legal environments influence stability over time.

Country risk is not static. It evolves. In a world where structural forces are reshaping risk faster than traditional models can capture, investors who do not rethink how they interpret country risk will increasingly misprice opportunity and vulnerability alike. A country that appears stable today may be building vulnerabilities beneath the surface. On the other hand, volatility in the short term may hide underlying strength. For practitioners, the challenge is not only to measure risk, but to interpret it and to distinguish between temporary shocks and structural shifts.

Emerging markets and developing economies have transformed the global economy over recent decades. The "great convergence" is changing the center of global growth and lifting hundreds of millions of people out of poverty. Despite these positive changes, the paths of these economies are still not smooth. Fiscal weaknesses, reliance on outside funding, exposure to climate change, demographic changes, and geopolitical shifts continue to cause different outcomes in different countries. In such an environment, capital must be deployed with discipline, and structural awareness, and investors must move beyond scoring models and develop a deeper understanding of how risks interact and change over time.

Richard Marney and Philipp Waelber give us a clear and practical framework for doing just that. Their emphasis on fundamentals—institutions, policy credibility, and broader structural context—directly tackles the challenges faced by investors operating in emerging markets. The Investor's Rutter framework presented in this book encourages a more dynamic perspective, one that embeds country risk analysis throughout the investment lifecycle rather than treating it as a one-off assessment.

I have had the opportunity to work with Richard at AGF, and I recognize in this book the same clarity of thought and practicality that he brings to our Investment Committee and Board discussions. This work reflects a practitioner's mindset: structured, disciplined, and grounded in real-world experience.

This book is a valuable resource for investors and development finance practitioners who seek to manage risk rigorously and responsibly and who understand that navigating emerging markets requires both rigor and perspective.

Constant Nzi, Group Chief Executive Officer (Interim), African Guarantee Fund

Nairobi, Kenya

Constant Nzi

Preface

It is better to be roughly right than precisely wrong.
Attributed to John Maynard Keynes et al.

The first question confronting an emerging markets investor when examining an opportunity is invariably: *"What about the country risk?"*

To answer this question, the investor typically begins with their own knowledge and experience of the geography, often supplemented by public and proprietary data, research reports, and third-party analyses. This initial assessment frames a "go/no-go" decision—whether to proceed to confirmatory diligence and, ultimately, investment approval.

At this stage, an economist is often enlisted to provide a detailed assessment of salient current and prospective country risks that could materially affect investment returns. The resulting analysis informs key assumptions in the financial model—revenue growth, interest costs, foreign exchange rates, and the like. For many investors, however, beyond a high-level sanity check on the implications for the investment's risk–return profile, the details of this analysis are skimmed in favor of a simplified "high–medium–low" country risk heat map. High-risk proposals become problematic, medium-risk cases may prompt modest tightening of structure or pricing, and low-risk countries tend to sail through.

Once approved, the investment often recedes into portfolio monitoring reports, where country risk factors are downplayed—if not forgotten entirely—until adverse economic, financial, or political developments trigger flashing red warning lights. At that point, urgent cross-departmental meetings are convened, but frequently the damage has already been done.

Not all stories unfold this way. Some institutions have developed effective capabilities to integrate country risk analysis throughout the investment lifecycle—from origination and investment committee approval to post-disbursement monitoring and, when necessary, proactive risk management. Yet if we were to grade the industry's overall performance in this regard, there remains a clear and widespread opportunity for improvement.

What explains this grade? A common culprit is the disproportionate focus on proximate rather than fundamental causes. Proximate causes relate to observable macro-financial outcomes—GDP growth or contraction, interest rate movements, exchange rate dynamics—and their immediate effects on revenues, cash flows, and valuations. Fundamental drivers, by contrast, look "under the hood" to explain *why* these proximate outcomes occur and whether they are sustainable.

Consider GDP growth. A proximate explanation may point to accommodative monetary policy or fiscal stimulus. A fundamental analysis probes deeper: a country's long-term investment in education, the quality of its institutions, the accumulation of human capital, and the incentives shaping productivity and innovation. Proximate causes are typically cyclical; fundamentals are structural. The former help explain yesterday; the latter inform tomorrow—and the days after tomorrow. For all but the shortest investment horizons, best practice requires identifying the fundamental drivers that determine whether current trends can endure.

A simple illustration makes the point. Suppose Countries A and B both fall into recession and respond with accommodative monetary policy and relaxed macroprudential constraints to encourage credit growth. In both cases, GDP recovers. How durable is that recovery? Country A operates under an independent central bank with strong policy credibility and an effective financial supervisory regime. In Country B, monetary policy is directed by the executive, and financial supervision is weak. All else equal, the odds strongly favor Country A. By examining institutional foundations—rather than headline growth figures alone—we gain a clearer view of whether recovery will prove sustainable or give way to inflation, credit impairments, and financial instability.

Yet much of the industry remains focused on static snapshots: current macroeconomic indicators, financial market metrics, political observations, and assessments of event risk—now increasingly supplemented by environmental and social considerations. These snapshots identify proximate drivers and extrapolate them forward, implicitly assuming continuity. What is often missing is a dynamic framework capable of capturing how political, institutional, economic, and financial forces interact and evolve over time. Widely used resources, such as sovereign credit ratings and standard scorecards, often lag real-time developments and overlook nonlinear risks. This reactive posture leaves investors exposed to abrupt shifts that static models fail to anticipate.

We argue for an alternative, process-oriented approach grounded in how investment professionals interpret country risk in shaping threats and opportunities. It begins with a country's fundamentals—geography, natural capital, climate exposure, demographics, and social characteristics: the *playing field*. Upon this foundation rest political, legal, and economic institutions—the *rulebook* governing behavior and incentives. Together, these shape macroeconomic and market outcomes, and ultimately investment returns in an EMDE space that presents unique and daunting challenges than developed markets, which often have more stable institutions and predictable policy frameworks, reducing the need for the same depth of dynamic country risk analysis.

But how can an investor systematically navigate this complex and evolving landscape? How can one move from static assessment to dynamic interpretation—anticipating inflection points before they erupt into headlines and market dislocations?

This book introduces the Investor's Rutter—a simple yet practical tool designed for market practioners to address these questions. The Investor's Rutter is intended to complement, not replace, sovereign credit ratings, macroeconomic models, and risk scorecards. It provides a structured, dynamic framework for interpreting political, institutional, economic, and financial signals over time. Rather than seeking to predict specific outcomes, the Rutter emphasizes disciplined interpretation: distinguishing temporary volatility from structural change, identifying emerging inflection points, and adjusting exposure as conditions evolve. And, importantly, the Rutter is consulted until the investment is finished.

The Investor's Rutter is not a predictive model but a practical decision framework that supports how investors interpret country risk across markets, asset classes, and investment horizons. This flexibility is especially valuable in EMDEs, where institutional and policy regimes can shift rapidly. Applied consistently across the investment life cycle, the Rutter integrates country risk into decision-making—not as an afterthought or crisis response, but as a core element of disciplined investment management. It is intended to complement, not replace, quantitative models and ratings by providing a structured way to interpret the signals they generate.

As we outline below, the book first surveys the economic, financial, institutional, and other topic areas underlying the elements of the Investor Rutter and then uses a series of short narratives and longer case studies to show how the Rutter assists in the navigation of the opportunities and risks created by these elements in the investment environment. In the latter, we provide a tool in the form of a flow diagram of the Investor Rutter process to assist the reader in their analysis of the respective investment cases.

At the time of going to press (March 2026), the war in the Middle East had escalated into a high-intensity confrontation, with the Strait of Hormuz largely closed to normal transit. Pressures were mounting to reopen this critical shipping route, but it was unclear how quickly a solution could be found and how durable it would be. This book does not aim to make short-term predictions. Instead, it focuses on the structural implications of geopolitical shifts and other longer-term dynamics, as discussed in Part II.

* * *

We divide the book into two broad sections.

In the first, we survey the topic areas underlying the elements of the Investor's Rutter, as follows:

- Part I (Chaps. 1–5): "Fundamentals" (macroeconomics, institutions, financial markets, and crises—causes and effects)
- Part II (Chaps. 6–10): "Context: A Changing World" (geopolitics, climate change, demographics, and artificial intelligence)

In the second, we demonstrate its use:

- Part III (Chaps. 11–13): "The Investor's Rutter: Concept and Application"
- Part IV (Chaps. 14–18): "Case Studies"

In Chap. 19, we close with a summary of key learnings.

Penang, Malaysia
Zurich, Switzerland

Richard Marney
Philipp Waeber

Acknowledgments Recognition fades; gratitude endures.

Anonymous

In writing a book of this kind, based as it is on decades of professional experience, the usual authors' acknowledgment's list of business colleagues, central bankers and financial supervisors, academics, policy makers, members of the judiciary and legal profession, and the media can easily grow to rival the length of a full chapter or more. As such, we will limit ourselves to express once again our heartfelt, but here private gratitude to a small number of individuals whose patience, generosity, and wisdom helped take this book from an initial idea to the finished product.

Competing Interests The authors have no competing interests to declare that are relevant to the content of this manuscript.

Contents

About the Authors

Richard Marney is a senior advisor for risk management with responsAbility Investments, Zurich. Over a nearly five-decade-long career, Richard has held senior management-level business development and fundraising, and executive management-level risk management and operating positions focused on EMDEs in (1) commercial and investment banking, (2) micro-finance, (3) impact investment asset management, and (4) private equity working in globally recognized financial services organizations, including BNY-Mellon and JP Morgan. Additionally, Richard has extensive experience on company boards of directors and investment and advisory committees across a broad range of sectors and regions. Along with Timothy Stubbs, he has published *Corporate Debt Restructuring in Emerging Markets: A Practical Post-pandemic Guide* (2021) and *Debt Restructuring in Emerging Markets: Effectively Navigating Local Institutional Frameworks* (2024), both with Palgrave Macmillan. Richard is a graduate of the Johns Hopkins University–School of Advanced International Studies, and University College London.

Philipp Waeber is the Lead Economist at responsAbility Investments, a leading impact asset manager specializing in private markets across diverse EMDEs. He advises the firm's credit and equity business on investment decisions and structuring to price and mitigate country risks. In close to two decades of experience as an economist, he has developed a profound understanding of what triggers crises, how they unfold, and where they leave corporates within a country. Philipp holds a bilingual master's degree in economics from the University of Fribourg, Switzerland, and is a CFA charter holder.

Abbreviations

ACWI	MSCI All Country World Index
AE	Advanced Economy
AGF	African Guarantee Fund
AI	Artificial Intelligence
ARA	Assessing Reserve Adequacy
BIS	Bank for International Settlements
CFM	Capital Flow Management
DFI	Development Finance Institution
DRC	Democratic Republic of the Congo
EECCA	Eastern Europe, Caucasus and Central Asia
EFF	Extended Fund Facility
EEZ	Exclusive Economic Zone
EMDE	Emerging Market and Developing Economy
ERM	Exchange Rate Mechanism
FCS	Fragile and Conflict-Affected State
FDI	Foreign Direct Investment
FSI	Financial Soundness Indicator
GFC	Global Financial Crisis
GFDD	Global Financial Development Database
GHG	Greenhouse Gas
IMF	International Monetary Fund
IFRS	International Financial Reporting Standard
IPCC	Intergovernmental Panel on Climate Change
MDB	Multilateral Development Bank
MENA	Middle East and North Africa
MSME	Micro, Small, and Medium Enterprise
NATO	North Atlantic Treaty Organization
NIIP	Net International Investment Position

PCI	Productive Capacity Index
SAFE	State Administration of Foreign Exchange
SDG	Sustainable Development Goal
SIDS	Small Island Developing State
TFP	Total Factor Productivity
TIC	Treasury International Capital
UNCLOS	United Nations Convention on the Law of the Sea
USD	United States Dollar
WGI	Worldwide Governance Indicator
WJP	World Justice Project
WTO	World Trade Organization

List of Figures

Part I

Fundamentals

EMDE Snapshots by Richard Marney

1

EMDEs' Macroeconomics: Growth Drivers, Policies, and Vulnerabilities

What is required for growth is not a larger pile of objects, but a different set of rules.
—Paraphrase of themes of P.M. Romer

EMDEs have undergone profound transformations over recent decades. While development and catch-up has been subject to regular setbacks and regional differences, the overall result is still remarkable. Billions of people have been lifted out of poverty and EMDEs have become a dominant contributor to global growth. In this chapter, we will take an in-depth look at EMDEs' growth trajectories and factors that have shaped them, first looking at the growth patterns and drivers, second at the role of domestic policies, and third at external vulnerabilities.

1.1 Growth Patterns and Drivers

From Crisis to Convergence

EMDEs' growth trajectory since the 1960s reveals several patterns. Initially, the way was paved with crises, starting with the 1973–74 oil shock, followed by the debt crisis in the 1980s, and concluding the century with the Asia Financial Crisis. While the oil shock hit high-income countries harder, particularly the 1980s and 1990s were rather dire for EMDEs as a whole. There is even talk of "lost decades" in Africa (1980s and 1990s) and Latin America (1980s). Aggregate real GDP per capita contracted or stagnated in these

R. Marney, P. Waeber, *The Emerging Markets Investor's Guide to Country Risk*,
https://doi.org/10.1007/978-3-032-26824-2_1

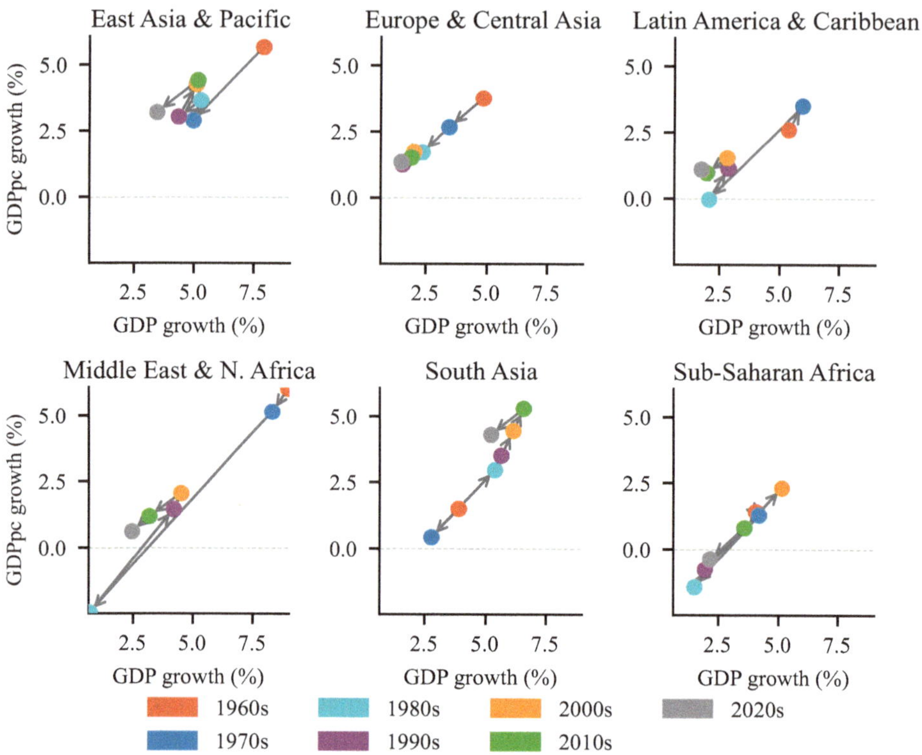

Fig. 1.1 GDP & GDP per capita growth by region (excl. High-income), decade averages. (Source: Authors' calculations based on World Bank)

regions for most of the 1980s, and only reverted to the 1980 level by the mid-1990s in the case of Latin America, and by 2010 (!) in the case of sub-Saharan Africa. The drivers of these "lost decades" were high debt burdens and tightened external financing conditions, compounded by weak institutions and policy volatility.[1] Conversely, supported by a mix of high investment, export-oriented industrialization and strong state capacity,[2] there was the "Asia miracle", in which many East Asian economies managed to sustain strong growth rates for decades (Fig. 1.1).

In 1960, East Asia had the same GDP per capita as sub-Saharan Africa, and only about half the level of Latin America. Today, East Asia has surpassed the other developing regions in terms of income levels by far (Fig. 1.2).

East Asia's per capita growth had already outpaced that of any other region by the turn of the millennium, only to accelerate further thereafter. China played a central role in that rise, after beginning market-oriented reforms in 1978 and joining the World Trade Organization (WTO) in 2001. Joining the

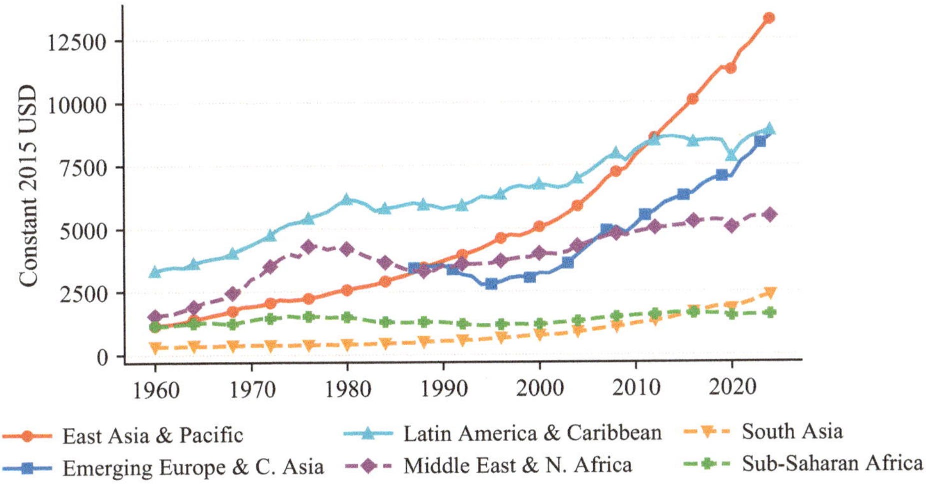

Fig. 1.2 Evolution of GDP per capita by region. (Source: World Bank)

WTO improved China's access to global markets by reducing both tariff and non-tariff trade barriers and unleashed a surge in foreign investment and technology transfer.[3] As a result, China integrated itself into the global economy and became the world's manufacturing center. China's success also lifted other EMDE, not least through its commodity hunger, benefiting commodity exporters across the world, including in Latin America and Africa.

The Asian Financial Crisis had also taught EMDE important lessons. The market trauma raised awareness not only of the benefits but also the risks of international capital flows. An earlier wave of financial liberalization was followed by policy enhancements, with many EMDEs accumulating important foreign exchange reserves and letting their exchange rates float to enhance their shock-absorption capacity. The perception of capital flow management also changed fundamentally. Economists have increasingly acknowledged risks associated with open capital accounts, including sudden stops (of capital inflows), credit booms, and asset price bubbles. There were further institutional enhancements. Included were measures, for example, aimed at greater inflation control, which helped explain greater macroeconomic stability and booming activity in EMDE since 2000. Crises also became fewer and shorter (see Chap. 4), which helped EMDE catch up with advanced economies (AE).[4] Economists coined the term "great convergence" to capture this effect, as EMDEs were finally able to narrow the income gaps to AEs. Paired with demographic shifts, rising income levels have greatly increased EMDEs' weight in the global economy, and their contributions to global GDP growth. In 2025 and measured in purchasing power parity terms, roughly 80% of

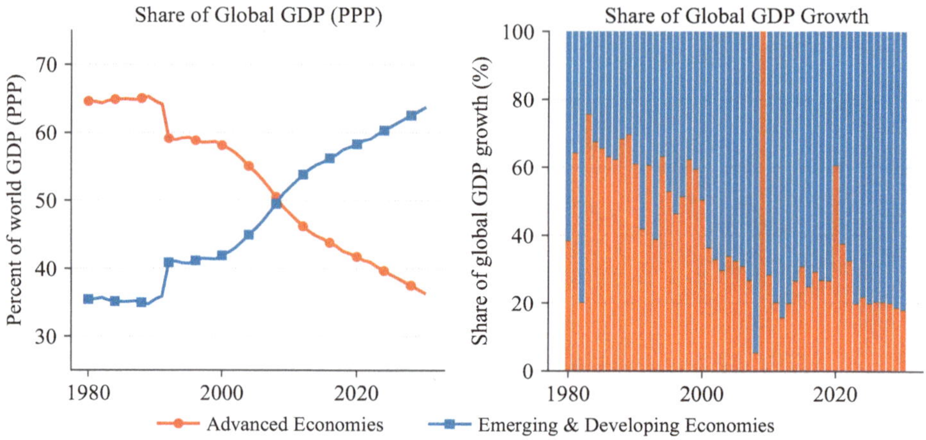

Fig. 1.3 EMDE's economic weight and their global growth contribution. (Source: IMF, authors' calculations)

global GDP growth originated in EMDE, compared to around one third in the early 1980s (Fig. 1.3).

Generally, EMDEs' annual growth potential is currently estimated at around 4%, compared to below 2% for AEs, or 3% versus 1.35% in per capita terms. Asia remains the global growth engine, contributing over half to global GDP growth in the mid-2020s. It is also the most populated region, being home to over half of the global working-age population. The heavyweights are obviously China and India, each hosting a population of about 1.4bn people, and close to one billion people of working age. Asia, too, has not been spared from a global trend of slowing population growth, an important factor weighing on the global growth potential. Only in sub-Saharan Africa does the working-age population continue to grow at a relatively steady and high pace (of around 3% p.a.), though even there total population growth displays a modest slowdown since 2010 (Fig. 1.4). How demographic shifts are expected to continue over the coming decades, and what repercussions they have on EMDEs' economic outlooks, will be subject of Chap. 8 of this book.

Asia's miracle and the generally improved EMDE growth performance since the turn of the century were accompanied by a broad-based improvement in social welfare in EMDE. For instance, extreme poverty greatly declined globally, from around 50% in 1960 to below 10% before the pandemic. Similarly, the share of global population living in low-income countries has been greatly reduced, from over 60% in 1990 to below 10% since the mid-2010s (Fig. 1.5). China's and India's reclassifications in 1997 and 2007

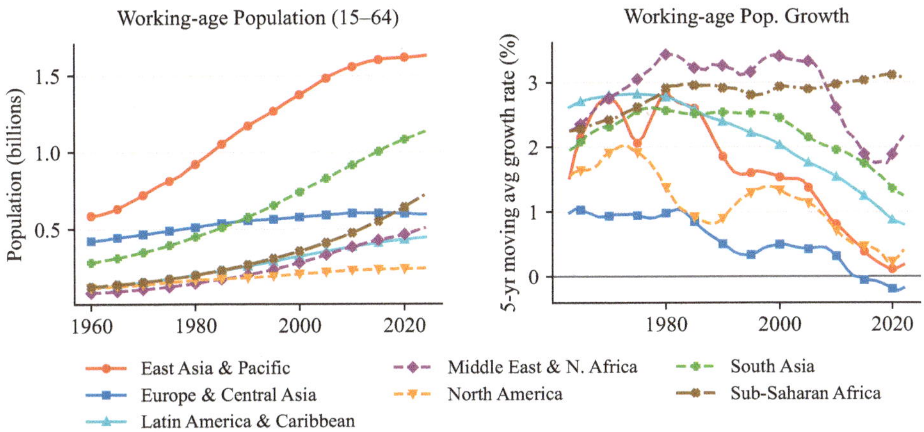

Fig. 1.4 Demographic shifts since the 1960s. (Source: World Bank, authors' calculations)

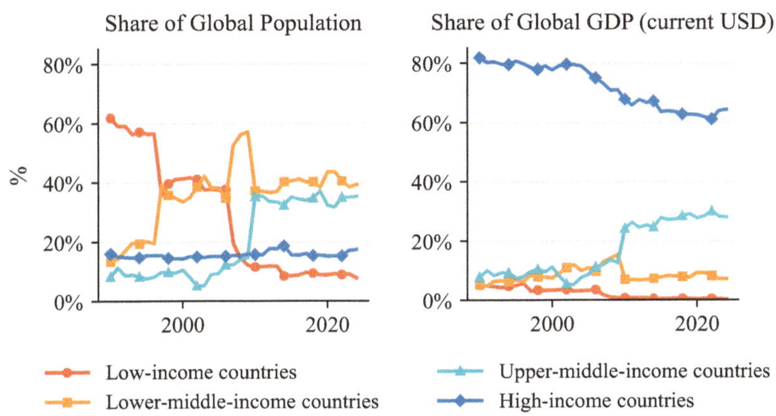

Fig. 1.5 Global population and output by income group. (Source: World Bank)

respectively explain the bulk of the improvement. Health and education indicators have also shown meaningful improvements, including rising life expectancy, declining child mortality, increased literacy, and almost universal basic education levels.

By the mid-2020s, i.e. the time of writing, EMDE were still outgrowing AEs, but some of the optimism about the great convergence was again being tempered. Furthermore, tectonic shifts were ongoing, creating much uncertainty about the global economic outlook, a topic covered in part II of this book.

Diverging Growth Trajectories Within EMDE

While the previous section of this chapter provided an overview of how EMDEs have grown in global importance since the 1960s, this chapter portrays the diversity within EMDEs. Progress has varied widely across regions and countries, with some powering ahead while others are falling behind. This heterogeneity limits the value of analyzing EMDEs solely through aggregate numbers.

Box 1.1: How China Distorts Aggregated Views on EMDE

China has grown tremendously since 1980. At the time, the Chinese economy only made up 2% of the global economy (in purchasing power parity terms). By the mid-2020s, its weight had increased to close to 20% of the global economy. Similarly, its weight within EMDE grew tremendously, from 6% in 1980 to 32.5% by 2025. With regard to GDP growth statistics, this has two important implications: First, for the period from 1990 to 2020, China's rise has lifted annual EMDE GDP growth by one percentage point a year. Second, China's structural slowdown since 2010 risks distorting aggregate EMDE growth numbers, but, somewhat surprisingly, it did not do so until the pandemic, meaning that EMDE excluding China slowed similarly to China. Only since the pandemic have the growth trajectories begun to diverge somewhat. Initially, China did much better by growing in the pandemic year 2020, when the world recorded the most synchronous economic downturn since at least the 1960s, with over 80% of countries seeing their output shrink. Not long after, China had to change course and abandon its zero-covid strategy, which depressed activity in 2022. With China's structural slowdown set to continue, the IMF's baseline projections suggest China will become a drag on EMDE growth by the end of the 2020s.China's heavy weight and its rather unique characteristics also distort many other EMDE aggregate measures. Among others, China's savings and investment rates are exceptionally high, the current account typically in surplus, external debt as a consequence very low, and the net international investment position (NIIP) even in surplus. The most exceptional—and somewhat worrying—feature though is China's indebtedness, the country having experienced a massive credit boom since the Global Financial Crisis (GFC).

In the mid-2020s, the median EMDE was growing by around 4.5%, and baseline projections by the IMF pointed towards a similar pace over the second half of the decade. Aggregate growth, though, was a bit higher, as some larger economies—including China—displayed stronger growth. In per capita terms, the difference between the GDP weighted (5.6% median) and unweighted (3.1%) growth distribution was even larger, above all because of Africa's dismal growth performance in per capita terms (Fig. 1.6).

But are these figures capturing the reality well? After all, EMDEs tend to have much larger informal economies, with the coexistence of formal and

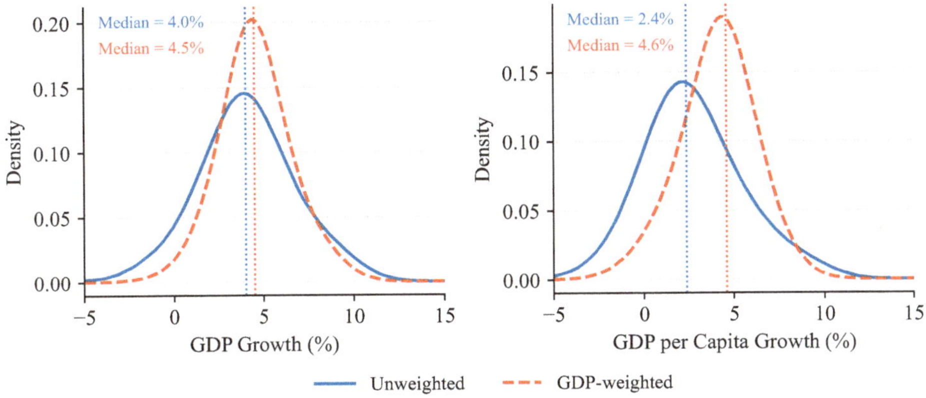

Fig. 1.6 Distribution of EMDE's growth performance in the recent past. (Source: authors' calculations based on World Bank)

informal sectors often referred to as *economic duality*. For instance, estimates show that the informal economy is much larger in EMDE (median of 37% in 2021–2022) than in AE (median 5%), with informality relatively stable over the past three decades, except for declining somewhat before the pandemic, but increasing quite meaningfully post-pandemic (Asllani et al., 2024)[5]. In terms of employment, the relevance of the far less productive informal sector is even more staggering: about 70% of total employment in EMDEs is informal.[6] The size of the informal economy is thereby negatively correlated with per capita income, with African countries generally topping the list in terms of informality. While official national accounts numbers include estimates on the size of the informal economy, it still adds a significant element of uncertainty regarding actual income levels. Poorer countries tend to have weaker statistical capacity. It does not come as a surprise that large revisions to GDP numbers are frequent in EMDE. A striking example was a revision in Nigeria, in 2014, shifting the base year from 1990 to 2010, and increasing the size of the economy in 2013 by 89%, thereby suddenly making Nigeria the largest economy on the continent. With the next shift in base year to 2019, the size of the Nigerian economy grew by another 34%. A more systematic look at IMF data over time reveals the extent of such revisions. Between 2015 and 2025, over 20 low- and lower middle-income countries have seen their 2013 GDP revised up by over 20%. Sub-Saharan Africa, small island states, and conflict-affected countries saw the largest revisions. But also some large EMDEs saw important revisions, such as Vietnam (+25%), Egypt (+12%), Kenya (+12), and Turkey (+16%), while GDP estimates for China, India, Brazil, and Mexico barely changed. In contrast to many EMDEs, revisions for AE were minor, i.e. typically within +/− 1%.

If we take GDP as a given, and assume that countries have a reasonable idea about the size of their population (though bear in mind that statistical capacity varies in EMDE), does GDP per capita serve as a good proxy for income levels in a given country? Obviously, GDP per capita ignores inequality, and as such, is somewhat misleading where inequality is high. Income inequality tends to be much higher in EMDEs than in AEs. In 2023, it was most pronounced in South Africa, Namibia, Colombia, and Mexico, where the top 10% of earners captured between 60% and 65% of total income, while the bottom 50% received only 6% to 8%.[7] The higher income inequality is, the less effective is GDP growth in alleviating poverty. While the share of the population living in poverty clearly declines with rising GDP per capita, there are still important differences in poverty rates at a given income level, particularly in low-income and lower middle-income countries. For instance, in 2022, at a GDP per capita of roughly USD 5000 (in 2017 prices), the share of population living in extreme poverty was estimated at around 5% in Pakistan, but 31% in Nigeria and 36% in Kenya.[8]

For any investor, inequality has two important implications. First, if an investment directly or indirectly targets a specific segment of the population, GDP figures may not be a good proxy for how the income levels of the target group evolve over time. For instance, a standard country-level assessment of economic strength in a highly unequal country is certainly better suited for a sovereign investment than for a loan to a microfinance institution targeting the bottom of the pyramid. Second, high inequality and widespread poverty pose important social and political risks.

Box 1.2: How Rating Agencies Assess Economic Strength[9]

Assessing economic strength is a standard building block of sovereign ratings and country risk scores. The large rating agencies—Fitch, Moody's, and S&P—focus in their approach on the following indicators:

1. Growth dynamics, with strong and steady GDP growth being preferred over slow and volatile growth trajectories.
2. Level of income as measured by GDP per capita, with higher income levels being associated with greater shock absorption capacity.
3. Economic scale and structure, where larger, more diversified economies are viewed as less prone to large shocks.

As such, agencies not only look at realized volatility (mostly over the past 10 years), but also at risk factors, such as a lack of economic diversification, high exposure to cyclical industries or potential sources of macroeconomic imbalances or instability that could heighten volatility in the future.

What Drives Growth in EMDEs?

The Composition of GDP

Before looking for what factors are conducive to economic growth, we will first examine the composition of GDP in EMDEs. Through the lens of the expenditure approach, GDP is the sum of public and private consumption, investment (including changes in inventories), and net trade (exports minus imports). In aggregate, roughly two thirds of GDP is consumption, and one third is investment, with net trade being quite small (contributing around one percent of GDP). Similarly, the split between public and private expenditure is roughly one third to two thirds. Hence, compared to AEs, investment spending and the private sector play a larger role in EMDEs. While the net trade is similarly small, EMDEs are slightly less open to trade than AEs, with total trade equaling roughly 50% of GDP in EMDEs and 60% in AEs.[10]

That said, a key point we consistently emphasize throughout this book also applies—there is wide variation among EMDEs. Ignoring fragile and conflict-affected states as well as small states, investment ratios in 2024 ranged from around 40% (China, Panama) to about 12% (Pakistan, Egypt, South Africa). Public expenditure likewise varied widely, from 43% in Bosnia & Herzegovina to less than 15% in Bangladesh and Guatemala. Furthermore, as mentioned earlier, with regard to overall investment spending in EMDE, China lifts the aggregate (by about 4.5 percentage points between 2015 and 2024) and somewhat distorts the picture. That said, EMDEs excluding China still display a higher investment ratio than AEs, which aligns with the intuition of large investment needs and growth opportunities.

Regarding the production approach, available aggregate data for EMDEs are not overly detailed, distinguishing only between agriculture, industry, and services. In aggregate, services dominate, making up roughly 60% of GDP, followed by industry (30%) and agriculture (10%). These numbers, though, tend to understate the importance of agriculture, as many smallholder farmers operate in the informal sector and hence may be outside the scope of national income accounting. The agricultural sector is characterized by a low productivity that still accounts for close to one third of total employment in EMDE and poses an important vulnerability with regard to climate change. Within industry, manufacturing plays a critical role in some EMDEs, most notably in parts of Asia that have followed an export-led growth model. In countries with high investment ratios, often linked to rapid urbanization, the construction sector also tends to be large. Finally, commodity-exporting countries typically have sizable mining sectors, which, though significant contributors to GDP, are generally capital intensive and offer fewer employment opportunities than their economic weight might suggest. Compared to AEs, both agriculture and industry play a larger role in EMDEs.

The Drivers of GDP Growth

After examining the composition of GDP, we now look at the drivers of GDP growth in EMDEs since the early 2000s. Again, we look at the expenditure and production approaches of calculating GDP but add the perspective of endogenous growth model.

It should not come as a surprise that investment spending is a bigger contributor to GDP growth in EMDEs compared to AEs, while consumption has a smaller weight. That said, consumption is still the largest contributor to GDP growth, having contributed about two thirds to overall growth since the early 2000s. What is a bit of a surprise is that external trade is not a consistently positive contributor to GDP and has played a minor role in EMDE overall. While some countries have successfully implemented an export-led growth model, these countries are counterbalanced by import-reliant economies where net trade is a negative growth contributor. It is also noteworthy that the divide between consumption and investment contributions has been quite stable in the reference period.[11]

There were, however, shifts in the sectoral contributions to GDP growth. The contribution of industry has declined after the Global Financial Crisis and the end of the last commodity super-cycle around 2014. Between 2014 and 2023, services contributed close to two thirds to EMDEs' GDP growth, industry contributed close to one third, and agriculture made up the remainder. Again, as one would expect, the industry sector has been subject to much greater fluctuations than the services sector and has overall been the largest contributor to GDP growth volatility, except for the Covid-19 pandemic year 2020. Compared to AEs, industry and agriculture are bigger contributors to growth, highlighting the importance of closely monitoring these sectors when assessing cyclical developments.[12]

An additional way to examine GDP growth drivers is through the lens of endogenous growth theory. Here we distinguish between the contributions of labor force expansion, capital deepening, and total factor productivity (TFP) growth.

What influences these three factors? The labor force expansion is above all driven by demographic trends. As outlined earlier, rapidly growing populations have expanded the labor force in many EMDE, increasing countries' production capacity. Capital deepening in turn is favored by high domestic savings and a good investment climate, i.e. a factor that is itself shaped by the quality of institutions (see Chap. 2). Meanwhile, TFP growth—capturing how efficiently labor and capital are used—is shaped by many subfactors. These include technology adoption, gains from structural transformation (not least as workers move from agriculture into higher-productivity sectors), investment in education and health supporting the accumulation of human capital, and, last but not least, urbanization, which creates efficiency gains.

IMF has pointed out that until the GFC, capital accumulation and TFP gains were quite strong thanks to technology diffusion and better resource allocation. However, since that time, there has been a major growth slowdown, both in EMDEs and AEs. IMF mainly attributed this to a notable decline in TFP growth, but to some extent also to moderating capital expenditure amid rising corporate leverage and weaker investor confidence. Meanwhile the working-age population has also been growing at a slower pace.[13]

Based on data from the Penn World Tables, TPF growth in EMDE has been disappointing in the past. Between 1960 and 2019, the average median growth rate of TFP in EMDE has been only 0.36%. In MENA, that number has even been negative, while it is zero in Latin America and only moderately positive in sub-Saharan Africa (0.24%). Only emerging Europe and Central, East and South Asia have consistently seen reasonable growth in TFP in the range of 0.8% to 1.1% during the observation period. Part of the great convergence mentioned earlier was also an increase in TFP growth. However, since the Global Financial Crisis, there has been a marked slowdown, with median TPF growth since 2015 hovering close to zero in EMDE. This slowdown has not been reserved to EMDE, but was also observed somewhat less pronounced in AEs. According to the IMF, this trend is likely explained by a combination of waning gains from information and communication technology, declining business dynamism, limited investments in new technology, a slower expansion of cross-border capital flows and trade since 2018, and lastly, reduced allocative efficiency of capital and labor.

Meanwhile, the view of growth theory has also evolved over time. In neoclassical growth theory, Solow emphasized capital accumulation and treated total factor productivity as an exogenous residual.[14] More recently, in endogenous growth theory, economists such as Lucas and Romer have focused on human capital, innovation, and technology as the explanation, where productivity growth reflects policy choices to invest in education to foster a knowledge-based and innovation-rich economy. Additionally, as we will discuss in greater detail in Chap. 2, the role of institutions is key. These are the building blocks of the economic, political, and legal rules of the game that create incentives and the means to drive innovation and heightened productivity.

Globalization

Yet another important growth driver over recent decades has been globalization. Above all thanks to trade liberalization and technological advances in transport and telecom, global trade flourished. Particularly in the 1990s and 2000s, global value chains emerged and deepened, with companies exploiting cost advantages of fragmenting production processes geographically. EMDEs were integral part of that process and benefited from a surge in FDI and associated knowledge transfer. Globalization and trade have accordingly also been major growth drivers, with virtually all country success stories featuring an integration into the global economy. Not all regions, however, participated equally. In particular, sub-Saharan Africa was greatly left behind. This performance reflected various factors, including a lack of infrastructure, lower levels of education, corruption, and civil conflict.

Since the Global Financial Crisis, however, globalization has stalled, with the trade intensity of the global economy trending broadly sideways since then. One important factor is that the creation of global supply chains had likely run its course. For instance, since around 2010, global goods trade has been growing at broadly the same rate as global industrial production, while before 2008 trade volumes clearly outpaced total production.

Furthermore, the current outlook is clouded by rising trade tensions, increased geopolitical risks, and technological advances. Strikingly, "peak globalization" around 2008 coincided with the high point of FDI inflows into EMDEs. Ever since, FDI inflows into EMDE have been trending down (as a percentage of GDP) markedly, with that ratio reaching in 2024 the lowest level since 1990. The weakening trend has been broad-based across EMDEs and raises important questions regarding further growth models and trajectories, which we will address in part II of this book (Fig. 1.7).

Geography and Natural Resources: Blessing or Curse?

Certainly, there are other factors affecting economic development that warrant investigation. One such factor that has entered the debate but does not enjoy

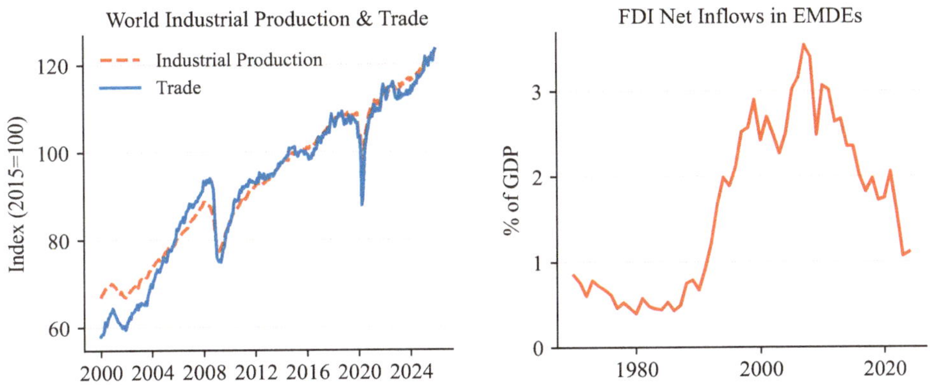

Fig. 1.7 Industrial production, global trade & FDI. (Source: Macrobond, Netherlands Bureau for Economic Policy Analysis (CPB), World Bank)

universal support as a significant driver is geography. Jeffrey Sachs has been one of the most prominent voices assigning geography an important role in development. In his most influential contribution on the matter titled "Geography and economic development", Sachs and his colleagues made a compelling case, arguing that a country's geographic location greatly affected its productive potential.[15] Parts of the argument were about geography affecting transportation costs (particularly in landlocked countries), disease burdens in the tropics (not least malaria, reducing worker productivity and life expectancy, thereby discouraging investment in education), and agricultural productivity (being lesser in the tropics amid less fertile soils and more climate hazards). Those arguments though were shortly afterwards countered by Daron Acemoglu and colleagues, with an influential paper arguing that the colonial disease environment shaped institutions, and that it was ultimately the institutions that determined long-run economic outcomes.[16] That said, ultimately, even in Acemoglu's view geography mattered for development outcomes, with the impact though being indirect. Geography, then, certainly plays a role. In some cases, though, the impact is different from what one might expect. For instance, one study found that rugged terrain, which normally poses headwinds to economic development by increasing transportation costs, proved beneficial in Africa by offering protection from the slave trade during colonialism, thereby preventing institutional collapse and social fragmentation.[17]

A second factor is natural resource endowment. What one would expect to be a blessing has proved often to be a curse. Numerous countries have failed to capitalize on their wealth of natural resources, often cited examples including the Democratic Republic of Congo, Sudan, and Nigeria. Comparably few are the contrasting examples, including Botswana and Chile. Explanations are manifold, including large rents from resources fostering corruption, patronage, and elite capture; the Dutch disease, in which booming commodity prices lead to real exchange rate appreciation, thereby hurting the price competitiveness of other export industries (such as manufacturing); and commodity price volatility often leading to boom-and-bust cycles. As so often in this book, the question on the resource curse brings us back to the relevance of institutions, because whether natural resource endowments support growth depends on institutional strength.[18] As such, the curse does not seem inevitable, but capitalizing on natural resources has historically proven very challenging.

As we have seen, both geography and natural resource endowments certainly affect countries' growth trajectories. These elements are included in the fundamentals of the Investor's Rutter, discussed below.

Income Convergence and The Middle-Income Trap

While we have seen how EMDEs have grown in the past and what their major growth drivers were, there remains the question of whether their income levels are catching up with high-income countries, with the United States being the most commonly used benchmark. Economists talk in this context of income convergence. In theory, convergence is expected to happen, thanks to initially lower capital stocks and technology adoption yielding higher returns on investment. In practice, however, convergence has only occurred sporadically and unevenly.

For most of the twentieth century, divergence—meaning that richer countries grew faster than poorer ones—was the dominant pattern, as well documented by Pritchett in this seminal work "Divergence, Big Time".[19] Different strains of literature[20] have attributed this divergence to limited technology diffusion, capital misallocation, and institutional weaknesses. Earlier development debates had also identified the so-called *poverty trap*, wherein a vicious cycle of low income, low savings, poor human capital, and weak institutions kept countries from escaping low-income levels. Toward the end of the century, however, some convergence finally emerged and accelerated further in the twenty-first century (Fig. 1.8).[21] Still, this process has been far from uniform. While many countries successfully transitioned from a low- to a middle-income status, they often struggled to further narrow the gap with high-income countries. This phenomenon is widely known as the "middle-income trap".

Convergence is thus rarely a steady process. Instead, there are periods of growth accelerations and reversals. Favorable external conditions, such as

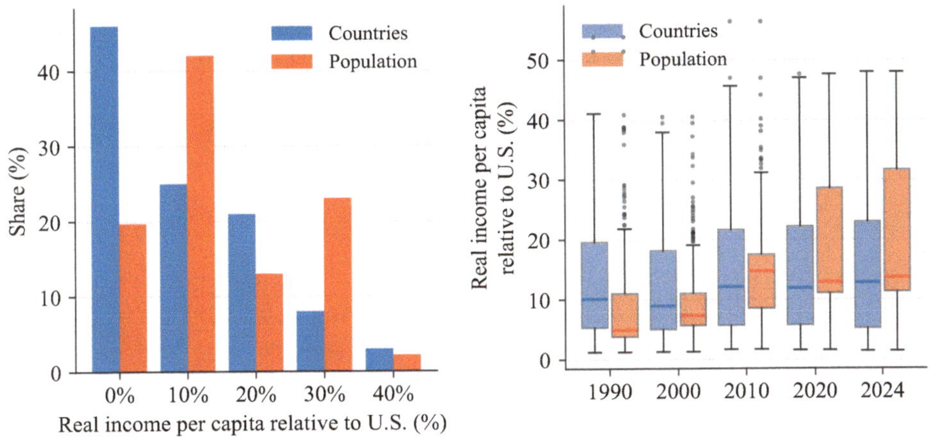

Fig. 1.8 EMDEs relative income per capita. Source: authors' calculation based on World Bank

strong external demand, cheap external financing conditions, and, for commodity exporters, high commodity prices, have played a major role in growth accelerations. Conversely, worsening external conditions often triggered growth reversals.[22] The "great convergence" between the early 2000s and mid-2010s, for example, coincided with robust demand from AEs, a commodity super-cycle and relatively benign global financing conditions. By contrast, external shocks have frequently precipitated growth reversals in EMDE, including sudden stops in capital flows (as during the 1997 Asian crisis), collapses in commodity prices (1985, 2014), or global recessions (early 1980s). Crises, more broadly, have often delayed or even derailed catch-up processes, with the "great convergence" notably occurring during a period characterized by fewer and shorter crises in EMDEs.[23] Nonetheless, crises can also present opportunities to recalibrate policies and lay the groundwork for further convergence in the future.[24]

While external forces create both opportunities and risks, domestic factors play an important role in countries' ability to capitalize on opportunities and mitigate risks. The World Bank's "World Development Report 2024" provided an in-depth analysis of the middle-income trap, offering critical insights on the role of domestic policies. Among its findings, the report highlighted that countries with weak institutions were more prone to growth slowdowns, that openness to foreign trade, investment and talent supported technological upgrading, and that development strategies must evolve as countries grow richer.[25]

Many of the aspects highlighted above will be explored in greater detail later in the book, including the role of institutions (Chap. 2), vulnerability to crises

(Chap. 4), and major developments shaping the outlook for EMDEs (Chaps. 6–10), all of which will help us explore the future of income convergence.

1.2 Domestic policies: shock absorber or multiplier?

Business cycles are a reality. Ideally, they are actively managed, with both fiscal and monetary policy measures playing a stabilizing role. For that to happen, countries need to have buffers and use them effectively, which ultimately is, once more, a function of institutional strength.

Varying Fiscal Space, Predominantly Pro-cyclical Policies

From an aggregate fiscal perspective, the picture is as follows: EMDEs are less indebted than AEs when looking at the public debt-to-GDP ratio but generally run larger annual deficits. Lower revenue generation capacity weighs on their debt-carrying capacity, implying that debt sustainability concerns typically emerge at a much earlier stage than in AEs. Their funding structure is also important. Historically, given a much smaller domestic savings pool to tap (except for a few exceptions such as China, India, and South Africa), external debt played quite a dominant role, with a combination of marketable debt (Eurobonds), multilateral funding, bilateral loans, and syndicated loans. Over the past two decades, domestic debt, however, gained a more prominent role, which is positive as it reduces foreign exchange risks, but comes at the expense of heightened sovereign-banking linkages. Since the Global Financial Crisis, EMDEs' public debt-to-GDP ratio has been on an upward trajectory, reaching the highest level in decades. That said, debt affordability, i.e. debt servicing costs as a percentage of public revenues, is a more relevant indicator when it comes to assessing debt sustainability. And debt affordability still compares favorably to most of recent decades. The combination of higher debt and interest rates implies that debt servicing costs will increase further going forward, with much depending on debt characteristics, particularly the share of marketable debt, its term structure, and the split between fixed versus floating rate debt. Baseline projections by the IMF point towards EMDE's spending on debt service crossing 10% of their revenues in 2027 and continuing to trend upward thereafter. While these levels compare favorably with the early 2000s, they may, in practice, test countries' willingness to serve their debt obligations in the context of large spending needs on health, education, and infrastructure.

As always, the aggregate view on EMDE masks substantial cross-country differences, with countries' fiscal strength and buffers varying considerably. To assess fiscal buffers, one can look at market pricing and sovereign ratings, at least for market access countries. What do these indicators tell us? Market pricing is, to a certain extent, sentiment-driven, and as such somewhat volatile, even more so for bonds with rather light trading volumes. While overall there is no clear trend in spreads, at times, differentiation between markets greatly increased. Particularly following the post-pandemic inflation and interest rate shock, market differentiation increased substantially. By July 2022, close to one third of sovereigns included in J.P. Morgan's EMBI indices had been priced to default (i.e. had spreads exceeding 1000 basis points). Since then, several sovereign defaults have actually occurred, and by 2025, the share of sovereigns priced to default had again declined to below 10%.

What about sovereign ratings? What does their distribution appear, and how has it changed over time? At the end of 2024, only about one third of EMDE sovereigns were rated at least BB-. Particularly since the pandemic, weaker sovereigns have come under significant pressure, with more than a quarter of EMDE sovereigns seeing their average rating declining by at least one notch by the end of 2024. Some countries faced heightened debt distress, including Ghana, Lebanon, Sri Lanka, and Zambia. On the other hand, very few sovereign saw their creditworthiness improving between 2015 and 2025. In fact, only three countries fell into that category: Jamaica (recovering from two sovereign defaults, one in 2010 and another one in 2013), Serbia, and Vietnam (Fig. 1.9).

Overall, we see that fiscal space is much more limited in EMDEs, but that there are large differences between markets. As such, it does not come as a surprise that fiscal policies in EMDE have predominately been procyclical in the past (although this is changing, as we discuss below), meaning that fiscal policy generally acted as an amplifier of business cycles.[26] Explanations for EMDE's procyclical fiscal policies focus on funding constraints (particularly during periods of stress), revenue volatility, and institutional weaknesses. Procyclical policies are generally negatively correlated with income levels (i.e. the poorer the country, the more procyclical its fiscal policy tends to be), and most pronounced in commodity exporting countries. There are important regional differences, with sub-Saharan Africa being the region with the highest degree of procyclicality while South and East Asia have generally followed a countercyclical stance.[27] On a positive note, procyclicality has weakened over recent decades, with policy recommendations such as greater use of automatic stabilizers, fiscal rules, and the

Fig. 1.9 EMDE sovereign rating transitions between 2014 and 2024. (Source: Authors' calculations based on World Bank Fiscal Space Database)

broadening of tax bases potentially helping to reduce it further.[28] That said, the Covid-19 pandemic once again demonstrated that EMDEs had much less fiscal space to enact countercyclical policies, enacting overall much less fiscal stimulus than AEs, and resumed fiscal consolidation much more quickly once there was a nascent recovery.[29]

Enhanced Monetary Policies, but Constraint Effectiveness

What about the cyclicality of monetary policy? If fiscal policy does not act as a shock absorber, does monetary policy at least play that role, with central banks tightening rates during booms, and easing their stance during busts?

Key for central banks delivering on their mandate of maintaining price stability is their independence. In EMDEs, central banks' independence has been on an uptrend since the early 1990s, according to various measures, not least the Central Bank Independence Index by Romelli, so that today EMDEs don't lag much behind AEs on average.[30] That said, existing measures of central bank independence can certainly be criticized, not least for their mostly arbitrary weighting of their sub-indicators and their focus on *de jure* rather than *de facto* independence.[31] Furthermore, it is noteworthy that there is no

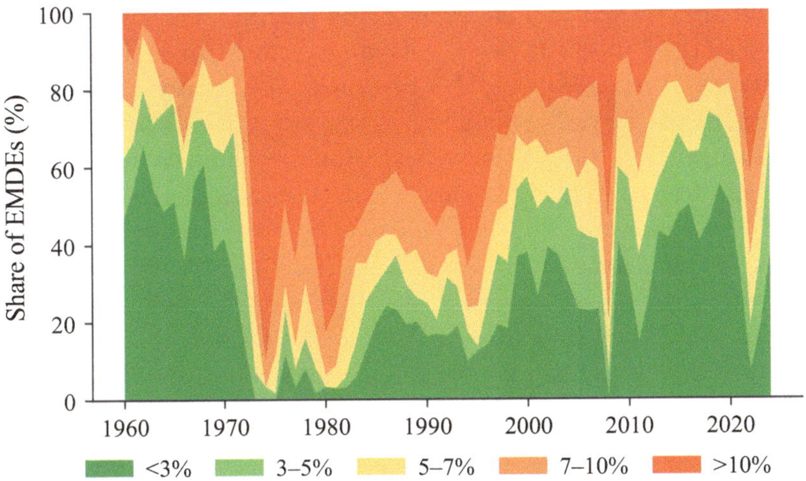

Fig. 1.10 Inflation in EMDEs since the 1960s. (Source: Authors' calculations based on World Bank)

clear connection either with countries' income levels or with governance indicators such as the rule of law, regulatory quality, or government effectiveness. Lastly, some individual countries' scoring challenges these indices' credibility, with Romelli's index assessing central banks in Bolivia, Turkey, and Venezuela as mostly independent.

A better way to qualify the work of central banks is hence to judge them based on their track record of maintaining price stability. In this regard, we clearly see improvements since the 1980s (Fig. 1.10). Just before the pandemic, roughly three quarters of EMDE maintained price stability effectively. Then the pandemic strained global production, through supply-chain disruptions and major shifts in demand (from services to goods and back). In addition, the escalation of geopolitical risks, and in particular Russia's invasion of Ukraine, further boosted both energy and food prices. Suddenly, not just EMDE but the entire world faced the worst inflation shock seen in many decades.

What was extraordinary was not only the macroeconomic turbulence that begun with the pandemic, but also the response by EMDE central banks. Some referred to it as a "quiet revolution in emerging market monetary policy", with EMDE central banks mimicking their AE counterparts by implementing countercyclical policies, but not stopping with interest rate cuts, but extending their toolkit to asset purchases.[32] What previously seemed unthinkable, suddenly became a reality, enabled by massive spillovers from ultra-expansionary monetary policies in AEs. Once the economic recovery kicked in and inflation started to increase, EMDEs' reaction was much more timely and forceful than their AE peers', allowing them to make relative gains in credibility, further reinforcing the perception of greatly improved policy frameworks since the early 2000s.[33]

One key obstacle to countercyclical monetary policies remains the still widespread "fear of floating" (a term coined by Guillermo A. Calvo and Carmen M. Reinhart in 2002),[34] whereby many central banks in EMDE hesitate to allow their exchange rates to fluctuate freely, worrying about a weakening currency driving up inflation, hurting balance sheets, and triggering capital outflows. According to the IMF's last classification of de facto exchange rate regimes (for the reference year 2022), only about 20% of EMDEs had a floating exchange rate, while all the others managed their exchange rates actively one way or the other, as illustrated below (Fig. 1.11). Being concerned about currency depreciation sparking inflation, triggering capital outflows or hampering financial stability, about half of EMDE central banks remain lukewarm about the prospect of a free-floating exchange rate. This reluctance often renders monetary policy pro-cyclical, with central banks hiking rates during downturns.[35]

Consistently, almost half of EMDEs have an *exchange rate anchor* as their monetary policy regime, although that share has been declining since 2010. *Inflation targeting*, which is the dominant monetary policy regime in AEs, is slowly spreading among EMDE, but still accounts for only about 25% of all regimes (Fig. 1.12).

Nevertheless, and somewhat surprisingly, a majority of EMDEs are seen as adopting countercyclical monetary policies, cutting policy rates in bad times and hiking rates in good times.[36] There is, however, one important caveat: the presence of a varying degree of dollarization undermines the transmission from policy to market rates and constrains central banks in their ability to steer domestic financing conditions. In that sense, global financial conditions, and above all US interest rates, still have important spillovers on domestic financial conditions in EMDEs. Furthermore, central banks' reaction function is not homogeneous, with central banks in countries with a history of high inflation needing to act more forcefully to deviations of inflation expectations from target in order to maintain price stability.[37]

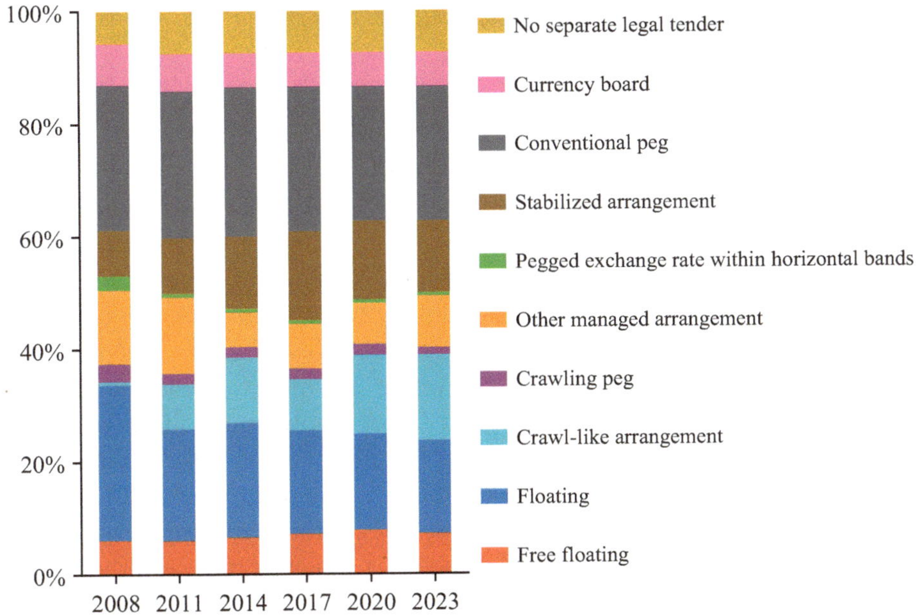

Fig. 1.11 Distribution of exchange rate regimes in EMDE. (Source: Authors' calculations based on IMF AREAER Database)

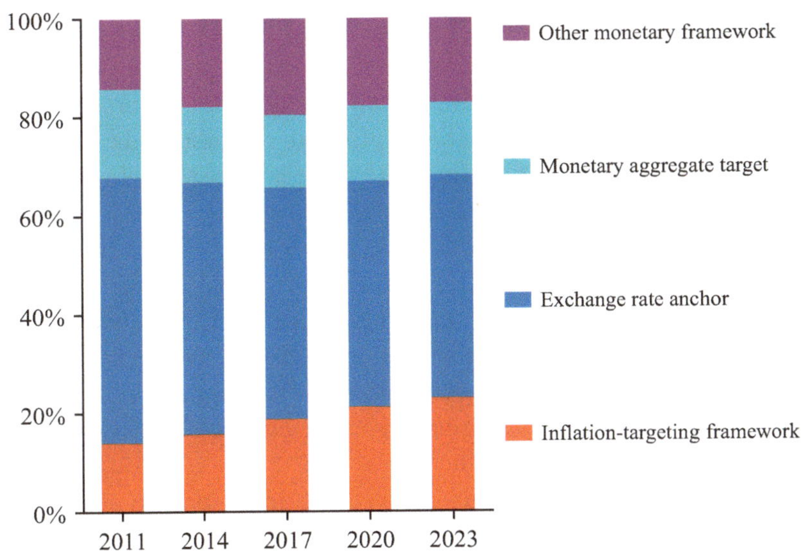

Fig. 1.12 Distribution of monetary policy regimes in EMDE. (Source: authors' calculations based on IMF AREAER Database)

1.3 External Vulnerabilities and Shock Absorbers

After having considered domestic policy options and applications, we will now look at EMDEs' external vulnerabilities, which tend to vary significantly between countries. Fundamentally, a majority of EMDEs can be categorized as countries with limited domestic savings and large investment needs. As such, the savings-investment balance, which equals the current account balance, is often negative, implying the country faces external funding needs—even in the absence of roll-over requirements. These funding needs can be covered by different sources, some of which are more reliable than others. These include foreign direct investment (more stable), portfolio investments (more volatile), and other investments. Furthermore, in case of insufficient funding, a country can draw from its foreign exchange reserves. Over time, external liabilities accumulate, with most EMDEs today featuring a negative net international investment position (NIIP), i.e. having more external liabilities than assets.

The Stock Perspective: Risks Related to Rollover Needs

The NIIP (as a percentage of GDP) varies widely, from −186% in Mongolia to +20% in Botswana (2024). Most EMDEs with a positive NIIP are commodity exporters, except for China (due, among other factors, to an exceptionally high savings rate, large trade surpluses in the past, and capital account restrictions) and Thailand (running large trade surpluses on both goods and services, especially tourism) (Fig. 1.13).

Headline NIIP figures, however, are not overly telling. In the case of Mongolia for instance, close to two thirds of external liabilities are foreign direct investment (FDI), which are roughly split evenly between debt and equity instruments. As mentioned earlier, FDI can be considered a stable source of funding, with a large stock of inward FDI signaling strength, rather than weakness. In Mongolia, another 30% of external liabilities are categorized as "Other Investment", which are—in the case of Mongolia—mostly loans to the government (i.e. non-marketable debt), non-financial corporations, and households. On the sovereign, concerns had greatly eased in 2023 thanks to a strong recovery in coal exports and prices allowing the country to replenish buffers and reducing its public debt-to-GDP ratio to an extent that Mongolia's EMBI spread touched an all-time low of 179 bps in January 2025. External debt statistics also showed that close to half of external debt was

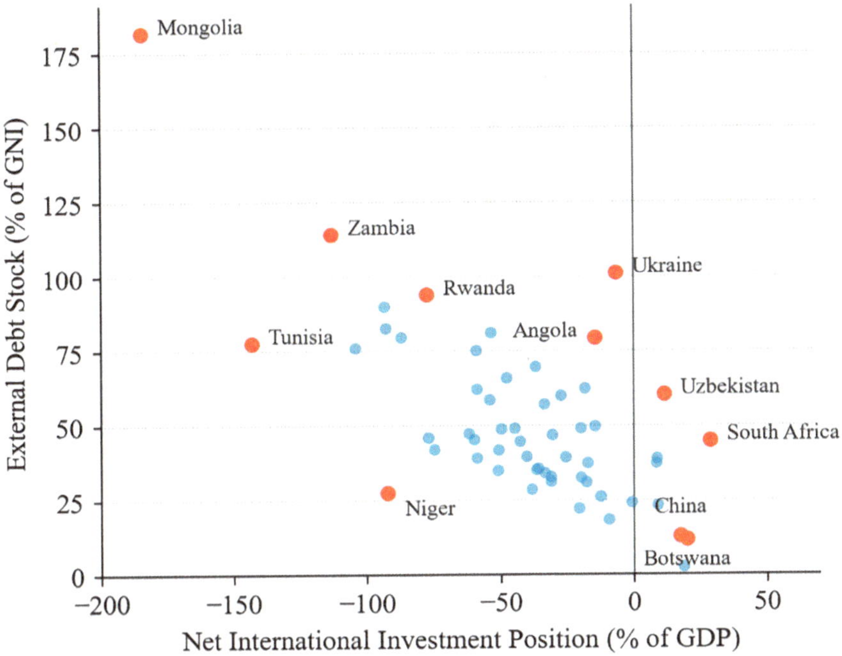

Fig. 1.13 Net International Investment Position & External Debt (2024). (Source: Macrobond, IMF, World Bank)

intercompany lending, again a stable source of funding, providing reassurance regarding the previously mentioned loans to non-financial corporates and households.

Instead of spending too much time on the NIIP, we suggest the reader take an in-depth look at external debt statistics. We look at the level, the borrower split, and the maturity structure. Once again, consider the case of Mongolia. External debt is high (158% of GDP at the end of 2024), and primarily split between intercompany lending (46%), general government (23%), and other sectors (20%; probably mostly non-financial corporations). Even if we have some comfort on intercompany lending and the sovereign (as alluded to before), there could still be reason for concern, if maturities were not spread out over time, but rather concentrated. In this regard, the fact that little short-term debt offers some comfort, but might be slightly misleading, as the classification of debt in short-term (less than one-year maturity) and long-term (more than one-year maturity) in the World Bank's International Debt Statistics is based on original maturity rather than remaining maturity. As such, it is equally important to analyze the maturity structure of long-term debt. In the case of Mongolia, external debt maturities were somewhat concentrated in the near-term, particularly for the private sector, but still not excessively high. The fact that average maturities of new external debt commitments had generally been above 10 years in recent years pointed towards both the public and private sector managing external debt liabilities well.

The Flow Perspective: Risks Related to Current Funding Needs

At times, it is not rollover needs but current funding needs that cause funding stress. The current funding needs stem from current account deficits, which occasionally widen sharply when an important source of external revenues suddenly dries up, or a surge in capital inflows boosts domestic demand.

In recent decades, EMDEs have experienced multiple boom-and-bust cycles in external financing, with booms occurring in the early 1990s (ending in the Asian Financial Crisis), the mid-2000s (ending with the Global Financial Crisis), and in the early 2010s (ending with the taper tantrum, i.e. the US Federal Reserve's tapering of asset purchases in 2013), often driven by global liquidity and high risk. These capital surges and reversals typically coincided with capital account liberalization and often increased macroeconomic instability. Eventually, views on capital flow management (CFM) measures shifted in response. While conventional wisdom of the early 1990s held that all countries should liberalize their capital accounts, the repeated boom-and-bust cycles prompted a rethinking and eventually induced a landmark shift in the IMF's institutional view in 2012, which recognized CFM measures as legitimate policy tools under certain conditions. Empirical studies suggest that CFM measures can be effective in reducing financial fragility and output volatility, not least by increasing the costs of borrowing from abroad.[38]

Besides volatile capital flows, major shifts in terms-of-trade can materially impact the current account balance, above all for economies dependent on commodity exports.

Since the pandemic, there have been a few examples of dramatic increases in current account deficits. Most striking, though not overly instructive, were the surges of current account deficits in Cambodia (to −47% of GDP in 2021)[39] and Kyrgyzstan (−42% of GDP in 2022). While Cambodia's current account balance was at least in part explained by large and highly volatile trade of gold and had normalized within two years, Kyrgyzstan's current account deficit remains very large (and mostly financed by "errors and omissions"), primarily due to unreported re-exports of goods to Russia. Both cases highlighted quality issues with official statistics, a matter that often also complicates proper assessments of risks in EMDE.

Regarding the current account balance, in the mid-2020s, the median EMDE had a deficit of roughly 2.5% of GDP, with the inter-quartile range between 0% and −5% of GDP. Often though it is less the level than change and deviation from the norm that points towards a build-up of vulnerabilities, not least as the level typically mirrors an economy's fundamental characteristics (such as being a commodity exporter like Azerbaijan, having a low savings rate like Turkey, or being an export hub such as China or Vietnam). This is also well reflected in the IMF approach to assess the external sector, which includes comparing the current account balance with what is deemed the normal level.

Mongolia, for instance, had in the mid-2020s a quite large current account deficit of around 10% of GDP. That deficit was a reflection of import-intensive mining projects (with the expansion of the world's largest copper mine Oyu Tolgoi involving sizeable imports of machinery and equipment), large dividend and interest payments to foreign investors (as a reflection of large external liabilities which we identified earlier), and a high reliance on imports (amid its landlocked geography and limited domestic production). The reliance on commodity exports, above all coal and copper, paired with large commodity price swings rendered Mongolia's trade and hence current account balance quite volatile.

Rollover needs and current funding needs together constitute a country's gross external financing requirements. Some analysts prefer to focus on net external funding needs, assuming that maturing debt will be rolled over. However, this assumption may not hold, especially when external liquidity tightens.

Shock Absorbers and Buffers

Typically, when US interest rates increased or financial markets went into risk-off mode, external liquidity tightens. When this situation arises, EMDE's operating with strong external liquidity, sound FX regimes, and domestic policy space can manage outflows or spikes in rates.

External imbalances can be contained by flexible exchange rates, though, as mentioned earlier, the "fear of floating" is still widespread in EMDE. Flexible exchange rates would help adjust to external shocks, such as a drop in export revenues or tightening global financing conditions. In response to such a shock, the exchange rate would weaken, making exports more competitive and imports more expensive. As a consequence, one should expect the trade balance and hence the current account balance to improve, at least in the medium term. That said, inflation and tighter monetary policy might offset some of the gains in competitiveness, while for price-inelastic exports (such as commodities), the volume effects might be limited. Furthermore, the strength of exchange rate effects is influenced by pricing and financing currencies, with the effects of currency weakening on the trade balance being more muted and mainly manifested in imports, where the US dollar has a dominant role in trade pricing and corporate financing.[40]

Another mitigant are foreign exchange reserves, which EMDEs started accumulating particularly after the Asian Financial Crisis in the late 1990s, which had uncovered the risks of open capital accounts paired with rigid exchange rates. To reduce external vulnerabilities, many countries pursued the build-up of reserves. Looking across EMDEs today, we see a general trend toward what the IMF's Assessing Reserve Adequacy (ARA) metric deems to be adequate levels. Though again as with most other aspects we zoom in on in this book, also here we have large differences across countries, with the bottom quartile having an ARA of less than 75% (with 100% to 150% being deemed adequate), while the top quartile has more than 150% (Fig. 1.14).

Coming back to Mongolia: external vulnerabilities were amplified by inadequate reserves, pro-cyclical fiscal policies, and a managed exchange rate (despite the Mongolian Tugrik *de jure* being a floating exchange rate). All this meant that the country certainly had important external vulnerabilities, which were at that point though somewhat contained by the fact that it had just experienced a boom and had partially replenished its buffers. Given the

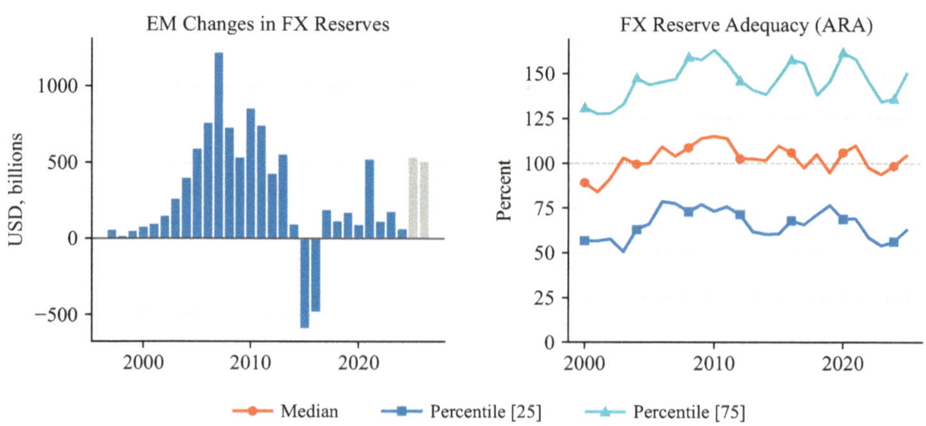

Fig. 1.14 EMDEs' fx reserves build-up and adequacy. (Source: Macrobond, IMF, Authors' calculations)

volatility in external receipts and rather weak institutions, it barely surprises that Mongolia in the past had occasionally to ask the IMF to come to the rescue, the IMF being the multilateral institution that helps countries resolve or prevent balance of payment crises by providing conditional funding accompanied by adjustment programs and reforms.

1.4 Conclusion

Let us recapitulate the major learnings from this chapter. EMDEs have made significant strides over recent decades and now account for a dominant share of global growth. That said, they remain a highly diverse group of countries, and not all have equally seized the opportunities offered by globalization and natural endowments. While policy frameworks have improved, domestic policies in many cases still risk acting as shock amplifiers rather than shock absorbers. A key takeaway is the persistent "fear of floating" across EMDE, which continues to constrain monetary policy effectiveness and limits countries' ability to adjust to external shocks. Lastly, there are important clouds on the EMDE's outlook amid demographic shifts, globalization having peaked and the middle-income trap continuing to bite. Yet, before turning to EMDEs' future prospects in Part II, we continue our assessment of their current condition by examining a pivotal factor in development: the quality of institutions.

Notes

1. See Sachs (1989), Easterly (2001) and Rodrik (2003). Easterly, W. (2001). *The Elusive Quest for Growth: Economists' Adventures and Misadventures in the Tropics*. Cambridge, MA: MIT Press. Sachs, J.D. (1989). 'The Debt Overhang of Developing Countries', in G. Calvo, R. Findlay, P. Kouri and J. Braga de Macedo (eds), *Debt, Stabilization and Development: Essays in Memory of Carlos Díaz-Alejandro*. Oxford: Basil Blackwell, pp. 80–102.Rodrik, D. (2003). *In Search of Prosperity: Analytic Narratives on Economic Growth*. Princeton, NJ: Princeton University Press.
2. World Bank (1993). *The East Asian Miracle: Economic Growth and Public Policy*. Oxford: Oxford University Press.
3. See Branstetter and Lardy (2006) and Naughton (2007).Branstetter, L. and Lardy, N. (2006). 'China's Embrace of Globalization'. NBER Working Paper No. 12373. Cambridge, MA: National Bureau of Economic Research.

   Naughton, B. (2007). *The Chinese Economy: Transitions and Growth*. Cambridge, MA: MIT Press.

4. Imam, P.A. and Temple, J.R.W., 2025. *Growth, Interrupted: How Crises Delay Global Convergence.* IMF Working Paper No. 25/116, International Monetary Fund.
5. Asllani, A., Dell'Anno, R., & Schneider, F. (2024). *Mapping the Informal Economy Around the World with an Enhanced MIMIC Approach: New Estimates for 110 Countries from 1997–2022.* CESifo Working Paper No. 11416, CESifo GmbH, Munich.
6. Ohnsorge, F. & Yu, S. (eds.) (2022) *The Long Shadow of Informality: Challenges and Policies.* Washington, DC: World Bank.
7. World Inequality Database, 2025. *World Inequality Database.* Available at: https://wid.world [Accessed 28 June 2025].
8. Our World in Data, n.d. *Share of population living in extreme poverty vs. GDP per capita.* Available at: https://ourworldindata.org/grapher/the-share-of-people-living-in-extreme-poverty-vs-gdp-per-capita [Accessed 28 June 2025].
9. Fitch Ratings (2024) *Sovereign Rating Criteria.* London: Fitch Ratings; Moody's Investors Service (2022) *Rating Methodology: Sovereign.* New York: Moody's.; and S&P Global Ratings (2017) *Sovereign Rating Methodology.* New York: S&P Global.
10. International Monetary Fund (IMF), 2025. *World Economic Outlook Database, April 2025.* Washington, DC: International Monetary Fund.
11. Own calculations based on data from IMF (2025).
12. Own calculations based on data from World Bank (2025).
13. IMF, 2024. *World Economic Outlook: Steady but Slow—Resilience amid Divergence.* Washington, DC: International Monetary Fund. Chapter 3: Slowdown in Global Medium-Term Growth: What Will It Take to Turn the Tide?
14. Solow, R.M., 1957. Technical change and the aggregate production function. *The Review of Economics and Statistics,* 39(3), pp. 312–320.
15. Gallup, J.L., Sachs, J.D. & Mellinger, A.D., 1999. Geography and economic development. *International Regional Science Review,* 22(2), pp. 179–232.
16. Acemoglu, D., Johnson, S. & Robinson, J.A., 2001. The colonial origins of comparative development: An empirical investigation. *American Economic Review,* 91(5), pp. 1369–1401.
17. Nunn, N. & Puga, D., 2012. Ruggedness: The blessing of bad geography in Africa. *Review of Economics and Statistics,* 94(1), pp. 20–36.
18. Frankel, J.A., 2010. The natural resource curse: a survey. *NBER Working Paper No. 15836.*
19. Pritchett, L., 1997. Divergence, big time. *Journal of Economic Perspectives,* 11(3), pp. 3–17.
20. See Kremer et al. (2022), World Bank (2024), and IMF (2018; 2024; 2025) for discussions of barriers to convergence.
21. Kremer, M., Willis, J. & You, Y., 2022. *Converging to convergence.* NBER Macroeconomics Annual, 36, pp. 337–380.

22. International Monetary Fund (IMF), 2018. *Growth accelerations and reversals in emerging market and developing economies: The role of external conditions.* IMF Policy Paper, October 2018. Washington, DC: International Monetary Fund.
23. Imam, P.A. & Temple, J.R.W., 2025. *Growth, Interrupted: How Crises Delay Global Convergence.* IMF Working Paper 25/116. Washington, DC: International Monetary Fund.
24. World Bank, 2024. *World Development Report 2024: The Middle-Income Trap.* Washington, DC: World Bank.
25. World Bank, 2024. *World Development Report 2024: The Middle-Income Trap.* Washington, DC: World Bank.
26. Bogetić, Ž. & Naeher, D. (2024) *Is Escaping the Fiscal Pro-Cyclicality Trap Possible? Evidence from the Middle East and North Africa*, Policy Research Working Paper, No. 10959. Washington, DC: World Bank.
27. Frankel, J.A., Végh, C.A. & Vuletin, G. (2019) *Why Some Countries Can Escape the Fiscal Procyclicality Trap and Others Cannot.* Policy Research Working Paper, No. 8963. Washington, DC: World Bank.
28. Arroyo Marioli, F. & Végh, C.A. (2023) *Fiscal Procyclicality in Commodity Exporting Countries: How Much Does It Pour and Why?* Policy Research Working Paper, No. 10428. Washington, DC: World Bank.
29. Alberola, E., Arslan, Y., Cheng, G. & Moessner, R. (2021) *Fiscal response to the COVID-19 crisis in advanced and emerging market economies.* Pacific Economic Review, 26(4), pp. 482–502.
30. Romelli, D. (2024) *Recent trends in central bank independence.* VoxEU.org, 26 February. Available at: https://cepr.org/voxeu/columns/recent-trends-central-bank-independence (Accessed: 23 July 2025).
31. Adrian, T., Khan, A. and Menand, L., 2024. *A new measure of central bank independence.* IMF Working Paper No. 24/35. International Monetary Fund.
32. Nagy-Mohacsi, P. (2020). *Emerging markets' new central bank orthodoxy.* Project Syndicate, 18 August. Available at: https://www.project-syndicate.org/commentary/emerging-markets-unconventional-monetary-policy-by-piroska-nagy-mohacsi-1-2020-08 [Accessed 24 Jul. 2025].
33. Evdokimova, T., Nagy-Mohacsi, P., Ponomarenko, O. and Ribakova, E. (2023). *Central Banks and Policy Communication: How Emerging Markets Have Outperformed the Fed and ECB.* Peterson Institute for International Economics, Working Paper No. 23–10.
34. Calvo, G. A. and Reinhart, C. M. (2002). 'Fear of Floating', *The Quarterly Journal of Economics*, 117(2), pp. 379–408.
35. Ahmad, A., McManus, R. and Ozkan, G. (2024). *Does fear of floating shape monetary policy and does it matter?* Economics Bulletin, 44(3), pp. 1055–1095.
36. De Leo, P., Gopinath, G. and Kalemli-Özcan, Ş. (2022). *Monetary policy cyclicality in emerging economies.* CEPR Discussion Paper No. 17748. London: Centre for Economic Policy Research.

37. Jácome, L.I., Imam, P., Quintero, A., and Sandri, D. (2025). *Inflation Targeting and the Legacy of High Inflation*. IMF Working Paper No. 25/14. Washington, DC: International Monetary Fund.
38. Erten, B., Korinek, A. and Ocampo, J.A., 2021. Capital controls: Theory and evidence. *Journal of Economic Literature*, 59(1), pp. 45–89.
39. Cambodia's current account deficit in 2021 was later revised down to 30% of GDP, mainly thanks to a sizable upward revision of the size of the economy. But even that number is still very high.
40. Adler, G., Casas, C., Cubeddu, L., Gopinath, G., Li, N., Meleshchuk, S., Osorio Buitron, C., Puy, D. and Timmer, Y., 2020. *Dominant currencies and external adjustment*. IMF Staff Discussion Note No. 2020/005. Washington, DC: International Monetary Fund.

2

The Foundational Role and State of Institutions

Outcomes follow incentives.
—A Common Saying

2.1 Institutions and Growth

Institutions

In this section, we introduce the concept of "institutions" and discuss the crucial roles they play in society, politics, and economics. For investors, the relevance will be clear. Economic growth and financial stability are intimately linked to the quality of the prevailing institutional framework. For example, the more secure the rule of law, all things being equal, the stronger and more sustainable will be capital formation, investment, innovation, productivity gains, and growth. This relationship is well recognized by the rating agencies whose sovereign rating methodologies incorporate institutional strength—such as rule of law, government effectiveness, corruption control, and policy credibility—as a core factor in their country ratings.[1] Throughout the book and, in particular, in the case studies that appear in Part IV: Chaps. 14–18, the important role of the institutions will be well demonstrated.

What Are Institutions and What Roles Do They Play?

Nobel Laureate Douglas North[2] begins his seminal work, "Institutions, Institutional Change, and Economic Performance" with the words,

R. Marney, P. Waeber, *The Emerging Markets Investor's Guide to Country Risk*,
https://doi.org/10.1007/978-3-032-26824-2_2

"institutions are the rules of the game in a society or, more formally, are the humanly devised constraints that shape human interaction. In consequence they structure incentives in human exchange, whether political, social, or economic. Institutional change shapes the way societies evolve through time and hence is the key to understanding historical change."[3] He continues, "*In the jargon of the economist, institutions define and limit the set of choices of individuals.*"[4]

For his part, the renowned economist, G.M. Hodgson,[5] reinforces the foundational role institutions play in shaping the rules by which a society operates. He wrote, "*Institutions are systems of established and prevalent social rules that structure social interactions [between individuals]. The term rule is broadly understood as an injunction or disposition, that in circumstances X, actors tend to, or are obliged to, do Y. A rule can be procedural (governing thought or other actions) or constitutive (allocating a function, position or status). Rules include norms of behavior and social conventions, as well as legal or formal rules.*"[6]

The reference to "individuals" highlights that institutions are built on the foundation of individuals and their behavior and require that society as a whole buy off. Samuel Huntington reminds us, *"Institutions are stable, valued, recurring patterns of behavior."*[7]

Institutions can take various forms, with a basic dichotomy being that between informal (taboos, norms, and customs) and formal (laws, regulations, constitutions). The change in informal institutions is a slow, evolutionary process. By contrast, formal ones can be created or modified sometimes more quickly by legislative or executive branch governmental action.[8] These private and public institutions range across the social, political, economic, and legal life within a society. A useful taxonomy appears in Williamson (2000),[9] where institutions are divided into four levels, the first two of these correspond to "informal" and "formal" (North, et al.) or in Williamson's language, "social institutions" and "institutional environment", respectively. Williamson introduces two further levels, first, governance, which includes issues of private order, and contract enforcement, and second, the economy, which includes issues of resource allocation and macroeconomic optimality analysis.

"Institutions" versus "Organizations"

In common practice, we use the words "institutions" and 'organizations" interchangeably. In fact, there is an important distinction, to which we will adhere.

The economist and scholar E.L. Khalil, well known for his work on the distinction between institutions and organizations, writes, "*Organizations are agents like households, firms, and states that have preferences and objectives. Institutions are formal and informal social constraints (rules, habits, constitutions, laws, conventions) which apparently reduce the total scarce resources.*"[10]

Hodgson digs deeper to highlight this difference, saying, "*Institutions must involve some shared conceptions, to make rules operative. Languages, money, law, weights, measures, traffic conventions, table manners, firms and all other organizations are institutions. All institutions are social structures, but not all social structures are institutions. For example, a demographic structure of a society is not necessarily an institution. Organizations are an important subclass of institutions, with the added features of boundaries, structure, membership criteria and principles of sovereignty.*"[11]

Using a sports analogy, Douglas North puts it more simply, likening institutions to the rules of the game, and organizations to the teams playing the sport.[12] Examples in North include: political bodies (parties, the Senate, regulatory agencies, ministries), economic bodies (firms, trade unions), social bodies (churches, clubs), and educational bodies (schools, universities).[13]

The Roles of Institutions

To understand why institutions are important to social cohesion, political stability, and economic performance (not to mention debt resolution), we should first focus on the roles they play. Institutions strive to achieve efficiency through the reduction of uncertainty and the provision of transparent and stable rules. Or in North's words, "*The major role of institutions in a society is to reduce uncertainty by establishing a stable (but not necessarily efficient) structure to human interaction.*"[14]

Unpredictability in actions and outcomes stands in the way of a reduction in transaction costs and hence hampers the attainment of greater economic efficiency. Institutions aim to make individual actions predictable. Dobler comments, "*Whether a formal rule or morals and norms – provide behavioral guidelines, which help an individual choose their own actions and predict others' behaviors.*"[15]

There is no steady state, no permanent, optimal set of institutional arrangements for a society over time, nor across societies. Institutions exist in a condition of constant change, albeit often impossible to perceive until history is written. North suggests, "*But the stability of institutions in no way gainsays the fact that they are changing. From conventions, codes of conduct, and norms of behavior to statute law, and common law, and contracts between individuals, institutions are evolving and, therefore, are continually altering the choices available to us."*[16]

Institutional change reflects the attempt of those in power to adapt to the evolution of the society, and its political and economic opportunities.[17] In a perfect world, this evolution is towards greater economic efficiency, for example via more secure property rights and contract enforcement throughout society. At other times, however politically powerful elements, direct institutional change, and resulting organizational development towards selective enforcement of such elements. The result is the creation of less efficient economic models. Below we discuss Acemoglu and Robinson's distinction between inclusive and extractive institutions,[18] as well as a Dercon's theory of the Development Bargain[19] to provide two perspectives on the creation or mitigation of less efficient economic models.

Box 2.1: "Things Are Not Always as They Seem"

A Cautionary Note—what's written is not always what happens!

One example—financial supervision. In all, jurisdictions have rules and regulations to protect the public, based on the concept that banks need to be subject to regulation, and that effective supervisory oversight is required to ensure compliance. The organizational structures, prudential policy technologies, and the like are similar. Yet, in practice, huge differences in effectiveness are apparent. The gaps are not just between countries (say, between Switzerland and the Democratic Republic of the Congo), but can arise over time in the same location, depending on politics, personalities, and market forces (say, in the USA, sometimes good, sometimes bad).

Another example—the judiciary. Countries that appear to have effective and equitable judiciaries—often scoring similarly on rule-of-law or judicial effectiveness indices—can nonetheless operate very different systems in practice. These differences arise because judicial outcomes are shaped not only by formal rules, but by informal power structures and political incentives that condition how those rules are applied.

Therefore, in our case studies and accompanying analysis, we make the effort to move beyond institutional form to their actual operation and practical impact on economic, political, legal, and financial activity.

2.2 The Role of Institutions in the Growth Story

Institutions and Growth

The question before policy makers is not "Do institutions matter" for economic growth, but "*which institutions matter and how does one acquire them?*"

(Rodrik—2000)[20] or North's questions of *"The central puzzle of human history is-to account for the widely divergent paths of historical change. How have societies diverged? What accounts for their widely disparate performance characteristics?"*[21]

Let's consider these questions from multiple angles.

First, according to Huntington's "Gap Hypothesis",[22] as societies experience social change and economic development, their governments must strive to manage the interaction of these forces and deliver stability and sustainable growth. Huntington addresses the risk that there is a lack of calibration between the aspirations for social and economic advancement (mobility) on the one hand, and the adequacy of the political institutions to sustain increases in national income and provide equality of opportunity for all citizens. When institutional development lags, members of the newly mobilized society fail to realize their heightened aspirations and grow frustrated. Further, there is typically a trend towards greater wealth and income inequality, and more pervasive corruption. This frustration generates political instability and creates headwinds to continued social and economic progress. Alternatively, the higher the degree of political institutionalization and political participation on the part of society, the more well developed and modern is the political community. In this case, the constructive calibration between social forces and institutions translates into a stable political community in which sustainable economic and financial development is more likely to be achieved. Political and economic institutions are mutually self-reinforcing, and hence in such a situation, economic and financial stability is enhanced. Additionally, Professor Huntington argues that *"the relation between the rate of economic growth and political instability varies with the level of economic development."*[23] Below a certain low level of economic development, people are more concerned about *"just getting by"*. Poverty acts as a barrier to the political instability that tends to develop at higher developmental levels where more affluent and better educated people mobilize to challenge the status quo.

Second, North spent much of his academic career investigating the question of why countries fail to converge to a common level of development, with the focus on institutions. His views evolved over time. In North and Thomas (1973)[24] he subscribed to the Alchian (1950) theory that competition would weed out inefficient institutions, and therefore, over time, all economies should converge. But as the evidence accumulated—say, Nigeria versus Singapore or even Malaysia/Indonesia—his thinking evolved, and he arrived at a point where he acknowledged the reality that not all countries achieve this convergence.[25] Positive institutional derives from pressures of the entrepreneurial class to modify the existing institutional framework for their benefit. Perception of necessary reforms and the political capacity to affect and sustain such changes, however marginally, are necessary preconditions. Successful economies engineer this positive institutional change; stagnant or declining economies do not. North develops this characterization of comparative, institutional evolution by juxtaposing successful developmental paths with examples of persistent failure.

Third, Fukuyama posited in "Political Order and Political Decay"[26] three, fundamental institutions, which he defined as stable, reoccurring patterns of behavior. These are the state, rule of law, and representative democracy.[27] He identified the rule of law and the quality of government—the capacity to fulfil the required functions—as essential to a stable and prosperous society.[28] Democratic participation acts as a useful check on corruption/rent seeking in government, which enhances economic efficiency.[29] Underdeveloped institutions mean an underdeveloped economy.

Fourth, Acemoglu, Johnson, and Robinson[30] ask the question of why some countries are poorer than others. The authors concur with North, and North and Thomas's views (see above) that the fundamental explanation of comparative growth are differences in institutions. On questions of culture, geography, and institutions as growth drivers the authors argue that the third predominates. They continue by discussing the nature of relevant institutions and argue that economic institutions matter for economic growth because they shape the incentives of key economic actors in society, they influence investments in physical and human capital and technology, and the organization of production. More than geography or culture, institutions determine not only the size, but also the division of the pie. Economic institutions are endogenous. They are determined as collective choices of the society, in large part for their economic consequences. Political factions compete to shape the economic institutions. The most powerful political groups determining the shape of these institutions. Implicit in the notion that political power determines economic institutions is the idea that there are conflicting interests over the distribution of resources and therefore indirectly over the set of economic institutions. Economic institutions are important because they influence the structure of economic incentives in society. Without property rights, individuals will not have the incentive to invest in physical or human capital or adopt more efficient technologies. Economic institutions are also important because they help to allocate resources to their most efficient uses, they determine who gets profits, revenues, and residual rights of control. The authors define "*good economic institutions as those that provide security of property rights and relatively equal access to economic resources to a broad cross-section of society.*"[31]

Fifth, Dercon refines the understanding of politics and the creation/strengthening of so-called good economic institutions.[32] The principal message of the book is a "development bargain" is necessary for growth. Successful developing countries pursue diverse economic, legal/regulatory, tax, and other related policies to arrive at similar developmental outcomes. There is no single, simple recipe. The common theme throughout "success stories" is that there is a durable commitment on the part of the political elite to focus on broad-based, sustainable economic development, as opposed to more insular or extractive model that maximizes the benefit to the elite over society as a whole—the smaller slice of a much bigger pie, and one that keeps coming. Hence, the pre-conditions for growth—both the institutions and the exercise of the organizations' mandates—are shaped to this end.

Sixth, the 2006 Nobel Laureate Edmund Phelps in the book "Mass Flourishing"[33] coined the expression of "endogenous innovation", the piston of growth of which supportive institutions are an essential component. Institutions condition society to encourage or discourage individual intellectual growth and personal achievement through which people and by extension their surrounding world prosper or stagnate. Phelps terms this "flourishing".[34] At the societal level, "mass flourishing", Phelps argues, "*comes from broad involvement of people in the processes of innovation: the conception, development, and spread of new methods and products—'indigenous innovation' down to the 'grassroots*[35]*'*". The casual chain can form into a virtuous positive feedback loop of values to institutions to innovation to growth and back again—think of the forward movement of a piston—or when negative institutions intervene, and act to reverse the direction of the piston. Phelps stresses, however, that supporting institutions alone are not sufficient. People must recognize that "*their prosperity depends on the breadth and depth of their innovative activity.*"[36] Micro-level innovations in technology, organization, finance, and commerce arise from this mass flourishing of striving to newness, supported by values and enabling institutions, Phelps' "indigenous innovation".

Seventh and last, Martin Wolf in the Crisis of Democratic Capitalism, cited above, echoes a similar theme, identifying "*elite self-interest*" as one of five drivers of the marriage of market capitalism to an expansion of liberal democracy, along with ideology, aspirations, empowerment, and influence.[37] He writes, "The ability and willingness of oligarchies to create and sustain effective political coalitions while tolerating genuine democracy is central to the story in this book."[38]

What does this all tell us? Consider two themes:

First, the authors provide similar answers to North's central question of what accounts for widely disparate economic outcomes, namely the presence of understandable, accepted, predictable, inclusive, and generally efficient rules of engagement (i.e., institutions), property rights, equal access to economic resources, supported by the relevant institutions and organizations that encourage and sustain innovation, with appropriate authority to regulate behavior and enforce compliance differentiate the successful from the underperformers. In particular, Fukuyama reaffirms the central role of the rule of law and the quality of government as essential to a stable and prosperous society, pointing to political participation as a guardrail against corruption/rent seeking in government.[39] Phelps argues for values that encourage the necessary curiosity and courage to drive individuals to innovate and take risks, within and upon a supportive institutional framework.[40]

Second, what determines when and how institutions develop in this ideal direction? Huntington[41] argues that society's values, aspirations, and institutions must be well-calibrated to ensure a stable political community in which sustainable economic and financial development is more likely to be achieved. How and when do institutions evolve? North[42] argues positive institutional development derives from pressures of the entrepreneurial class to modify the existing institutional framework for their benefit. Wolf agrees that the decisions of the elite, their "self-interest", determine the path of institutional development. Dercon[43] argues that successful outcome result when there is a lasting commitment on the part of the political elite to focus on broad-based, sustainable economic development, as opposed to more insular or extractive model that maximizes the benefit to the elite over society. Lastly, beyond a certain, take-off point, broad-based indigenous innovation fuels economic success, as Phelps suggests.

Box 2.2: Why We Are Poor? (F. Sionel Jose)

The renowned Philippine novelist and essayist F. Sionel Jose spent a lifetime observing and writing about the inequality and grinding poverty of his homeland, while marveling at the great achievements of the Philippine diaspora, estimated at some 6.1 million.[1] In the essay, "Why we are poor?"[2] he once wrote, "The basic question really is why we did not modernize fast enough and thereby doom our people to poverty?[3]" He identified the failure to develop inclusive institutions that create a sense of one country, with equal opportunities and protections for all. The obstacles to such an equitable, modern society do not arise from the global economy, resource endowments, or Acts-of-God, he argued, but rather the failure of Filipinos themselves to recognize that "We are our own enemy. And we must have the courage, the will to change ourselves."[4]

And what did F. Sionel Jose feel must be changed? Without using the same words, he implied "institutions", saying, "We condone cronyism and corruption, and we don't ostracize or punish the crooks in our midst. Both cronyism and corruption are wasteful but we allow their practice because our loyalty is to family or friend, not to the larger good."[5] *That is, lacking the political, legal, and economic institutions that sustain dynamic and equitable development, Filipinos retreated into their own fiefs, tribes, and families, where parochial interests superseded those of the nation. In their own country, Filipinos' economic and social wellbeing lagged that of their neighbors elsewhere in Asia for so much of the past half century. This stood in stark contrast to their formidable achievements, indeed often over-performance, in academics, medicine, industry, and finance in their new, adopted homelands. The difference? Not the people, but the institutional environment of the countries in which they had come to live. This case is a compelling example of the central role of institutions in development. It is noteworthy how impressively the Philippines has progressed economically, and the institutional framework matured in recent years. This record provides yet another validation of the connection between growth and institutional development.*

1. *See* https://worldpopulationreview.com/country-rankings/immigration-by-country#
2. F. Sionel Jose, "Why we are poor" in Termites in the Sala, Heroes in the Attic, published by Solidaridad Publishing House: Manila, 2005.
3. F. Sionel Jose, *op. cit.*
4. F. Sionel Jose, *op. cit.*
5. *See* https://liberaleconomy.wordpress.com/2006/11/23/fsionil-joses-why-are-filipinos-so-poor/.

Before concluding, let's consider one example that should resonate with many if not all—politics. What government does or fails to do fills our lives. Sound, stable politics create a more supportive environment than will be the case where a society is plagued by severe degrees of political instability, characterized by erratic policy making, drastic changes in the nature and direction of administrations/regimes, and reoccurring, fundamental rewriting of society's rules of engagement. A country where people have the ability and confidence to expend the time and expense in education, develop new technologies, raise and invest capital, and operate in safe, inefficient, and predictable markets will achieve higher and more sustainable growth than countries where the opposite is the case. In the research of Aisen and Veiga,[44] the authors concluded that, "*Higher degrees of political instability are associated with lower growth rates of GDP per capita,*" and argued there to be multiple transmission channels, including lower productivity, and physical and human capital accumulation.[45] At its base, their conclusion is there is a clear association between instability in politics and higher uncertainty in future economic policy.[46]

Closing Messages

First—institutions are important for investment and growth.

As many have written that institutions are important to sustainable economic growth is beyond dispute. What institutional framework is most appropriate for each country and how these institutions affect the macroeconomy and the financial system varies. Notwithstanding jurisdictional differences in form, the presence of a core set of strong institutions in the areas of law, politics, economics, and finance is a necessary condition for growth and, relevant to this book's purpose, in the creation of a positive investment climate. To preserve the key message of this chapter, take a mental photograph of a selection of countries excerpted from the World Bank's Worldwide Governance Indicators (Fig. 2.1):[47]

The data only goes back to 1996, hence underemphasizing the point, but still deliver a clear message. The success stories (Singapore, Malaysia, Botswana)

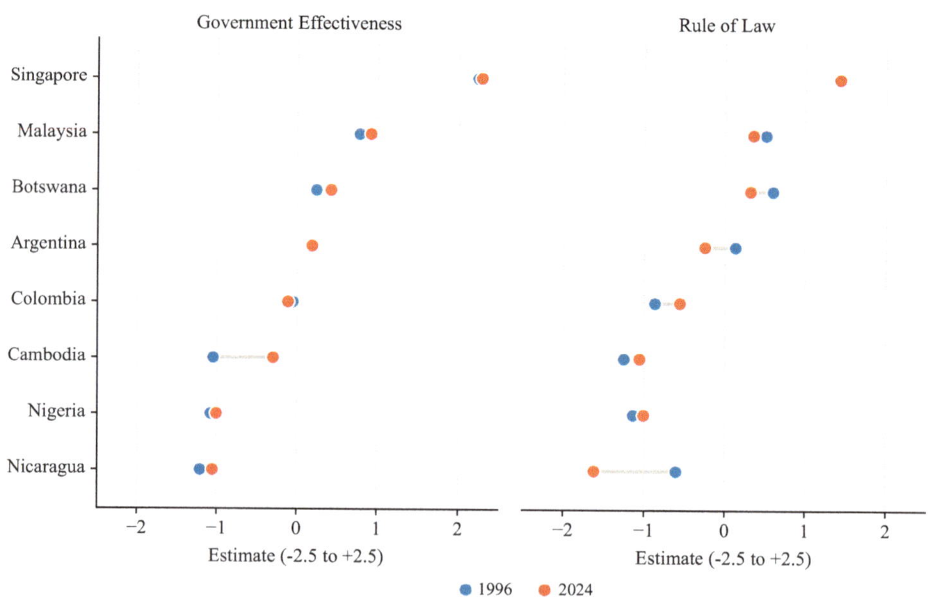

Fig. 2.1 Evolution of selected Worldwide Governance Indicators. (Source: The World Bank)

show higher ranks in government effectiveness and rule of law than the remaining countries. The former have outperformed economically and have higher sovereign ratings. Noteworthy is the observation that two countries—Argentina and Nicaragua—have experienced declines in their rankings over the period, a timeframe in which their economies have struggled.

Second—the EMDE institutional development is diverse.

The EMDE panorama is diverse, and hence a comparison of institutions between AEs and EMDEs a daunting task. While a generalized "charcoal sketch" might appear, the reader is advised to ascertain the characteristics of each investee country. As the IMF counsels (Fig. 2.2):

> *Developing countries are a heterogeneous group with different structures, vulnerabilities, and policy frameworks. They differ markedly in their levels of development, macroeconomic performance, institutional quality, and integration into global markets.*[48]

Element	AE	EMDE
Institutional strength	Resilient, able to weather political change and external shocks	Ranging from moderately resilient to fragile
Political governance	Typically democratic, with institutionalized checks and balances	Diverse forms ranging from democracies to authoritarian regimes, with weak checks and balances
Rule of Law	Strong	Generally weaker, with inconsistent application and transparency
Judiciary	Independent, competent, and impartial	Ranging from partially independent to politically-controlled
Bureaucracy	Professional and meritocratic	Mixed. In weaker cases, clientelist
Human capital development	High quality, with wide access	Mixed. Often underfunded with poor outcomes
Property rights	Strong protections and contract enforcement	Mixed – moderate to weak protections and contract enforcement
Control of corruption	Low incidence, with strong enforcement	Higher incidence with weaker enforcement
Infrastructure	Physical and technological assets well developed	Less developed

Fig. 2.2 Comparison of institutions between AEs and EMDEs. (Source: The Authors)

2.3 Institutions and the Investment Climate

Definition

The World Bank defines the investment climate as "*The set of location-specific factors shaping the opportunities and incentives for firms to invest productively, create jobs, and expand. It includes macroeconomic stability, governance, infrastructure, labor skills, and the regulatory and institutional environment.*"[49]

In its 2004 study, "Improving the Investment Climate for Growth and Poverty Reduction",[50] the World Bank concludes that a "healthy investment climate" is essential for sustainable and inclusive growth. Governments have central parts to play in strengthening the institutional framework, constructing necessary infrastructure, supporting human capital development, and implementing policy measures aimed at encouraging innovation and investment/risk-taking by the private sector. Similar to the view of institutions as a growth driver, we can argue there is no real debate that a positive environment for investors is good for business, and stronger, appropriate institutions are core.

Elements

The factors contributing to a positive investment climate are many and dynamic. In the Matrix below, we catalogue these elements ("Investment Climate Elements") and link them to their respective prerequisites and summarize the benefits of each. To enhance an understanding of how these elements relate to each other, we divide them into four levels, shown graphically here, in this "Investment Climate Roadmap" (Fig. 2.3):

At the base sits a country's "endowment", consisting of its climatic conditions (temperatures, rain patterns, exposure to extreme weather events, and the like) and its natural resources. For example, consider natural capital endowments in advanced economies like Australia, Canada, Norway, and Singapore, and EMDEs like Brazil, Jamaica, Nigeria, and the Philippines. The diversity is manifest and alone cannot predict economic outcomes. Think of natural resource-rich countries like Norway and Nigeria or natural resource weak (island) economies such as Singapore and Jamaica. The economic outcomes (and hence investment potentials overall) depend on how a country uses its natural capital or reacts to its lack to fashion a sustainable economic outcome. Again, what explains Norway v. Nigeria, Singapore v. Jamaica?

We argue—institutions—and hence in this model, resting on this foundation are these informal and formal rules by which society operates, politics are

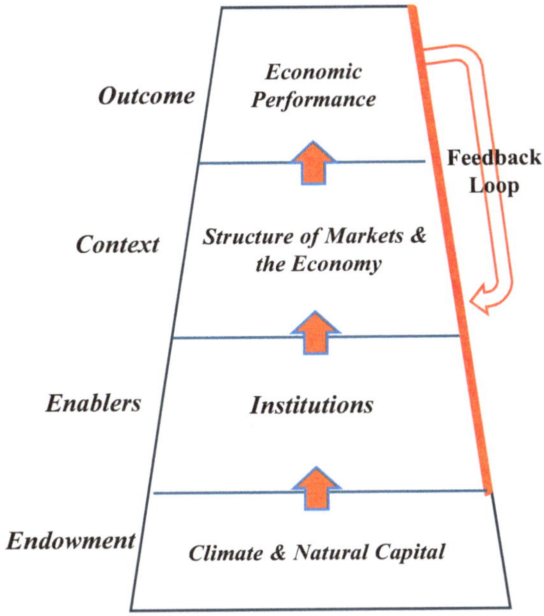

Fig. 2.3 Flow of the investment climate. (Source: The Authors)

framed, and human activity ensues. Education and health are essential ingredients for the development of human capital, which enables creativity and innovation in a constructive risk-taking space secured by strong rule of law and supported by social and political stability.

On the third level, this potential plays out in a national context, where efficient markets and a balanced well-functioning economy facilitate capital formation, mobilization, and its application in productive investments. Flash again—Norway v. Nigeria, Singapore v. Jamaica.

On the fourth level, the institutional framework, the structure of the economy, and the efficiency of markets translate into actual macroeconomic performance and stability over time. In this state, of course, not all new investment projects succeed, just as like a rugby team on the pitch for which not all matches end well. However, while both the investor and the fly-half accept this, they both expect the environment to support the activity, and defined rules of engagement to be respected. Only in this situation will investors risk their capital (and rugby players their bodies).

We defer a more-in-depth discussion, including a series of case application to the investment analysis and underwriting process to the chapters which follow.[51]

A Global Perspective

We use the IMD World Competitiveness Rankings as a proxy for the relative strength of countries' investment climates[52]. In 2025, IMD covers 69 countries, basing its ranking on a proprietary methodology[53]. In simple terms, the approach uses four main factors: (1) economic performance; (2) business efficiency; (3) government efficiency; and (4) infrastructure. These main categories are then divided into sets of subfactors, using a combination of hard data (e.g., national income, trade accounts, etc.) sourced from international, regional, and national statistical services, and soft data focusing on relevant competitiveness indicators sourced from surveys. The hard data contributes roughly two-thirds of the ranking. The Competitive Factors and Subfactors consist of the following: (1) Economic Performance—domestic economy, international trade, international investment, employment, and prices; (2) Business Efficiency—Productivity, labor market, finance, management practices, attitudes, and values; (3) Government Efficiency—public finance, tax policy, institutional framework, business legislation, and social framework; and (4) Infrastructure—basic infrastructure, technological infrastructure, scientific infrastructure, health and environment, and education.

The 2025 ranking appears in Fig. 2.4.

The entirety of the EMDE cohort is not covered owing to data availability, methodological consistency, and the IMD's high standards of quality control. Notwithstanding, the data permits the conclusion that the critical mass of the missing EMDE countries would rest in the bottom third of the table.

Rank	Country	Score	Rank	Country	Score	Rank	Country	Score
1	Switzerland	100	24	Belgium	74.6	47	Jordan	57.8
2	Singapore	99.4	25	Czech Republic	73.7	48	Hungary	56.7
3	Hong Kong SAR	99.2	26	Austria	73.6	49	Romania	56.6
4	Denmark	97.5	27	Korea Republic	73.4	50	Greece	55.3
5	UAE	96.1	28	Oman	72.9	51	Philippines	54.9
6	Taiwan	93.7	29	United Kingdom	71.9	52	Poland	53.9
7	Ireland	91.3	30	Thailand	71.3	53	Croatia	51.2
8	Sweden	90.2	31	New Zealand	70.2	54	Colombia	49.7
9	Qatar	89.9	32	France	69.9	55	Mexico	49.8
10	Netherlands	89.8	33	Estonia	69.7	56	Kenya	48.3
11	Canada	88.7	34	Kazakhstan	69.0	57	Bulgaria	48.0
12	Norway	86.2	35	Japan	68.7	58	Brazil	46.4
13	USA	84.3	36	Kuwait	68.7	59	Botswana	46.1
14	Finalnd	83.8	37	Portugal	67.8	60	Peru	45.9
15	Iceland	83.5	38	Latvia	67.0	61	Ghana	44.2
16	China	82.1	39	Spain	65.8	62	Argentina	42.8
17	Saudi Arabia	82.1	40	Indonesia	64.3	63	Slovak Republic	42.8
18	Australia	78.4	41	India	64.2	64	South Africa	42.0
19	Germany	78.2	42	Chile	62.5	65	Mongolia	40.9
20	Luxembourg	78.2	43	Italy	62.5	66	Turkiye	40.4
21	Lithuania	77.7	44	Cyprus	61.8	67	Nigeria	39.7
22	Bahrain	76.6	45	Puerto Rico	61.0	68	Namibia	37.5
23	Malaysia	74.8	46	Slovenia	59.1	69	Venezuela	25.5

Fig. 2.4 IMD World Competitiveness Ranking 2025. (Source: IMD)

Classification	IMD Rank	WGI - Government Effectiveness	WGI - Rule of Law	WGI - Control of Corruption
Advanced Economies	8.0	1.8	1.8	1.9
EMDE	58.0	(0.4)	(0.5)	(0.5)

Fig. 2.5 AE vs. EMDE—Average IMD and WGI scores. (Source: IMD, World Bank WGI, the Authors Calculations)

Above, we used the WGI as an indicator of general institutional strength and the quality of governance. For this purpose, this tool is more effective than the IMD Ranking, whose focus is a broader measure of national economic competitiveness in which the WGI themes enter as subfactors. These measures are highly complementary. We argue above in this chapter that the strength of institutions is the primary driver of differences in economic outcomes over time, and will link below their vital importance to the investment underwriting and management process. In general, the stronger the institutional framework, the better is the investment climate, and the better the investment climate, the more competitive the country. Hence at the AE vs. EMDE level, the IMD (ranking) and WGI (scored between −2.5: weak governance and +2.5: strong governance) approaches should deliver a broadly similar result, as they do (Fig. 2.5).

Here our operative assumption will be that the institutional framework in the EMDE cohort is generally less well-developed than AEs. Conditions vary from country to country, and fluctuate over time. Weak rule of law, judiciaries, policy-making design and implementation, control of corruption, and the like represent challenges to successful investment outcomes. We use the word "challenge" and not "obstacles" or "blocks" intentionally. Our intention is to highlight the need to understand and attempt to mitigate the damaging effects of impaired or missing institutional elements. Our discussion below and the use of case studies in this book will not result in a comprehensive and definitive mapping of the risk topography and applicable structural mitigants. Instead, the objective is to provide a form of seafarer's rutter or compass to help navigate the institutional shoals that exist more in EDME markets than in the AEs.

2.4 Implications for Investors

Introduction

In this section, we pick up the navigational tools and begin the process to understand how they can be used. The approach we follow is to outline a standard investment life cycle, which encompasses the work from origination to divestment (or when things go awry, special operations). In each phase, we describe the major tasks, identify the institutional linkages, and point out the resulting challenges to investors. The treatment will be intentionally cursory, with the hope that the structure and approach will identify major challenges (not all), but more importantly provide an evaluative method employable throughout the book.

Investment Life Cycle: The Five Phases

Our five phases appear as follows:

First: Origination
Investment sourcing, evaluation, structuring, and approving
Second: Deployment
Documentation, fulfillment of conditions precedent/subsequent, including all requisite approvals and legal actions (e.g., perfection of security, registrations, etc.), and disbursement(s).
Third: Holding Period
Monitoring, on-going analysis and evaluation, covenant compliance checks (debt or certain forms of hybrid capital), miscellaneous, requisite investment management activities, board and other shareholding activities (equity)
Fourth: Divestment
Final maturity and last installment / other amounts (debt or certain forms of hybrid capital), exit (equity)
Fifth: Special Operations (when necessary)
Restructurings, recapitalizations, judicial liquidation, and other requisite actions.

The impact of macro-level, market, legal and regulatory institutions is felt throughout the investment cycle, with the resulting transactional challenges depending on the jurisdiction, the nature of the investment, the actors, and the context. A simplified exposition appears below. We reemphasize that the institutional linkages and resulting challenges cited below are intended to demonstrate the thought process, not to be exhaustive. We add to the breadth and depth of the evaluation of the impact of institutions below and in Chap. 5 and in the case studies in Chaps. 14–18.

Phase	Institutional linkages	Challenges
1. Origination	• Pertinent law and regulation • Governance and accounting standards • Regulatory regime • Market supervisory regime and enforcement powers • Credit bureau and other market data sources	• Accuracy of the numbers • Reliability of the credit and/or business history • Clarity of pertinent legal provisions • Registration and enforceability of security arrangements • Shareholder rights and protections • Foreign investor protections
2. Deployment	• From (1) above • Security and other contract enforcement capabilities	• Failure to perfect security interests • Governance failures at the investee level to document correctly the transaction to ensure binding obligations
3. Holding period	• From (1) above • Macroeconomy and investment climate	Events that negatively affect performance and financial condition: • Systematic risks • Governance failures or fraud • Legal and/or regulatory changes • Political instability
4. Divestment	• From (1) and (3) above • Investor (including foreign) rules • Capital repatriation rules • Foreign exchange regime	• Generalized moratoria on foreign capital outflows • Discriminatory FX, tax or other treatment of foreign lenders/investors
5. Special operations	• From (1), (3), and (4) above • Specialized extra-judicial and judicial legal and regulatory treatment and processes for debt resolution or investor dispute	• Underdeveloped or inefficient resolution environment • Failure of the government to adhere to debt and investment resolution law and regulation in a non-discriminatory manner to foreigners • Slow and ineffective legal processes • Politically connected parties exploiting the resolution process to the detriment of lenders or investors

To anticipate the subsequent, more rigorous treatment of the institutional challenges confronting EMDE investors, we choose one example for the moment—debt default and workouts. Here we borrow from Richard Marney and Timothy Stubbs—*Emerging Markets Debt Restructuring: Effectively*

Navigating Local Institutional Frameworks[54] In this book, the authors frame "ten observations" on the practical and formal characteristics or challenges confronting foreign lenders in debt distress situations, based on their decades of experience in the EMDE as investors, legal counsel, and restructuring specialists. These are:

1. Heightened volatility in economic activity, with greater frequency / depth of recessions, and higher incidence of systemic or broad-based crises (banking, debt, and/or currency) creating more challenging credit conditions and potentially higher default rates.
2. Underdeveloped institutions, contributing to pervasive flaws in rule of law, regulatory supervision, and corporate governance.
3. Greater severity when the financial distress case is disclosed or recognized.
4. Higher incidence of secured, collateral-based lending versus unsecured, cash flow-based lending.
5. Absence of, or inadequate, institutional arrangements to support effective judicial restructurings (hybrid or full).
6. Material challenges in organizing a group of participating creditors, generally and more in particular consisting of both local and foreign lenders
7. Poor enforcement of stakeholder rights, notably in the case of foreign shareholders and/or lenders.
8. Actions by politically connected interests or other corrupt actors which impede equitable outcomes.
9. Underdeveloped debt resolution practices, personnel, and financial transaction structuring technologies.
10. Limited access to capital in amount, duration, and legal structure.

The observations principally reflect underdeveloped legal and judicial institutions.[55] However, in the cases of (1) and (10), the impact on macroeconomic performance and stability and financial development is indirect. Central to these challenges is the level of development of the insolvency framework, which importantly reflects the maturity of the jurisdiction's institutions.

Marney and Stubbs presented a grading or ranking of the quality of the EMDE insolvency frameworks (borrowing from the Clint Eastwood classic western, the "Good, the Bad and the Ugly"). This ranking used: (1) the use of the INSOL principles pertaining to consensual, out-of-court restructurings; (2) the degree of development of specialized and complete legal arrangements for judicial restructurings; and (3) the actual outcomes of debt restructurings, giving higher credit for less-costly out-of-court and going-concern outcomes.

The ranking appears in Fig. 2.6.

	Good	Bad	Ugly
INSOL Principles known and/or observed	Known and observed in practice	Typically not known and observed in practice	Not known/observed in practice
Standalone Insolvency Law with provisions for judicial restructuring	Yes Includes modern hybrid and full judicial restructuring procedures, cross-class cram down and DIP finance similar to US Ch. 11. There is a highly professional and competent insolvency office holder (IOH) community. There are specialised bankruptcy courts with experienced, commercially-minded judges. The courts are generally efficient, despite occasional delays. There is a relatively reliable rule of law. Stigma is no longer an issue for borrowers.	Yes, but process plagued with inefficiencies resulting in delays and poor execution The insolvency law includes restructuring provisions, but in practice these are not widely used. A long observation period (1-year, subject to extension) also hinders restructurings. There is no hybrid procedure nor DIP finance. Insolvency proceedings are heard by commercial courts (but not specialised bankruptcy courts). Courts are sometimes unpredictable and slow with overloaded dockets, with non-commercially-minded judges. However, this tends to vary depending on whether courts are in the capital city or provinces. The IOH profession is still weak (though improving slowly). Stigma is a persistent issue for borrowers.	No standalone law and limited practical experience with judicial restructurings Decades-old insolvency provisions are contained in various different legal acts (civil and commercial codes) and are significantly out of step with international bankruptcy practice. Insolvency proceedings are heard in courts of general jurisdiction (which also hear criminal, family law and civil matters), hence not commercially-minded. Courts are notoriously slow, unpredictable, non-independent and subject to outside influence and corruption. The IOH profession is weak and unreliable, focused in virtually every proceeding on liquidation. Stigma is a significant issue for borrowers.
Consensual restructurings	Common	Less-common	Rare
Outcomes	Ranging from "going-concern" to liquidation, depending on the circumstances	Reorganization outcomes *less* frequent	Reorganization outcomes even *less* frequent to the point of liquidation being the expected result

Fig. 2.6 Quality of EMDEs' insolvency frameworks. (Source: Marney and Stubbs—Emerging Markets Debt Restructuring (2024))

Regime / Episode	Ugly	Bad	Good
Severe	Case 1	Case 2	Case 3
Mild	Case 4	Case 5	Case 6

Fig. 2.7 Insolvency episode heatmap. (Source: Marney and Stubbs—Emerging Markets Debt Restructuring (2024))

In the opinion of Marney and Stubbs, few of the EMDEs fit into the "Good" category, a moderate group is solidly in the "Bad", while the majority are in the lower "Bad" to "Ugly" range. The expected loss implications are material. Figure 2.7 shows a heat map which estimates the loss (green is low, red is high) as a function of the severity of the shock and the development level of the insolvency framework:

The progression from red to green depicts the increasing challenges to achieving a successful outcome and limiting credit losses, depending on the type of case (mild vs. severe) and the relative stage of institutional development (Good, Bad, or Ugly). This is one example of the material impact that the level of institutional development can have on investment results. More will follow.

Notes

1. Moody's Investors Service (2022). *Sovereign Ratings Methodology*. November 2022; Standard & Poor's Ratings Services (2021). *Sovereign Rating Methodology: Incorporating Political Institutions and Governance*. Update Note; Fitch Ratings (2023). *Sovereign Rating Criteria*. March 2023.
2. *Dr.North shared the 1993 Nobel Prize in Economic Sciences with Robert Fogel for applying economic theory and quantitative methods to explain long-term economic and institutional change.*
3. North, Douglass C., Institutions, Institutional Change and Economic Performance (Cambridge University Press, 1990), p. 3.
4. North (1990), page 4.
5. *Dr. Hodgson is best known for his work on evolutionary economics and the theory of institutions.*
6. Hodgson, G.M. (2023) The Wealth of a Nation—Institutional Foundations of English Capitalism: Princeton University Press, page 191.
7. Huntington, Samuel P., Political Order in Changing Societies (New Haven, Yale University Press, 2006), page 9.
8. Notably, however, laws and regulatory regimes cannot race forward so quickly as to be too far out ahead of a society's informal norms. As Elizabeth Cady Stanton has said, "To make laws that man cannot and will not obey, serves to bring all law into contempt. It is very important in a republic, that the people should respect the laws, for if we throw them to the winds, what becomes of civil government?"
9. Williamson, O. E. (2000) *The New Institutional Economics: Taking Stock, Looking Ahead,* Journal of Economic Literature, 38(3), pp. 595–613.
10. Khalil, E.L., 1995. Organizations versus institutions. *Journal of Institutional and Theoretical Economics,* 151(3), pp.445–466.
11. Hodgson, G.M. (2023 op. cit., page 192.
12. North (1990), page 4.
13. North (1990), page 5.
14. North (1990), page 6.
15. Dobler, C.(2019) The Impact of Formal and Informal Institutions on Economic Growth in Hohenheimer Volkswirtschaftliche Schriften. 65, page 10.
16. North (1990) *op. cit.* Page 6.

17. North (1990) *op. cit.* Page 7.
18. Acemoglu, D. and Robinson, J.A. (2012) Why Nations Fail: The Origins of Power, Prosperity, and Poverty: Crown Publishers.
19. Dercon, S. "Gambling on Development", Hurst and Company, London, 2022.
20. Rodrik (2000) Institutions for High Quality Growth - NBER Working Paper No. 7540.
21. North (1990) *op. cit*, page 6.
22. Huntington (1984) *op. cit* pages 53–55 Samuel P., "Political Order in Changing Societies", 1968, Yale University Press, New Haven
23. Huntington (1984), *op. cit.*
24. North, Douglass C. and Robert P. Thomas, "The Rise of the Western World: A New Economic History", 1973, Cambridge University Press, Cambridge UK.
25. North (1990). page 7—His fuller answer to the question concerning divergent growth trajectories appears: *"The answer hinges on the difference between institutions and organizations and the interaction between them that shapes the direction of institutional change. Institutions, together with the standard constraints of economic theory, determine the opportunities in a society. Organizations are created to take advantage of those opportunities, and, as the organizations evolve, they alter the institutions. The resultant path of institutional change is shaped by (1) the lock-in that comes from the symbiotic relationship between institutions and the organizations that have evolved as a consequence of the incentive structure provided by those institutions and (2) the feedback process by which human beings perceive and react to changes in the opportunity set. The increasing returns characteristics of an institutional matrix that produces lock-in come from the dependence of the resultant organizations on that institutional framework and the consequent network externalities that arise. Both the formal and the informal institutional constraints result in particular exchange organizations that have come into existence because of the incentives embodied in the framework and therefore depend on it for the profitability of the activities that they undertake."*
26. Fukuyama, F. "Political order and Political Decay—From the Industrial Revolution to the Globalization of Democracy", (2014,) Profile Books, London.
27. Fukuyama (2014), *op. cit* .pages 37–9.
28. Fukuyama (2014), *op. cit.* Pages 37, 52–3.
29. Fukuyama (2014), *op. cit* .pages 81–84.
30. Acemoglu, D., Johnson S., and J. Robinson 2004. "Institutions as the Fundamental Cause of Long-Run Growth".
31. Acemoglu, D., Johnson S., and J. Robinson, (2004) *op. cit,* page 9.
32. Dercon,(2022) *op. cit.*
33. Phelps, E.S. (2013) Mass Flourishing - How Grassroots Innovation Created Jobs: Princeton University Press.
34. Phelps (2013*) op. cit,* page 5.
35. Phelps (2013*) op. cit,* page 6.

36. Phelps (2013*) op. cit,* pages 7–8.
37. Wolf, M, (2023) *op. cit,*pages 22–7).
38. Wolf, M. (2023), *op. cit,* page 27.
39. Fukuyama, (2014) *op. cit* pages 61–63.
40. Phelps (2013*) op. cit,*
41. Huntington, (1984) *op. cit*
42. North ((1990) *op. cit.,*
43. Dercon, (2022) *op. cit.,*
44. Aisen A. and Jose Veiga, F.V. (2011) How Does Political Instability Affect Economic Growth? IMF Working Paper
45. Aisen and Veiga (2011) *op. cit.*
46. Aisen and Veiga (2011) op. cit. The authors cite several studies that have identified a negative relation between political instability and investment (Alesina and Perotti, 1996; Mauro, 1995; Özler and Rodrik, 1992; Perotti, 1996).
47. https://www.worldbank.org/en/publication/worldwide-governance-indicators
48. International Monetary Fund (2014). *World Economic Outlook: Legacies, Clouds, Uncertainties*. Washington, DC: IMF.
49. World Bank. (2005). *World Development Report 2005: A Better Investment Climate for Everyone*. Washington, DC: World Bank.
50. World Bank (2004). Improving the Investment Climate for Growth and Poverty Reduction. Washington, DC: World Bank.
51. We reference Chap. 4 (Crises), Chap. 5 (A Holistic View: Implications for Investors) and especially Chaps. 14–19 (the four case studies and Summary Learnings).
52. https://www.imd.org/centers/wcc/world-competitiveness-center/rankings/world-competitiveness-ranking/
53. https://www.imd.org/centers/wcc/world-competitiveness-center/rankings/world-competitiveness-ranking/methodology/
54. Marney, R. and Stubbs, T., 2024. *Emerging Markets Debt Restructuring: Effectively Navigating Local Institutional Frameworks*. London: Palgrave Macmillan.
55. Marney, R. and Stubbs, T., 2024. *Emerging Markets Debt Restructuring: Effectively Navigating Local Institutional Frameworks*. London: Palgrave Macmillan; Chapter 3 for a complete discussion.

3

EMDEs' Financial Development: Depth, Structure, and Stability

Finance is like a knife. You can use it to cut your food or to stab your neighbor
—Paraphrase of themes of R. Rajan

3.1 The Role of the Financial System in Development

The financial system plays a vital role in development. Or in the words of the World Bank: "Countries with more developed financial systems can better allocate capital and risks and enjoy higher, more sustainable economic growth and larger reductions in poverty and income inequality."[1] Access to financial services allows individuals to smooth consumption, build human capital, and scale businesses. Appropriate capital also improves resilience against shocks. The core functions of the financial system include mobilizing savings, allocating capital, monitoring investments and facilitating risk management, including through diversification.[2] When the financial system expands and strengthens these functions, as reflected in greater access, depth, and efficiency, this is referred to as financial development.

Empirical research clearly establishes a significant, causal impact of finance on growth. This impact, however, tends to diminish as financial systems expand and income levels rise, and may eventually even turn negative. According to the Bank for International Settlements (BIS), once the credit-to-GDP ratio exceeds 100%, the share of firms qualifying access to finance as a major business constraint does no longer decrease with higher levels of credit, implying that additional credit rather serves those firms that already enjoy

R. Marney, P. Waeber, *The Emerging Markets Investor's Guide to Country Risk*,
https://doi.org/10.1007/978-3-032-26824-2_3

ample access to finance. Most EMDEs, however, are still far from reaching that level, implying further potential of financial deepening to support economic activity.[3]

This relevance is reflected in financial inclusion being part of the Sustainable Development Goals (SDGs). SDG 1, ending poverty establishes that everyone should have access to financial services (target 1.4), while SDG 8, decent work and economic growth aim at strengthening the capacity of domestic financial institutions to encourage and expand access to banking, insurance, and financial services for all (target 8.10).[4]

What factors facilitate and typically impede financial development? At its core, financial development hinges on the quality of institutions, in particular how well the legal and regulatory environment protects property rights, allows for contract enforcement, and strengthens creditor rights.[5] These institutional underpinnings of financial development are discussed in detail in this chapter. Further, financial liberalization, defined as loosening restrictions on credit allocation, interest rates, foreign bank entry, and capital flows, was widely promoted as a way to accelerate financial development. As documented by the IMF's Financial Liberalisation Index, EMDE greatly liberalized their financial systems between the mid-1980s and the early 2000s.[6] Capital account openness, as measured by the Chinn-Ito Index, likewise increased during that time, though EMDE remained divided between countries that kept their capital accounts rather closed and those that opened up. Yet financial liberalization proved no panacea: it could foster growth, but also fragility. Ultimately, it is the quality of institutions that makes the difference, with financial liberalization working best when paired with sound supervision, rule of law, and strong creditor rights.[7]

In many EMDEs, institutional weaknesses continue to constrain financial development. What has greatly improved is account ownership for individuals, which has jumped from 42% in 2011 to 75% in 2024, with digitalization making financial services more accessible and affordable. In 2024, however, only 40% of people in EMDEs saved formally using an account, 60% made digital payments, which suggests that usage was still lagging account ownership.[8] Furthermore, many Micro, Small and Medium Enterprises (MSMEs)—which account for a large portion of total employment in EMDEs—are still credit-constraint, with their financing gap even increasing between 2015 and 2019.[9]

Limited progress is also visible in the IMF's Financial Development Index, with EMDEs stagnating since the 2010s, despite the gap with AEs remaining very large. That said, there are large differences among EMDEs, with financial development being strongly correlated with income levels, meaning that

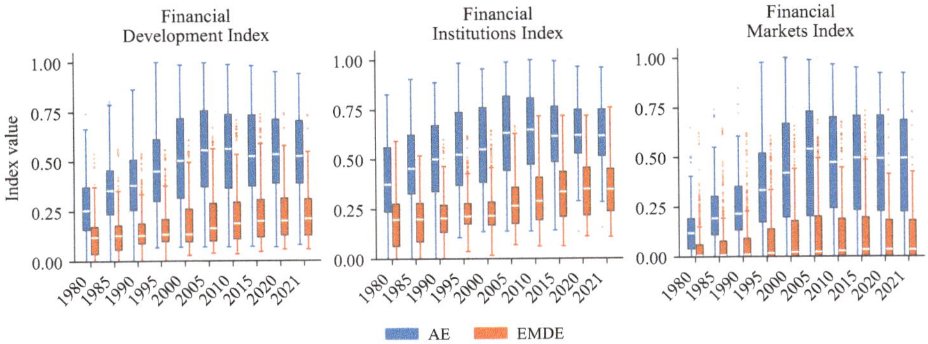

Fig. 3.1 Financial Development Indicators, AEs vs. EMDEs. (Source: IMF)

higher income is generally associated with higher financial development. The IMF's index is composed of two subindices looking at the development of financial institutions and financial markets, assessing in each case the depth (size and liquidity), access (of individuals and companies to financial services), and efficiency. As the development of domestic capital markets will be subject to sub-section 3.3, the focus here is on financial institutions. Generally, EMDEs do much better on the development of financial institutions than financial markets, and with regard to financial institutions, there has been more progress on access while particularly the depth remains shallow in most cases. Where EMDEs score comparably well is on efficiency, which is somewhat surprising given that banking sectors are typically highly concentrated, with concentration having further increased over the past decade. By 2023, on average, the three largest banks per country controlled 64% of total banking sector assets (Fig. 3.1).[10]

Countries that saw the biggest increase in the Financial Development Index since 2000 tend to be larger EMDEs that were at least somewhat successful in developing domestic financial markets, such as China, Thailand, and Brazil. When looking only at the development of financial institutions, countries like Bolivia, Georgia, Peru, and Romania show the strongest improvement. We are hesitant to call these cases success stories, however, as the actual picture is often more nuanced than the index suggests. As of 2024, leverage in China and Thailand appears very high, while Romania has been deleveraging since 2010, and Bolivia's domestic credit trajectory has resembled boom-and-bust cycles. At the other end of the spectrum, the picture is clearer: many low-income countries and fragile states have recorded hardly any financial development. But there are also some middle-income countries where financial development has remained shallow. A particularly striking case is crisis-prone

Argentina, where decades of poor policymaking have caused extreme macroeconomic volatility, ultimately preventing the financial sector from growing sustainably.

3.2 Key Characteristics and Differences of EMDE Financial Sectors

EMDE financial sectors feature both similarities and differences to their AE peers. Unless otherwise noted, the following discussion draws on insights from the IMF's Financial Soundness Indicators and the World Bank's Global Financial Development Database. We stress again on the key constraints in EMDE financial sectors—data scarcity and limited transparency/reliability. Data impairment is especially problematic with respect to asset quality in many jurisdictions.

Financial sectors in EMDEs tend to be much smaller than AEs' and dominated by banks, despite non-bank financial institutions (NBFIs) having gained importance since the turn of the century. Within the broad category of NBFIs, it is useful to distinguish between traditional NBFIs such as such insurance companies and pension funds which are generally regulated and long-term oriented and so-called shadow banks which engage in bank-like credit intermediation but operate outside banking regulation. While the former can provide stability by mobilizing long-term savings, the latter may—despite often filling gaps left by banks—introduce vulnerabilities through riskier lending, less stable funding, and weaker regulation.[11] At the same time, fintech is reshaping the financial sector landscape in many EMDEs, with mobile money platforms such as M-Pesa in sub-Saharan Africa, digital banks like Nubank in Latin America, and large payment ecosystems such as Alipay in China expanding access to finance for hundreds of millions of people. Yet, while fintech boosts financial inclusion, it also poses challenges in areas like consumer protection, cyber-security, and systemic oversight.[12]

Despite these developments, reliable cross-country data on NBFIs remains scarce, making a proper assessment difficult. The available data displays important cross-country differences in terms of financial sector composition, with banks' share of total financial system assets—in a survey by the BIS covering only a small sample of relatively developed EMDEs—ranging from close to 90% in Indonesia to roughly 35% in South Africa.[13] South Africa, however, is more of an exception, with NBFIs' assets typically making up only about 6% of GDP (median across 35 low- and middle-income countries for

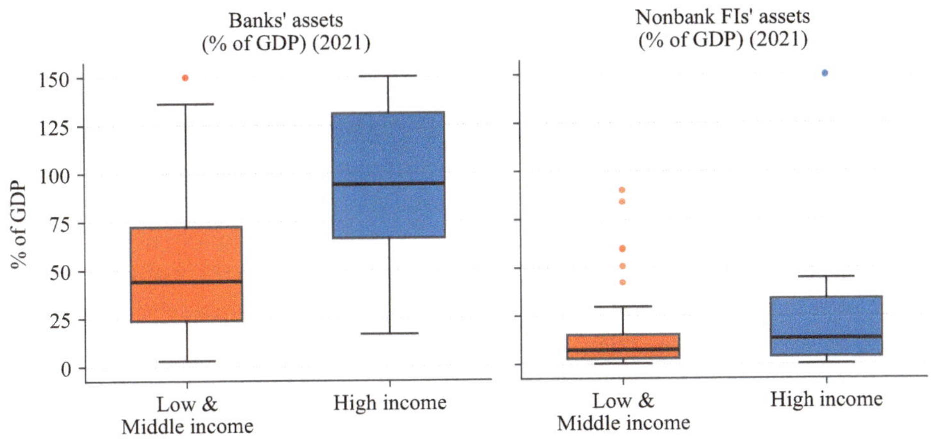

Fig. 3.2 Financial system assets relative to GDP. (Source: World Bank, Global Financial Development Database (GFDD). Note: The sample of countries in the chart above is not constant, as data on NBFIs is quite scarce. For low- and middle-income countries, the sample shrinks from 91 countries in the case of banks' assets to 35 countries (NBFIs' assets))

which data is available). As such, an analysis of EMDE's financial sectors can focus on banks (Fig. 3.2).

One tends to expect that foreign banks have a bigger presence in EMDE. Indeed, market liberalizations, increased trade and investment linkages, and changing perception of market opportunities led to a surge of foreign bank ownership in EMDE between the mid-1990s and the Global Financial Crisis, with the median share of foreign banks more than doubling from 20% in 1995 to 44% in 2009. In terms of assets, at that point, foreign banks' share was at 34% in the median EMDE. The GFC though proved a structural break, inducing Western banks to focus on their core business. What followed was less a retreat from internationalization than a slight shift in composition, with South-South banking and regionalization gaining importance at the expense of Western banks.[14] Eventually, Chinese banks became more important players,[15] primarily through cross-border lending. In any case, the increased presence of international banks is thought to have advantages such as stronger competition, better risk sharing, and improved efficiency. However, it also comes with risks by exposing countries to foreign shocks as seen in the global financial crisis, when foreign banks cut their lending activity more than domestic banks and amplified global economic headwinds.[16] Ultimately, it is once more the quality of institutions that makes a difference, with benefits dominating in well-regulated environments, while increased foreign presence can amplify fragility in weaker institutional settings.[17]

When comparing EMDEs to AEs though, foreign banks' market share is only slightly larger in EMDEs (median at 27% vs 23% in 2021). If it is not bank ownership, could it be a reliance on foreign wholesale funding that differentiates banking sectors in EMDE from AE peers? It is, though actually somewhat contrary to intuition, with banks in EMDE actually having much lower external debt compared to their counterparts in AEs. EMDEs' external debt is in most cases below 10% of GDP, the median being at (only) 4% of GDP, compared to a median of close to 30% in AEs.

Often it is said that EMDE banking sectors are more concentrated than their AE peers. However, when looking at the share of total sector assets of the three and five largest banks, that assessment proves to be wrong. At worst, the sector concentration is about the same in both country groupings, with the usual disclaimer: EMDEs are very diverse. Somewhat larger is the difference in the market share of state-owned banks, with AEs (17%) displaying a lower ratio than middle-income (28%) and low-income countries (22%). The conventional view has been that state-owned banks undermine financial development and growth. Recently, however, this view has been questioned, as state-owned bank lending tends to be less pro-cyclical and thus supportive of macroeconomic stability.[18]

On paper, EMDEs typically look safer when it comes to their net stable funding ratio (NSFR), i.e. a key metric comparing duration mismatches of assets and liabilities. That said, to a large extent this reflects their asset structure, with EMDEs providing far fewer long-term loans and holding more government securities (which typically carry a lower weight in the calculation of the ratio) compared to their AE peers. That said, also the funding structure plays a role, with EMDE banks typically predominantly funded by deposits, and a lower reliance on wholesale funding. As such, NSFRs in the range of 130% to 150% (the regulatory minimum typically being 100%) provide some comfort. What the NSFR ignores is deposit concentration. While numbers are scarce, indications are that these concentrations are higher in EMDEs than in AEs. The collapse of Silicon Valley Bank in the US in March 2023 served as a reminder of risks from concentrated deposits, with depositors withdrawing about 60% of total deposits in a single day.

Loan concentration also poses important risks, though here we have a clearer picture thanks to better data availability. In aggregate (median), EMDEs display larger credit concentrations, with large exposures roughly equaling regulatory capital. That said, both in EMDE and AE, cross-country differences are very large, with the large-exposure-to-capital ratio in 2021 ranging from 2% (Ethiopia) to 700% (Bangladesh) in EMDE, and 1% (Denmark) to 500% (Israel) in AEs.

On average, EMDE banking sectors broadly seem as resilient as their AE peers. Looking at banking sectors' so-called z-score, which combines capitalization, profitability, and earnings volatility into a single indicator of resilience, medians of AEs and EMDEs are about the same. However, at the weaker end, vulnerabilities are clearly more pronounced in EMDEs than in AEs, with countries such as Azerbaijan, Colombia, Kazakhstan, and Indonesia persistently scoring relatively badly in the early 2020s.

3.3 The State of Local Capital Markets

Since the turn of the century, many EMDEs have strived to develop their local capital markets. We noted earlier that progress has been uneven, and overall rather muted. Here we present a more detailed look at EMDEs' financial market development.

Public Equity Markets

Despite EMDEs' growing share of global output, their share of global equity market capitalization has remained rather stable on a comparably low level of around 20%, with China and India accounting for the bulk of it.[19] EMDEs' weight is even lesser in global benchmark equity indices such as the MSCI All Country World Index (ACWI), where EMDEs only make up about 10% of the index. As such, there is remarkable discrepancy between EMDEs' economic weight, and their relevance in financial markets. To some extent this simply reflects lesser financial development, with total market capitalization of listed domestic companies being almost three times that of AEs when measured as a percentage of GDP (63% vs 171% in 2024). Another factor is the tendency of larger EMDE firms to list on AE stock markets.[20]

Besides being shallower, EMDEs' equity markets also have the reputation of being less liquid. However, on the back of passive investing and the rise of institutional investors, market liquidity in AEs has been trending down ever since the Global Financial Crisis, while market liquidity in EMDEs, and particularly upper-middle income countries, has trended up and today is much higher than in AEs.

With regard to the investor base, EMDEs equity markets differ quite meaningfully from AEs. In particular, ownership is much more concentrated, with

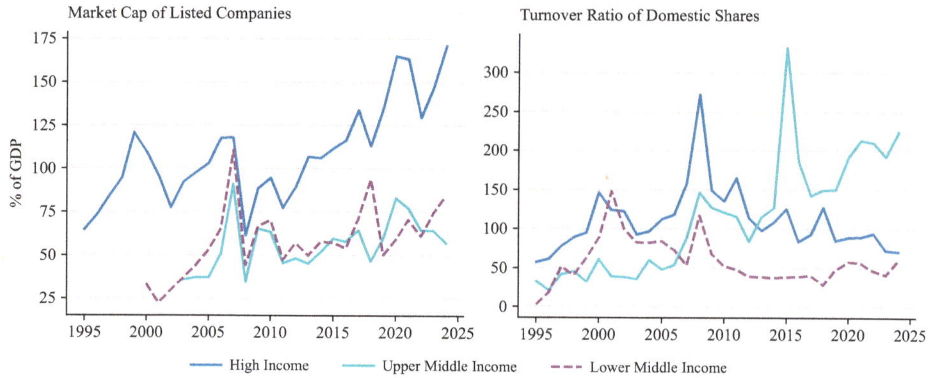

Fig. 3.3 Market capitalization and turnover ratio of domestic stocks. (Source: World Bank)

the top three shareholders having a majority in more than half of listed companies. One large shareholder is the public sector—having on average a 30% stake in EMDEs' equity markets—not least as partial stock market listing of state-owned enterprises is a popular approach for divestment. In contrast, institutional investors play a much lesser role than in AEs, owning roughly 12% (compared to a global average of 47%) (Fig. 3.3).[21]

When it comes to equity returns, the widespread perception is that EM do not pose an overly attractive investment opportunity, or at least have not offered compelling returns in the past. One only has to look at the fact sheet of the MSCI Emerging Market Index to get that view confirmed. It shows that the MSCI Emerging Markets Index has, over the past 10 years, delivered lower annual returns (8.86% by December 2025) than the MSCI World (12.74%), the latter index only featuring AEs. Furthermore, the lower returns came with higher volatility, suggesting indeed that at least over the past decade, the risk-return profile of EMDE equities was not overly attractive.

That said, the performance of these two benchmark equity indices also shows that market timing has played an important role. Since inception in 1987, the MSCI Emerging Market Index has outperformed the MSCI World, with EM outperformance mostly limited to two phases, one in the early years of the index (until 1993), and one in the 2000s. Since, EM outperformance has become rather scarce, which in turn has weighed on investor appetite and translated into persistently lower valuation.

Furthermore, it is important to know the composition of these indices. In terms of markets, in the EM index, there are four that make up over 80% of the total market capitalization: China (27.6% in December 2025), India (15.3%), South Korea (13.3%), and Taiwan (20.6%).[22] Roughly a third of the index is hence composed by two countries, South Korea and Taiwan, that the IMF defines as AEs, and the World Bank as High-Income Countries. Meanwhile, through the MSCI World, we mostly look at the US stock market performance, the US market weight being 71.9% as of December 2025.[23]

In terms of sectors, the largest two are in both indices information technology (28%/27%) and financials (22%/17%). Compared to the MSCI World, the MSCI EM has an underweight in health care (−6.7 percentage points), industrials (−4.1 pp), and consumer staples (−1.5 pp), while it is overweight in financials (+5.2 pp), materials (+3.9 pp), and consumer discretionary (+1.7 pp). Overall, the index has thus larger exposure to more cyclical sectors, providing one explanation for the higher volatility in its returns.

Given that companies included in benchmark indices tend to be quite large, an important question is how much of their revenues are generated domestically. For the MSCI EM Index, with around 70%,[24] the bulk of revenues is generated in companies' home markets, implying that investors' exposure through the MSCI EM Index is indeed predominantly towards EM. The domestic exposure varies between sectors, being particularly large real estate, utilities and financials, while at the lower end of the scale for information technology and materials.[25] Somewhat ironically, the index's single largest constituent that accounts for roughly 10% of the index, TSMC, earns the vast majority of its revenues outside its home country Taiwan.

So why have EM equities performed so poorly since the global financial crisis, while EMDEs maintained a positive GDP growth differential against AEs? The answer to this question is multifaceted. On the macro level, it certainly played a role that EMDEs growth potential was continuously revised down ever since. Back in 2008, the IMF saw EMDEs' growth potential at around 7%. By 2025, that number had come down to around 4%. Another crucial element is that EMDEs' outperformance in terms of GDP growth has not translated into faster earnings growth of listed EMDE companies. The relative performance of earnings per share was even worse due to persistent share issuance in EM against widespread share buybacks in the US.[26] What did not help either is that China's equity market as the largest index constituent has performed relatively poorly in the past. It is quite telling that for instance J.P. Morgan, the world's largest bank, in its Strategic Asset Allocation does not have any equity exposure to China at all, arguing amongst others that corporate profitability is less of an objective there than elsewhere, not least on the back of different policy priorities.[27] Equally telling is the rapid rise of dedicated EM equity funds that exclude China, fueled by concerns over regulatory crackdowns, governance issues, and geopolitical tensions.[28] Lastly, weakening EM currencies have not helped either in delivering compelling returns, with roughly 40% of the MSCI EM Index total returns since 2010 in USD being eaten away by fx losses.

Public Bond Markets

EMDE's local bond markets have expanded importantly over the last two decades. The development and depth of local markets though vary substantially between countries. To function efficiently, capital markets require a certain scale, implying that larger economies have an easier job developing local markets.[29]

By providing a benchmark for pricing assets, a well-functioning government debt market facilitates the development of other market segments.[30] Given that most EMDEs' financial markets are still nascent, it does not come as a surprise that governments tend to be the largest issuers. As domestic markets have deepened, maturities lengthened and local currency borrowing increased. There are EMDEs that predominately fund themselves in local currency, such as China, India, Thailand, and Brazil. Furthermore, some countries have quite successfully reduced their reliance on foreign currency borrowing, including Vietnam, Peru, and Armenia. Nevertheless, borrowing in foreign exchange continues to make a sizeable share of total borrowing in most EMDEs, the median being roughly 50% in 2025[31] and the ratio tending to be higher for smaller countries and markets with a history of macroeconomic volatility.

Many EMDEs have enjoyed both, a growing domestic investor base as well as increased foreign participation in local markets. The latter was supported by improving fundamentals, easing capital account restrictions, and—before the pandemic—the search for yield.[32] That said, foreign investor interest in local currency bonds has peaked before the pandemic, and has since been rather trending down. Among a rather small sample of larger EMDEs with more developed local bond markets, foreign holdings of local currency bonds have roughly halved since peaking in early 2018 (Fig. 3.4).

Corporate bond markets tend to be smaller than government bond markets, even in countries with relatively developed local markets, with China being a major exception. While corporate bond markets increased quite meaningfully since the Global Financial Crisis, first, they came from a very low base, and second, much of EMDEs growth in corporate bonds was driven by China. As such, corporate bond markets remain rather small in most EMDEs, the most notable exceptions being China, Brazil, Malaysia, and Thailand.

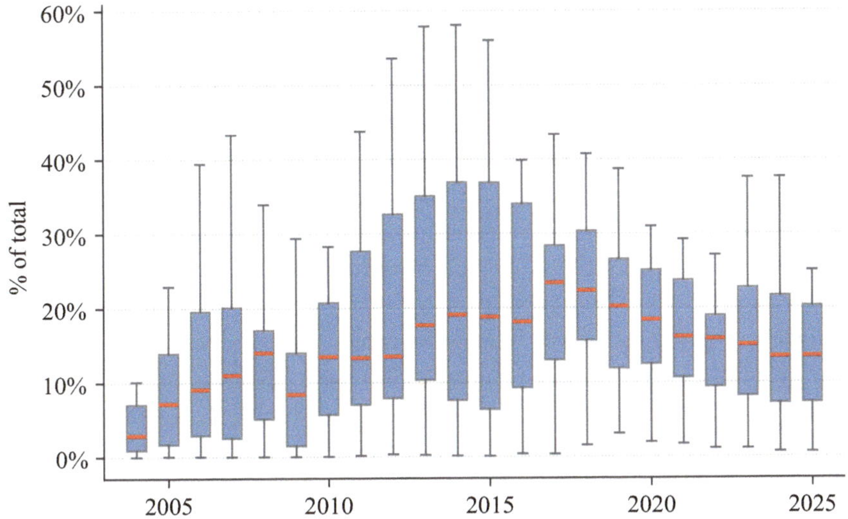

Fig. 3.4 Foreign investors' holding of central government debt securities denominated in local currency. (Source: IMF Sovereign Investor Base Dataset)

In most cases, EMDEs' domestic markets remain less liquid than AEs. This is reflected in larger bid-ask spreads, price moves in response to trades, and a slower return of bid-ask spreads to long-run levels after shocks. Most liquid are markets that enjoy a broad and diversified investor base, and well-developed complementary markets such as for repos and derivates. On the investor base, pension funds and insurance companies tend to have a long-term focus and hence play a stabilizing role. However, again, there are only a few markets where these players are large (such as South Africa), suggesting that the development of them would also benefit the development of local capital markets. Having foreign investors is also beneficial, as they not only tend to provide additional funds, but also bring different views and needs. The latter is important, as for markets to function well, there needs to be a variety of beliefs and strategies so that not all market participants want to buy or sell at the same time.[33]

What does not help with attracting international investors is that over the past decade, total returns of emerging markets' local currency bond indices have yielded relatively poor total returns and risk-adjusted returns. Above all, this was a result of fx losses amid a strong dollar cycle.[34] Also, for foreign investors, local currency bond returns tend to be amplified in hard currency by exchange rate moves, with EM currencies typically weakening when local yields rise.[35]

Private Markets Filling Gaps

Local capital markets offer clear benefits by channeling capital to its most productive use and facilitating risk-sharing. Their development will hence remain a policy priority going forward.

In the meantime, large financing gaps persist, which has given rise to private markets as a complementary channel of capital provision. Multilateral Development Banks (MDBs), Development Finance Institutions (DFIs), and impact-oriented asset managers play a central role in that area. Historically, they have managed to deliver relatively stable returns alongside high impact.

The publication of Global Emerging Markets (GEMs) database by a consortium of MDBs and DFIs[36]—featuring comparably low default and high recovery rates of their loan portfolios—made some headlines in 2024 about credit risks in EMDEs being widely overstated. However, the data merely allows for statements about MDBs' and DFIs' loan books that can hardly be generalized, not least as borrowers have strong incentives to remain current on obligations towards such reliable and affordable lenders. As such, rating agencies have mainly taken it as a confirmation for some of these institutions' preferred creditor status.[37]

3.4 Macro-Financial Stability

Improving Regulation and Supervision

Generally, macro-financial stability has greatly improved in EMDE since the Asian Financial Crisis in the late 1990s. Ever since, the occurrence of banking crises has dramatically reduced in EMDEs. The improved resilience is often attributed to better economic performance (as outlined in Chap. 1) supported by globalization and mostly favorable external funding conditions. Part of the explanation though are also policy enhancements following two decades of crisis in the 1980s and 1990s. These enhancements included tightened banking regulation and supervision, greater central bank independence, and improved policy frameworks guiding central bank action in response to swings in capital flows and exchange rates.[38]

The quality of regulation though varies widely across countries, as documented by the World Bank's Business Ready report. While only starting in 2024 and country coverage still being ramped up, the report clearly portrays important differences across EMDEs when it comes to the "quality of

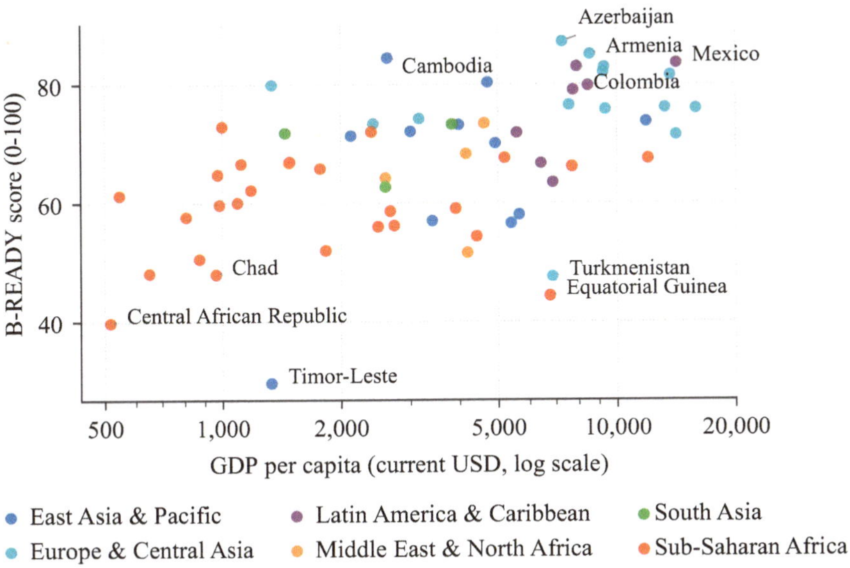

Fig. 3.5 Quality of regulation of financial services. (Source: World Bank, Business Ready Report 2025)

regulations for financial services". Markets that are viewed quite favorably include Armenia, Georgia, Mexico, and Rwanda, while Ecuador, Paraguay, and Tunisia score relatively poorly. What makes the World Bank score interesting is its low correlation with other indicators (and thus provides additional insights), including GDP per capita and Regulatory Quality assessed by Worldwide Governance Indicators (Fig. 3.5).

Since the Global Financial Crisis, macroprudential policies have been widely adopted and generally been perceived as effective.[39] However, bank failures in the US and Switzerland in 2023 highlighted persistent vulnerabilities even in AEs' financial systems, underscoring the need for persistent vigilance in monitoring emerging risks globally. Interestingly, in 2023, EMDE banks emerged largely unscathed, not least as they had much lower unrealized losses on bond holdings (related to the sharp increase in interest rates between 2022 and 2023) than their AE peers.

Banking Sectors Predominantly Healthy

According to the IMF's Financial Soundness Indicators (FSIs), banking sectors in EMDE generally appear well capitalized, profitable, and liquid. This is confirmed by the World Bank's Finance and Prosperity report 2024, which

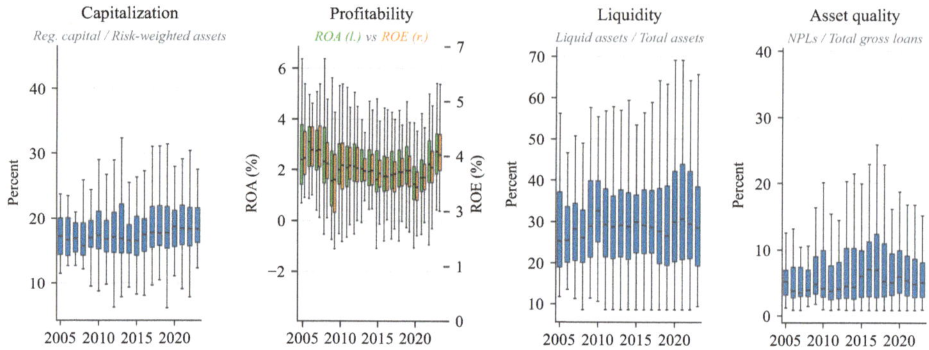

Fig. 3.6 Key financial soundness indicators across EMDEs. (Source: IMF FSI)

assesses that financial sector risks were predominantly moderate in the near-term, and that most EMDE banks could withstand sizable shocks. That said, several risks were identified, notably related to sovereign exposures in countries with heightened public debt sustainability concerns, lagged effects of higher interest rates, and asset quality challenges. Furthermore, a non-negligible number of banks in lower-income countries were deemed vulnerable to significant but plausible deteriorations in asset quality and haircuts of sovereign holdings. Lastly, what accentuated risks was that almost 70% of EMDEs facing "high" financial sector risks were deemed ill-prepared to handle financial stress (Fig. 3.6).[40]

An important question is how reliant these FSIs are. There are several elements here. First, in some cases, banks might deliberately try to hide their weaknesses and vulnerabilities. Second, regulatory forbearance measures by the regulator might distort some of metrics. And third, current regulatory standards do not properly account for sovereign risks in banks' balance sheets, a topic we cover further below.

Box 3.1: The IMF and the Financial Sector

The IMF's Financial Sector Assessment Programs (FSAPs) often highlight practices such as evergreening of loans—i.e. rolling loans over for borrowers that are unable to repay a loan to avoid classifying it as non-performing—or regulatory action that cloud the interpretation of FSIs. These assessments are conducted every five to ten years for financial sectors considered as systemically important, few of which are EMDEs. For the rest of EMDEs, these assessments are conducted upon request by national authorities, potentially encouraged by the IMF/World Bank, often during periods of heightened vulnerabilities or major reform. In these reports, the IMF frequently flags that report non-performing loans (NPLs) and provisions may understate risks. Factors such as weak classification rules,

(continued)

(continued)

forbearance, and loss deferrals frequently mask asset problems, leading the IMF to recommend independent asset quality reviews (AQR) or supervisory action. Recent examples of the IMF finding evidence of or risk of understated asset quality and calling for stronger provisioning rules, better data, or independent AQRs to increase transparency include Bangladesh, Ecuador, Kazakhstan, and Turkey.

Even without FSAPs, the IMF's annual Article IV reports provide useful insights into data limitations and broader financial sector risks.

What is the relevance of healthy financial systems? Where banks are sound and supervision is strong, financial systems are more likely to cushion shocks rather than amplify them. As will be discussed in the next chapter, banking crises impose particularly high costs, typically causing deep recessions and slow recoveries.

Households' Financial Resilience

Yet another angle to look at financial resilience, at least of households, is to look at people's ability to access additional money in case of a sudden need. The Findex survey raises exactly this question (among many others), and deems people resilient if they can access 5% of their country's per capita income within 30 days without major difficulty. According to that definition and the latest Findex survey (2025), 56% of people in EMDEs are considered financially resilient. While financial resilience tends to increase with rising national income, the relationship is far from perfect. In some low-income countries, a surprisingly high share of people indicate being able to raise additional money without major difficulties, such as Burkina Faso (62%) and Togo (61%). On the other hand, there are some upper-middle-income countries, where that number is surprisingly low, including South Africa (31%) and Botswana (31%). Mostly, people would rely on family and friends for raising emergency funds. The wealthier a country, the more people rely on savings, and the less they depend on selling assets (Fig. 3.7).

The flipside, however, is that 36% of people across EMDEs are financially vulnerable, struggling to raise additional money in case of a sudden need.

All this is relevant because households' financial resilience ultimately supports banks' asset quality and private consumption in times of crisis. Resilient households are better positioned to continue servicing debt obligations and to smooth consumption, even when confronted with some income losses. Where resilience is low, downturns are amplified, as households increase precautionary savings and banks tightening lending standards in response.

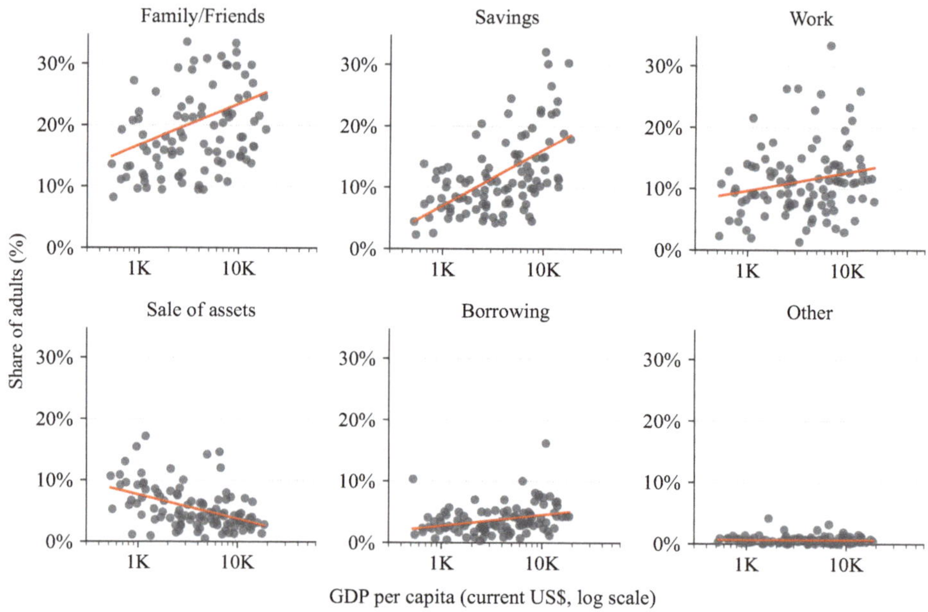

Fig. 3.7 Main source of emergency funds (within 30 days) vs. GDP per capita. (Source: Global Findex Survey 2025, World Bank. Note: Each country marks a dot)

Financial Deepening vs. Credit Bubbles

When assessing financial deepening, it is important to distinguish between healthy expansion and credit bubbles. Looking at EMDEs, several patterns stand out. First, the higher the income, the higher domestic credit. While the connection is not perfect, it works very well for country aggregates by income status. Second, dynamics differ by income status, with upper-middle-income countries seeing a relatively strong upward trend, particularly since the Global Financial Crisis. In contrast, the domestic credit-to-GDP ratio has been mostly trending sideways in low- and high-income countries, while lower-middle-income countries only recorded a moderate uptrend over the past two decades. However, as mentioned in Chap. 1, the number for upper-middle-income countries is heavily distorted by its largest member: China. In 2008, its domestic credit made up 100% of GDP. Fast forward 16 years, that ratio has almost doubled to 194% in 2024. Given China's economic weight, its figures clearly distort the upper-middle-income aggregate. Excluding China shows that domestic credit as a share of GDP has barely increased in this group since the mid-2010s. Domestic credit still remains substantially below

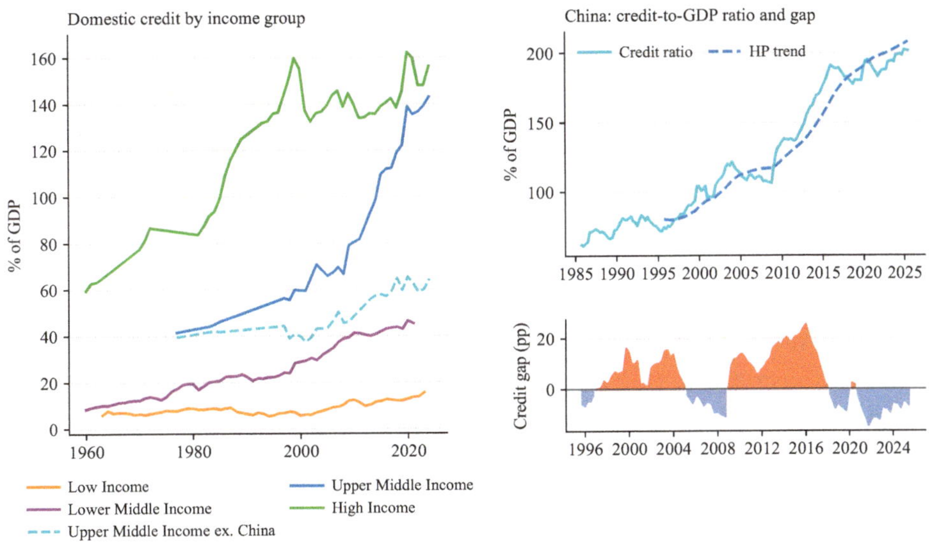

Fig. 3.8 Domestic credit by country income group and China's credit gap. (Source: Macrobond, World Bank, BIS, authors' calculations)

AEs' levels, suggesting that there is still ample room for financial deepening in EMDEs excluding China (Fig. 3.8).

Economists' preferred metric to assess credit overheating is the so-called credit gap, whereby the actual credit-to-GDP ratio is compared to its trend. According to its logic, it is not the actual level per se, but rather an acceleration in financial deepening that signals a build-up of risks. This approach has its merits, with the credit gap being the single most powerful leading indicator for banking crises,[41] which, among other factors, explains why Basel III—the current gold standard of global banking regulation—uses the credit gap as a guide for setting countercyclical capital buffers. That said, also the credit gap has its shortcomings to keep in mind when using it to assess credit dynamics. First, during a prolonged, but steady leveraging cycle the gap will eventually narrow, even though risks likely have not receded. China, for instance, at the end of 2024 had a negative credit gap,[42] despite the earlier mentioned leveraging cycle. Second, in short sample periods, the estimate is sensitive to the starting point, particularly if it is near the peak or trough of a financial cycle. Lastly, in many EMDEs, a lack of data does not allow for the calculation of the credit gaps. As a rule of thumb, quarterly domestic credit numbers need to be available for at least 10 years, to calculate the gap.[43]

What matters though is not only how quickly credit expands, but also what it is used for. Credit directed toward productive investments supports long-term growth, while concentrated lending for consumption or real estate development may at best support current activity, and at worst create financial fragilities that ultimately deepen downturns.

Probably the most obvious credit bubble over the last decade unfolded in Cambodia. In 2011, domestic credit to the private sector was at 23% of GDP. Within 12 years, it had increased to a staggering 130% of GDP. Between 2014 and 2021, typically between 25% and 30% of adults reported having borrowed from financial institutions over the past year, which is quite high. At the same time, information about borrowers was scarce, with credit bureau coverage initially only at 21% of adults. Coverage increased to 52% by 2019, yet credit histories were still not easily available for many borrowers. As such, credit underwriting standards certainly were not overly prudent. There were growing reports of borrowers taking loans from multiple institutions and cases of over-indebtedness leading to suicide. Regulatory forbearance measures introduced during the pandemic allowed financial institutions to continue reporting sound asset quality through 2021. By the end of 2024 though, the non-performing loan (NPL) ratio had surged to 7%, and the domestic credit-to-GDP ratio had started to decline. The country has so far avoided a recession, but GDP growth had clearly slowed.

3.5 The Role of Foreign Exchange

In most EMDEs, banks' assets and liabilities are denominated not only in local currency but also, to varying degrees, in foreign currency. The degree of financial dollarization varies greatly, not least depending on a country's inflation and exchange rate history that crucially determines people's confidence in local currency deposits as a store of value. Furthermore, trade openness and remittances are typically conducive to dollarization, as they come along with higher foreign currency inflows. Lastly, financial sector development and regulation certainly play a role, with lower levels of development typically coming along higher levels of dollarization (Fig. 3.9).[44]

The crucial element of dollarization—beyond undermining the monetary policy effectiveness and reinforcing the "fear of floating"—is that it poses risks to financial stability, mainly through funding and credit risks. Funding risks stem from the fact that central banks' ability to provide liquidity support in foreign currency is—unlike in domestic currency—limited, or, as economists tend to say, constrains the central bank's ability to act as a lender-of-last-resort. Meanwhile credit risks stem from potential fx mismatches, as borrowers' repayment capacity might be impaired by a weakening exchange rate if a

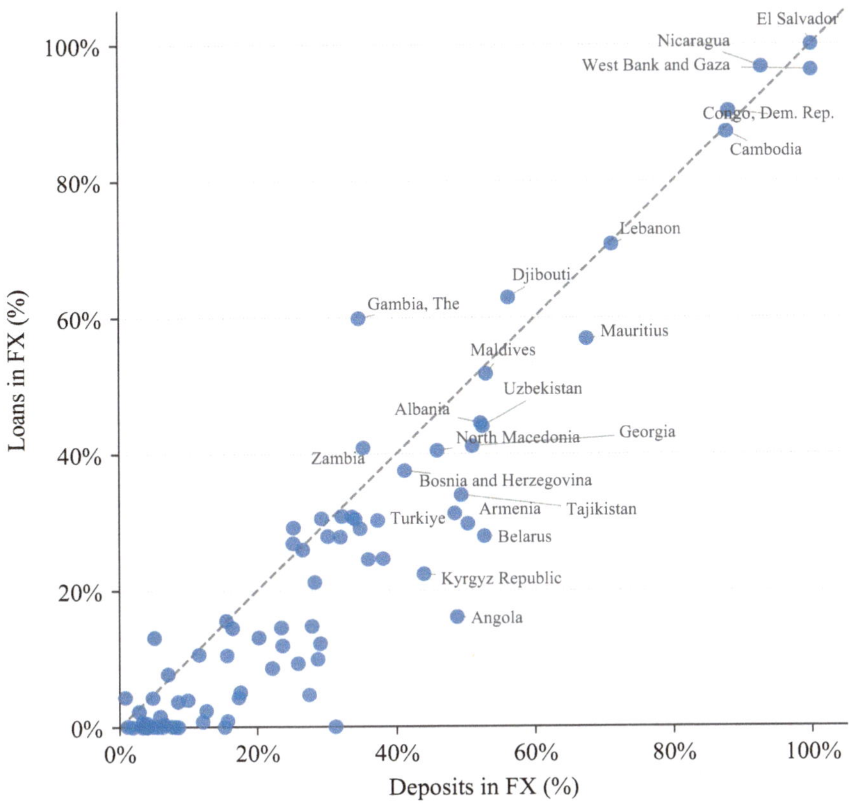

Fig. 3.9 Loan and deposit dollarization in 2023 in selected EMDEs. (Source: IMF, Moody's)

loan is in foreign exchange and the borrower's income is in local currency, i.e. if a borrower has no "natural hedge".

While these risks clearly exist, effective regulation can certainly play at least a mitigating role. For instance, credit risks can be mitigated by bans of certain types of fx lending (to borrowers without a natural hedge) and stricter prudential requirements such as higher debt-service-to-income ratios and loan-to-value ratios for fx loans. Furthermore, banks can be more resilient against the risk of higher credit losses due to loan dollarization by imposing additional capital requirements on (unhedged) fx loans.[45] Turkey illustrates how effective such regulation can be. Despite currency crises having become more the norm than the exception, and with 25–40% of bank loans in fx, Turkish banks reported hardly any NPLs on their fx loan book, see charts in Fig. 3.10. This was only possible thanks to tight regulation on fx lending, with Turkey

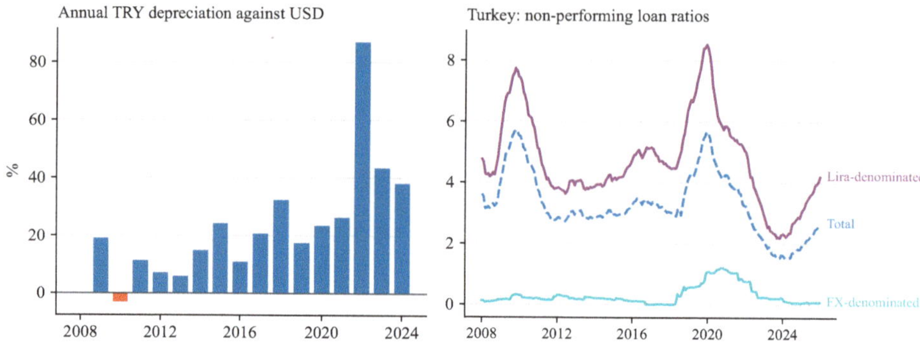

Fig. 3.10 Currency depreciation and non-performing loans in Turkey. (Source: World Bank, Banking Regulation and Supervision Agency of Turkey (BRSA), Macrobond)

banning fx loans to households in 2009, and tightening corporate eligibility rules for fx loans in 2018.

Mitigating funding risks is more difficult, but stricter liquidity requirements for fx liabilities combined with central banks holding adequate foreign exchange reserves can certainly help. This is particularly important for fully dollarized countries, including Ecuador, El Salvador, and Panama in Latin America, Kosovo and Montenegro in Eastern Europe, and Zimbabwe in sub-Saharan Africa.

Lastly, regulators should impose limits to open currency positions, i.e. limit mismatches between foreign currency assets and liabilities, so that large swings in exchange rates have a limited impact on banks' profitability.

3.6 The Sovereign-Bank Nexus

As we have learned in Chap. 1, the pandemic has left important scars particularly on EMDEs' sovereign balance sheets. Public debt is at a multi-decade high, and debt servicing costs are rising amid central banks' response to the post-pandemic inflation shock. These costs will likely continue to increase as maturing debt is rolled over at higher interest rates and large annual deficits add to the debt stock—pressures reflected in the pronounced downgrades of EMDE sovereign ratings since the pandemic.

We have also learned that EMDE sovereigns increasingly tap domestic funding sources, which on the one hand reduces their vulnerability to weakening exchange rates, but on the other hand increases the so-called sovereign-bank nexus, whereby banks' financial health is increasingly tied to that of the sovereign. Banks' sovereign exposure furthermore tends to increase in the run-up to sovereign defaults, with the sovereign losing access to external funding sources. This creates a negative feedback loop: when sovereign creditworthiness deteriorates, banks' balance sheets weaken through (often not fully recognized) losses on their sovereign holdings and worsening macroeconomic conditions. In turn, the prospects or need for bank support further strain sovereign finances, which amplifies banks' losses on their sovereign portfolios.

As domestic banks typically hold domestic debt, the question quickly becomes whether domestic debt would be included in a sovereign debt restructuring. Historically, sovereigns have more often defaulted on external debt than on domestic debt, but domestic debt restructurings have become more frequent over time, not least as domestic debt grew in importance. Nowadays, they are as frequent as external debt restructurings.[46] Similarly, gaps between local currency and foreign currency sovereign ratings have narrowed, and today rarely exceed one notch.[47]

Under which circumstances should we expect domestic debt to be included in a sovereign debt restructuring? According to the IMF, domestic debt-only restructurings tend to occur in countries with low external debt to private creditors and shallow financial systems, i.e. when there is not much external debt that can be restructured, and when domestic debt restructurings do not risk causing much collateral damage. In the past, mostly low-income countries and small states opted for this resolution. When both domestic and external debt are high, external debt is mostly owed to private creditors and banking systems have a certain size, troubled sovereigns are likely to opt for a comprehensive debt restructuring covering both domestic and external debt.[48]

When sovereign debt is restructured, domestic and external alike, maturity extensions and a reduction in interest rates are very common. Face value reductions, in contrast, are rare, even more so in domestic debt restructurings. While domestic debt restructurings are typically resolved faster (taking 10 quarters, instead of 13 quarters), they entail slightly higher losses (42% of net present value vs. 37%).[49]

What is particular with sovereign exposure is that it is standard practice to consider it risk-free, even when sovereign creditworthiness deteriorates. As the World Bank has put it: "Bank prudential requirements largely ignore the fact that local currency sovereign exposures carry default risks." This has important implications. In the run-up to sovereign defaults, financial stability indicators typically misstate the underlying strength of the sector. With sovereign exposure often valued at face value, income statements ignore losses in market value, thereby overstating profitability. Somewhat ironically, thanks to higher rates on new sovereign exposure, profitability might even increase. Capital adequacy ratios (CAR) are also misleading, as the numerator (capital) benefits from persistent profitability (through retained earnings), while the denominator (risk-weighted assets) is gravely misstated due to a zero-risk weight of sovereign exposures. Lastly, liquidity risks are greatly understated, with sovereign debt qualifying as high-quality liquid assets (HQLA) even when they have become illiquid amid shallow or distressed markets. As if that was not enough, banks have limited disclosure requirements on their sovereign exposure, further limiting the transparency of their balance sheets.[50]

There is one last aspect to consider: In 2024, the World Bank concluded that a majority of EMDEs that faced high financial sector risks was ill-prepared to handle financial stress amid outdated or weak financial sector safety nets and supervisory frameworks. This in turn increased the likelihood and severity of crises.

In the next chapter, we will examine the frequency of sovereign and banking crises, and explore in greater detail how they interact.

All in all, where sovereign creditworthiness is under pressure, investors should pay special attention to banks' sovereign exposures and their underlying health.

3.7 Summary and Outlook

In sum, financial sectors play a vital role in development, are dominated by banks, and—with a few exceptions—banks appear mostly healthy. In most countries, financial deepening has further legs to run, with high leverage remaining a particular concern in China. While EMDEs typically display higher levels of dollarization, associated risks can be managed. Whether they are properly managed is not least a question of institutional strength.

What is the outlook? In the BIS's view, maintaining macro-financial stability will be more challenging going forward, for several reasons.[51] First, important challenges loom for EMDEs including geopolitical fragmentation, climate change, and the risks of interest rates staying higher for longer. Second, while macroprudential tools are geared towards banks, technological developments might shift business towards NBFIs. We would add that the development of Artificial Intelligence (AI) also poses important risks for cybersecurity. Lastly, fiscal risks might become more important, in the context of spending pressure amid population ageing and climate change, but also higher debt servicing costs. We concur that EMDEs are currently undergoing many major shifts that could affect their financial stability. These trends were a key motivation for writing this book, and Part II will examine them in detail.

Notes

1. World Bank (2024) *Finance and Prosperity 2024*. Washington, D.C.: World Bank Group.
2. Levine, R., 2005. Finance and growth: theory and evidence. In: P. Aghion and S. Durlauf, eds. Handbook of Economic Growth. Vol. 1A. Amsterdam: Elsevier, pp. 865–934.
3. Bank for International Settlements (2024) *Keeping the momentum: How finance can continue to support growth in EMEs.* BIS Papers No. 148. Basel: Bank for International Settlements, September.
4. United Nations (2015) *Transforming our world: the 2030 Agenda for Sustainable Development.* A/RES/70/1. New York: United Nations General Assembly. Available at: https://sdgs.un.org/2030agenda (Accessed: 30 July 2025).
5. Levine (2005).
6. Abiad, A., Detragiache, E. and Tressel, T., 2010. A new database of financial reforms. *IMF Staff Papers*, 57(2), pp. 281–302.
7. Sahay, R., Čihák, M., N'Diaye, P. and Barajas, A. et al., 2015. *Rethinking financial deepening: Stability and growth in emerging markets.* IMF Staff Discussion Note SDN/15/08. Washington, DC: International Monetary Fund.
8. Klapper, L., Singer, D., Starita, L. and Norris, A., 2025. *The Global Findex Database 2025: Connectivity and Financial Inclusion in the Digital Economy.* Washington, D.C.: World Bank.
9. International Finance Corporation (2025) *MSME Finance Gap: An Updated Estimation and Evolution of the Micro, Small and Medium-Enterprises (MSME) Gap in Emerging and Developing Markets.* Washington, DC: International Finance Corporation, March.
10. World Bank (2024)
11. Albuquerque, B., Ahnert, T., Dobler, M., Huang, W. & Jassaud, N. (2025) *From Banks to Nonbanks: Macroprudential and Monetary Policy Implications.* IMF Working Paper WP/25/96. Washington, D.C.: International Monetary Fund.
12. World Bank (2022) *Fintech and the Digital Transformation of Financial Services.* Washington, D.C.: World Bank.
13. Bank for International Settlements (2024)
14. World Bank (2018). *Bankers without Borders: Globalization and Banking.* Washington, DC: World Bank.
15. Claessens, S. & Van Horen, N. (2020). *Banking across borders: Are Chinese banks different?* IMF Working Paper No. 20/285. Washington, DC: International Monetary Fund.

16. Cull, R., Martínez Pería, M.S. & Verrier, J. (2012). *Foreign Banks: Trends, Impact and Financial Stability*. IMF Staff Discussion Note SDN/12/10. Washington, DC: International Monetary Fund.
17. Detragiache, E., Tressel, T. & Gupta, P. (2008). Foreign banks in poor countries: Theory and evidence. *Journal of Finance*, 63(5), 2123–2160.
18. Panizza, U., 2023. State-owned commercial banks. *Journal of Economic Policy Reform*, 26(1), pp.44–66.
19. World Bank, 2025. *World Development Indicators* [database]. Series: Market capitalization of listed domestic companies (current US$, code: CM.MKT.LCAP.CD). Washington, DC: World Bank. Available at: https://databank.worldbank.org/source/world-development-indicators (Accessed: 11 January 2026).
20. Banerjee, R., Mehrotra, A. & Zampolli, F., 2024. *Keeping the momentum: how finance can continue to support growth in EMEs*. BIS Papers No. 148, Monetary and Economic Department, Bank for International Settlements, September 2024.
21. OECD (2025). *Supporting emerging markets and developing economies in developing their local capital markets*. OECD Policy Brief. Paris: Organisation for Economic Co-operation and Development.
22. MSCI, 2025. *MSCI Emerging Markets Index Factsheet (USD)*, MSCI Inc. Available at: https://www.msci.com/documents/10199/c0db0a48-01f2-4ba9-ad01-226fd5678111 (Accessed: 11 January 2026).
23. MSCI, 2025. *MSCI World Index Factsheet (USD)*, MSCI Inc. Available at: https://www.msci.com/documents/10199/178e6643-6ae6-47b9-82be-e1fc565ededb (Accessed: 11 January 2026).
24. Goldman Sachs Asset Management (2025). *Emerging Markets Equity Fund: Investment Commentary Q2 2025*. Goldman Sachs Asset Management, July 2025.
25. Nakamura, J-L. & Bindschädler, M. (2025). *Emerging market equities are more domestic than you think*. Vontobel Asset Management. Available at: https://am.vontobel.com/en/insights/emerging-market-equities-are-more-domestic-than-you-think (Accessed 18 January 2026).
26. Rao, A. & Gupta, R. (2025). *Long-Term Investing in Emerging Markets: Identifying Drivers of Total Shareholder Return in Emerging Market Equities. The Journal of Beta Investment Strategies*, Winter 2025, Volume 16, Number 4.
27. Wise, A. (2025). *EM bonds price more climate risk than EM equities*. J.P. Morgan Global Markets Strategy, The Long-term Strategist, June 2025.
28. Caquineau, M. (2025). *The Rise of Ex-China Funds*. Morningstar, 1 July 2025.
29. World Bank Group (2020). *Capital Markets Development: A Primer for Policymakers*. Washington, DC: World Bank Group.
30. Bank for International Settlements (2024). *Towards Liquid and Resilient Government Debt Markets in Emerging Market Economies*. Basel: BIS.

31. Authors' analysis based on: Moody's Investors Service (2025). *General Government Foreign-Currency and Foreign-Currency Indexed Debt as a share of General Government Debt (%), 2004–2025*. Fundamental Data & Metrics database.
32. Bank for International Settlements (2020). *Implications of Financial Market Development for Financial Stability in Emerging Market and Developing Economies*. Basel: BIS.
33. Bank for International Settlements (2024)
34. International Monetary Fund (2025) *Global Financial Stability Report, October 2025: Global Shocks, Local Markets: The Changing Landscape of Emerging Market Sovereign Debt* (Chapter 3), International Monetary Fund, Washington, DC, 14 Oct.
35. Bank for International Settlements (2020)
36. European Investment Bank (EIB) (2024) *Private and public lending 1994–2023: Default and recovery statistics*. Luxembourg: European Investment Bank, for the Global Emerging Markets Risk Database (GEMs) Consortium.
37. Moody's Ratings (2025) *Multilateral Development Banks—Global: MDB default statistics confirm strength of preferred creditor status*. Moody's Investors Service, 17 April 2025. Fitch Ratings (2025) *MDBs' sovereign loan performance highlights preferred creditor status: New data support Fitch's approach of capturing PCS in MDBs' capital adequacy*. Special Report, 18 February 2025.
38. Bank for International Settlements (2024)
39. International Monetary Fund (2023) *Macroprudential Policy Effects: Evidence and Open Questions*. IMF Policy Paper No. 2023/014. Washington, DC: International Monetary Fund.
40. World Bank (2024)
41. IMF (2024) *Staff Guidance Note on Macroprudential Policy—Detailed Guidance on Instruments*. Washington, D.C.: International Monetary Fund.
42. Bank for International Settlements (2025) *Credit-to-GDP gaps: China (actual-trend)*. BIS Data Portal. Available at: https://data.bis.org/topics/CREDIT_GAPS/data (Accessed: 9 August 2025).
43. Drehmann, M. and Tsatsaronis, K. (2014). The credit-to-GDP gap and countercyclical capital buffers: questions and answers. BIS Quarterly Review, March, pp. 55–73.
44. Vargas, M. and Sanchez, J., 2023. *Taming Financial Dollarization: Determinants and Effective Policies—The Case of Uruguay*. IMF Working Paper No. 23/244. Washington, D.C.: International Monetary Fund.
45. Cakir, S., Atamanchuk, M., Al Riyami, M., Sharashidze, N. and Reyes, N., 2022. *Reducing Dollarization in the Caucasus and Central Asia: What Could Help Make Further Progress*. IMF Working Paper No. 22/154. Washington, D.C.: International Monetary Fund.

46. Erce, A., Mallucci, E. & Picarelli, M., 2024. Sovereign Defaults at Home and Abroad. *CEPR Discussion Paper Series* 18,739. London: Centre for Economic Policy Research (CEPR).
47. Amstad, M., Packer, F. and Shek, J., 2018. *Does sovereign risk in local and foreign currency differ?* BIS Working Papers No. 709. Bank for International Settlements.
48. International Monetary Fund (IMF), 2021. *Issues in restructuring of sovereign domestic debt.* IMF Policy Paper, December 2021.
49. Erce et al. (2024).
50. World Bank (2024)
51. Bank for International Settlements (2024)

4

Financial Crises in EMDEs: Types, Frequency, and Interactions

Crises are not random, exogenous shocks; they are the result of predictable policy and market failures.
—Paraphrase of themes of Roubini & Mihm

A painter strives to develop the technique to depict the various states of the sky, ranging from the pure cerulean blue of an engaging summer afternoon to the indigo, greys, scattered whites, and blacks of an approaching storm. The changing visuals may be challenging to create, but easy to interpret.

An Approaching Storm—Painting by Richard Marney

R. Marney, P. Waeber, *The Emerging Markets Investor's Guide to Country Risk*,
https://doi.org/10.1007/978-3-032-26824-2_4

In contrast, for policy makers and investors, the task of looking into the evolving macroeconomic and financial panorama to anticipate coming threats can be enormously challenging. Many rigorous early-earning systems have been developed to predict the market equivalent of a summer thunderstorm (or worse), with varying degrees of success. Our aim is more modest. This chapter divides its work into three major parts. First, we provide a brief history of financial crises—taxonomy, incidence, sequencing, and the like. Second, we walk through the life cycle of a crisis, touching on the drivers, transmission channels, triggers, and aftereffects of crises. Third, we apply these learnings to a set of investment underwriting narratives to highlight their impact on analysis and structuring.

4.1 Overview

Taxonomy

The term "financial crisis" employed here denotes three principal crisis types:[1] (1) banking; (2) currency; and (3) debt. All three have occurred in the EMDE space, often together. Over time, the incidence and clustering of the crisis types have varied. In contrast, in the AEs, currency crises are rare events, debt crises are more frequent, and banking crises take place more often, most recently during the Global Financial Crisis.

Banking Crisis[2]

Such a crisis occurs when a significant portion of the banking system is unable to redeem its deposits for currency at par, and the supervisory authority undertakes widespread bailouts and closures. Key here is the term "significant portion". There are cases where an increase in bank failures occurs or (as discussed above) market stresses lead to credit rationing, but the sum does not rise to the level of a "crisis". These lesser evils are also relevant to the purpose this book.

As noted above, financial institutions fail in non-banking crisis situations. For an investor, this distinction is of obvious importance whether as a borrower, depositor, or shareholder. So even short of an outright "crisis", potential, systemic weaknesses in the financial sector are of material concern to investment decisions and hence crisis warning signals are important plots on the radar screen.

In Systemic Banking Crises Data Base II (L. Laeven and F. Valencia 2020),[3] the authors defined a banking crisis as meeting the following conditions: *first*, signs of distress for a significant portion of the financial system; and *second*, significant intervention by the government to stabilize the system, when at least three of the following occur: deposit freeze/bank holiday, significant bank nationalizations, bank restructuring costs of 3% or more of GDP, extension of liquidity support equal to at least 5% of GDP, widespread use of government guarantees, and asset purchases from the banks of at least 5% of GDP.

Currency Crisis[4]

Such a crisis occurs when the central bank is unable to redeem its notes for foreign exchange at par, in the context of a rapid currency depreciation or a series of strong devaluations. A currency crisis typically follows a failed attempt to maintain a form of fixed exchange rate regime, where the currency, once allowed to move more freely, depreciates markedly. The definition of Frankel and Rose[5] is followed by Laeven and Valencia, who establish two thresholds for annual depreciation against the US dollar: *first,* a depreciation of at least 30%; and *second*, a depreciation rate that is at least ten percentage points higher than the previous year. Currency crises are the most frequent and are often linked to other crisis types given EMDE vulnerabilities.[6]

In the economic literature, currency crises have been divided into "three generations" corresponding to historical episodes where exchange rate regimes came under pressure and reached critical stages: (1) related to the Latin America crisis period of the 1980s—where central bank monetary policy inconsistency with the maintenance of the fixed FX regime leads to the collapse of the FX regime, "with a bang" following rational speculation by investors;[7] (2) related to the Exchange Rate Mechanism (ERM) crisis (Black Monday in 1992) where the UK failed to keep its exchange rate above the lower limit, showing that market skepticism about a government's willingness to defend its exchange rate leads to multiple equilibria and crisis, where speculators act because they believe others will; [8]and (3) related to the Asian Financial Crisis in 1997–1998, where (balance sheet) vulnerabilities due to the currency and duration mismatches broke currency pegs under self-fulfilling speculative pressures and ushered in periods of rapid and severe depreciation.[9] Related to these third-generation models with their focus on balance sheet mismatches is the work around so-called sudden stops, produced by a change in investor sentiment, such as a risk-off moment as the infamous 2013 "Taper Tantrum",[10] with pressure on reserves and the exchange rate developing as external capital flows reverse.[11]

Debt Crisis[12]

A "debt" crisis develops when a government is unable or unwilling (preventatively) to honor its obligations fully in the agreed transaction currency, and a moratorium and rescheduling ensues. Such a debt crisis was historically understood to be related to external, sovereign debt, but is increasingly relevant to domestic government debt as well.[13] The historical record in Fig. 4.1 shows that crises can occur in isolation or in combination, and that in the latter situation, the order can vary depending on the circumstances.

Incidence

There is a vast literature cataloguing past crises.

First, for the period up to 2016, we rely on Laeven and Valencia (2018, 2020).[14] Their database covers all three crisis types and the period 1970 to 2016.

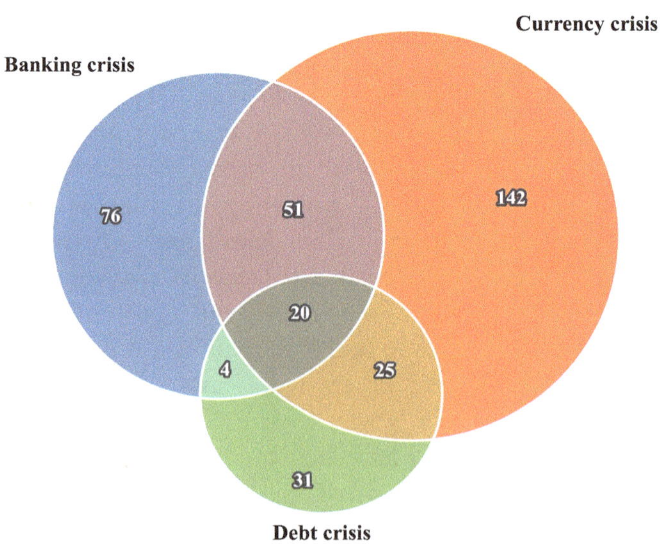

Fig. 4.1 Coincidence of banking, currency, and debt crises, 1970–2017. (Source: Laeven and Valencia (2020))

The key findings are as follows:[15]

- There were 151 banking crises (EM: 128 and AE:23), 229 currency crises (EM:215 and AE:14), and 66 debt crises (EM:65 and AE:1)
- Most crises occurred in the emerging markets: 85% of banking crises, 94% of currency crises, and 98% of debt crises.
- The 1990s was a crisis filled decade, with roughly 15 events per year, with currency and banking crises predominating. This observation is further supported by the World Bank's 2019 study, "Waves of Debt" (Fig. 4.2):
- Until the wave of sovereign debt crisis around the pandemic (below), the majority of debt crises occurred in the 1970s and 1980s.
- Currency and banking crises occur in clusters, with the former often, but not always, preceding the latter.
- Most notable episodic clusters for the EM cohort included the: (1) the Latam Debt Crisis of the 1980s; (2) the Mexican Tequila Crisis 1994/5; (3) the Asian Financial Crisis of 1997/8.
- The negative impact on the real economy was unambiguous, with the severity and duration, depending on the nature of the crisis and the policy responses; from above, three EM crises, the 1980's LatAm Debt Crisis resulted in a lost decade, while the affected countries in Southeast Asia bounced back quickly.

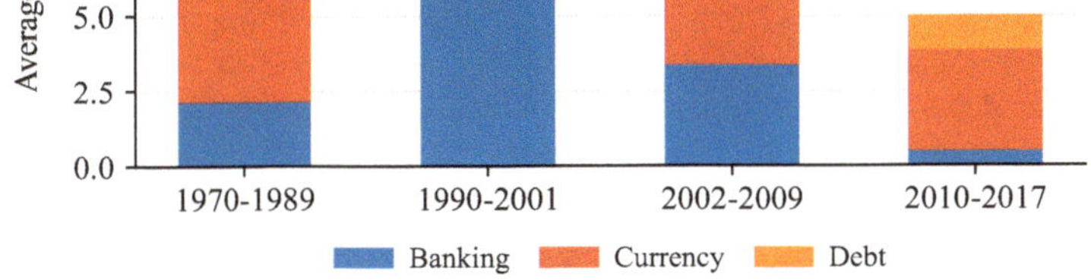

Fig. 4.2 Average number of crisis onsets per year, by sub-period. (Source: Laeven and Valencia (2020))

Second, for the period after 2016 to the present, there has been a relative uptick in the incidence of crises. This increase reflected the convergence of the pandemic and its macroeconomic after-effects, monetary policy tightening in the US, and US dollar strengthening. The largest wave of sovereign debt crises since the 1980s has occurred, with roughly half seen in sub-Saharan Africa (Ghana, Chad, Ethiopia, Mozambique, and Zambia), and other noteworthy cases including Venezuela, Lebanon, and Sri Lanka. Six countries have experienced severe devaluations/depreciations episodes, of which four—Argentina, Turkey, Egypt, and Pakistan—confronting multiple events, and two—Nigeria and Ghana—individual episodes. The underlying causes included the aforementioned factors, as well as idiosyncratic failures such as Turkey, where unorthodox monetary policy execution unnerved investors. There have been several banking stress episodes—Lebanon, Sri Lanka, Ghana, and Argentina—none of which arguably rose to the level of a full-blown banking crisis.

Box 4.1: Montiel and Financial Crises

A digression to touch on an abstraction of the technical financial crisis definition offered above.

To capture the fundamental or unifying cause underlying the concept of a financial crisis, P. Montiel defines a crisis "as a situation in which the credibility of some economic agent's (or agents') commitment to discharge a financial obligation that the agent had previously undertake is called into question by the market – that is, by other economic agents who have come to rely on that commitment". His meaning is that in a well-functioning market, exchange (buying and selling, lending/borrowing and repayment, etc.) will generally occur in an ordered manner—save for idiosyncratic episodes of insolvency—reflecting contractual terms and agreed values. However, when the macroeconomy and/or market conditions as a whole cease to operate normally or a systemic agent like the central government or the Central Bank fails to perform then the capacity and/or willingness of individual agents to fulfill their exchange commitments "raises the prospect of sudden discrete changes in relative asset prices". Think about the behavior of investors as the 2008 GFC played out after the collapse of Lehman Brothers. Fear that financial counterparties could not or would not perform plunged financial markets into maelstrom of panic selling, asset price collapses, and insolvencies. That is, a financial crisis! Or more specifically, a form of banking crisis where we observed: (1) a loss of trust among depositors/lenders leading to bank runs, and seizing up of the interbank market; and (2) credit / investment stops reflecting risk aversion and the collapse in collateral values. Relating this breakdown in ordered, market exchange to the definitions of the three types of financial crises noted above, we now understand better their natures: (1) "banking crisis"—when a significant portion of the banking system is *unable to redeem its deposits for currency at par*; (2) "currency crisis"—when the central bank is *unable to redeem its notes for foreign exchange at par*; and (3) "debt" crisis—when a government is *unable or unwilling (preventatively) to honor its obligations fully in the agreed transaction currency.*

Montiel, P.J., 2014. *Ten Crises: Macroeconomic Policy and Financial Stability in Emerging Markets*. New York: Routledge.

Sequencing

The preceding section showed there've been many financial crises. Before we dig into the causes, warning signals, effects, and policy responses—this chapter's primary objective given the relevance for investors—we provide a historical snapshot of the incidence and sequencing of these events (Fig. 4.3).

For ease of presentation, we borrow from Laeven and Valencia, whose cataloguing represents a crucial source in the field.[16] Through their analysis of the historical data, the authors identified common themes in clusters of financial crisis episodes, "waves", as they label them, and posited that each was associated with global or regional shocks, and spread across multiple countries, which shared similar institutional, economic, and financial characteristics, and generally adhered to similar sequencing whereunder banking crises happen simultaneously with, or prior, to currency and debt crises. Their findings conform with the conclusions of Kaminsky and Reinhart (1999), Fratzscher et al. (2011), Reinhart and Rogoff (2011), and Gourinchas and Obstfeld (2012), despite these other studies covering different sample periods and employing different definitional parameters.[17]

4.2 When Crises Hit

In this section, we discuss aspects of the workings of financial crises to highlight the process (the "cycle") in which vulnerabilities build up in the pre-existing macroeconomic and financial conditions to a critical point where

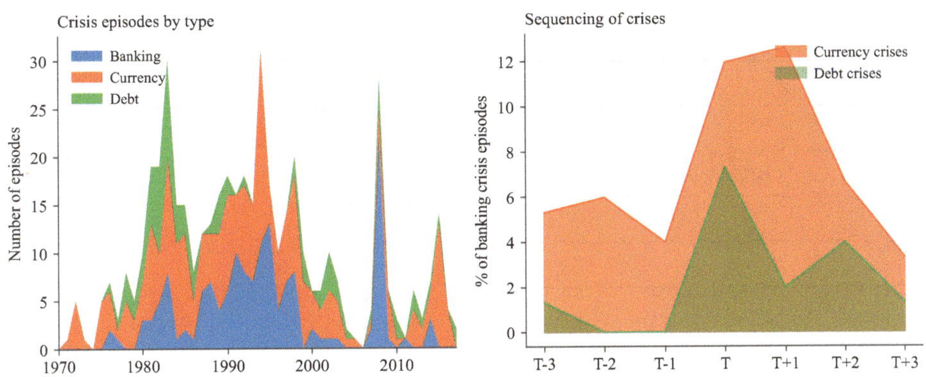

Fig. 4.3 Crisis episodes by type and sequencing relative to banking crises, 1970–2017. (Source: Laeven and Valencia (2020). Note: Right panel shows the share of banking crisis onsets coinciding with a currency or debt crisis onset within a ±3-year window)

events trigger a crisis. *First*, we present a five-stage "crisis life cycle" illustrating the process by which an economy moves from stability through crisis outbreak and ultimate resolution/recovery. The movement through the cycle is defined as the crisis' "transmission". Three summary cases demonstrate the operation of this cycle. *Second*, we evaluate the fundamental and proximate causes of the crises in these same, three cases. *Third and last*, we identify the institutional, structural, and/or policy "circuit-breakers" involved in countering the impact of the crisis. In this last exercise, we use a counter-factual to highlight the role of such circuit breakers in crisis management.

Box 4.2: A Personal Tale

A few weeks before shipping off to Brazil as a young banker in the halcyon days prior to the outbreak of the 1980s Latin American Debt Crisis, one of the authors was called into the office of the chief risk officer (CRO) and given a copy of James Michener's novel "Chesapeake" and told, "Read this!" Bemused, the junior dutifully raced through the book and reported back days later, expecting a useless, university-style literary discussion. Instead, the CRO asked, "How does the story of Devon Island help you understand Brazilian country risk?"

For those who don't recall (or haven't read this work), in the novel Devon is a fictional island in the Chesapeake Bay near Washington D.C. Over four centuries the island gradually succumbs to coastal erosion, rising waters, and violent storms, including devastating hurricanes. One night, the island, now uninhabited, disappears under the storm waters.

Without waiting for a response, the CRO said, "I just want you to remember one thing. Country fundamentals—the institutional framework, the financial system, the structure of the economy, public finances, and such are like the geological foundations of Devon Island. Strong country fundamentals ultimately determine a country's resilience in economic storms—everything from effective bank supervision, the level of corruption, the coherence of macroeconomic policy, to the exchange rate regime and beyond. These fundamentals influence materially the economy's performance, strength of the FX regime, the external liquidity posture and debt sustainability, financial sector stability, and the like." Then, pointing to a map of South America on the wall, "A storm is looming—the debt-funded current account deficits are not sustainable in the long-term and if Volker follows through with his monetary policy plans, then 'bang', the delicate balance blows up, and you," smiling wryly, "may be spending the foreseeable future as a restructuring specialist!"

The CRO was prescient on a number of counts. On the 20 August 1982, Mexico declared a foreign debt moratorium, and a race to the bottom ensued throughout the regions. For Brazil, weak fundamentals—underdeveloped institutions, structural defects, and macroeconomic imbalances—left the country highly vulnerable to a vicious, downward cycle of capital outflows, loss of foreign reserve, and stained investor confidence. Eventually, in February 1983, just days after all of us in the country had celebrated the annual Carnival festival, Brazil completed arrangements with its foreign creditors and the hated IMF. After enjoying one caipirinha too many the night before, the young banker penned an airmail letter to the CRO. The worn, yellowed original still rests in a scrapbook four decades later. Several lines remain etched in memory and have guided the banker's approach to country risk management ever since—"Devon Island collapsed into the Chesapeake Bay because it was built on faulty geological foundations. A hurricane was merely the trigger event – the proximate cause. In the case of Brazil today, indeed, the Mexican contagion and its impact on investor confidence has strained the country's fragile debt sustainability to the breaking point. But to find the true villain we have to look deeper. Brazil has fallen prey to the crisis, gone beyond the breaking point, due to faulty institutional, economic and financial foundations, exacerbated by poor policy choices which had placed the country in this position of vulnerability." The CRO finally got his answer! And the junior did spend a great deal of time in debt restructurings.

Crisis Life Cycle

A suggested cycle appears as shown in Fig. 4.4.

First, the pre-existing country conditions or their fundamentals. As expected, these elements are the institutional framework as described in Chap. 2, the structure and the key performance indicators of both the domestic and external macroeconomy and the financial sector. We continue our use of the sovereign credit rating as the differentiating grade, and all things being equal, the proxy for susceptibility to crisis. Using the case of Brazil of the late-1970s/early 1980s, we identify an underdeveloped institutional framework, a bloated public sector, structural dependence on a small number of commodity exports, import substitution policies, and a reliance on foreign capital, with the results that the country was plagued by weak policy capacity, and a degree of political instability with an increasing unpopular military dictatorship.

Second, from this beginning state we transition into the phase where vulnerabilities build up. This movement is driven by a diverse set of idiosyncratic and exogenous factors reflecting the country characteristics and the sources / channels of vulnerability. The rate, duration, and direction of movement

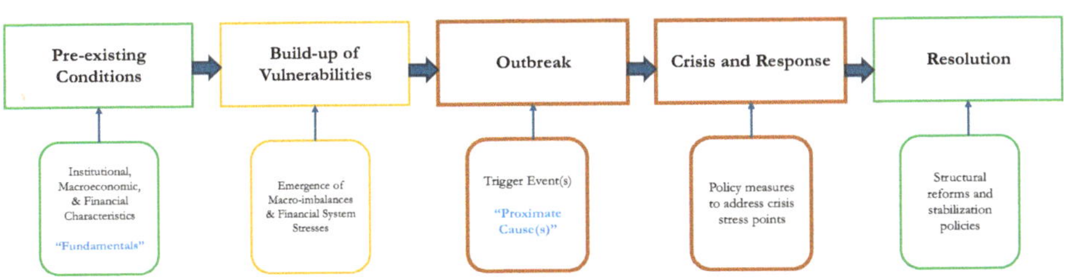

Fig. 4.4 Crisis life cycle. (Source: The Authors)

vary according to the country characteristics, the external context, and the nature and efficacy of the policy response. Overall, the transition in non-linear and subject to reversal. In Brazil, the emergence of serious vulnerabilities began first with the second oil price shock in 1979, which increased markedly the import burden at a time when export prices softened. The deterioration in the country's terms of trade contributed to a widening in the current account deficits and an increase in the external financing requirement. Thereafter, the tightening of US monetary policy in responses to an inflationary surge drove up interest rates, raising the debt service burden on the country's stock of foreign debt, much of which was priced on a floating Libor basis. Economic growth slowed down markedly from the beginning of the decade.

Third, there is the outbreak, the occurrence of the trigger event(s). This takes the form of one or more events that tips the situation into a crisis mode. For example, in the case of Brazil, the declaration of a payments moratorium in August of 1982 by Mexico adversely affected investor sentiment and set in motion the debt crisis.

Fourth, in the aftermath of the Mexican announcement, Brazil saw most foreign banks, the major source of debt capital to the country, curtailing lending new term debt (the Resolution 63 and Law 4131—to banks and corporates, respectively), and begin to run-down their short-term trade finance and interbank lines of credit. These developments resulted in FX reserve depletion and pressures on the crucial export trade. Brazil did not immediately follow Mexico, but instead began conversations with its foreign creditors, leading to the proposal of a four part (project) plan to roll-over maturing term loans, commit to the maintenance of short-term trade and interbank lines, and provide a quantum of new money.

Fifth, in the resolution phase, the hope is that the policy responses and structural reforms fix the situation. This does not always happen, or at least not in one step. In the case of Brazil, the first restructuring simply "kicked the can down the road" and the "can" did not stop rolling until 1994. In the interim, multiple subsequent restructurings took place, before the government negotiated its participation in the Brady Plan, and regained market access. Economic reform was slow going in the 1980s, punctuated by the Sarney administration, a hyperinflation episode, and the ill-fated Plano Cruzado.[18] Later under the management of President Itamar Franco and Finance Minister Fernando Henrique Cardoso, progress was made in addressing the fundamental challenges of the economy, a task that continues to this day.

Three Cases

Let's now walk through the life cycle in three hypothetical cases.

Crisis Life Cycle

	Currency Crisis	Banking Crisis	Debt Crisis
1. Pre-existing conditions	• Commodity exporter • Modest current account deficit • Low external debt burden, as government has funded chronic and expanding fiscal deficits with short-duration LC treasury bills (TBs) • Foreign funds are significant buyers of the TBs • Local politics are unsettled, with challenges to consistent and coherent fiscal, monetary, and FX policies • FX regime: Loosely pegged to the USD	• A traditional, agriculture-based economy with structural transformation aspirations into manufacturing • Capital account is tightly controlled • A highly regulated and predominantly public-sector-dominated financial sector • Credit activity is heavily collateral based, with SMEs having limited access • Economic metrics are generally in a safe zone—Low, but steady growth, stable prices, moderate fiscal deficit and public debt, a modest trade surplus, and minimal external debt.	• A diversified economy, based on a public-sector-led development model • Robust growth rates over the recent past • Domestic savings insufficient to cover investment, which has been funded largely by external debt as a result • Most of the external debt was borrowed by the public sector • Persistent current account deficit • Rising external debt, with most contracted on a floating rate basis • Operates a peg to a basket of currencies modelled on their major trading partners

(*continued*)

(continued)

Crisis Life Cycle	Currency Crisis	Banking Crisis	Debt Crisis
2. Build-up of vulnerabilities	• Global episode of stagflation results in a general monetary policy trend midst slowing growth; similar trends present in local economy • Reduced demand for major commodity export product lowers trade surplus, leading to a wider current account deficit • Rising local interest rates weigh further on economic activity, but are insufficient to counter the beginnings of capital outflows • The fiscal deficit expands in the slowing economy • In the upcoming elections, a left-of-center opposition party, whose party platform is seen as populist, including proposing a hefty W/T on interest paid to non-resident investors is ahead in the polls	• A program of financial liberalization is undertaken, consisting of: (i) relaxation of capital account controls; and (ii) increase in the number and type of financial intermediaries, reduction in minimum capital requirements, elimination of limits on LTV, sector and single borrower concentration, etc. • As a result, credit extension volumes rise dramatically, with a marked relaxation of lending standards • Over time, systemic asset quality deteriorates, and provisioning coverage levels decline. • A subtle flight to quality develops, with smaller and newer banks especially affected, although rumors of hidden bad debts even in the larger, more established institutions	• The economy has achieved high growth for over a decades, but debt levels have creeped up to levels the IMF has characterized as raising the prospect of debt distress • Despite a significant REER appreciation, the government resists a devaluation; speculative pressures build up in anticipation of the peg breaking and the country begins to run down its FX reserves in defense

(continued)

(continued)

Crisis Life Cycle			
	Currency Crisis	Banking Crisis	Debt Crisis
3. Outbreak	Capital out-flows accelerate as non-resident investors unwind their positions in TBs due to the economic developments and fear of an opposition victory	A central bank audit of the second largest bank uncovers significant under-provisioning of problem loans. The news spills out into the market producing a run on this institution, which spreads, leading to a systemic crisis	As reserve coverage declines to a dangerous level and foreign lenders begin to withdraw support, the rating agencies downgrade the country. Market access ends.
4. Crisis and response	The central bank undertakes a series of policy steps centered around the decision to allow the currency to float freely	The deposit insurance corporation (DIC) intervenes 7 of the country's 16 commercial banks, increases the covered amount of insured deposits, and relaxes temporarily the collateral requirements at the discount window.	The central bank declares a moratorium on payments of interest and principal, establishes requirements concerning exporters' obligation to sell FX proceeds to the central bank, and tightly rations FX to importers and travelers. At the same time, the government begins conversations with the IMF in anticipation of initiating negotiations with the Paris Club and its private creditors

(*continued*)

(continued)

Crisis Life Cycle	Currency Crisis	Banking Crisis	Debt Crisis
5. Resolution	• The central bank maintains the floating rate regime, although intervening tactically to mute bouts of volatility • After its victory over the opposition, the incumbent government promulgates a balanced program of revenue mobilization measures aimed at narrowing the fiscal deficit, with no discriminatory treatment of non-resident investors • The Ministry of Finance phases in a new debt management strategy, replacing short-duration TBs with long-term bonds • Overtime, on the back of stronger global demand, commodity prices rebound, and the country's trade surplus rises, the current account deficit narrows, and FX reserve increases	• The DIC liquidates two banks, supports the merger of two others, and places three other in a supervised regime where preferred shares are sold to the government to buttress capital buffers • The central bank tightens prudential limits to address the recent, reckless lending practices and strengthens its supervisory powers to ensure adherence to best-practice governance, accounting, and reporting standards. • The emergency liquidity backstop measures are slowly phased out as the market stabilizes	• The parties agree that a long-term solution requires: a combination of: (i) Structural reforms to address the underlying causes of the over indebtedness; and (ii) debt restructuring providing a menu of maturity prolongation and interest rate / principal reduction provisions to calibrate better debt service requirements with payment capacity and economic requirements • A multi-year arrangement with the IMF is agreed as part of the debt restructuring to ensure adherence to the structural reform agenda

Causation

As noted above, the newspaper headline of the "why" of a financial crisis typically falls into the category of proximate causes, commonly known as "triggers", and is connected to one or more shocks. However, central to our work is to identify the fundamental drivers which lay the groundwork permitting the shocks to transform the vulnerabilities into a crisis.

In the case of Brazil, the Mexican moratorium and the negative impact on investor risk-appetite were the triggers. Not all shocks lead inevitably to the outbreak of a crisis. The strength of the institutional framework, the resilience of the structure of the economy, and the efficacy of the government's policy response determine the degree of susceptibility to crisis, that is, how vulnerable is the country to the effects of the shock. The stronger these "circuit breakers", the lower the susceptibility to crisis. For Brazil, had the country's current account been in surplus or even in a moderate deficit, with no or only limited dependence on foreign capital flows, then the Mexican episode would have been inconsequential for the country. As matters stood, Brazil was highly exposed to the risk of a sudden stop in capital flows and the government's capacity to respond effectively and definitively resolve matters was limited. So, ensued the crisis and the Lost Decade. In the case of banking crisis above, the fundamental cause was a botched liberalization of the financial system, and the various knock-on effects. The proximate causes were the disclosure of the real state of the asset quality / under-provisioning in one large (arguably systemically important) bank created a crisis of confidence in the stability of the system and necessitated the government's response. In the case of the currency crisis, the core, fundamental cause was a USD-currency peg resulting in an overvalued REER that discourages the development of non-commodity export businesses, price inflation in the non-tradable goods sectors, and the entry of short-duration, speculative portfolio capital, while the proximate cause was the reversal of capital flows.

Examples from recent crises include: (i) Russia 1998—(a) Fundamental: weak fiscal discipline, dependence on energy exports, and short-duration debt profile; (b) Proximate: fall in oil prices, leading to sovereign default; (ii) Brazil 1999—(a) Fundamental: high public debt and fiscal deficits, dollarization, and weak financial sector supervision; (b) Proximate: currency crisis and capital flight; (iii) Turkey 2018—(a) Fundamental: economic overheating, high corporate foreign currency debt, erosion of Institutional Independence: (b) Proximate: deteriorating relations with the United States, threat and imposition of tariffs, and subsequent collapse in investor confidence.

These events catalyzed capital outflows, rollover risk in external debt markets, and a sharp depreciation of the lira—effectively a run on the currency.

The build-up of institutional, macroeconomic, and financial vulnerabilities that create the pre-conditions for the break-out of a financial crisis is a complex process. The progression, composition, timing, and the ultimate impact of these drivers have varied among crisis episodes, sometimes morphing into storms, other times not.

To capture this complexity, we have prepared following matrix, which shows the pre-conditions or events that increase the probability that triggers or shocks will either push the economy into crisis or, by themselves, cause a non-linear or sudden shift from calm to storm. The elements and the discussion in the matrix that follows are collected from the vast literature on this subject, a limited collection of which is contained in the bibliography at the end of this chapter and reconfirmed from the author's observations of crisis incidents since 1982.

Category / condition or event	Description	Impact
Institutional framework		
Weak rule of law	Imperfect scope, substance, adherence, and enforcement of laws governing finance and economic activity; absence of a well-functioning, competent, and independent judiciary	Impedes capital mobilization and investing due to concerns of property rights and contract enforcement with the result of increasing, all things being equal, financial fragility and susceptibility to crisis
Corruption	Violation of law and rent seeking for self-enrichment and/or impairment of efficient markets and exchange	
Lack of data / transparency	Economic and financial data collection and publication deficiencies	Business, financial, and legal decision making is impaired
Policy mismanagement	Ill-conceived and/or poorly executed public policies creating or exacerbating sub-optimal economic outcomes	Contributes to uncertainty about the future, so complicating the formulation of business strategy and the evaluation of investment risks, with the result of increasing, all things being equal, financial fragility and susceptibility to crisis
Lack of policy credibility	Structure and/or past execution of public policy having diminished confidence in policy efficacy or true government commitment	
Political instability	Frequent change in administrations, uncertainty in policy and overall direction, polarization, tendency to social unrest, even violence/conflict	

(*continued*)

(continued)

Category / condition or event	Description	Impact
Financial system		
Weak regulation / Supervision	Poor design and incomplete coverage of necessary provisions, combined with ineffective and/or biased enforcement	Lays the groundwork for the development of operational and financial / credit risks and impedes the capability to monitor, identify, enforce, and remedy breeches
Incomplete / shallow markets	Underdeveloped markets, which fail to provide the scope, scale, and depth to ensure necessary capital mobilization and intermediation over the cycle	Contributes to conditions of financial fragility and, once in a crisis phase, dilutes the response capability
Poor governance / Risk management	The lack of the necessary structure, policies, and procedures, resources, and ongoing stakeholder commitment to avoid and/or effectively mitigate all aspects of enterprise risk	Weakens the capacity to avoid / limit the occurrence of the full range of enterprise risks before they metastasize into systemic risk events
Excessive credit growth	Credit growth exceeds the productive requirements of the economy and begins to fuel high-risk and speculative activities	Contributes to a host of economic and financial problems and threats including asset price bubbles, over indebtedness, inflationary pressures, banking sector fragility, and when funded with external debt, FX and external liquidity risks
Bank—Sovereign Nexus	Bank exposure to the government through loans or the purchase of government securities	Impact on the asset quality, provisioning levels, profitability and ultimately solvency due to a government default or restructuring that impairs value.

(*continued*)

(continued)

Category / condition or event	Description	Impact
Poor asset quality / inadequate credit loss provisioning	Weak origination and investment underwriting standards / execution, and portfolio management; and the failure to provision correctly against expected losses	Impedes overall economic efficiency and performance, contributes to the development of solvency, liquidity, ALM risks that could threaten enterprise viability and lay the ground work for crisis development
Currency and duration mismatches	Treasury and portfolio management policies and/ or execution	
Inadequate liquidity and solvency buffers	Limited / insufficient protection for businesses (investees) / financial institutions against situations of illiquidity and/or insolvency	
Macroeconomy		
Growth underperformance	GDP fails to achieve its potential either on a short-term cyclical basis or for the longer-term due to structural constraints	Reduction in the national income and wealth with adverse impacts on economic and financial stability
Lack of economic diversification / commodity dependence	A reliance on a small number of activities, typically within the primary sector (e.g. energy, minerals, agricultural commodities).	Subject to greater prices volatility, with negative knock-on effects on the balance of payments, and economic activity
Prices—Deflation, hyperinflation, volatility	Price stability or moderate levels of inflation give way to chronic price volatility, deflation, or high / hyperinflationary episodes	Exercises negative influence on economic planning and performance, and heightens financial risks
Asset price overvaluation	Speculation drives real estate, equity, and other asset prices to levels not justified by their fundamentals	The formation of such asset bubbles impairs the efficient allocation of capital, and their subsequent bursting poses serious threats to financial stability with knock-on effects to the broader economy

(*continued*)

(continued)

Category / condition or event	Description	Impact
High and chronic fiscal deficits	Weak revenue mobilization and/or high levels of government expenditure result in overall (and primary) fiscal deficits	Contributes to crowding out effects, impairing the efficient allocation of capital in the economy, inflationary pressures, and the build-up of public debt to unsustainable levels; and when funded by "printing money", inflationary pressures
Unsustainable public debt	Debt service obligations exceed the PV of projected fiscal surpluses, hence creating a situation where incremental indebtedness required to service existing obligations	Vulnerability to sudden stops / reduced flows of requisite capital and hence a sovereign debt crisis
Overvalued REER	As measured against a country's trading partners, the currency is stronger than justified by fundamentals	Reduces export competitiveness / incentivizes imports and foreign capital inflows, hence weakening external liquidity and increasing susceptibility to crises. When present in the case of pegged exchange rate regime, the stage is set for possible speculative attacks and the breaking of the peg, and subsequent, severe financial damage to exposed (short FX positions) parties, with potential for broader risk dissemination, even to the point of full scale banking and/or sovereign debt crises; associated with "boom and bust" episodes

(continued)

(continued)

Category / condition or event	Description	Impact
High and chronic current account deficits	Reflecting (domestic and external) structural imbalance evidences higher import expenditures and investment costs than export revenue and investment income, and hence the shortfall to be covered by running down FX reserves and/or contracting new foreign debt or equity capital	Weakens external liquidity (FX reserves and debt capacity) and hence increases the susceptibility to currency and sovereign debt crises
External shocks		
Sudden stop—Capital flows	Cessation of external capital supply, due to local or global factors	Decreases external liquidity producing heightened risk of currency and sovereign debt crises, and to the degree financial institutions and end borrower are reliant on such funding, banking crises
Increase in global interest rates	Complicates economic policy making for small, open economies without an independent monetary policy and can reduce the supply of external capital	Potentially affects negatively both the cost and availability of capital, with the predictable knock-on effects.
Market contagion event	Investors translate risk concerns from events / fears found in other markets to a specific market	Creates pressures on existing points of vulnerability, hence raising the likelihood of crisis
Negative terms of trade shock	A sudden and large reduction in the ratio of a country's export to import prices, signaling a potential deterioration in the trade balance	Similar overall effect on external liquidity
Predatory tariff actions	A sudden reduction in export competitiveness for a particular market, even to the degree of a de facto embargo	

(*continued*)

(continued)

Category / condition or event	Description	Impact
Acts of God		
Geopolitics	War, terrorist attacks, sanctions	Severe, albeit typically short-duration, impacts on the economy with knock-on effects on the financial system
Natural disaster	Flood, tempest, earthquake and the like	
Pandemic	Ranging from SARS to COVID-19 type events	
Climate event	Degradation / loss of land and water resources	Reduction in productive capacity and welfare
Crisis interaction		
Twin or triple crisis episode	A severe form of "knock-on" effect where, say, a currency crisis leads to a banking crisis	See the transmission discussion (below) in this chapter

Impact

Crisis impact on the economy and the financial system depends on the type, characteristics, feedback loops, and the duration of the episode, and is highly contextual. However, as a generalized guide, we have prepared a heat map as shown in Fig. 4.5 to assist in an understanding of the relative impact on selected macro-level economic and systemic financial variables.[19]

Banking Crisis

In general, of the three primary crisis types, banking crises have the potential for being the most damaging to economic activity for longer, but can be seen as second to sovereign debt crisis. When they occur, the failure of institutions and the subsequent disruption to credit intermediation, including the impact

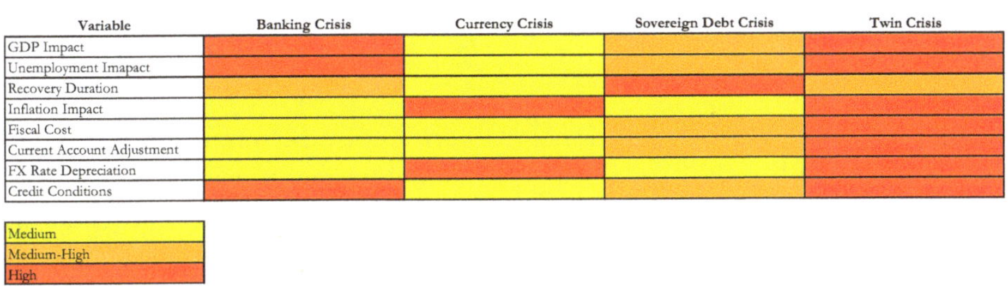

Fig. 4.5 Heat map on crises. (Source: The Authors)

of weaker demand (macroeconomic fallout) and supply (funding constraints and increased risk aversion), weigh heavily on the macroeconomy. The restoration of the *status quo ante* requires time.

Currency Crisis

The degree of impact of a currency crisis depends on the level of external openness of the economy, the role that foreign currency assets and liabilities play in the local economy and financial markets. Generally, they are less malign than the other varieties. Inflation is typically more affected than in the others. As noted below, the circuit breakers of limited mismatches on financial institution and corporate balance sheets, and the capacity and willingness of the government to support the financial sector, will determine whether a currency crisis morphs into a banking crisis (Twin Crisis) or vice versa.

Sovereign Debt Crisis

These events result in a long-term hit to investor confidence and hence can generate protracted periods of sub-optimal economic performance that can severely weaken the mobilization and intermediation of capital. During this slow recovery, the economy is subject to other headwinds and the building up of structural imbalances, of which the "Lost Decade" in Brazil is such an example.[20]

Twin Crises

The most common and notorious variety is banking-currency. For understandable reasons, this crisis type is the most damaging to the macroeconomy.

How It Plays Out

In this section, we present a fictional twin crisis episode to trace the path from the identified vulnerabilities, through the shock(s) that precipitates the crisis, to how the crisis plays out (this episode will be used in Sect. 4.3, where we examine the same fact set from the perspective of debt and equity investors).

Pre-Existing Conditions

1. At the outset, the country was BB-/Ba3 rated middle-income country. Its Rating Scorecard showed below average Economic Strength (reflecting low average GDP growth), slightly weaker "Institutions and Governance Strength" (although with concerns voiced about rigor of financial sector supervision, lax reporting, and a deficient credit bureau), but well above-average "Fiscal Strength" (reflecting low debt levels and ample fiscal policy space). External vulnerability risk was deemed slightly lower than the peer group (modest currency account deficit, with low but adequate reserve coverage, and historically limited external debt). The Macro Profile was rated as a Moderate (numerical level—9).
2. The government undertook a series of measures meant to liberalize the financial system, increase competition, and hence improve access to finance. Historically, the sector was dominated by a handful of large commercial banks, and lending and funding activities tightly controlled. Post-implementation— on the positive side, the implementation of these measures did result in a moderate increase in the number, type, and activities of the system's financial institutions. However, on the negative side, there was a significant rise in systemic leverage, credit standards were generally relaxed, and reflecting competition the new entrants were forced to rely on wholesale funding and to lend to the more risky segments—real estate and early growth stage companies—historically avoided by the incumbent banks. On the liability side, a further source of risk began to build up. The elimination of controls on foreign borrowings led to a significant increase in external capital inflows as banks and corporates accessed this cheaper source of debt capital. This practice became a double-edged sword—bolstering reserves on the one side at a time when the capital flows caused the REER to become overvalued and the trade balance deteriorated, but creating potential currency mismatches on borrower balance sheets / systemic exposure to capital outflows on the other.
3. As many had feared, sector governance and supervision lagged. The program failed to upgrade the resources of the financial supervisory commission to match the prerequisites of the larger and more complex, liberalized market and the country was slow in adopting the new international accounting standards. Unlike most in the region, the authorities allowed local companies to continue to use national GAAP rather than IFRS.
4. The increase in capital inflows in the context of the country's managed exchange rate regime (a form of peg) led to the progressive overvaluation of the REER, which further encouraged foreign borrowings.

Vulnerabilities

1. To compete, the more aggressive of the new entrants had begun to use short-duration, variable rate wholesale money from local and international lenders to fund long-duration loans primarily to real estate developers. Increasingly, this became the market practice. During the good times, this combination of playing the yield curve to build a portfolio of high yield loans created wide earnings spreads, which has helped further by an appreciating nominal and real exchange rate, and the robust economy's limited NPLs.
2. During this phase of rapid growth and aggressive credit/treasury practices, the poor reporting standards became a serious challenge for the supervisory function as well as for investors.
3. In time, the economy began to overheat, and the central bank was forced to hike interest rates. Earning spreads narrowed. Additionally, the monetary tightening was accompanied by fiscal consolidation. The two developments squeezed the real estate sector and NPLs mounted. The combination of narrowing net interest margins and increased cost of risk (loan loss provisioning) reduced profitability and caused several covenant breaches.

Outbreak

Thereafter, the largest of the new entrants defaulted on a local note issuance facility. The event triggered Cross Default provisions across all their debt, most notably the foreign-sourced credits. Investors to the new entrant sector slowed renewals, hence creating liquidity pressures throughout the cohort. Even the incumbent banks began to experience depositor and lender retreats. Most worrisome was the onset of outflows of foreign portfolio capital, as these foreign funds doubted the government had means to support the financial sector. Pressures built up on the government to allow the currency to float.

Crisis

The government recognized the country confronted a twin crisis: (1) banking: insolvency of a number of new entrants and liquidity pressures for the solvent institutions; and (2) currency: if even a moderate portion of the foreign funders decided against renewing, the country's reserve would fall to a dangerous level, and the currency peg would be unviable. The country's sovereign rating was changed to a negative outlook, and the periodic update of the Macro Profile was adjusted down one level to a Weak + (10).

Resolution

Banking: *First,* the government addressed the immediate threat of bank runs throughout the sector by promulgating a series of liquidity support measures that combined expanded access to the central bank discount window, and as necessary emergency funding lines to cover maturing lines of credit. The new entrant default that had sparked the crisis was cured through the latter. Initially, nervous lenders took the public money and left. Soon, when the market realized the government not only had the fiscal space and new debt capacity to fund aggressively such a program, and intended to use it, they began to return and the status quo was reestablished for the moment. *Second,* the financial supervisory commission was instructed to examine the causes of the financial sector "weaknesses" and suggest reforms. Experts from the IMF were called in to assist in the work. Two major themes emerged: (1) The business model of the new entrants was deemed unsustainable. In a manner like the Bank of England response in the so-called Secondary Banking Crisis in the 1970s,[21] the local central bank in this case rigorously audited the sector and based on this evaluation divided the cohort into the "good, the bad, and the ugly". The "good" were allowed to continue to operate independently, but with stricter prudential standards and oversight. The government assumed direct control of the "bad", guaranteed their liabilities, and groomed them for eventual sale to stronger shareholding groups in the domestic and international financial sector. The "ugly", fortunately small, were liquidated, with equal recovery treatment for local and foreign creditors.[22]

Currency: While in the end, the effective response to quell the emergent banking crises also had the benefit of stemming the outflow of foreign capital, the government accepted it had been a "close call". Fortunately, the role of foreign debt capital in the financial sector was helpful but not essential. The country operated with a modest current account deficit, the cover of which from foreign direct investment was typically just enough to achieve a moderate balance of payments surplus, and maintain reserve coverage at three months of imports. Domestic savings levels and financial markets could be relied upon to fund loan growth, albeit at lower levels than in the recent past. Rather than shut down the foreign pipeline, the government promulgated a series of measures, most notably: (1) setting open currency limits as a low percentage of equity (previously, no limits); (2) mandating a minimum tenor of one year for foreign currency loans (previously no minimum); and (3) establishing a mandatory approval process for all foreign sourced loans, which would allow the government the discretionary power to moderate inflows as warranted (previously no such approvals were necessary).

As a post-script, identifying the fundamental and proximate causes is straightforward. The "boom and bust" flavored, foundational causes of the episode revolved around the financial sector liberalization, from which an unsustainable business model for the new entrants evolved in which duration, interest rate basis, and currency mismatches, and higher risk lending emerged. As long as market conditions safeguarded asset quality and liquidity, the cohort prospered, and systemic stability was assured. When macroeconomic developments—inflationary pressures—necessitated a restrictive monetary and fiscal policy response, this changed. The combination of higher interest rates and reduced public spending were the proximate causes—the catalyst, if you will—of the crisis, which precipitated the increase in NPLs, heightened cost of risk, narrowing of net interest margin, and ultimately the decline in net profitability.

4.3 Significance for Investors

The Closing: A Collection of Brief Narratives

We take here the Twin Crisis case in the preceding section of this chapter as the backdrop for four, brief narratives, as follows:

Narrative 1: Foreign debt investment in a new entrant financial institution.
Narrative 2: Foreign equity investment in a different, new entrant financial institution.
Narrative 3: Foreign debt investment in a local property development company.
Narrative 4: Foreign equity investment in a different, local property development company.

We assume the investments were made soon after the financial liberalization was announced by the government. In each narrative, we introduce the country risk considerations incorporated into their original investment analysis and investment approval (the "Underwriting"). In the case studies presented in the next chapters, we develop this analysis in greater detail and extend the work throughout the investment life cycle to eventual exits.

Narratives 1 and 2

Common Facts

The country risk analysis teams at both investors correctly evaluated the potential benefits and risks of the financial liberalization program, and the macro-economic/financial stability implications. In particular, they focused on: (1) the historical weaknesses in financial supervision; and (2) the expected risk management considerations—mismatches and lower credit quality—inherent in the new entrants' business strategies. How they interpreted the impact on their investments differed, as discussed below.

Underwriting

Investor 1: The decision to provide debt capital to the new entrant cohort reflected the search for increased yield. The incumbents were generally rated just below the sovereign ceiling, while the implied ratings in the new entrant sector were several notches below. To mitigate the risks, lending was FX denominated, secured by portfolio (incumbent lending was generally unsecured), carried a tighter set of financial covenants, and an overall shorter duration (than in the incumbent sector). The last consideration assured the investor that, should the idiosyncratic credit risk slip and/or systemic threats arise, they could exit at par. Projected FX reserve levels were deemed to be adequate to neutralize transfer and convertibility risks.

Investor 2: Increased returns also motivated this private equity investor. Financial institution private equity investment returns in this country and indeed elsewhere had become unexpressive. The new entrant market promised to be far more risky, but these very same elements provided the possibility of markedly higher returns. The risk of foreign capital generating a destructive "boom and bust" sequence leading to instability in the banking and currency markets was discounted, and the projected investment returns would compensate.

Narratives 3 and 4

Common Facts

The real estate sector was a clear target for the new entrants (and indeed was one of the government's objectives), and the prospect of increased supply of debt capital mobilized great interest on the part of property developers. These companies were predominantly subsidiaries of major regional developers. Up to this point, property prices had never declined materially for a long period and hence the downside was discounted in what promised to be a robust sector.

Underwriting

Investor 3: This experienced international lender to the sector operated within a narrow business model—providing FX denominated construction phase funding against partial secure purchase commitments. For the rest of the exposure, they would depend on the developer, whose financial wherewithal should be adequate to retire the debt. While they recognized the possibility of the market overheating and any knock-on effects destabilizing the financial sector or worse, the in-house economist argued that the government's ample fiscal space would allow it to stabilize the situation as necessary. As such, they felt themselves protected against any future market downturn or systemic disturbance, as they would be able to curtail new lending and retire outstanding exposure before conditions deteriorated.

Investor 4: This highly successful, regional property conglomerate had recently gone public. Its lofty valuation reflected an aggressive growth strategy, which included a significant contribution from this local market. Years of profitable expansion in their stable home market had created a sense of disaster myopia, which resulted in their glossing over any potential market or macroeconomic instability.

Messages from the Brief Narratives

On the financial institutions side, three significant, direct investment risks loomed: (1) the sequence of portfolio quality deterioration pressuring profitability and ultimately solvency; (2) duration mismatches calling into question the capacity to meet liquidity requirements; (3) currency and interest rate basis mismatches affecting the net interest margin, lowering profitability, and ultimately pressuring solvency. For these institutional level risks to morph into a broader, systemic crisis, a critical mass had to form. As noted above, once the market called into question the solvency of the new entrant sector writ large, lenders began to pull their funding, precipitating a liquidity crisis. This flight spilled over to the currency market as non-resident investors moved to convert their local currency into FX. The country's reserves and the sustainability of the currency peg were threatened.

On the property developer side, their travails fed into the portfolio quality deterioration experienced by the lenders. The fundamental calculus always present in real estate—matching supply and demand, and hence projecting price points—appears not to have been handled proficiently. Too much was built too soon, and we can surmise that the boom times attracted more financially fragile development companies into the market.

Overall, debt investors benefited from the structural mitigants and payment priority not available to the equity and highlight the fact that, all things being equal, the latter are more exposed to country risks than are the former.

At the macro level, the policy response had to address the fundamental drivers—the structural weaknesses of the new entrant market and the inability of the supervisory regime to keep these characteristics in check—as well as to relieve the pressure on the exchange market. Investors recognizing the potential for the flaws in the liberalization program and weak financial supervision resulting in the market mess that ensued might have been expected, but the focus on institutions and the secondary/tertiary effects of government policies in this context is often absent in investment analysis.

These highly simplified narratives were not intended to exhaust the full range of possible scenarios in which the vast number of country risk variables can play out and affect investment performance, whether the market environment has reached a crisis state. Instead, at this point, the reader should take away one major learning. This deals with the interplay of fundamental and proximate causes. There is a tendency to focus on the immediate country risk drivers which may explain eventual investment outcomes. As we have shown in this and preceding chapters, an understanding of: (1) the foundations of the macroeconomy and financial system, most notably the institutional framework and the underlying, structural characteristics; and (2) the implications of these factors for actual performance is crucial for the effective evaluation of risks and the resulting transaction structuring. In the case studies and general commentaries that follow, we will increase the complexity of the situations in which the investment underwritings occur but will always rely on the essential distinction between fundamental and proximate causes, and the need to speculate on how the fundamentals influence if not determine the outcome.

Notes

1. For interested readers, please see 3(i)(c) below for a more detailed discussion of crisis types.
2. Demirgüç-Kunt, A. and Detragiache, E., 1998. The determinants of banking crises in developing and developed countries. *IMF Staff Papers*, 45(1), pp. 81–109.; and Demirgüç-Kunt, A. and Detragiache, E., 2005. *Cross-country empirical studies of systemic bank distress: A survey*. IMF Working Paper No. 05/96. Washington, DC: International Monetary Fund.
3. Laeven, L. and Valencia, F., 2020. *Systemic Banking Crises Database II*. IMF Economic Review, 68(2), pp. 307–361.
4. Flood, R.P. and Garber, P.M., 1984. Collapsing exchange-rate regimes: Some linear examples. Journal of International Economics, 17(1–2), pp. 1–13. Flood, R.P. and Marion, N.P., 1997. Perspectives on the recent currency crisis literature. International Journal of Finance & Economics, 2(1), pp. 1–26.
5. Frankel, J.A. and Rose, A.K., 1998. *The currency crisis: A retrospective on the causes and consequences of the 1997–98 Asian currency crisis*. NBER Working Paper No. 6833, National Bureau of Economic Research.
6. See: Eichengreen, B. & Bordo, M., 2002. *Crises now and then: What lessons from the last era of financial globalization?*NBER Working Paper No. 8716. Cambridge, MA: National Bureau of Economic Research: Laeven, L. & Valencia, F., 2008. *Systemic banking crises: A new database*. IMF Working Paper No. 08/224. Washington, DC: International Monetary Fund.; and Laeven, L. & Valencia, F., 2018. *Systemic banking crises revisited*. IMF Working Paper No. 18/206. Washington, DC: International Monetary Fund. Additionally
7. Krugman, P., 1979. A model of balance-of-payments crises. Journal of Money, Credit and Banking, 11(3), pp. 311–325; and Flood, R.P. and Garber, P.M., 1984. Collapsing exchange-rate regimes: Some linear examples. Journal of International Economics, 17(1–2), pp. 1–13.
8. Obstfeld, M., 1986. Rational and self-fulfilling balance-of-payments crises. American Economic Review, 76(1), pp. 72–81; Flood, R.P. and Marion, N.P., 1997. Perspectives on the recent currency crisis literature. International

Journal of Finance & Economics, 2(1), pp. 1–26. and Claessens, S., Kose, M.A. and Laeven, L., 2012. *Financial Crises: Causes, Consequences, and Policy Responses*. IMF Working Paper No. 12/28. Washington, DC: International Monetary Fund.

9. A rich literature including Burnside, C., Eichenbaum, M. and Rebelo, S., 2001. *Hedging and financial fragility in fixed exchange rate regimes*. European Economic Review, 45(7), pp. 1151–1193; Chang, R. and Velasco, A., 2001. *A model of financial crises in emerging markets*. Quarterly Journal of Economics, 116(2), pp. 489–517; Krugman, P., 1999. *Balance sheets, the transfer problem, and financial crises*. In: P. Isard, A. Razin and A. Rose, eds. *International Finance and Financial Crises: Essays in Honor of Robert P. Flood Jr.* Boston: Springer, pp. 31–44; and Calvo, G.A., 1998. *Capital flows and capital-market crises: The simple economics of sudden stops*. Journal of Applied Economics, 1(1), pp. 35–54.
10. Taper Tantrum: https://www.investopedia.com/terms/t/taper-tantrum.asp
11. Calvo, G.A., Izquierdo, A. and Mejía, L.F., 2004. On the empirics of sudden stops: The relevance of balance-sheet effects. NBER Working Paper No. 10520. Cambridge, MA: National Bureau of Economic Research.
12. Reinhart, C.M. and Rogoff, K.S., 2011. From financial crash to debt crisis. American Economic Review, 101(5), pp. 1676–1706
13. Recent episodes of domestic debt crisis include: Russia (1998), Argentina (2001–2), Ukraine (2010), Ghana (2022); and Sri-Lanka (2023).
14. Laeven, L. and Valencia, F., 2018. *Systemic Banking Crises Revisited.* IMF Working Paper No. 18/206. Washington, DC: International Monetary Fund. and Laeven, L. and Valencia, F., 2020. *Systemic Banking Crises Database II.* IMF Economic Review, 68(2), pp. 307–361.
15. See 3(ii) below for a more detailed, historical survey, "Waves of Crises Since 1980".
16. Laeven, L. and Valencia, F., 2020. Systemic Banking Crises Database II. IMF Economic Review, 68(2), pp. 307–361.
17. Kaminsky, G.L. and Reinhart, C.M., 1999. *The twin crises: The causes of banking and balance-of-payments problems.* American Economic Review, 89(3), pp. 473–500; Fratzscher, M., Lo Duca, M. and Straub, R., 2011. *Asset price booms, credit booms, and financial crises.* ECB Working Paper No. 1347. Frankfurt: European Central Bank.; Reinhart, C.M. and Rogoff, K.S., 2011. *From financial crash to debt crisis.* American Economic Review, 101(5), pp. 1676–1706; Gourinchas, P.-O. and Obstfeld, M., 2012. *Stories of the twentieth century for the twenty-first.* American Economic Journal: Macroeconomics, 4(1), pp. 226–265.
18. Pang, E.-S. and Jarnagin, L., 1997. *The Cruzado Plan and the politics of economic stabilization in Brazil.* In: E.-S. Pang, ed. *The International Political Economy of Transformation in Argentina, Brazil and Chile since 1960.* London: Palgrave Macmillan, pp. 101–127

19. Sources consulted: Laeven, L., & Valencia, F. (2020). Systemic Banking Crises Database II. IMF Economic Review, 68(2), 307–361.Reinhart, C. M., & Rogoff, K. S. (2009). This Time Is Different: Eight Centuries of Financial Folly. Princeton University Press.Kaminsky, G. L., & Reinhart, C. M. (1999). The Twin Crises: The Causes of Banking and Balance-of-Payments Problems. American Economic Review, 89(3), 473–500. Calvo, G. A., Izquierdo, A., & Mejía, L. F. (2004). On the Empirics of Sudden Stops: The Relevance of Balance-Sheet Effects. NBER Working Paper No. 10520. Eichengreen, B., & Hausmann, R. (1999). Exchange Rates and Financial Fragility. NBER Working Paper No. 7418.

    Demirgüç-Kunt, A., & Detragiache, E. (1998). The Determinants of Banking Crises in Developing and Developed Countries. IMF Staff Papers, 45(1), 81–109. Montiel, P. (2014). Ten Crises. Oxford University Press. Frankel, J. A., & Rose, A. K. (1996). Currency Crashes in Emerging Markets: An Empirical Treatment. Journal of International Economics, 41(3–4), 351–366. Baldacci, E., Gupta, S., & Mulas-Granados, C. (2009). How Effective Is Fiscal Policy Response in Systemic Banking Crises? IMF Working Paper No. 09/160. Claessens, S., Kose, M. A., & Laeven, L. (2014). Financial Crises: Causes, Consequences, and Policy Responses. IMF Working Paper No. 14/28.
20. "Brazil's "lost decade"was generally the 1980s, the final years of the country's military dictatorship and the first years of civilian government. It was a period of economic stagnation, hyperinflation, and crippling foreign debt".
21. See: (i) Reid, M., 1982. *The Secondary Banking Crisis, 1973–75*. London: Macmillan; (ii) Capie, F., 2010. *The Bank of England: 1950s to 1979*. Cambridge: Cambridge University Press.; and (iii) Bank of England, 1976. *The Secondary Banking Crisis of 1973–75: A Report to the Court of Directors of the Bank of England*. London: Bank of England.
22. Unequal treatment of foreign versus local creditors is a reoccurring problem in the EMDE space, as local regulators /supervisors are torn between local politics and financial stability considerations, on the one hand, and international investment obligations on the other. A recent, notable case was that of Chase Bank Kenya in 2016.

5

A Holistic View: The Investment Climate

Nations fail today because their extractive economic institutions do not create the incentives needed for people to save, invest, and innovate.
—Paraphrase of themes of Acemoglu and Robinson

5.1 Introduction

In the preceding chapters, we summarized the macro-economic, institutional framework, and financial market characteristics of EMDEs, along with their susceptibility to crisis. These were generalized sketches—broad strokes in charcoal. Now, we begin to refine the images, by categorizing EMDE country types to depict their investment climates: current states, trajectories, and the opportunities and threats they present.

The challenge for investors is to identify and evaluate these country risks, and then to balance their likely impact on investment returns. The question for investors is how to go about it. In this chapter, we start the work of answering this question.

This chapter is organized as follows:

First, we reprise the description of a sound investment climate outlined in Chap. 2, the so-called Investment Climate Roadmap.

Second, we walk the reader through a suggested investment climate classification for a selected set of EMDEs and test this classification system against public sources such as sovereign credit ratings and the World Bank "B-Ready".

R. Marney, P. Waeber, *The Emerging Markets Investor's Guide to Country Risk*,
https://doi.org/10.1007/978-3-032-26824-2_5

Third, we position the Investment Climate Roadmap in the investment structuring and approval process, before walking through a narrative to demonstrate the application of the Roadmap.
Fourth, we end with brief closing remarks.

5.2 Investment Climate: The Concept

Definition

In Chap. 2, we cited the World Bank definition, which we repeat here. A country's investment climate consists of: "The set of location-specific factors shaping the opportunities and incentives for firms to invest productively, create jobs, and expand. It includes macroeconomic stability, governance, infrastructure, labor skills, and the regulatory and institutional environment."[1]

Elements

As noted above, the factors contributing to a positive investment climate are many and dynamic. In Chap. 2, we depicted the composition and the interaction of these factors graphically in the Investment Climate Roadmap (Fig. 5.1).

The logical flow is:

1. A country's inherited endowment is the base from which society develops.
2. Development is "enabled" by the informal and formal rules that influence how society operates, politics are framed, the economy evolves, and law and organizations to govern markets are formed.
3. Supported by these institutions, the economy and markets mature, enabling creativity and innovation in a constructive risk-taking space secured by strong rule of law and supported by social and political stability.
4. Lastly in this context, efficient markets and a balanced, well-functioning economy facilitate the formation / mobilization of capital to support productive investment, from which growth and further capital formation / mobilization ensues, creating a virtuous (or vicious) circle or feedback loop.

What determines direction and strength? The macroeconomic and market outcomes create a feedback loop, as society and the political class react to evolving opportunities and threats. The speed and nature of change in the enablers and the context are a function of a country' characteristics, and

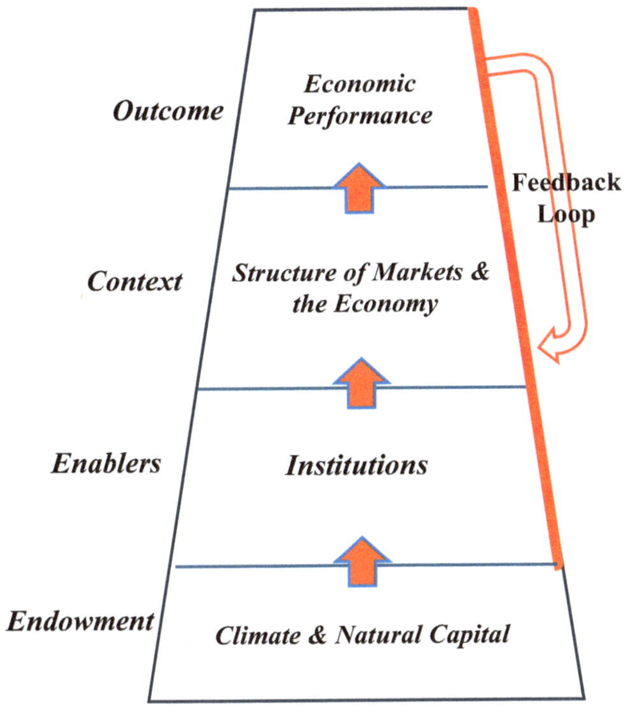

Fig. 5.1 Flow of the investment climate. (Source: The Authors)

endogenous factors particular to the country. How does this work? One example is how high- and worsening-income inequality acts as drag on consumption and aggregate demand, weighing on the pace of GDP growth. In a country where political engagement is low and the relevant institutions used to change government priorities and policies ineffective, a negative feedback loop (or just inaction) allows this weak economic outcome to persist. Another example is where chronic underinvestment in education, health, intellectual property protections, and the like hamper human capital development, and limit innovation and increases in factor productivity, with obvious, negative knock-on effects on economic growth. As we will share in our first case study in Chap. 14, post-independent Marcadia acted to break this negative feedback loop by prioritizing quality, universal education through the tertiary level, and strengthening intellectual property laws, among other measures.

In its 2004 study, "Improving the Investment Climate for Growth and Poverty Reduction",[2] the World Bank concludes that a "healthy investment climate" is essential for sustainable and inclusive growth. Governments have central parts to play in strengthening the institutional framework, constructing necessary infrastructure, supporting human capital development, and implementing policy measures aimed at encouraging innovation and investment/risk-taking by the private sector. Like the view of institutions as a growth driver, we can argue there is no real debate that a positive environment for investors is good for business, and stronger, appropriate institutions are core.

A Sketch: The Good, the Bad, and the Ugly

In practice, a healthy investment climate falls into the category of things captured by the famous quip of a US Supreme Court justice on the concept of obscenity: *"I shall not today attempt further to define the kinds of material I understand to be embraced within that shorthand description and perhaps I could never succeed in intelligibly doing so. But I know it when I see it."* As above, general characteristics, detailed lists of components, and as we do below, comparative country rankings can be elaborated. But in the end, like all complex ecosystems with intangible qualities where subjectivity and human judgement are operative, whether we are policy makers, investors, or entrepreneurs, we will "know it when we see it".

Notwithstanding, as a frame of reference rather than a formal rating tool, we will fashion a classification system in Sect. 5.3. As a preamble, we provide another charcoal sketch employing "the good, the bad, and the ugly" ranking method used by Marney and Stubbs (and others) (Fig. 5.2).

When reviewing this table, consider: *first*, the rating categories and individual components sit along a continuum; *second*, for a country, specific components can rest in different categories; *third*, not all components carry the same significance or weight in each country; and *fourth*, the impact of feedback loops will also vary by country.

With these caveats in mind, let's assume overall that investment grade countries fall solidly into the "good" category, along with selected, ascendant BB-rated countries. The "bad" category encompasses the remaining BB and selected B-rated countries, with the "ugly" label applying to the remaining weaker B-rated sovereigns and below.

Before moving on to Sect. 5.3, we suggest the reader undertake an exercise. Randomly choose a dozen countries, and stick a G, B, or U label on each. Base the grade on your perception of the attractiveness of the country-risk characteristics of the jurisdiction as a destination for your next investment (all things being equal). Then, next to each grade, note a few reasons for your choice. Keep this with you throughout the rest of the book. Spoiler alert—it will repeatedly come in handy.

	Good	Bad	Ugly
I. Endowment			
1. Climate Vulnerability	Degree can vary, but adaptive capcity is satisfactory	Degree can vary, adaptive capacity not fully adequate	High post-adaptation vulnerability
2. Geography	Variable characteristics, but not an economic obstacle	Location/characteristics possible drag on economic performance	Location/characteristics possible drag on economic performance
3. Demography	Supportive	Moderate degree of pressure on fiscal conditions and civil stability	High degree of pressure on fiscal conditions and civil stability
4. Natural Resources	Variable characteristics, but not an economic obstacle	Access to all essential inputs incomplete	Lack of access to essential inputs a drag on growth
II. Macroeconomy			
Domestic			
1. GDP per capita	Medium to high; satisfactory growth characteristics	Low to medium; weaker growth characteristics	Low
2. Price Stability	Low inflation	Moderate to high inflation; bouts of volatility	Moderate to high inflation; bouts of volatility
3. Business cycle volatility	Minimal beyond garden variety economic cycles	Moderate to high	Moderate to high
4. Wealth and income inequality	Moderate	Moderate to high	Moderate to high
5. Size of the informal economy	Limited	Moderate to high	Moderate to high
6. Size of primary sector	Variable characteristics, but not an economic obstacle	Moderate dependency	High
7. Savings - Investment Balance	Surplus or a manageable deficit	Deficit, requiring external funds	Deficit, requiring external funds
8. Revenue mobilization and public finances	Strong	Weak to moderate	Weak
9. Fiscal policy space	Strong	Limited	Reliant on external / concessional funds
10. Monetary policy capacity and credibility	Strong	Weak to moderate	Weak
11. Diversification	High	Moderate	Limited
12. Total Factor Productivity	Increasing	Stagnant	Stagnant
External			
1. Commodity export dependence	Variable characteristics, not an economic obstacle	Moderate; TOT volatility	High
2. Current account	Surplus or a manageable deficit	Deficit creating liquidity / debt sustainability risks	Reliant on external / concessional funds
3. Balance of payments	Surplus or a manageable deficit	Deficit creating liquidity / debt sustainability risks	Reliant on external / concessional funds
4. Access to external capital markets	Full	Limited	No acccess
5. External shocks	Limited but high degree of resilience	Susceptible, only moderate degree of resilience	Highly susceptible; weak resilience
6. FX regime	Free or managed float	Managed float, currency peg; FMV deviation	Inconvertible

Fig. 5.2 Investment climate—The Good, Bad and Ugly. (Source: The Authors)

III. Institutions			
1. Economic duality	Very limited	Low to moderate	Moderate to high
2. Civil liberties	Full	Partial	Impaired
3. Political engagement	High	Low to moderate	Low
4. Political stability	High	Low to moderate	Low
5. Rule of law	Strong	Weak to moderate	Impaired
5. Judicial system	Well-developed and effective	Underdeveloped, with inefficiencies	Impaired
6. Regulation	Well-developed and effective	Underdeveloped, with inefficiencies	Impaired
7. Corruption and rent-seeking	Low	High to moderate	Pervasive
8. Civil violence	Low	High to moderate	High
9. Infrastructure and other public goods	Ample and adequate	Underdeveloped with gaps	Inadequate, with major gaps
10. Ease of doing business	High	Low to moderate	Low to highly problematic
11. Education	High quality and satisfactory access	Inconsistent quality and access	Low quality and limited access
12. Healthcare	High quality and satisfactory access	Inconsistent quality and access	Low quality and limited access
13. Government effectiveness	Strong	Weak to moderate	Largely dysfunctional
14. Public financial management	Strong	Weak to moderate	Largely dysfunctional
IV. Financial Markets			
1. Depth and breadth	Strong	Weak to moderate	Weak
2. Regulation and supervision	Strong	Weak to moderate	Weak
3. Payment/ transfers and credit information	Strong	Weak to moderate	Weak
4. Financial inclusion	Strong	Weak to moderate	Weak
5. Governance	Strong	Weak to moderate	Weak
6. Financial sector performance and stability	Strong	Weak to moderate	Weak
7. Restructuring / insolvency capacity	Strong	Weak to moderate	Weak
V. Crises			
1. Incidence crises	Low	Moderate to high	High
2. Crisis reponse capabilities	Strong	Weak to moderate	Weak
3. Vulnerability to sudden stops	Low	Moderate to high	Extreme, when there is access to external capital
4. Sensitivity to FX market changes	Low	Moderate to high	Extreme, when currency is convertible
5. Bank / sovereign nexus	Low	Moderate to high	High

Fig. 5.2 (continued)

5.3 Country Investment Climate Classifications

There exist many different approaches to assess countries' investment climate. Typically, they strive to assess how conducive a country's institutional, regulatory and macroeconomic environment is to private investment. In doing so, they tend to focus on the business environment, the strength of institutions, macroeconomic stability, infrastructure quality, and policy predictability. The main indicators include:

- B-Ready report by the World Bank: Based on enterprise surveys and administrative data, B-Ready provides a worldwide, annual assessment of the business and investment climate. It assesses how easy it is to start, operate, and close a business, and focuses on three pillars: regulatory framework, public services, and operational efficiency. B-Ready is the successor of the well-known Ease of Doing Business report and was launched in 2024 with a partial country coverage. By 2026, it targets full country coverage.
- Heritage Foundation's Index of Economic Freedom: This index strives to assess how conducive policy frameworks are to entrepreneurial activity and private investment. It does so by aggregating a broad range of policy and institutional variables under the themes of rule of law, government size, regulatory efficiency, and market openness. Published annually, it covers most EMDEs.
- Worldwide Governance Indicators (WGIs) by the World Bank: We encountered these indicators earlier in Chap. 2. They are published annually for over 200 countries, and feature six dimensions: rule of law, control of corruption, regulatory quality, government effectiveness, political stability, and voice and accountability. What is important to know is that they are perception-based (i.e. rely on surveys of firms and experts), and provide a relative assessment of each dimension, year after year.
- Rule of Law Index by the World Justice Project (WJP): This index is a survey-based assessment of laws and institutions delivering on accountability, just law, open government, and an accessible and impartial justice. The annually published index was first piloted in 2008 and today covers over 140 countries.
- Sovereign ratings: Their focus is different, as they assess sovereign creditworthiness rather than the attractiveness of doing business. Still, sovereign scorecards incorporate many factors that matter for the investment climate, such as macroeconomic stability, institutional strength, political risks, and

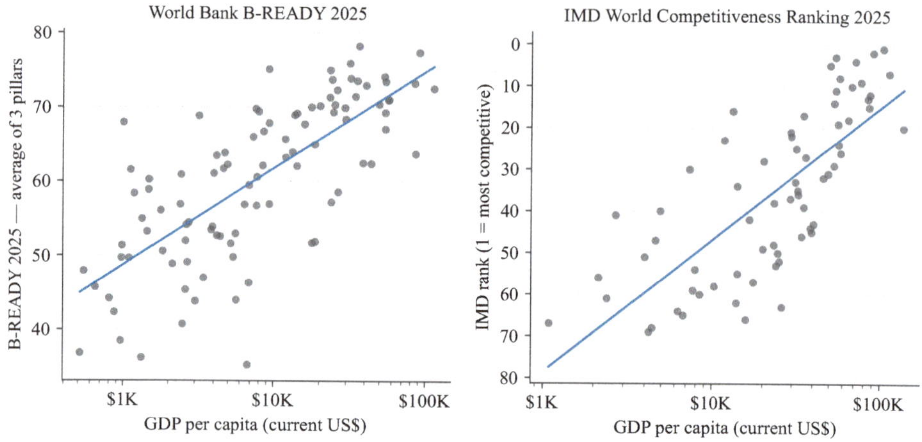

Fig. 5.3 Business environment and competitiveness relative to income level. (Source: World Bank, IMD)

external vulnerabilities. Furthermore, sovereign ratings serve as an anchor of creditworthiness in any economy. Accordingly, they provide a useful complementary perspective to other approaches.

- World Competitiveness Ranking by IMD: This index combines hard data with survey-based perceptions of executives, to derive an annual assessment of countries' competitiveness. It is based on four pillars: economic performance, government efficiency, business efficiency, and infrastructure. The major drawback is its rather narrow country coverage among EMDEs.

All these indicators have one thing in common: they correlate relatively strongly with GDP per capita, meaning that the richer a country, the better its institutions and investment climate. This resonates well with the feedback loop described earlier, between enabling factors and outcomes. Figure 5.3 visualizes this pattern for two indicators, the B-ready and IMD competitiveness ranks.

That said, the correlation is not perfect, and there are both, countries that score persistently better than their income level would suggest and others that do persistently worse. An interesting exercise is therefore to run regressions, explaining the various investment climate indicators with GDP per capita, and then to look at the residuals, i.e. to which extent countries perform systematically better than their income level would suggest.

The results point to significant heterogeneity among EMDEs, as visible in Fig. 5.4. The positive standouts include Botswana, Costa Rica, Georgia, Jamaica, and Rwanda. All these countries score significantly and persistently

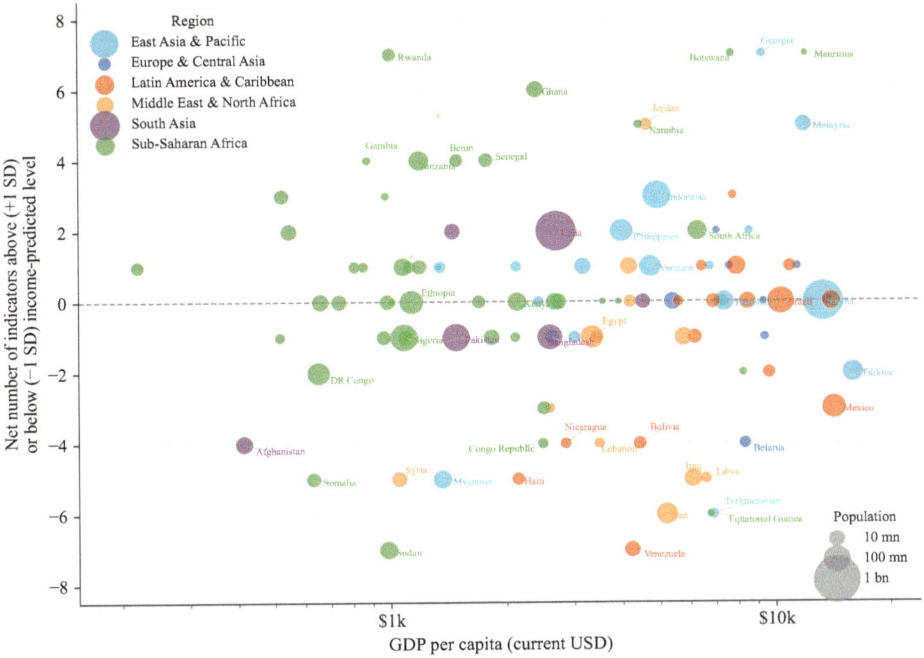

Fig. 5.4 Investment climate—over- and underperformers relative to income level. (Source: World Bank Worldwide Governance Indicators (WGI, 2024); WJP Rule of Law Index (2025); Heritage Index of Economic Freedom (2026); World Bank Business Ready (B-READY, 2025); World Bank WDI. Note: Each country's net score counts the number of indicators where performance exceeds the income-predicted level by more than one standard deviation, minus those falling below. Indicators draw on partly overlapping source data)

above expectations. In contrast, there are a number of countries that underperform, most of which are not very prominent in investors' minds, including Belarus, Bolivia, Iran, Iraq, Myanmar, and Somalia.

While these quantitative indicators help with assessments and comparisons, they should be complemented by qualitative gauges. The U.S. Department of State's Investment Climate Statements are a key resource in this regard, offering country-specific insights on foreign investment restrictions, legal frameworks, and the protection of property risks, among others.

But does a comparably better investment climate actually translate into higher Foreign Direct Investment (FDI) inflows? The relationship between the two is very weak. While some reform-oriented countries such as Rwanda and Georgia attract relatively high FDI inflows, there are others that attract even higher FDI despite offering a worse investment climate, such as Mozambique or Mauritania. This result is not unexpected, considering that

FDI is influenced by other factors, including resource endowments and market potential. Moreover, large investors often mitigate certain risks, including political and expropriation risks, through risk insurance and contractual safeguards.

Ultimately, while the investment climate fails to explain short-term capital allocation, it remains a critical long-term determinant of private-sector development. Unlike endowments, the investment climate is a factor that countries can improve, with payoffs in terms of productivity, entrepreneurship, and investment in the longer run.

5.4 Investment Climate Roadmap and the Investment Approval Process

Before exploring further how the Investment Climate Roadmap works in practice, let's digress briefly by incorporate this Roadmap into the investment structuring and approval process. A highly, simplified view appears in Fig. 5.5.

In this graphic, we see an "Investment Proposal" travel through four, analytic "doorways" to arrive at the "Transaction Structure & Economics". The first of the four doorways—Country: Investment Climate—is the concept discussed above. The remaining three are: (1) Global Conditions—the macroeconomy, capital and currency markets, commerce and trade policy; (2) Sectoral Conditions and Outlook—growth prospects and challenges of the sector in which the investee operates; and (3) Company Conditions and Outlook—the investee's strengths, weaknesses, opportunities, and threats. In each room, the preliminary indicative terms and conditions of the proposed investment are adjusted to conform to what the country, global, sector, and investee facts dictate or permit, until the parties decide whether there is a deal or not, and if yes, what are the agreed terms and conditions.

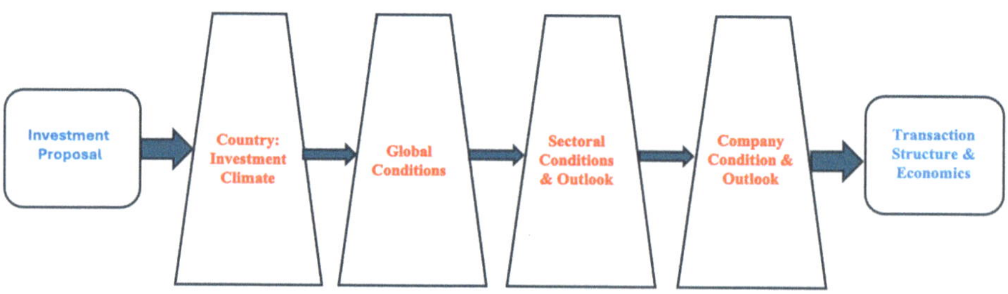

Fig. 5.5 Investment process roadmap. (Source: The Authors)

To understand how this process works in practice, we present a short narrative in Sect. 5.5.

5.5 A Narrative

How does the impact of the investment climate play out in practice? As all seasoned investors know, there is no single, correct answer and Monday's response may prove outdated come Tuesday. In this section, we attempt a preliminary answer, nonetheless.

Our approach is to walk through a hypothetical investment in the form of a global private debt fund providing senior secured debt to a local property development company. We examine this case using the Investment Climate Roadmap in the context of different sovereign rated countries.

To be clear, the focus is on the initial investment decision—the "go or no go" question and the reasons underlying this determination. Later in the book, we will extend the discussion to cover the life of the investment—performance, monitoring, and in selected cases, workouts / recapitalizations, and the like.

The Opportunity

A shortage of affordable, residential housing exists. A major constraint is the availability of finance. The shortage is present in both the construction and post-completion (buyer) phases. In this case, a global private debt fund examines the viability of a senior, secured construction phase credit facility to a local property development company.

Transaction: Prerequisites

Key to the financial and legal terms and conditions on which an approval of the transaction will be predicated is positive evaluation of a set of elements outlined in the Investment Climate Roadmap.

These include:

1. Sustainable economic growth.
2. Sufficient, effective demand for housing.
3. Access to commercial financing.
4. Supportive and stable government housing sector policies.

5. Land availability and infrastructure (water & sewage, energy, etc.)
6. Efficient zoning, permitting, and approval processes.
7. Sound legal foundations of housing construction and ownership, including the protection of property rights, contracts, and lender security interests.
8. Competent judiciary and efficient judicial processes to enforce the rights of the parties in (7).
9. Protections against political interference or corruption.
10. Predictable financial regulations.

A Heat Map

The impact of these elements on transaction structuring and ultimately approval will vary according to the country's endowment, stage of development of the enabling institutions, the resulting economic, political, and legal context, and lastly the macroeconomic and market outcomes that drive investment performance.

As noted above, we position the investment in the four sovereign rating cohorts (BBB, BB, B, and Caa) and evaluate the impact of the selected investment climate elements on the investment decision. This heatmap is highly simplified as one would expect, as it uses sovereign ratings to aggregate diverse economies into a single group despite their varied characteristics and places a single grade on each (High to Very Low, shown by the color gradations from green to red). However, for our purposes we believe this gets the basic messages across (Fig. 5.6).

Interpretation

We will use the BBB-rated level as the baseline.

I. Endowment

The relevant risk is the impact of climate change events on the availability of natural capital resources involved in community development (e.g., land and water), after taking into consideration a government's adaptive capacity. We argue that as a country's credit rating declines, all things being equal, this risk is heightened. In lower rated sovereigns, the financial capacity and policy capabilities to address the effects of rising sea levels, changing rain patterns, extreme weather events, and the like are weaker or completely absent. The

Fig. 5.6 Investment climate metrics by rating level. (Source: The Authors)

impact on the property development company is to decrease the size of their market opportunity and potentially lower their top line and raise their costs.

II. Enablers

Three are identified:

1. Government Policies that Support and Regulate Home Construction and Ownership

   These actions reflect the objectives, policy effectiveness, and fiscal capacity of the government. We argue that the latter two weaken as the sovereign rating declines, as political cohesion / stability and the necessary financial resources to fund operating expenses, fixed capital, and tax subsidies decrease. The impact of these risks is to lower top line growth as both supply and effective demand, and operating margins are impacted negatively.

2. Infrastructure

   Community development and housing construction require a series of public goods, including roads, water and sewage systems, electrical grids, schools, and the like. The provision of these public goods requires government commitment and adequate financial means. As noted above, fiscal space declines as the sovereign rating decreases. The impact of inadequate infrastructure is to constrain growth in the housing stock which may lower top line growth or in an extreme case shift the responsibility to the property development company for essential infrastructure with significant cost implications.

3. Rule of Law

   Construction and home buying and the concomitant financing rely on a variety of contracts, established property rights, security arrangements, and the like, as well as a developed body of law and, for defaults and disputes, an efficiently functioning judicial system. The strong and effective presence of these institutions will decline as the sovereign rating decreases. At some point in this continuum, commercial and financial transactions require measures that raise the cost of mitigating actions to a point where the business becomes unviable, or alternatively the lack of appropriate legal foundations blocks transactions at any cost.

III. Context

1. *Judicial Processes*

   Laws on the books are just words, unless judicial processes permit enforcement of rights and sanctions with respect to the judiciary's capability to support contract enforcement, protect property rights, and ensure the sanctity of security is essential to business in general, and this is especially true in the construction and real estate sectors. As we move down the sovereign rating ladder, the effectiveness, timeliness, objectivity, and transparency of the role of the judiciary become weaker and weaker. At the lower levels, investors must question the capability of the judicial system to protect their just interests in a timely manner, if ever. These concerns act to limit the amount and duration of investments, and in many cases result in economically attractive being abandoned

2. *Permitting and Approvals*

   Land use zoning, construction permits, and occupancy approvals are essential steps in the development of housing stock. These actions require clear rules and procedures, competent implementing organizations, and measures to protect against manipulation by political influences or corrupt parties. As sovereign ratings decline, the speed and impartiality of these actions deteriorate, reflecting same weaknesses observed in legal processes in general. When the system doesn't function, business slows and may even result in increased costs when builders must engage in under the table payments to "grease the wheels"

3. *Corruption*

   Corruption leads to increased transaction costs and inefficiency, creates greater uncertainty, introduces heightened risks, and distorts competition across the economy, including in the property development sector. While corruption exists in all countries, its pervasiveness and the weakness of government and society in combatting its negative impacts are greater in lower rated sovereigns

4. *Financial System*

   A broad, deep, and financially sound financial system is crucial to the functioning of the economy. For the property development sector, access to construction phase funding for the builders and mortgages for the buyers is especially important. As we move down the rating scale, financial systems become less well developed, are often less financially resilient, have weaker funding bases, and operate with more constrained and risk averse lending practices. The loan amounts are lower, durations shorter, loan to value requirements more conservative, and pricing higher. A form of credit rationing ensues. The impact on the property and real estate sectors is predictable. In this current narrative, these factors have prompted the global private debt fund's discussions with our hypothetical property development company

5. *Financial Regulation*

   Underpinning the operation of a sound financial system is a body of clear and predictable regulation, overseen by a professional supervisory authority acting to ensure compliance. As with all businesses and investors, the two parties in our narrative depend acutely on this model. Like law and the judiciary above, the quality of financial regulation deteriorates as we move down the sovereign rating ladder

IV. Outcome

As discussed above, well-developed and appropriate institutions are essential building blocks of a healthy (or positive) investment climate. In turn, there is an indisputable, positive correlation between a healthy investment climate and strong, sustainable economic growth and national development. Over the long-term, economic outcomes are stronger and less volatile, along with a lower susceptibility to event risk in higher- than in lower-rated sovereigns. For our property development company, a stronger economic outcome exercises direct and, through the heightened confidence and more robust financial means of the end-buyers of the residential units being built, indirect benefits to financial performance and investment returns. All things being equal, as we move down the sovereign rating scale, the picture becomes less favorable for the industry and participants like our company.

A Simulation

Let's assume a make-believe scenario where the investment committee of the private debt fund has two proposals on the agenda. Both are for property development companies, whose only differentiating characteristic is the country in which each is located. The first is in a BBB (positive outlook) sovereign, while the second is in BB- (negative outlook) country. The proposal for each is a 48-month term, local currency (LC) senior-secured construction phase credit facility.

For the first, the following summary outline is presented using the four "analytic doorways" depicted in the simplified investment analysis diagram found in Sect. 5.4.

- **Country**: BBB (positive outlook), supportive institutions, solid macroeconomy, increasing middle-class household incomes.
- **Global**: Stable markets and an open trading system.
- **Sector**: Large growth potential due to an expanding middle class home demand, tax & financial incentives, credit available, but not sufficient to meet increasing demand.
- **Company**: Established and profitable player in sector, major constraint is construction phase financing, as local mortgage credit supply is ample.

For the second, this summary outline appeared:

- **Country**: B+ (negative outlook). Institutions are relatively underdeveloped with result that domestic and external, economic fundamentals are weaker, high degree of income inequality, with a limited middle class.
- **Global**: Same as above.
- **Sector:** More limited growth potential as middle-class purchasing power is weak.
- **Company**: Established player, but with a spotty profitability record due to the more volatile market environment and more limited market focus, credit constraints exist in both the construction phase and mortgage financing areas.

The key differences between the two cases were:

1. Sovereign credit rating (BBB v. B+).
2. Institutions (supportive v. underdeveloped).
3. Economic fundamentals (solid & improving v. weak).
4. Housing demand (expanding v. stagnant middle class).
5. Sector (high v. low growth outlook).
6. Borrower (stronger v. weaker credit fundamentals)

The outcome of the IC was:

- **Transaction 1**: The requested amount and terms were approved—a 48-month, senior secured, LC-denominated credit.
- **Transaction 2**: The original proposal was rejected in favor of a smaller facility with a 12-month, senior secured, FX-denominated credit, with a reduced LTV ratio, tighter financial covenants, and a guarantee from the local shareholders.

What would you have done?

5.6 Closing Remarks

We opened this chapter by referencing the challenge for investors to identify and evaluate country risks, and then to balance their likely impact on investment returns. The question for investors is how to go about it. In this chapter, we began the task of answering this question of how to go about it.

We started first by continuing the discussion of the concept of the "investment climate", begun in Chap. 2—Institutions. Its introduction in Chap. 2 was to highlight the central role that these informal and formal "rules of the game" exercise in how investments play out. In our presentation of the investment climate, we suggested a continuum from a country's natural endowment through these institutions as enabling agents supporting efficient market development and sustainable economic growth, and ultimately driving market, macroeconomic, and investment performance. Second, we inserted the step of analyzing the nature and impact of the investment climate into a broader investment evaluation process, in which we added the subsequent steps of considering the impact of global market conditions, sectoral growth opportunities and challenges, and lastly the idiosyncratic characteristics of the investee. The discussion was intentionally very high level to permit a clearer focus on structure and process (methodology).

In Part III (Investor's Rutter), we will extend and deepen the analytic tools by which we apply country risk analysis to the investment process and then in Part IV (Case Studies), we will use these tools in a series of cases. Before doing this, however, we now move to Part II, "A Changing World". An investor must be sensitive to potential changes in geopolitical, global market, macroeconomic, technological, demographic, and climatic conditions (to name a few). In this next set of chapters, we will survey a selection of such sources of changes in the country risk panorama and then overlay their effects on our analysis model.

Notes

1. World Bank. (2005). *World Development Report 2005: A Better Investment Climate for Everyone*. Washington, DC: World Bank
2. World Bank (2004). Improving the Investment Climate for Growth and Poverty Reduction. Washington, DC: World Bank.

Part II

Context: A Changing World

EMDE Panorama by Richard Marney

6

Geoeconomic Recalibration: Risks and Opportunities for EMDEs

Geopolitics is back—and it is now a bigger driver of global markets than at any time since the Cold War.
Paraphrase of themes of I. Bremmer.

6.1 Introduction

As we have learned earlier in Chap. 1, turbo-charged globalization was a key feature of the 1990s and the 2000s. Eventually, globalization, measured by the share of global exports and imports in percent of GDP, peaked around the Global Financial Crisis. Not least the slow recovery from the Global Financial Crisis promoted a debate about who had benefitted from it, with the benefits not evenly spread. Surveys show that attitudes towards globalization had become less supportive in the Western world, and before long, politicians started addressing these concerns. Free trade agreements have become less frequent, trade negotiations at the World Trade Organization (WTO) came to a halt, and trade barriers surged after 2017. By that time, Russia had forcefully taken Crimea from Ukraine, and the first Trump administration in the US had started a "trade war" with China as part of its "America First" agenda. Still, the occasionally heated rhetoric had failed to translate into visible shifts in trade patterns, with globalization not reversing, but slowing (giving rise to the term "slowbalization").

Then the pandemic arrived, an immense global public health crisis. To contain it, governments were quick in introducing both, mobility and export restrictions, the latter concerning particularly medical goods such as masks. Global supply chains, that had grown increasingly complex by the time, faced

R. Marney, P. Waeber, *The Emerging Markets Investor's Guide to Country Risk*,
https://doi.org/10.1007/978-3-032-26824-2_6

unprecedented disruptions. While the health crisis was eventually contained thanks to an incredibly fast development of effective vaccines, the pandemic still had taught the world many lessons. One of them was that global supply chains were vulnerable to disruptions, and posed important risks for corporates. Yet another was that in times of crisis, countries might not rely on others for the supply of critical goods. The public discussion hence shifted, from *offshoring* to *near-shoring* and *friend-shoring*, and from *just-in-time* to *just-in-case*. It was *resilience* that became the dominant paradigm, replacing *efficiency*.

Russia's invasion of Ukraine, which it started in 2022, reinforced these lessons from the pandemic, particularly for Europe, that was highly reliant on energy imports from Russia at the time, and saw itself subsequently confronted with an energy crisis when Russia cut it off from its gas supplies.

The next, and for now the last pivotal moment has been the re-election of Donald Trump as US president in 2024. Part of his continuous "America First" agenda was economic nationalism, and before long he had introduced sweeping import tariffs on many countries. Average US import tariffs surged to levels not seen since World War II (Fig. 6.1). On top, the US had—even before Trump's return—started introducing some export restrictions on China, most notable on cutting-edge semiconductors, which the Trump administration subsequently tightened. In 2023, Jake Sullivan, at the time National Security Advisor of President Biden, in an often-cited speech[1] talked about a "small yard and high fence" US strategy when it comes to "foundational technologies", with American leadership in computing-related technologies, biotechnologies, and clean energy considered "a national security imperative".[2]

But not only the US has its aspirations of greater autonomy in areas of national interest. For instance, also Europe has its agenda of "strategic autonomy", formalized around 2016, and refined after the pandemic, which strives for creating the capacity to act autonomously in strategically important policy areas such as defense, energy, and digital capacities. Ursula von der Leyen, President of the European Commission, has repeatedly talked about the EU's intention to de-risk and diversify supply-chains while not aiming for decoupling.[3] Along similar lines, China had introduced the "Made in China 2025" initiative in 2015, targeting technological self-sufficiency and global leadership in key industries.

All in all, it is obvious that the world is changing, with international cooperation and free trade no longer being the ruling paradigms of our time. A new "Washington consensus" has emerged, with national security and resilience at its core, even when it comes with reduced efficiencies and higher costs. This is also reflected in a new field of scientific research having emerged.

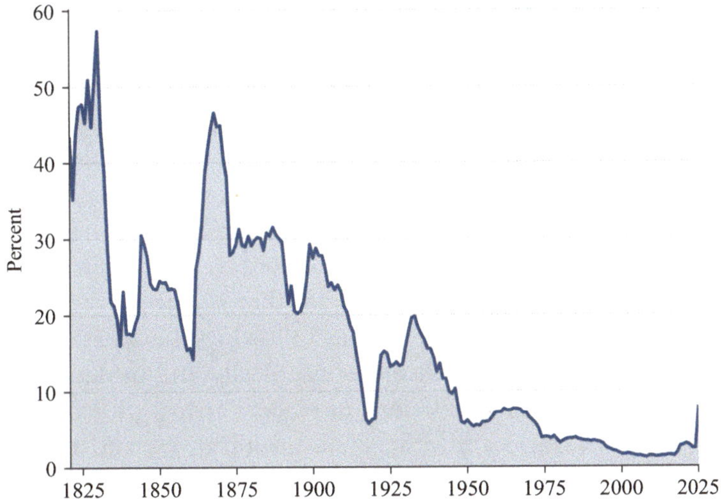

Fig. 6.1 US average tariff rate on all imports, 1821–2025. (Source: US International Trade Commission (USITC))

Geoeconomics studies "how international political rivalry (including war) shapes economic policies and outcomes – and vice versa."[4] This chapter takes an in-depth look at what has been labelled *geoeconomic fragmentation*, i.e. "a policy-driven reversal of global economic integration often guided by strategic considerations",[5] by assessing the prospects for disintegration for global trade and finance, and their potential economic impact for EMDEs.

6.2 The Geoeconomic Toolbox

As the definition suggests, geoeconomic fragmentation is driven by policies. So what are the policy tools that are likely to be deployed more frequently going forward? In times of peace, the toolbox includes import tariffs and controls, export and investment restrictions, as well as foreign aid. Such measures are increasingly common and often openly disclosed. In times of war, actions go even further, including outright embargoes, sabotage, and cyberattacks.

Trade Restrictions

Import tariffs have recently been championed by the United States, while the rest of the world—accounting for roughly 85% of global trade—for now sticks to moderate import tariffs (of around 3% on average). Import tariffs are mostly considered a protectionist tool aimed at a domestic audience. That said, the second Trump administration clearly weaponized it to get concessions from targeted countries, although the ultimate objectives were not always being clear to the public.

Tariffs are not the only policy tool affecting imports. In some cases, there have been outright bans of imports. A prominent example is the restriction, if not outright ban, of equipment from the Chinese 5G telecoms champion Huawei in many Western countries, due to concerns over espionage and vulnerabilities in critical infrastructure. Yet another example are Western countries bans of most imports from Russia following the Russian invasion of Ukraine, aimed at weakening Russia economically and undermining its war efforts. But also China has restrictions in place, barring government agencies from using Western devices in official communications and blocking many Western social media platforms.

Countries not only steer imports but also exports, either promoting or restricting them. For much of the 2000s, discussions focused on unfair export subsidies and trade disputes fought at the World Trade Organization (WTO). China, for instance, was repeatedly accused of violating trade rules by subsidizing its exports. In 2019 the WTO's dispute settlement system was effectively paralyzed when the United States blocked appointments to the Appellate Body, arguing that it had exceeded its mandate. Since then, the number of new disputes has dropped sharply, with the absence of a functioning appeal mechanism eroding the credibility and enforceability of multilateral trade rules.

That said, what really stood out in recent years was the increasing number of outright export bans. During the pandemic, many countries banned exports of medical equipment, such as medical masks. Then, in response to Russia's war against Ukraine that started in 2022, the West imposed many export restrictions on Russia, with Russia responding by stopping its gas exports to Europe, thereby creating an energy crisis there. Lastly, the rivalry between the US and China further accentuated, with the US restricting high-technology exports to China, and convincing others like Japan and the Netherlands to do the same, limiting among others exports of advanced semiconductors and equipment for the production of such. China itself weaponized its dominant position in the production of some raw materials, for instance temporarily banning the export of key minerals. All that is happening in the context of WTO rules allowing for export restrictions to prevent or relieve critical shortages of essential products, and policies to protect national security interests.[6]

Investment Restrictions

It is not only trade restrictions that are on the rise, but also investment restrictions. Motivated by a growing number of foreign takeovers in critical sectors, many countries have put in place mechanisms to monitor and restrict inward foreign investment.[7] Areas in focus include defense, critical infrastructure, emerging technologies (such as AI, semiconductors, or quantum computing) as well as energy, raw materials, and food security. On the back of national and economic security concerns, also restrictions on outward investment are on the rise. Most notably, since 2020, the US introduced and tightened regulation around outbound investment, with the EU following suit by introducing a framework to monitor outbound investments in critical sectors. Predominantly, these measures aim at preventing the transfer of sensitive technologies to "countries of concern".[8]

Foreign Funding

Yet another tool used to exert influence in a fragmenting world is foreign aid, whether in the form of grants or loans. While rarely openly disclosed, empirical research is indicative of both the direction and timing of foreign support being shaped geopolitical considerations.[9] Not least China emerged as what some call "an international lender of last resort", providing loans to countries in debt distress.[10] That said, its funding is often rather opaque, and channeled through central banks and other state-controlled institutions.[11] Historically, the great powers of their time have been the biggest official lenders, with hegemons seen as insuring the world not least by lending big during global shocks. Official lending is hence not only large, but remarkably counter cyclical, with "sudden stops" in private capital flows often accompanied by "sudden spikes" in official capital flows.[12]

War Games

In times of war, the toolbox expands to include more drastic measures, first and foremost embargoes, whereby a country completely halts economic exchange with the target state. Russia's invasion of Ukraine led many Western countries to cut economic relations with it, severely restricting trade, cutting it off from the international payment system, limiting access to hard currency, and freezing its central bank reserves.

Russia though is hitting back, by influencing foreign elections, stirring dissent among Western allies, testing NATO by targeted violations of members' airspace, as well as inflicting harm through cyberattacks and sabotage. All these actions increase public spending pressures, and increase the likelihood of operational disruptions in rival power blocs going forward.

6.3 Global Trade—Fracturing in Sectors of Strategic Importance

While the world arguably is growing more protectionist amid rising trade restrictions, actual trade data show only a stabilization of global trade on an elevated level, rather than a decline in trade openness (Fig. 6.2). As such, at least for now, global trade has proven surprisingly resilient, and there are no signs of deglobalization.

Changing Trade Patterns in the Recent Past

The aggregate data, however, hides underlying shifts. Underneath the surface, there is evidence of trade patterns starting to fragment between a US-centered and a China-centered bloc.[13] One of the most obvious and pronounced shifts has been China's loss of market share in the US. In 2018, 21% of US goods imports originated from China. By 2025, that figure had fallen to below 10%.

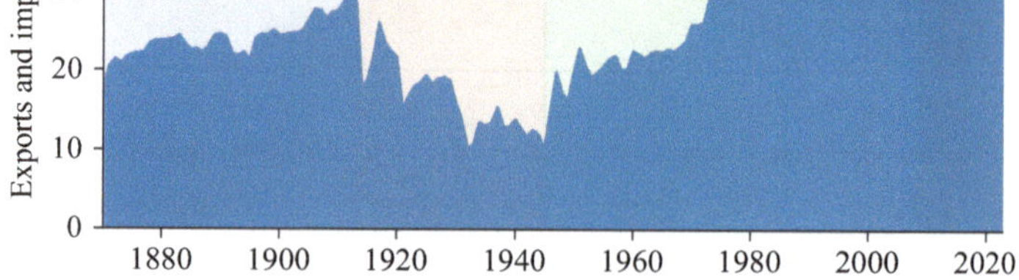

Fig. 6.2 World trade openness, 1870–2023. (Source: Klasing & Milionis (2014); Penn World Tables; World Bank, World Development Indicators—via Our World in Data. Note: Era periodization follows IMF (2023). Pre-1960 estimates are based primarily on advanced economies; post-1960 series cover a broader country sample)

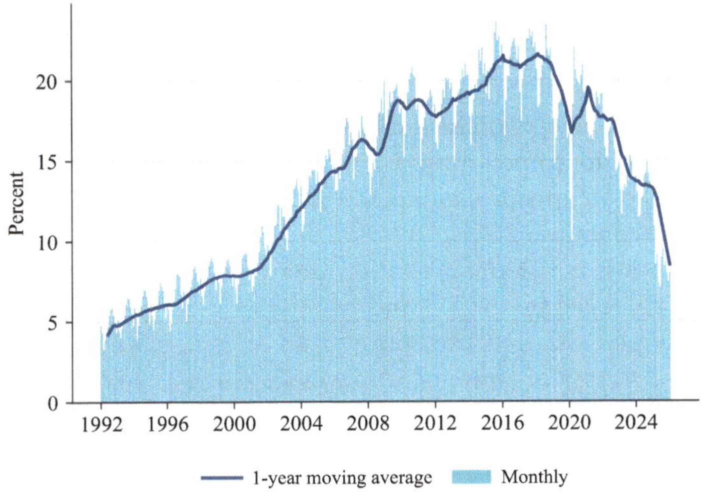

Fig. 6.3 China's share of US goods imports. (Source: US Census Bureau via Macrobond)

This suggests that both the US-China trade war and the pandemic had lasting repercussions (Fig. 6.3).

The question then became whether Chinese exports were merely rerouted through other, so-called connector countries, with minimal value added there, or whether there was trade reallocation, with production shifting to those countries. So far, most evidence points to the latter. Mexico, for instance, became the US' largest trading partner in 2023 after receiving significant FDI—mostly from the US—in sectors where tariffs were applied on Chinese imports.[14] Similarly, Vietnam benefitted from trade reallocation, raising its domestic value added in exports to the US in strategic sectors such as electronics and chemicals. Here too, increased production was at least partially a result of rising FDI, not least from China, but also from Japan, Korea, and the US.[15]

These developments are likely a consequence of both US trade policies and shifting paradigms regarding global supply-chains, after the pandemic exposed inherent fragilities. While in the pandemic, there was talk about a paradigm shift from "just-in-time" to "just-in-case", and from "offshoring" to "near-shoring", the US-China trade war introduced the term "friendshoring."

By historical comparisons, not least to the Cold War era, goods trade between the different blocs remains substantial.[16] Could that change in the not-too-distant future, and could the Cold War era potentially serve as a blueprint for what a new equilibrium might look like?

Contours of a New Trade Order

Arguably, it is difficult to know how geoeconomic fragmentation will continue, and what a new equilibrium might look like. One plausible and well-developed scenario comes from Neil Shearing, author of "The Fractured Age – How the Return of Geopolitics Will Splinter the Global Economy", published in September 2025.[17]

His key thesis: while the global economy will fracture into two blocs, one Western bloc led by the US and one with China at its core, "fracturing is not simply globalization in reverse".[18] In Shearing's view, fracturing will mainly affect sectors of strategic importance, such as advanced electronics and ICT, green technologies, critical raw materials, as well as health and life sciences. In these areas, governments will pressure firms to secure supply chains within their respective blocs. Everything else, and hence over 95% of global trade, will be unaffected, with Western consumers continuing "to fill their homes with goods that are made in China".[19] Meanwhile, each bloc's boundaries will remain somewhat fluid and potentially change over time. For now, the Western bloc is likely to include most of Europe, Canada, Japan, Korea, and Vietnam, while China's bloc will include Russia, Iran, and Venezuela. Commodity producing countries will be courted by both blocs. While their economic ties might currently be stronger with China (given its resource-intensive growth model), their political systems, as well as social and cultural ties, are often closer to the West. What about India, the world's most populated country? Its position is not yet fully determined, but it may eventually end up in the Western bloc, not least as choosing that side in a fracturing world might offer economic opportunities. Exemplary is Apple's move to shift the iPhone production for the US market from China to India.

With the US having become more protectionist under the second Trump administration, and China facing much higher US import tariffs than all other countries, ultimately more than 5% of global trade might be affected by fracturing. But reshoring production to the US or Europe will mainly remain talk, because even if governments were to sever ties with China in other areas, production would most likely be relocated to another low-cost country in the Western bloc, as is happening with Apple's iPhone. As such, Shearing presents fracturing also as a process that offers opportunities for some countries, including Mexico, Vietnam, India, and Poland.

Strategic Nodes in Global Trade

In a world of geopolitical rivalry, control over global production suddenly becomes an instrument of power that risks being exploited. When the US tightened restrictions on advanced semiconductor exports to China in 2025, the latter responded by restricting exports of rare earths, thereby leveraging its global dominance in the production of these. There are other minerals where China plays a critical role in global production, including lithium and cobalt. But China's influence expands beyond raw materials, not least as it has become the dominant manufacturer of green technologies, including solar panels, wind-turbine components, and lithium-ion batteries. Countries that are serious about the green transition, many of which are situated in Europe, hence critically rely on China.

For investors, understanding such chokepoints is essential. On the one hand, they pose important vulnerabilities to businesses and countries, but on the other hand, they offer also opportunities as the Western bloc strives to reduce its over-reliance on China and to diversify their suppliers.

6.4 Global Finance – Western Payment Infrastructure Rivalled

Part of the latest wave of globalization has been a surge in cross-border capital flows. As outlined earlier, many EMDEs liberalized their capital accounts and opened up to foreign capital, which helps explain this surge. What will geoeconomic fragmentation mean for global finance?

Building on the ideas on how global trade might evolve, it is likely that cross-bloc flows in strategically important areas will decline because of investment screening processes and investment restrictions. That said, already today, inter-bloc capital flows do not seem overly large, with around four-fifths of all global cross-border capital flows happening within the US-centered bloc.[20] Furthermore, to the extent that the fragmentation process will lead to trade reallocation, it will likely temporarily increase cross-border flows, both within blocs and across them, not least with Chinese firms building factories in third countries to serve the US market and circumvent high import tariffs. Moreover, the split between public and private capital flows is likely to change, with public flows gaining importance.[21]

As Edward Fishman lays out in "Chokepoints",[22] the United States' dominance of the global financial system—as reflected in its position as the global

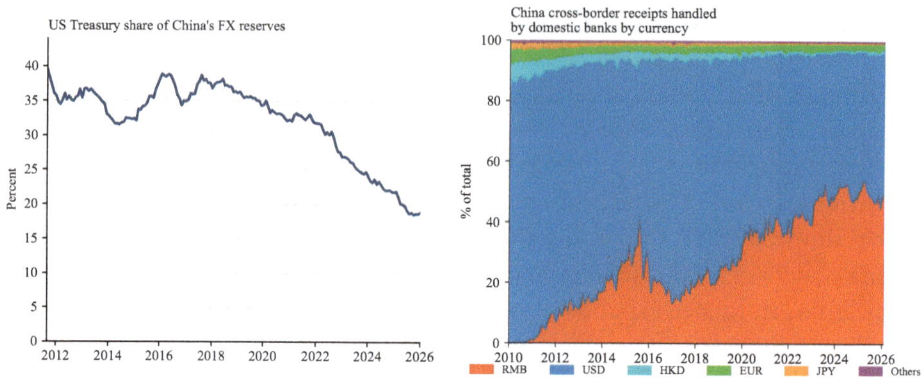

Fig. 6.4 China's declining financial exposure to the United States. (Source: US Treasury, Treasury International Capital (TIC) system; State Administration of Foreign Exchange (SAFE); People's Bank of China; via Macrobond)

reserve currency and the USD's dominance in trade finance and forex transactions—provides it with significant leverage over adversaries. It has used that leverage increasingly over the past two decades, with the campaign against Iran's nuclear program in the mid-2000s marking the start and sweeping financial sanctions against Russia following its assault on Ukraine in 2022 representing the peak. The United States has demonstrated its ability and willingness to effectively cut off countries from the global financial system and freeze their foreign exchange reserves. In doing so it has spurred its rivals to work on reducing their financial vulnerabilities and the US' leverage. Among others, China "is ditching the dollar, fast",[23] launching its own payment system in 2015 (CIPS, Cross-Border Interbank Payment System) and a multi-central bank digital currency platform (called mBridge) that aims to enable instant cross-border payments and settlements in 2021. Most strikingly, by mid-2025, China settled more than 50% of its total cross-border receipts in its national currency, whereas back in 2010 hardly any of these payments were denominated in yuan (see Fig. 6.4). That the Western response to Russia's invasion of Ukraine in 2022 acted as a catalyst for financial decoupling is also evident in Chinese banks' overseas lending, all of which is since denominated in yuan, whereas previously only about 15% of such loans were in yuan. Along similar lines, China has been drastically reducing its US treasury holdings as part of its foreign-exchange reserves.

That said, despite China's economy rivaling that of the US and Eurozone in size, the international usage of its currency remains far behind the USD and EUR. In particular, China's relatively closed capital account and weaker rule-of-law are holding it back. As such, most observers remain skeptical about the renminbi's ability ultimately rival the USD as the dominant global currency.[24] Furthermore, the biggest threat to USD dominance arguably at present comes from within, with actions by US President Trump undermining central bank independence and the rule of law.

6.5 Economic Impact of Geoeconomic Fragmentation

Geoeconomic fragmentation affects global growth prospects through multiple channels. Trade restrictions are typically associated with economic costs, as they reduce efficiency, resulting in higher production costs, weaker export performance, and negative employment effects. Trade openness is also seen as stimulating innovation by increasing domestic competition, improving technology adoption, facilitating the transfer of knowledge, and enhancing the skill base of workers. As such, fragmentation could hamper technology diffusion and innovation. Lastly, the process of fragmentation is associated with heightened uncertainties, which risk weighing on consumption and investment, with households increasing precautionary savings and firms postponing investment decisions.

There have been multiple attempts to quantify the potential economic impact of geoeconomic fracturing. These analyses all rely on assumptions and/or scenarios of how fragmentation might unfold. Some assume an end to trade in high-tech manufacturing and energy across blocs. Others, under a severe fragmentation scenario, a complete halt in inter-bloc trade. All emphasize that their estimates are subject to considerable uncertainty.[25]

Estimates of the long-run impact of geoeconomic fracturing vary widely, ranging from around 1% of global GDP under a benign scenario to as much as 12% under a severe fragmentation scenario. In the end, the deeper the fragmentation, the higher the costs. With regard to the global distribution of income losses, researchers often argue that EMDEs will be most affected, as they rely more on external demand and technological transfer. This view, however, is not entirely intuitive. Few EMDEs have large, strategically important sectors, and even fewer belong to the Chinese bloc and export the output of these sectors to the West. In fact, only China itself comes to mind. While many EMDEs rely on Chinese imports and may seek to reduce this dependence in certain sectors, overall external demand should remain intact, if not strengthen as a result of geoeconomic fragmentation, provided they fall into the Western bloc.

6.6 War Risks

At the same time as globalization lost momentum and eventually stalled, armed conflicts and the associated death toll have been on the rise globally. In 2024, the number of conflicts involving the state reached the highest level since 1946, with conflicts in Africa nearly doubling within a decade and accounting for almost half of all conflicts globally, followed by Asia and the Middle East. The early 2020s also marked the most violent years since the Cold War, with particularly the wars in Ethiopia, Ukraine, and the Middle East in particular causing heavy casualties. Meanwhile, the number of interstate wars remains relatively small, making it difficult to determine whether there is an uptrend or just some volatility.[26]

Globally, more than one billion people live in what the World Bank qualifies as fragile and conflict-affected states (FCS). While both the absolute number and the share of the global population living in FCS have been on the rise over the past decade, this is due less to new countries being added to the list (such as some Sahel countries in the late 2010s and, more recently, Ukraine and Venezuela), and more to strong population growth within existing FCS. Geographically, FCS are most prevalent in Africa (50% of all FCS, 63% of the FCS population), with most of the remainder located in MENA and Asia. Of these conflicts, most in Africa are internal insurgencies, while those in the Middle East are often interstate and proxy conflicts. Predominately, FCS are low-income countries and generally receive limited foreign investment, as investors are deterred by violence and weak institutions. Exceptions include resource-rich countries such as Democratic Republic of the Congo (DRC) and Nigeria, where foreign investment still flows into oil, gas or mining projects. Notable exceptions also include today's major wars, above all Russia's invasion of Ukraine and the escalation of violence in the Middle East. Together with China's assertive ambitions in the South China Sea and its growing pressure on Taiwan, these conflicts represent the major geopolitical flashpoints of today's world, posing significant risks for international investors.

China—Growing Ever more Assertive on its Territorial Claims

Alongside its economic rise, China has significantly increased its military power and become more assertive about its territorial claims in the South China Sea and its ambitions regarding Taiwan. Large territorial claims in the South China Sea are demarked by the so-called Nine-Dash Line, whose origins date back to 1947 and which China formally submitted to the UN in 2009 (albeit without clearly defining the legal nature and precise coordinates of the claim, thus leaving its interpretation ambiguous).[27] Since then, China has underpinned its claims by building military bases on artificial islands atop of reefs across the South China Sea, ignoring a landmark ruling by the United Nations Convention on the Law of the Sea (UNCLOS) in 2016, which concluded that Beijing's maritime claims were inconsistent with international law.[28] The US accuses China of using gray zone operations by applying a wide variety of coercive operations somewhere in between peace and war, allowing it to exert control over the region without triggering a military response by opponents.[29]

The global concern about China's claims in the South China Sea stems from the fact that they overlap with Exclusive Economic Zones (EEZs, i.e. maritime zones established under UNCLOS that extend up to 200 nautical miles from a country's coastline and grant coastal states sovereign rights over natural resources) of at least five nations: the Philippines, Vietnam, Malaysia, Brunei, and Indonesia. Of these, the Philippines has a mutual defense treaty with the US, while Vietnam and Indonesia are strategic partners. As such, any escalation risks drawing the US and China into a direct military confrontation, which both countries would seek to avoid but which could still happen due to miscalculation or mistakes.

Even more acute, however, are the risks surrounding Taiwan. Beijing has long sought reunification, and most analysts agree it is a core objective to China's Communist Party. China has also grown increasingly assertive in recent years, with senior US officials voicing concerns about a potential military invasion within the next few years. Some scholars argue that the "window of opportunity" for China lies in the near-term, as delay risks placing it in a weaker position.[30] That said, many of the considerations are open to interpretation. For instance, do China's current economic difficulties make an invasion less likely or more? One might assume the former, but history shows that leaders often rally nationalist sentiment in times of domestic economic weakness. Similarly, Taiwan's outsized role in the global production of advanced semiconductors, which the west tries to curb, raises the stakes. On one hand, this strengthens the US resolve to defend Taiwan; on the other, it makes the island an even more attractive target for China, whose access to these semiconductors is being curtailed by Western export controls. A further layer of uncertainty stems from large-scale purges of the PLA's senior leadership that President Xi Jinping undertook since 2022. While the purges strengthen political control, they have likely weakened operational readiness in the near-term by removing experienced commanders and creating leadership gaps.[31]

If China were to advance its claims on Taiwan by force, it could take many forms—from a blockade to a full-scale invasion—but in any case would ultimately risk drawing the two superpowers into a direct military confrontation. The US has for long maintained a policy of "strategic ambiguity" towards Taiwan, leaving open the question of how it would react to a Chinese invasion. Under President Trump, however, there is greater uncertainty about Washington's willingness to intervene. In contrast to election campaign rhetoric about keeping the US out of foreign conflicts, the second Trump administration has engaged in a series of military operations abroad. Together, these actions point to a selective and transactional use of force, often undertaken with limited coordination with allies or multilateral frameworks. Furthermore, Trump has previously argued that Taiwan "stole" the US' chip industry and should pay for its own defense.[32] Beyond willingness, recent military operations in the Middle East—by consuming critical munitions, degrading inventories, and stretching naval deployments—have also raised questions about the US' military capacity and readiness in the Indo-Pacific in the near term.[33] This greater uncertainty about the US stance increases the risk of an invasion.

Even if a direct confrontation were avoided, the economic implications would be profound. Taiwan dominates the global production of advanced semi-conductors which are vital inputs for AI, automotive manufacturing, and consumer electronics. Moreover, the ensuing Western sanction regime could cause major disruptions, while global consumer and business confidence would likely plummet, sending markets into off-risk mode.

When it comes to Western sanctions, the question is whether they would follow the "Russia playbook". Western countries would certainly build on the lessons learned from the sanctions imposed on Russia, but it is doubtful that they would go as far, given China's much stronger economic and financial ties with the West. Western nations would design sanctions that exert maximum pressure on China while minimizing the collateral damage to their economies. Such a sanction regime would likely include restrictions on new investments in China, tighter export controls on sensitive technologies, as well as targeted asset freezes and travel bans.

Overall, it is safe to assume that the global economic fallback from a Chinese invasion of Taiwan would be immense. In 2024, Bloomberg estimated that the global economy could contract by around 10% of GDP, which is roughly twice the shock experienced during the Global Financial Crisis and the Covid-19 pandemic.[34] What is noteworthy about these estimates is that they show a much bigger near-term hit to China (−17%) than the US (−7%), with East Asia generally being the worst affected region due to disruptions in regional trade networks and the regions export orientation. Countries such as

Vietnam, Malaysia, and Thailand might see GDP contractions of up to 20%, while Indonesia and the Philippines could experience declines of 12–14%. The drag would be somewhat milder, but still substantial, for India, thanks to its less open and more diversified economy.

Russia—Restoring Lost Greatness?

Russia's war against Ukraine, that started with the forceful annexation of Crimea in 2014 and continued with the attempted full-scale invasion in 2022, marks one of the key geopolitical escalations of recent times. While the Western reaction in 2014 was still relatively muted, the full-scale invasion triggered a decisive rupture, with Western nations imposing heavy sanctions on Russia and seeking to isolate it economically. Russia, in turn, exploited Europe's reliance on its gas supplies to engineer an energy crisis there.

At the time of writing, the war in Ukraine remains ongoing, with no end in sight. Russia's actions extended beyond Ukraine, including interference in elections in Romania and Moldova, airspace incursions by drones in Europe that cause operational disruptions, efforts to map critical infrastructure such as undersea cables carrying global internet and communications (potentially as a prelude to sabotage), and the launch of frequent cyberattacks. As such, Russia persistently threatens to cause operational disruptions, particularly in Europe.

Ultimately, the question is what Russia's foreign policy objectives are. Vladimir Putin has repeatedly labelled the collapse of the Soviet Union "the greatest geopolitical catastrophe of the 20th century" and has sought to portray himself as the singular leader capable of restoring Russia's lost greatness. He also claims a responsibility to protect ethnic Russians in former Soviet states. Furthermore, Putin views NATO's eastward expansion as an existential threat to Russia's security, despite NATO being a defensive alliance, and presents Russia as a defender of those who oppose what he calls the "degrading West".

In a fragmenting world, with the US showing signs of retrenchment and Europe rushing to reassert its defense capabilities, Putin's Russia will likely remain focused on resisting further eastward expansion of NATO while seeking pretexts to interfere in former Soviet states with sizable Russian minorities. It will also continue undermining Western cohesion and fueling internal divisions. Countries most at risk include Moldova, the Baltics, and Georgia, with risks to the latter currently contained by its pro-Russian government. The risk of other countries facing direct Russian military aggressions also seems contained as long as the war in Ukraine, which absorbs substantial resources, continues.

For the time being, Russia will therefore likely rely primarily on hybrid warfare, seeking to weaken its perceived opponents while avoiding direct military confrontation. While both Russia and NATO likely want to avoid such a confrontation, there remains a tail risk that miscalculation or accident could trigger one, the consequences of which could be devastating, given both sides possess nuclear weapons.

Middle East—New Power Balance, Persistent Tensions

Following Hamas' assault on Israel in October 2023, tensions in the Middle East escalated sharply. Israel responded by waging a war against Hamas in Gaza, carrying out attacks on Hezbollah in Lebanon and targets in Syria, and even conducting military strikes against Iran. In 2026, the conflict broadened further, with the US and Israel launching large-scale strikes on Iran, and Iran responding by disrupting critical infrastructure and trade routes across the region in an effort to raise the economic costs of the conflict.[35]

Israel has emerged as the dominant regional military power, supported by direct US involvement, while Iran's network of proxies has been significantly degraded. Doubts, however, remain over whether Israel can and wants to sustain the role of the regional hegemon.[36] While opposing forces are currently much weakened, there is a substantial risk that the extensive use of force could sow the seeds of future backlash. As such, the Middle East is likely to remain prone to recurring escalations of tensions and violence.

For EMDE, the risks are mostly indirect—with only a few countries directly involved in the conflict—but increasingly systemic. With about a third of the world's seaborne oil supplies passing through the Strait of Hormuz, it remains one of the most critical chokepoints of global energy supply.[37] The 2026 events have highlighted the vulnerability of these flows to disruption,[38] and the risk the region's security situation poses to global energy[39] and trade systems. Regional disruptions to shipping routes and supply chains can have major repercussions for inflation dynamics, external balances and growth prospects globally, particularly for energy importers. Furthermore, large-scale military operations risk straining global defense resources and increasing uncertainty in other regions. Even if tensions were to ease, the 2026 episode underscores the structural fragility of critical trade routes and suggests a higher geopolitical risk premium on energy and transport going forward.[40]

6.7 Implications for Investors

Strive for Security Makes the World Riskier

As outlined throughout this chapter, a new "Washington Consensus" is emerging, with national security interests playing an ever-larger role as US hegemony is challenged by China. Under a baseline scenario, this means that a US-led Western bloc and a China-centered bloc will seek to decouple in sectors of strategic importance. That decoupling is driven in part by a security dilemma: as one bloc enhances its economic security, the other feels less secure and is pushed to invest in its own. Once trust is lost, the likely consequence is an arms race for resilience.[41]

A relevant concept in this regard is Edward Fishman's adaption of the "Impossible Trinity", which argues that only two of the following three elements can co-exist: (1) economic interdependence, (2) economic security, and (3) geopolitical competition. With competition now a reality and the scramble for economic security under way, interdependence will likely continue to unravel.[42]

Ironically and worrying, reducing the reliance on geopolitical rivals also lowers the perceived cost of conflict. The consequence of de-risking global supply-chains and decoupling in strategically important sectors is therefore a troubling rise in global war risks.[43] Consistently, in the Atlantic Council's latest Global Foresight survey among leading geostrategists and foresight practitioners, 40% of respondents expected "another world war, involving a multifront conflict among great powers" over the next decade.[44]

Tracking Escalation Risks

With the relevance of geopolitical risks established, is there a way to track them and possibly anticipate an escalation? Most immediately, mobilizations and troop movements provide important signals. In the case of Russia's invasion of Ukraine, reports about a build-up of Russian troops close to the Ukrainian border began appearing almost four months before the invasion started, though many observers initially believed it was merely a negotiation tactic and downplayed the likelihood of war. That said, in the case of China, military exercises around Taiwan have increased in recent years to such an extent that a "fig leaf of an exercise" could actually mask the preparation for an attack (Fig. 6.5). According to US defense officials, the People's Liberations Army Navy could "move into a blockage posture in a matter of hours".[45]

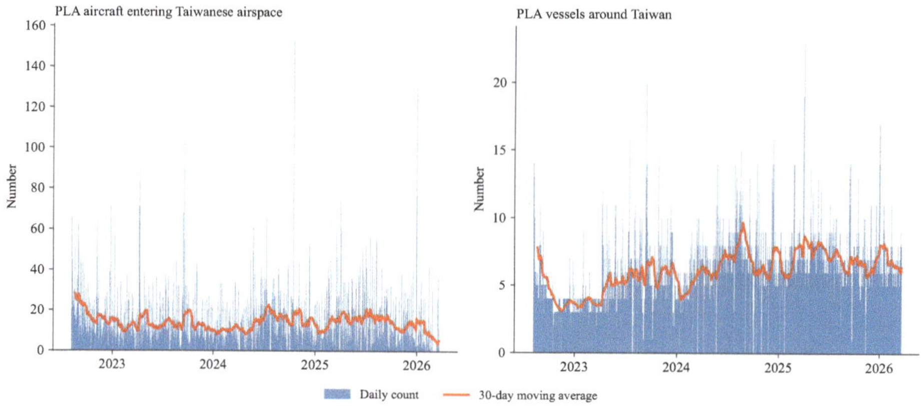

Fig. 6.5 PLA military activities around Taiwan. (*Source: Taiwan Ministry of National Defense*, via *Macrobond*)

As such, when it comes to Taiwan, one must look for other early-warning indicators. Trade data can offer early signals, with China likely to stockpile vital goods it depends on, above all: energy (oil, gas, and coal); raw materials such as iron ore, copper, and nickel; food items such as soybeans for animal feed; and potentially some high-tech components. Given the granularity of available trade statistics, analysts can leverage these data to identify potential signs of war preparations. At the time of writing, import data did not indicate such preparations were accelerating (Fig. 6.6).

Yet another area to monitor is the extent to which China is becoming "sanction-proof" against a potential US weaponization of financial dominance, for instance by further reducing its holdings of US Treasuries and expanding the use of the renminbi in bilateral trade settlements. That said, given the size of China's annual current account surpluses, it will remain a net creditor to the world in general, and the US in particular, with the latter arguably being the only market large enough to absorb China's external surpluses.

Gray Zone Operations - a Persistent Threat, though Exposure Varies

Beyond the outright escalation of geopolitical tensions, "gray-zone" operations such as state-sponsored cyberattacks—which have been on the rise in recent years—can cause significant economic harm. While research typically focuses on major countries and geopolitical conflicts, and therefore leaves

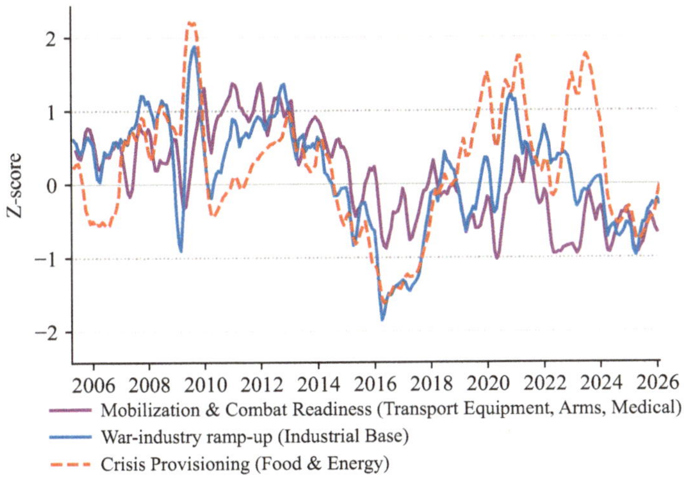

Fig. 6.6 China's strategic import pressure index. (Source: Authors' calculations based on data from China General Administration of Customs. Z-scores of deflated and detrended import categories, smoothed with a three-month moving average. Values above +1 signal import surges that deviate significantly from long-term structural patterns; values below −1 indicate unusual import compression)

aside most of EMDEs, many of them—particularly those outside the contested regions discussed in the previous subchapter—combine relatively low exposure with high vulnerability.

The lower exposure stems from their limited relevance to the strategic interests of major powers, given their often modest economic size and geopolitical importance. Moreover, exposure varies across sectors: firms in critical industries such as energy, finance, and communication arguably face the highest risk. The higher vulnerability of many EMDEs, meanwhile, reflects weaker institutional capability, including less advanced intelligence capabilities, limited preparedness, and gaps in governance and regulation. Given these heightened vulnerabilities, investors need to carefully assess the risks to their portfolios arising from gray-zone operations.

Risks and Opportunities for Investors

Absent major geopolitical escalations or grey-zone operations, trade frictions pose both risks and opportunities for investors. The risks arise when chokepoints in global supply-chains are exploited by geopolitical rivals. Tensions between the US and China intensified throughout 2025, with each exploiting its respective leverage over critical nodes in global value chains.

China remains a complex investment case. On the one hand, investors are attracted by low valuations on Chinese equities and the global ambitions of firms such as BYD, which combine technological leadership with unmatched price competitiveness. On the other hand, there is mounting opposition to Chinese companies, particularly in sectors of strategic importance. On the back of data security concerns and state access, several Western governments have increased political and regulatory scrutiny of Chinese technology firms, including AI developers such as DeepSeek, super-apps like WeChat, and entertainment apps such as TikTok. As a result, the international success of Chinese products risks being held back by geopolitical tensions.

The currently ongoing reconfiguration of global supply chains offers opportunities but also comes with risks. Investments in manufacturing businesses in countries like Mexico or Vietnam benefit from trade relocation away from China, but face scrutiny over trans-shipment practices that could ultimately result in higher US tariffs. India positioned itself as an alternative electronics producer for the US market but eventually got hit by high US tariffs for importing lots of Russian oil. Meanwhile, Poland is successfully positioning itself as a near-shoring hub for Western Europe, attracting electronics and battery producers. However, many of the supply-chains still run through China and therefore remain exposed to disruption from geopolitical frictions.

Outside near- and friend-shoring hubs, investors must navigate competing spheres of influence. Panama offers a recent example: under US pressure, it tightened the scrutiny of Chinese investments and ultimately sided with the US. Others, such as Nicaragua, being pressured by Western sanctions over human rights abuses, have drifted closer to Beijing. In that case, push factors were at work. In other instances, it is more about pull factors, with the promise of Chinese infrastructure projects and financing for instance inducing Honduras in 2023 to drop its recognition of Taiwan.

Commodity exporters such as Chile, Indonesia, and several African nations are being courted by both blocs, as demand for critical minerals and supply-chain diversification soars. For these countries, it is a balancing act, and missteps risk causing pressure from one side or the other.

Meanwhile, when considering investments in Eastern Europe, heightened defence spending raises fiscal pressures and potentially corporate tax burdens, while Russian grey-zone operations—ranging from cyberattacks to sabotage—add operational risks. Several countries also remain torn between their populations' aspirations of a Western lifestyle and deep economic ties with Russia, the most prominent examples being Armenia, Georgia, and Moldova. The Georgian elections in 2024 were a testament of how torn these countries are, and how difficult this balancing act is, with the ruling party winning likely rigged elections on the promise of peace through rapprochement with its past aggressor, Russia.

In the Middle East and Africa we see geopolitical tensions having knock-on effects. For instance, Egypt has suffered greatly from reduced shipping through the Suez Canal, and heightened security concerns pose persistent risks to its large tourism sector. Elsewhere on the African continent, Russia seems happily supporting regimes or military juntas, providing political backing for access to natural resources, further undermining regional security.

What all these examples illustrate is that geopolitics has become a key factor for international business prospects. Vulnerable firms will strive to mitigate risks by maintaining larger inventories, yet as long as one side controls substantial shares of global supplies of critical inputs, recurring supply disruptions are likely. The companies most at risk are those operating in sectors of strategic relevance, such as advanced electronics and ICT, green technologies, critical raw materials, and health and life sciences. International investors must assess these risks carefully, even when dealing with companies outside the critical sectors.

Notes

1. Sullivan, J. (2023) *Remarks by National Security Advisor Jake Sullivan on Renewing American Economic Leadership at the Brookings Institution*, 27 April. The White House. Available at: https://bidenwhitehouse.archives.gov/briefing-room/speeches-remarks/2023/04/27/remarks-by-national-security-advisor-jake-sullivan-on-renewing-american-economic-leadership-at-the-brookings-institution/ (Accessed: 5 October 2025).
2. Sullivan, J. (2022) Remarks by National Security Advisor Jake Sullivan at the Special Competitive Studies Project Global Emerging Technologies Summit, 16 September. *The White House.* Available at: https://bidenwhitehouse.archives.gov/briefing-room/speeches-remarks/2022/09/16/remarks-by-national-security-advisor-jake-sullivan-at-the-special-competitive-studies-project-global-emerging-technologies-summit/ (Accessed: 5 October 2025).
3. See for instance **von der Leyen, U. (2023)** Statement by President von der Leyen at the joint press conference with President Michel following the EU-China Summit, 7 December. *European Commission.* Available at: https://ec.europa.eu/commission/presscorner/detail/en/STATEMENT_23_6409 (Accessed: 5 October 2025).
4. Mohr, C. & Trebesch, C. (2025), 'Geoeconomics', *Annual Review of Economics* (forthcoming); Kiel Working Paper No. 2279.

5. International Monetary Fund (IMF), 2023. *Geoeconomic Fragmentation and the Future of Multilateralism.* Staff Discussion Note SDN/2023/001. Washington, DC: IMF.
6. Bown, C. P. (2023) 'The Challenge of Export Controls'. *Finance & Development,* June. Washington, DC: International Monetary Fund.
7. Mohr, C. & Trebesch, C. (2025).
8. OECD (2024). *Managing security implications of international investment.* Paris: Organisation for Economic Co-operation and Development.
9. Mohr, C. & Trebesch, C. (2025).
10. Horn, S., Reinhart, C. M., Trebesch, C. & Parks, B. C. (2023). *China as an international lender of last resort.* NBER Working Paper No. 31191, April.
11. Horn, S., Reinhart, C. M., Trebesch, C. & Parks, B. C. (2023).
12. Horn, S., Reinhart, C. M. & Trebesch, C. (2024). *International lending in war and peace.* Preliminary draft, October 2024. Kiel Institute / Harvard University.
13. Gopinath, G., Gourinchas, P.-O., Presbitero, A. F. & Topalova, P. (2024) *Changing Global Linkages: A New Cold War?* IMF Working Paper No. 2024/076.
14. Arizala, F., Mineyama, T. & Tuesta, H. (2025) *Relocation of Global Value Chains: The Role of Mexico.* IMF Working Paper WP/25/180.
15. Schulze, T. & Xin, W. (2025) *Demystifying Trade Patterns In A Fragmenting World.* IMF Working Paper WP/25/129.
16. Gopinath, G., Gourinchas, P.-O., Presbitero, A. F. & Topalova, P. (2024).
17. Shearing, N. (2025) *The Fractured Age: How the Return of Geopolitics Will Splinter the Global Economy.* London: John Murray Business.
18. Shearing, N. (2025), p. 8.
19. Shearing, N. (2025), p. 15.
20. Shearing, N. (2025).
21. Mohr, C. & Trebesch, C. (2025).
22. Fishman, E. (2024) *Chokepoints: How Global Power Is Reshaped by Economic Weapons.* New York: Oxford University Press.
23. The Economist (2025) 'China is ditching the dollar, fast: Officials believe that the yuan has finally come of age', *The Economist,* 10 September.
24. See for instance Shearing (2025), Fishman (2025) and von Beschwitz, B. (2024) *Internationalization of the Chinese renminbi: progress so far and outlook.* FEDS Notes, Board of Governors of the Federal Reserve System, 30 August. Available at: https://www.federalreserve.gov/econres/notes/feds-notes/internationalization-of-the-chinese-renminbi-progress-and-outlook-20240830.html (Accessed: 19 October 2025).
25. International Monetary Fund (IMF), 2023.
26. Rustad, S. A. (2025) *Conflict Trends: A Global Overview, 1946–2024.* PRIO Paper. Oslo: Peace Research Institute Oslo (PRIO).

27. Permanent Mission of the People's Republic of China to the United Nations (2009) *Note Verbale CML/17/2009*, 7 May. Available at: https://www.un.org/Depts/los/clcs_new/submissions_files/mysvnm33_09/chn_2009re_mys_vnm_e.pdf (Accessed 12 October 2025).
28. The Republic of the Philippines and The People's Republic of China (2016) *The South China Sea Arbitration: Award of 12 July 2016*, Reports of International Arbitral Awards, Vol. XXXIII, pp. 153–617. Available at: https://docs.pca-cpa.org/2016/07/PH-CN-20160712-Award.pdf (Accessed 12 October 2025).
29. Helmus, T.C., Grocholski, K.R., Liggett, T., Rhoades, A.L., Savitz, S. and Palmer, K. (2024) *Understanding and countering China's maritime gray zone operations*. Santa Monica, CA: RAND Corporation.
30. Moore, G.J. (2025) 'Xi Jinping's Taiwan dashboard: Considering Xi's calculus for a possible move on Taiwan', *Journal of Indo-Pacific Affairs*, 8(1), pp. 15–34.
31. China Power Project (2026) *The purges within China's military are even deeper than you think*. Center for Strategic and International Studies (CSIS), February.
32. Hille, K. (2024) 'Donald Trump calls for Taiwan to "pay" for its own defence', *Financial Times*, 17 July.
33. The Economist (2026) *The Iran war could sap American military power for years*. The Economist, 18 March.
34. Welch, J., Leonard, J., Cousin, M., DiPippo, G. and Orlik, T. (2024) 'Xi, Biden and the $10 trillion cost of war over Taiwan', *Bloomberg*, 9 January.
35. England, A. and Bozorgmehr, N. (2026) *Iran sets its price to end the war*. Financial Times, 19 March.
36. The Economist (2025) 'An unrestrained Israel is reshaping the Middle East: its quest for hegemony will strain domestic cohesion and foreign alliances', *The Economist—Briefing*, 26 March.
37. Wilson, T. (2025) 'Why oil traders are watching the Strait of Hormuz: crude prices surge over potential for disruption to the narrow waterway', *Financial Times*, 13 June.
38. Ratcliffe, V., Jilani, H. and Dempsey, H. (2026) *World faces gas supply cliff edge as Gulf's final LNG shipments approach ports*. Financial Times, 22 March.
39. Moore, M. (2026) *Iran war is the greatest threat to global energy 'in history', warns IEA*. Financial Times, 20 March.
40. The Editorial Board (2026) *Iran war will scar the global economy*. Financial Times, 20 March.
41. Fishman, E. (2025) *Chokepoints: American power in the age of economic warfare*. Ncw York: Portfolio/Penguin.
42. Fishman, E. (2025) *Chokepoints: American power in the age of economic warfare*. New York: Portfolio/Penguin.
43. Mohr, C. & Trebesch, C. (2025).

44. Atlantic Council (2025) *Global Foresight 2025*. Washington, DC: Atlantic Council.
45. Hille, K. & Sevastopulo, D. (2025) 'China improves ability to launch sudden attack on Taiwan, officials say', *Financial Times*, 26 May.

7

Climate Change: EMDEs' Exposure and Mitigants

Climate change is a global problem with grave implications: environmental, social, economic, political and for the distribution of goods. It represents one of the principal challenges facing humanity in our day.
Paraphrase of themes of Pope Francis.

7.1 Introduction

If truth be told, the first time one of authors really thought about climate change was in the aftermath of the catastrophic 2004 Boxing Day tsunami. Sitting in the university common room, he overheard a conversation between two professors that went something like this:

"*Do you see these foolish people? Didn't they realize the rapid retreat of the sea was the warning that a tsunami was coming*?" said the one, a social sciences lecturer, as he waved a picture of three beachgoers venturing across the exposed seabed off the coast of Thailand.

R. Marney, P. Waeber, *The Emerging Markets Investor's Guide to Country Risk*,
https://doi.org/10.1007/978-3-032-26824-2_7

Authors' collection; original source unverified

"A tragedy, of course," replied the other, a mathematician. "Since the day, I've been thinking how pictures like this serve as a perfect metaphor for a far bigger calamity, one that should be equally obvious."

"And that is?"

"Global warming, of course! There's enough evidence to convince all but the willfully ignorant of the approaching climate change tsunami. Yet, like those poor souls in your picture, the world wanders recklessly towards a terrible fate."

For years after this chance encounter, the picture remained a vivid reminder of what lies ahead for the international community should mitigation actions fail to address global warming and its effects on society and the economy. Today, even with a dramatic turn from denial and sometimes feckless efforts by the well-intentioned, we may be too late. For financiers and investors, the reality of climate change, most notably physical risks but increasingly transition risks, is now with us. These elements are already affecting debt service capacity and credit ratings at both the sovereign and corporate levels, equity valuations, and portfolio allocations. However, structures often fail to address effectively the risks to operational performance, financial sustainability, and brand, and do not adequately price in the risk.

In this chapter, we provide a brief survey of the topic—evidence for climate change, a global snapshot of relative degrees of vulnerability, a risk taxonomy extending down to the firm level, a sketch of the implications for investors—followed by a set of short narratives to demonstrate the role of physical and transition risks in transaction structuring. The nature of the book and the limited number of pages available will necessarily shortchange what is arguably the paramount longer-term risk confronting not just investors but society as whole. Therefore, many topics will be either referenced only in passing or omitted all together. To remedy this in part, we include a number of sources for further reading in the endnotes to the chapter.

7.2 The Evidence

In this section, we rely in great measure on the "Synthesis Report" (2023) Intergovernmental Panel on Climate Change (IPCC) Sixth Assessment Report (AR6).[1] The report was released in multiple parts by different working groups between 2021[2] and 2023. Our discussion reflects the data, evaluation, and conclusions contained therein, with which the authors agree.

The evidence is clear and compelling—"unequivocal" in the words of the Synthesis Report—that human activity is responsible for increases in the temperatures in the atmosphere, on land, and in the ocean. The Report indicates, *"Global surface temperature was 1.07 [0.8–1.3]°C higher in 2010–2019 than in 1850–1900."*[3] Heightened Green House Gas (GHG) emissions due to our economic activity and land use changes are the primary cause of this increase in global temperatures (Fig. 7.1).

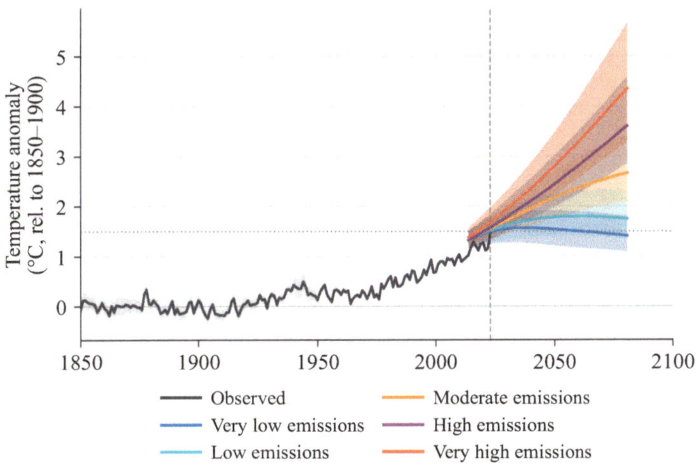

Fig. 7.1 Global mean surface temperature anomaly, observed and projected. (Source: IPCC Sixth Assessment Report, Working Group I (2021). Note: Shaded bands show the 5th–95th percentile of assessed model projections. Shared Socioeconomic Pathway projections from 2014. The dashed vertical line marks the end of the observed record (2023))

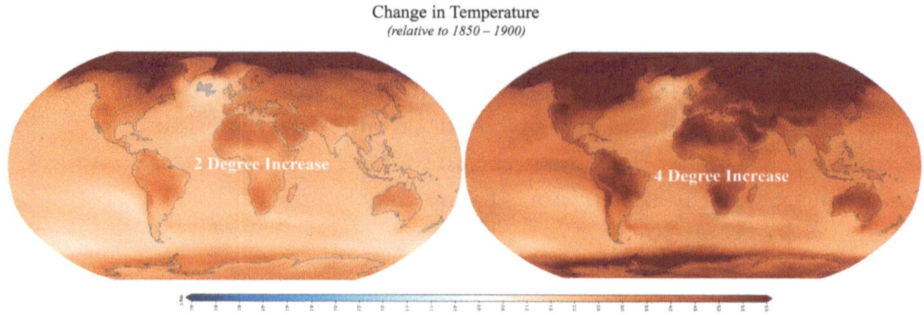

Fig. 7.2 Projected global temperature patterns under 2 °C and 4 °C warming

The observed temperature increase in the decades leading up to the end of the twentieth and the early years of the new century attest to this clear trend. Other authoritative sources[4] support the IPCC conclusions. This development has resulted in rapid changes throughout the world in the atmosphere, cryosphere, and biosphere.[5] The consistent, progressive, multi-decadal rise in temperature has altered global meteorological patterns, leaving the troposphere, land, and water warmer, with certain areas of the globe, such as the arctic, more affected, inducing variation across the seasons—winters warming faster than summers on the whole—and raising the incidence of extreme weather events. Additionally, other observed phenomena include melting glaciers and sea ice, resultant rising sea levels, and heightened ocean deoxygenation and acidification.

Climate change affects regions and countries differently and this variation will widen over time as temperatures rise further, and the knock-on effects develop and intensify. *First*, the direct impact of rising temperatures can be seen in Figs. 7.2.

These exposure and ultimate vulnerability to these knock-on effects or better called, the physical risks, vary according to geography, topography, demographics, and economic structure, and are discussed in greater detail in Sect. 7.3 (Risk Effects) and Sect. 7.4 (Country Exposure). For the moment, a few examples will suffice to prove the point that, even before considering the more complex factor of adaptive capacity, and the economic and institutional underpinnings (covered in Sects. 7.3 and 7.4), climate change affects regions, countries, and even locations within countries differently. Densely populated South Asia confronts the risks of changing precipitation (monsoon) patterns, higher incidence of extreme weather events, increasing glacial melt, and greater severity of heatwaves, whilst agrarian sub-Saharan Africa must overcome the combination of drought and extreme heat threats to agriculture and animal husbandry, and archipelago-intensive countries in South-East Asia and the so-called Small Island Developing States (SIDS) face the menaces of sea-level rise, storm surges, coastal flooding, and coral bleaching.

The future becomes increasingly fraught, as outright climate change denial and economic, political, and institutional constraints to addressing mitigation and adaptation priorities stymie a timely and effective global response. The IPPC Report warns: *"Global surface temperature will continue to increase until at least the mid-century under all emissions scenarios considered. Global warming of **1.5°C and 2°C will be exceeded during the 21st century unless deep reductions in CO_2 and other greenhouse gas emissions occur in the coming decades."*[6] In this scenario, changes in the global climate system will become more pronounced over time, heightening exposure to chronic and acute risks, with developing countries increasingly challenged to implement effective adaptation responses. As discussed below, the EMDE cohort will require such actions in order to reduce the threat to the systemic stability, sustainable economic growth, and positive welfare outcomes on which a positive investment climate depend. At the firm level, climate-related risks—physical, transitional (adaptation and mitigation), and natural capital[7]—create a layer of complexity and challenge to traditional credit and investment analysis, which we treat below.

7.3 Risks

Why should we be concerned about the threat of climate change? At a high level, the answer is obvious—despite the bemusing scene of seeing a U.S. senator standing on the floor of the chamber holding a snowball to prove it a hoax. The physical effects of rising temperatures, a higher incidence of extreme weather events, frequent and more severe coastal flooding are commonplace events in our daily news feed. The purpose in this chapter is not to reaffirm the obvious fact these developments are real, increasing, and serious threats to sustainable economic development and human welfare.

Instead, our aim is to share recent work on climate risk taxonomies, the interplay of physical risks and adaptation/mitigation actions, and the differentiated impacts at the country level as a result. This discussion is the overture to the main event—climate change and the implications for investment performance.

In this section we present: (1) basic concepts; (2) an example of a risk taxonomy; and (3) the risk impact at the firm-level.

Basic Concepts

Here we define certain key terms that will be used in this chapter and throughout the book.

Physical Risks: Direct climate change effects, arising from "acute" events (e.g., floods, heatwaves, etc.) and "chronic" developments (e.g., rising sea levels, temperature increases, etc.)

Exposure: To understand this concept, just remember the question heard in many boardrooms—"Are we in harm's way?" In our context, exposure captures the extent to which the economy or a business is potentially affected by physical risks of a changing climate. The degree of exposure is primarily a function of geographic and physical characteristics, but over time can reflect the effects of institutions, economic structure, demographics, and the like.

Sensitivity: Another question "How easily will we be harmed" helps us understand the meaning. The concept captures the degree to which the economy or firms are actually affected, reflecting the degree of dependency on sectors and activities sensitive to the effects of climate change, and the existing infrastructure and other measures addressing these risks.

Vulnerability: Given a country or firm's exposure and sensitivity to climate change, what's the end result after measures are taken to mitigate the risk impacts. The measures in question are adaptation policies (see below).

Transition Risks: The socio-political, legal, reputational, economic, and financial risks present in the transition to climate resiliency, which arise from policy responses, technologic change, litigation actions, and the like.

Adaptation: Actions to "adjust" to climate change with the objective of lessening the impact of potential damages and exploiting opportunities. These actions are intended to manage unavoidable near-term or longer-term consequences of climate change for society and the economy. Examples include: (i) adoption of drought resistant crops or the development of more efficient irrigation in agriculture; or (ii) man-made or natural infrastructure works to lessen the impact of storm surges or progressive rises in sea levels.

Mitigation: Measures to reduce GHG emissions and/or enhance carbon sinks. These actions are aimed at preventing or lessening conditions, whose materialization in the medium and long term would seriously threaten social and economic stability.

Adaptive Capacity: The capacity and willingness of a country to frame and implement the requisite policies. ND-Gain terms this as "readiness", which they measure according to a country's economic, governance, and social readiness.[8]

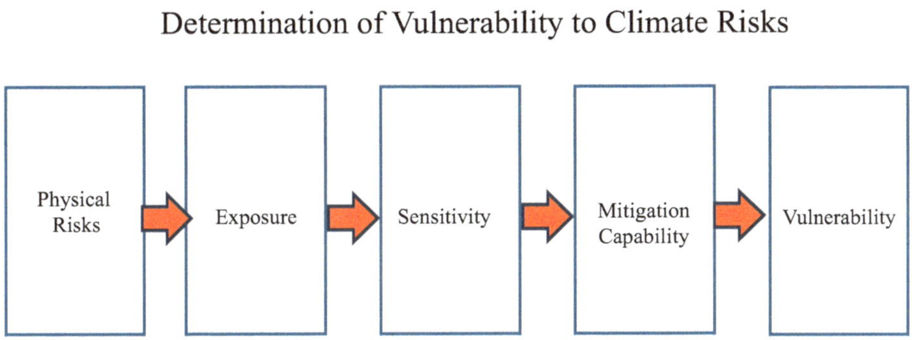

Fig. 7.3 Determination of vulnerability to climate risks. (Source: The Authors)

The simple schematic in Fig. 7.3 depicts the process by which a country (or for that matter a firm, see below) arrives at their degree of vulnerability to climate change.

Climate change produces two primary risks: the physical (resulting from the changing climatic structure) and the transitional (resulting from the movement towards climate resilience). At the core rest these physical risks which lead to a country's sensitivity to these risks. To arrive at the actual level of vulnerability, consideration is given to a country's capability to implement mitigation measures to lessen the impact of climate change.

Using the definitions in (1) above, let's consider some country cases.

One significant physical risk—sea level rise or storm surges—creates exposure for countries worldwide which are situated along coastlines. By virtue of its particular topography (low-lying and flat), the Netherlands is highly exposed, but due to an advanced and well-prepared set of existing actions—strong early-warning and emergency, flood protection, and land use measures—is less sensitive to these same climate change risks. However, as indicted above, the Netherlands boasts a very strong mitigation capability—ample financial means, technological sophistication, strong community engagement, and policy effectiveness to enhance resilience to sea level rise and storm surges—which has succeeded in reducing the country's vulnerability to a low level.

In contrast, take Bangladesh. The country's exposure to rising sea levels and storm surges is extremely high, even worse than in the Netherlands. Bangladesh sits predominantly in a floodplain, situated along a low-lying coastline, and at the confluence of several major rivers, hence increasing the risk from sea level rise, tropical storms, and storm surges. The country's sensitivity to these climate change hazards is very high. This condition reflects high population density in exposed areas, heightened dependence on rain-fed agriculture, deficient flood control infrastructure, amongst other factors. Bangladesh's adaptive capacity is moderate to low. The country lacks the financial means, institutions, infrastructure, and policy effectiveness to mitigate these risks to a degree similar to the Netherlands. As a result, Bangladesh ranks among the more climate-vulnerable countries globally.

In summary, both countries have a high exposure to sea level rise and storm surge risk. Netherland differentiates itself from Bangladesh in having a high adaptive capacity that positions the country as one of the least vulnerable to this set of climate change risks (indeed more generally), whilst Bangladesh, whilst improving, can only muster limited adaptation responses leaving the county in a still vulnerable place.

In Sect. 7.4, we discuss a number of approaches to evaluating and ranking countries' exposure, sensitivity, and vulnerability to climate change, which put the discussion on Netherlands and Bangladesh in more perspective.

Taxonomy

We present here an example of a simplified risk taxonomy. This approach follows a standard model of dividing climate change risks into two categories—the physical and transitional risk types—for which examples of risk elements and the nature (chronic/acute) are identified. Lastly, in anticipation of the discussion of the financial impacts at the enterprise level, we proffer a set of indicative effects on businesses (Fig. 7.4).

That the impact of too much or too little water, more frequent and severe storms, or debilitating heatwaves can be bad for business is obvious. Slightly less so, but no less important, are the risks present in the transition to a more resilient, climate-friendly economy to companies' operational performance, financial condition, and attraction to investors. To explain the actual impact, the analysis must go deeper than these (quite obvious) headline risks, first by focusing on the sectoral level, but ultimately analyzing the impact on individual firms.

In the penultimate section of this chapter—Sect. 7.5: Implications for Investors—we will do this, by *first* surveying a number of sectors in the economy to highlight the effects of selected risk elements, *second*, by outlining the financial impact of these risks on several hypothetical enterprises, and lastly, by discussing analytic and structuring challenges. However, before getting to this, it will be helpful to evaluate relative country vulnerabilities.

Category	Risk Type	Risk Element	Chronic v. Acute	Business Impact
Physical	Water Stress	Supply	Chronic	Operationsl disruptions, increased operating costs, supply chain regulatory compliance costs
		Waste Water Disposal	Chronic	Increased capex and financial costs, challenges affecting production and operating margins, potential legal penalties
	Heat Stress	Elevated Temperatures	Chronic and Acute	Operational disruptions, increased operating costs, heightened supply chain vulnerabilites
		Wildfires	Acute	Operational disruptions, physical damage, financial replacement costs, insurance costs, reputational damage to brand
	Extreme Percipitation	Floodiing	Chronic and Acute	Operational disruptions, physical damage, financial replacement costs, insurance costs,
		Drought	Chronic and Acute	Water scarity (supply shortages in water stress, above) and its implications
	Ice/Glacier Melting	Sea Level Rise	Chronic	Similaar to flooding above, but with the additional risks of salinization of ground water supplies and the risk of permanent loss of land, infrastructure and fixed assets necessary for operations, business continuity risks
		Water Security	Chronic	See Water Stress - Supply, above
	Extreme Weather Events	Incidence	Chronic and Acute	Damage to infrastructure, workijng capital, and fixed assets, operational disruptions, financial losses, insurance pressures, business continuity risks
		Severity	Chronic and Acute	Intensification of "incidence" factors
	Ocean Acidification	Coral Bleaching	Chronic	Loss of reef-based fish stocks, reduction of tourist appeal, increase in costal erosion, decline in property values, increased insurance and other costs
		Ecosystem Impairment	Chronic	Driven by coral bleachin, above.

Fig. 7.4 Climate change risk taxonomy. (Source: The Authors)

Category	Risk Type	Risk Element	Chronic v. Acute	Business Impact
Transition	Technology	Cost of Adoption	Chronic	Technological obsolesence, technology transition costs, supply chain disruptions, regulatory conformity requirements, market and competition pressures, reputation risks
		Development or Adoption Failure	Chronic	Business sustainability risks
	Regulatory	Cost of Compliance	Chronic	Increased direct and indirect operating expenses
		Business Disruption	Chronic	Temporary or permanent business sustainability risks
	Operational Impairment	Process	Chronic	Business disruption, increased direct and indirect operating expenses, human resources requirements
		Forwad & Backward Linkages	Chronic	Similar risks affecting supply chains and customers
	Loss of Subsidies	Energy / Emissions	Chronic	Taxes and levies increased and/or subsidies remeoved/lowered with knock on effects on supply and cost
		Water Use	Chronic	Similar to Energy, above
	Access to Capital	Deterioation in Metrics	Chronic	Real reducrtion in historical and /or expectations of future deterioration in operational, debt service, equity valuation metrics impair access to, and/or increase the cost of capital
		Investor Reputational Concerns	Chronic	Lack of conformity to sustainable environmenteal standards result in a reduction in a decline in investor interest in the company
	Business Sustainability	Transition - Adoption Cosrs	Chronic	Overall impact of changes in technology, regulation, operating systems, capital structuuring / access to capital, and the losss of subsisidies on the performance and sustainability of the business, including changes in public perception and demand for the company's products
		Cash Flow Deterioration	Chronic	Reflecting theTransition - Adoption Costs, above

Fig. 7.4 (continued)

7.4 Evaluating Country Vulnerability

Introduction

We touched earlier on the distinctions between exposure, sensitivity, and vulnerability to climate change risks, and compared snapshots of two countries—the Netherlands and Bangladesh—using sea-level rise and flooding as risk threats. These two coastal nations emerge at divergent points of the climate change vulnerability spectrum. In this section, we expand this analysis by turning to the ND-Gain[9] a composite index designed to measure and rank a country's readiness to strengthen resilience and vulnerability to climate change. There are many indices in use today to gauge the nature and degree of climate change risk.[10] They vary according to the methodology, scope, and components. Two major distinctions amongst the indices are, first, whether they include just physical risks or incorporate adaptive capacity into the calculus, and second, whether the focus is forward looking or not. We have chosen the ND-Gain due to their measuring vulnerability after considering a country's adaptive capacity (readiness) and the forward-looking nature of the index.

The ND-Gain Index[11]

This index has been developed by the University of Notre Dame's Global Adaptation Initiative.[12] The composite score is the difference between the "Readiness Score" and "Vulnerability Score". The Readiness Score assesses the country's capability to mobilize investment capital to support climate adaptation efforts. The score is based on three components: (i) economic readiness—business climate, financial systems, and investment freedom; (ii) governance readiness—political stability, control of corruption, and legal systems; and (iii) social readiness—education levels, ICT infrastructure, and civil society engagement.

The Vulnerability Score aims to express a country's exposure, sensitivity, and adaptive capacity across six life-supporting sectors:

1. Food—covering agricultural production, food security, and nutrition.
2. Water—focusing on water availability, access, and sustainability.
3. Health—addressing public health systems and climate-sensitive diseases.
4. Ecosystem Services—assessing the health and function of natural ecosystems.

Sector	Exposure component	Sensitivity component	Adaptive Capacity component
Food	Projected change of cereal yields	Food import dependency	Agriculture capacity (Fertilizer, Irrigation, Pesticide, Tractor use)
	Projected population change	Rural Population	Child malnutrition
Water	Projected change of annual runoff	Fresh water withdrawal rate	Access to reliable drinking water
	Projected change of annual groundwater recharge	Water dependency ratio	Dam capacity
Health	Projected change of deaths from climate change induced diseases	Slum population	Medical staffs (physicians, nurses and midwives)
	Projected change of length of transmission season of vector-borne diseases	Dependency on external resource for health services	Access to improved sanitation facilities
Ecosystem services	Projected change of biome distribution	Dependency on natural capital	Protected biomes
	Projected change of marine biodiversity	Ecological footprint	Engagement in International environmental conventions
Human Habitat	Projected change of warm period	Urban concentration	Quality of trade and transport-related infrastructure
	Projected change of flood hazard	Age dependency ratio	Paved roads
Infrastructure	Projected change of hydropower generation capacity	Dependency on imported energy	Electricity access
	Projection of Sea Level Rise impacts	Population living under 5m above sea level	Disaster preparedness

Fig. 7.5 ND-Gain summary of indicators. (Source: Chen, C., Noble, I., Hellmann, J., Coffee, J., Murillo, M. and Chawla, N., 2015. *University of Notre Dame Global Adaptation Index: Country Index Technical Report*. Notre Dame, IN: University of Notre Dame. pp. 14–15)

5. Human Habitat—including infrastructure quality and exposure to natural hazards (e.g., flooding, sea-level rise).
6. Infrastructure—evaluating the robustness of energy, transport, and communication systems.

A summary of the indicators appears in Fig. 7.5.

All of the indicators are normalized and scored on a scale of 0 (lowest) to 1 (highest). Composite ND-Gain scores are calculated for each country and ranked accordingly. Data sourcing uses publicly available, internationally comparable, and peer-reviewed data from the World Bank, UNDP, WHO, Freedom House, etc. A simple graphic from the ND-Gain Technical Report depicts the progression and the meaning for varying score levels (Fig. 7.6).

There are 172 countries ranked[13]. At the high end are advanced economies, with countries such as Norway, Finland, Switzerland, Denmark, Sweden, NZ, Austria, Germany, Iceland, and Ireland making up the top 10. At the bottom are the EMDE countries, with the lowest ten all from Africa. Recalling the cases of the Netherlands and Bangladesh, the rankings are 12 and 64 (Fig. 7.7).

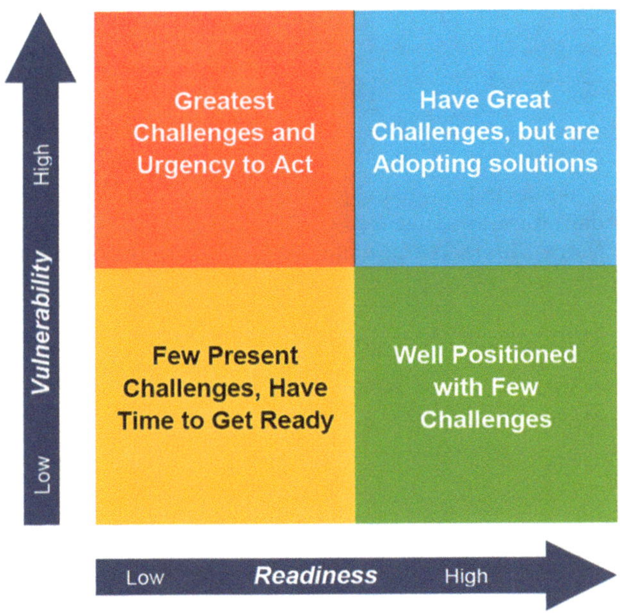

Fig. 7.6 ND-*Gain readiness and vulnerability.* (Source: Chen, C., Noble, I., Hellmann, J., Coffee, J., Murillo, M. and Chawla, N., 2015. *University of Notre Dame Global Adaptation Index: Country Index Technical Report*. Notre Dame, IN: University of Notre Dame. p. 12)

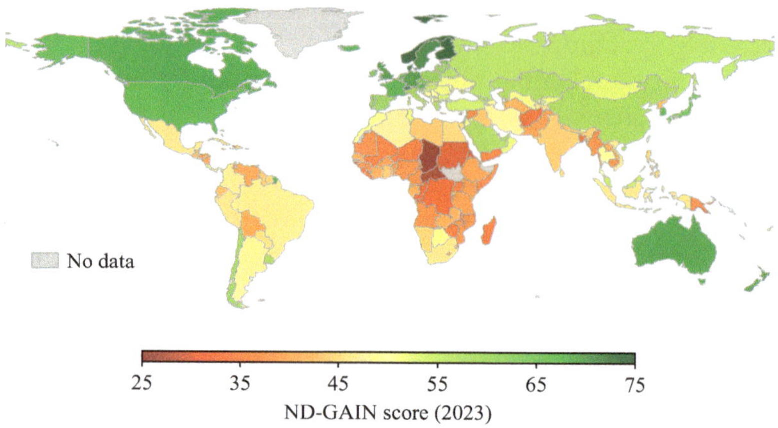

Fig. 7.7 Climate vulnerability and resilience worldwide. (Source: ND-GAIN Country Index (2023))

Rank	Country	ND-GAIN Score	Vulnerability Scor	Readiness Score	Exposure	Sensitivity	Adaptive Capacity	conomic Readine	vernance Readin	Social Readiness
38	Argentina	72.6	0.49	0.45	0.33	0.57	0.44	0.73	0.56	0.76
44	Brazil	71.4	0.78	0.56	0.77	0.39	0.57	0.61	0.51	0.7
48	India	70.6	0.67	0.52	0.78	0.78	0.37	0.47	0.31	0.62
50	Indonesia	70.2	0.6	0.45	0.7	0.69	0.7	0.33	0.35	0.74
52	Vietnam	69.8	0.38	0.61	0.45	0.77	0.34	0.46	0.32	0.7
53	Peru	69.6	0.38	0.37	0.35	0.75	0.79	0.46	0.62	0.39
60	Kenya	68.2	0.33	0.45	0.64	0.6	0.69	0.66	0.46	0.75
61	Ghana	68	0.73	0.48	0.52	0.76	0.4	0.62	0.55	0.57
62	Nigeria	67.8	0.6	0.53	0.36	0.34	0.3	0.74	0.75	0.7
64	Bangladesh	67.4	0.65	0.69	0.55	0.4	0.71	0.54	0.42	0.75
88	DRC	62.6	0.31	0.4	0.32	0.32	0.65	0.36	0.51	0.46
106	Uzbekistan	59	0.78	0.56	0.75	0.46	0.66	0.66	0.68	0.36
108	Tajikistan	58.6	0.72	0.6	0.43	0.49	0.69	0.68	0.41	0.41
110	Armenia	58.2	0.41	0.32	0.63	0.44	0.34	0.58	0.34	0.51
111	Georgia	58	0.39	0.6	0.46	0.71	0.48	0.69	0.44	0.71
124	Ecuador	55.4	0.39	0.39	0.56	0.48	0.36	0.55	0.38	0.73

Fig. 7.8 ND-Gain—Selected countries. (*Source: University of Notre Dame, 2023.* Notre Dame Global Adaptation Initiative (ND-GAIN) Country Index Rankings. *Notre Dame: University of Notre Dame.* https://gain.nd.edu/our-work/country-index/; *Authors' Preparation*)

To provide a deeper understanding of the workings of the index, we take a subset of the country universe selecting 16 EMDE market from Latam, Asia, Africa, and Central Asia & the Caucuses (Fig. 7.8).

For the countries noted above, summary commentary appears in order of ranking:

- Argentina

– Argentina has moderate vulnerability and moderate readiness, with strengths in governance but weaknesses in economic adaptability. Drought and water stress *in the west, along with agricultural sensitivity, are top concerns.*

- Brazil
  - Brazil's vulnerability is rising, due to deforestation, urban flooding, and heat stress. Readiness is moderate, with strengths in institutional capacity but weaknesses in social inclusion and long-term planning. Preserving the Amazon is a key resilience factor.
- India
  - India exhibits moderate vulnerability and moderate readiness. High exposure to extreme heat, water stress, and flooding make it especially climate-sensitive. While governance structures are improving, infrastructural and social readiness gaps remain. Investment in urban resilience and water resource management is critical.
- Indonesia
  - Indonesia's vulnerability is high, particularly to sea-level rise, flooding, and biodiversity loss. Despite decent governance readiness, infrastructure and health systems are weak in adapting to rising risks. Coastal protection and improved urban planning are urgent needs.
- Vietnam
  - Vietnam faces high exposure to coastal and riverine flooding due to its low-lying delta regions. Its vulnerability is high, though adaptive capacity is relatively strong, with good agricultural and water resource strategies. Investment readiness is moderate.
- Peru
  - Peru exhibits high exposure to glacial retreat and water shortages. Readiness is low, especially in economic and infrastructure areas. Mountain ecosystem vulnerability and urban water stress are major challenges.
- Kenya
  - Kenya has moderate vulnerability, primarily from drought, floods, and health risks. It scores relatively well in social readiness but lacks infrastructure resilience. Climate-smart agriculture and better health infrastructure are high priorities.
- Ghana
  - Ghana's vulnerability is moderate to high, with exposure to temperature variability and flooding. Governance and social readiness are improving, but infrastructure lags. Continued investments in water systems and urban adaptation are needed.

- Nigeria
  - Nigeria faces high vulnerability, driven by floods, droughts, and conflict-prone regions. Despite some readiness in governance, social and economic readiness are weak. Long-term strategies for urban resilience and energy transition are critical.
- Bangladesh
  - One of the world's most climate-vulnerable countries, Bangladesh has high exposure to cyclones, flooding, and salinization. Adaptive capacity is stretched despite strong social readiness. Low economic readiness remains a barrier to scaling resilience.
- Democratic Republic of Congo (DRC)
  - One of the least ready and most vulnerable countries, DRC struggles with poor governance, limited adaptive capacity, and high sensitivity to environmental and social stressors. International support is vital for basic infrastructure and institutional reform.
- Uzbekistan
  - Uzbekistan shows moderate to high vulnerability, especially from water stress and agricultural sensitivity. Readiness is constrained by economic and governance challenges. Strengthening regional cooperation on water resource management is vital.
- Tajikistan
  - Tajikistan experiences high vulnerability due to its mountainous terrain and water dependence. Readiness is low, with limited infrastructure and economic capacity to respond effectively to climate risks.
- Armenia
  - Armenia has moderate vulnerability and relatively higher governance readiness. Its sensitivity to droughts and extreme temperatures is mitigated by its institutional capacity, but infrastructure remains underdeveloped.
- Georgia
  - Georgia shows moderate vulnerability and strong governance readiness. Exposure to floods and landslides poses risks, but institutional stability supports adaptation planning.

- Ecuador
  - Ecuador's vulnerability is moderate to high, with exposure to floods, landslides, and biodiversity loss. Social readiness is reasonable, but economic constraints limit adaptation. Targeted investment in rural resilience is needed.

7.5 Implications for Investors

Introduction

Climate change poses a serious and increasing threat to economic growth, business performance, and ultimately political stability and social welfare. For investors, much is beyond their control. Material actions to mitigate global warming certainly require the bold and concerted involvement of governments. Similarly, adaptation on a meaningful scale requires organizational, technical and financial resource beyond the means of private sector enterprises. In short, adaptive capacity reflects the government's commitment and available resources to facilitate a smooth transition to an environmentally sustainable economic model.

EMDE countries are more vulnerable, due to the combination of heightened climate exposure in many cases, and limited adaptive capacity, given, weaker institutions, lower national wealth, and constrained fiscal capacity. As referenced above, the adaptive capacity in this cohort will be challenged to match the growing threat of global warming, damaging changes in precipitation patterns, sea-level rise, and the increased incidence and severity of extreme weather events. This reality will figure in the calculus.

Notwithstanding, there are measures that private enterprises can take to minimize or even neutralize certain physical, climate change risks. Examples are adopting more drought-resistant crops in the agriculture sector or relocating a production facility away from a flood zone. Additionally, all things being equal, the greater the financial resilience of an enterprise, the greater their capacity to absorb the top-line and cost impacts of physical risks, and fund necessary adaptation-focused operating and capital investments. In this section, we look to elaborate on this last thought—that companies can differentiate themselves from their competitors not only in dealing with the risks of climate change, but also in certain cases, the opportunities that may arise.

The remainder of this section is organized as follows. *First,* we frame the market context by discussing climate change, credit ratings and access to capital. *Second,* we sketch out a view of the differing, sectoral impact of the physical and transitional risks identified in Sect. 7.3. *Third,* we present a set of short narratives, with varying country sovereign ratings, climate change exposure/vulnerability characteristics, economic sector activities, stand-alone financial strength features, and distinct investment instruments/structures. The purpose of these narratives is to bring to life the interplay of climate change risks and firm-level operating and financial performance. The treatment will be intentionally quite high level in form, but will equip the reader with learnings that will figure importantly Case Studies in Part IV, Chaps. 14–18.

Credit Ratings and Access to Capital

All three major rating agencies have reached similar conclusions with respect to the negative credit impact of climate change and environmental degradation. Moody's notes this increasingly prominent role of climate change in forward looking credit risk analysis, and estimates that roughly a quarter of rating actions reflect the role of physical and transitional climate change factors.[14] Sovereigns are more often influenced by these risk elements, but the effect on corporate issuers is on the rise. The threat will only rise unless governments act. In their 2025 outlook, Moody's comments that, "the *Countdown to 2030 decarbonization targets highlights implementation gaps and investment risks. Redoubled global efforts to meet targets – or backtracking – will have significant and distinct implications for credit strength across sectors and financial markets.*"[15] The stakes are high. A "significant" portion of the debt capital market is exposed to carbon transition risk, as the graphic in Fig. 7.9 shows.

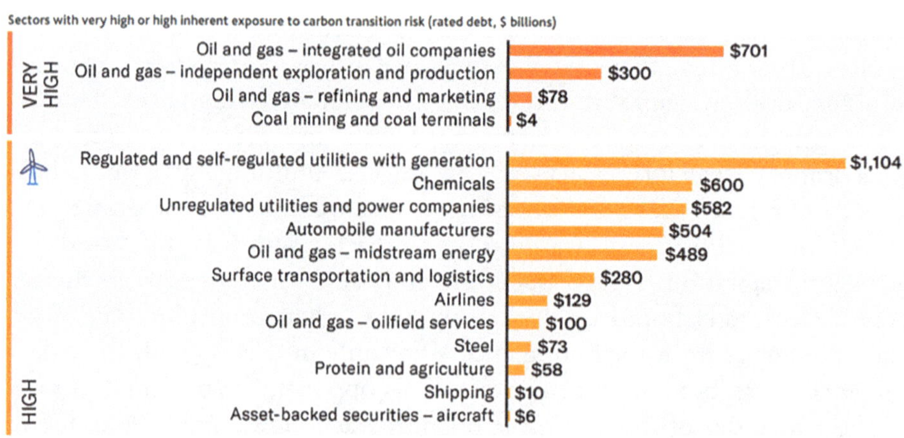

Fig. 7.9 Sectoral exposure to carbon transition risk. (Source: Moody's ratings. Note: As of November 2024)

In a similar vein, S&P and Fitch highlight the growing influence of climate change on both sovereign and corporate credit ratings. S&P identifies physical and transitional risks as important drivers of rating actions. The impact of these risks is to erode productive capital and growth potential, especially in the EMDE, leading to a deterioration in a country's debt sustainability.[16] In the case of corporates, the damage is more pronounced in high emission, resource-intensive, and water-dependent sectors.[17] Fitch[18] characterizes climate change as a structural risk to sovereign creditworthiness. EMDEs with climate-sensitive economies and weak adaptive capacity are most vulnerable. These prevailing conditions increase the risk of economic instability, fiscal deterioration, and debt distress, and lead to credit rating downgrades. Strengthening of institutional frameworks and supportive fiscal action to develop climate adaptation capacity act as credit buffers. Like with Moody's and S&P, Fitch identifies companies in climate-sensitive sectors as more likely candidates for negative credit rating actions. In a 2023 paper written by Klusak, Agarwala, Buke, Kraemer, and Mohaddes[19] simulate the effect of climate change on sovereign credit ratings for 109 countries, creating a form of predictive, climate-adjusted sovereign credit rating model. Their key findings include: (i) material downgrade risks under high emission scenario (by 2030—average rating decline of 0.6 notches globally and by 2100—average decline of 2.4 notches, with EMDEs most affected in both cases); (ii) low-emissions scenario greatly mitigates losses; (iii) high emissions could increase borrowing costs by ~150 basis points by 2100; and (iv) strengthened adaptive capacity reduces rating declines.

In focusing on the impact on capital market access and pricing, the views of the rating agencies are generally mirrored amongst sell-side analysts and academic research. For example, a summary of the views of JP Morgan[20] includes the commentary that climate change represents a long-term drag on global economic growth, in particular for the more vulnerable countries. EMDEs face a disproportionately perilous future, given limited adaptive capacity. In the bank's view, climate risks are already affecting corporate default probabilities, spreads, and insurance costs. Goldman Sachs follows the same general set of views, and shares the basic message that climate risks are already with us, are materially credit-relevant, yet are not consistently priced appropriately.[21] An IMF Working Paper written by Cevik and Jalles (2020) affirms these analyses.[22] Their paper provides a rigorous analysis of the impact of climate change on sovereign bond spreads with a focus on differences between AEs and the EMDEs. Using a 98 country sample for the period 1995 to 2027, the authors found that sovereign borrowing costs did rise in response to climate shocks more in the EMDE cohort, leading to weaker fiscal and debt dynamics, and reflected less-well developed institutions and lower fiscal buffers. The sectoral analysis conforms to the views of the rating agencies outlined above. Further, Kling, Volz, and Murinde (2021)[23] investigated the question of the impact on the cost of capital at the firm level. Employing a data set covering 4000+ firms in 68 countries over the period 2000–2018, the authors found that EMDE access to capital declined and its cost, especially for debt, increased. Climate vulnerability acted as a credit constraint, with the effect more pronounced for younger and smaller firms, with markets pricing in a sovereign-level climate-sensitivity risk premia into these corporate credits. Lastly, Buhr et al. (2018)[24] concluded that highly vulnerable EMDE countries face higher risk premia as investors required compensation for the heightened uncertainty, and that this climate vulnerability acted as a deterrent to inflows of FDI and portfolio flows.

Sectoral Impacts

As in the case of sovereign-level discussion above, sectors within countries present variable levels of vulnerability to climate change. A sectoral risk ranking appears in Fig. 7.10.

The underlying factors driving the suggested ranking are complex. We provide in the endnotes a suggested set of sources for the interested reader to dig deeper into this topic.[25]

A brief review of a selection of physical risk drivers helps to understand this ranking (Fig. 7.11).

The rise of global temperatures creates direct chronic (progressive increases) and acute (heat waves) threats that affect agricultural productivity even when water supply constraints are limited. This results in making outside labor activity in agriculture, agribusiness, and construction for example less productive and even dangerous for workers' health, requiring increased capital and operating expenses to deal with the heat, and even leading to production

High	Medium	Low
• Agriculture / Agribusiness • Water-intensive Industrials & Manufacturing • Conventional Energy • Real Estate / Construction • Tourism / Hospitality	• Mining • Transport / Logistics • Retail • Forestry	• Media /Telecom • Financial Services • Health Care • ICT/Digital Service • Renewable Energy

Fig. 7.10 Sectoral risk rankings. (Source: *The Authors*)

Illustrative Risk Types and Impacts	
1. Temperature	• Reduced Crop Yields in agriculture • Lower Worker Productivity in outside work • Heightened Capex/Opex – cooling systems in multiple sectors • Production Disruption in multiple sectors
2. Water Stress	• Reduced Crop Yields in Agriculture • Increased Capex/Opex – Irrigation, Water Rights - in Agriculture and Water-intensive industrial and manufacturing activities • Production Disruption in multiple sectors
3. Extreme Weather	When located in higher-risk areas • Business interruption in multiple sectors • Increased capex for repairs • Higher Insurance expenses, when available
4. Sea Level Rise	When located in higher-risk areas • Expenses related to protective measure • Relocation – expense and business interruption
5. Reef Bleaching	When located in higher-risk areas • Reduction in tourism • Marine ecosystem impairment / destruction - fishing and aquaculture

Fig. 7.11 Climate risk types and economic impacts. (*Source: The Authors*)

interruptions. Elevated temperatures also produce indirect impacts, for example, driving polar and glacial ice melting and contributing to sea level rises. Water issues are central of course to agriculture/agribusiness performance but can also reduce productivity and increase costs for secondary sector activities heavily reliant on water. Extreme weather events affect a wide range of regions and countries, where tropical storms produce wind-damage and destructive storm surges that result in disruption of activity and significant financial outlays to repair damage. We tend to think about tourism first, but the scope of affected activities includes a long list of primary, secondary, and tertiary activities when located in the high-risk zone. Sea level rise is likewise associated with tropical tourism, but in fact figures as a threat to a wide range of economic activities when located in low-lying coastal areas. Varying adaptive capacities (think the Netherlands v. Bangladesh) play a key role in determining the final vulnerability outcome and hence for this risk element adaptive capacity rather than the sector itself is the important consideration. Reef bleaching predictably affects tourism, fishing, and aquaculture in island and coastal regions adjacent to coral reefs.

The sectoral story is not all gloom and doom. In a changing climate world, there are also opportunities. There are many, and include renewable energy and clean power infrastructure, climate smart agriculture, water security, waste management, EV transportation, green construction, to mention a few. The capacity and willingness of government to provide tax, financial and regulatory support and the public acceptance of the long-term benefits of these areas are necessary for their development. AEs are generally in the positive camp, although the backsliding of the MAGA movement sets the US apart. In the EMDE space, there are noteworthy proponents throughout the globe, led by China and India. In Africa, the AfDB is active in pursuing a green energy campaign.

Narratives

Brief Remarks on Climate Change and Debt Versus Equity

Lenders worry about borrowers meeting a set schedule of payments of principal and interest for a contractual loan amount. Equity investors have a more complicated task, having to agree on an initial valuation, the terms of the investment, the management of subsequent equity rounds that could result in dilution under certain circumstances, and then the timing and terms of one or more liquidity events/exits. Debt can range from overnight to ten years (or more), but contractually has a pre-set life save for certain types of hybrids. On the other hand, equity's ex ante lifespan is indeterminant. The range of climate-related risks are relevant and material for all levels of the capital structure. However, the channels by which they affect transaction risks and hence structure, pricing, and value vary. In both areas, for reasons covered above, the situations are more fraught in the EMDE.

For debt, the task is to evaluate the impact of climate risks and necessary adaptation measures on leverage, profitability, and cash flow. An agricultural company whose harvest fails due to drought in a given season reduces current cashflow, but is able to drawdown short-term lines and use existing cash balances to meet its debt obligations. A manufacturing group whose high-energy intensive production processes must be adapted to conform with new emission standards and to quell an expanding consumer boycott is forced to increase leverage to fund the requisite at a time when sales are declining, and experiences a progressive decline in debt service capacity to a point where a payment default occurs, and a restructuring exercise becomes necessary. A tropical hotel chain's attempt to finance an expansion program with debt falters as lenders require significantly more equity to calibrate projected operating cash flows to debt service requirements, given the projected costs of building protective walls and other structural improvements to address the threat of rising sea levels. In these three examples, the focus is on whether given all the expected climate risk effects, the debt can be serviced. In the first, other liquidity is available to resolve the current year problem (another bad harvest would be another matter). In the second, default occurs, a restructuring becomes necessary, and bankruptcy/liquidation looms. In the third, prospective lenders force a change in the capital budget (more equity, less debt) as a condition for participating in the funding program.

Equity is more complicated. Let's use the same three examples from above. Assume each looks to tap the equity markets. The agricultural company must address investor (hence valuation) concerns about water security. Do measures like an investment program in irrigation assets, the purchase of expanded water rights, a change to more water-resistant crops, and the like credibly resolve this risk or not? And if so, at what cost and how does the resulting net financial burden affect valuation metrics and exit prospects. For the second, how does the necessary adaptation investments to transition to a lower-carbon energy model and the rebranding of the group as an environmentally friendly business influence valuation and investor interest. For the third, are investors willing to take the chance of investing in the tourism sector in areas at risk of sinking below the sea at any price? And if so, how do the imponderables translate into a valuation calculus and exit scenarios?

Four Narratives

For each of the four narratives, we start with a summary of certain common facts on the country and sector's vulnerability to specified climate risk elements, then present a debt and an equity transaction for the same company, with assumed financial characteristics and sensitivities to the specified climate risk elements. We end with summary comments. The selection of the characteristics of the narratives is meant to cover a wide range of sectors and risk elements. As noted above, the detailed case studies in Part V will present a far more detailed treatment of investment cases with various risk factors, including climate change.

The First

1. Background

Oceania is situated along the trade routes between east and west. The government established an industrial zone adjacent to its central port into which they attracted the final assembly facilities for major global electronic brands. Oceania's strength—location and ease of shipment—is also their vulnerability, as the low-lying topography and geographic position in a typhoon alley exposes the country to the increasing incidence and severity of these storms, as well as the creeping rise of the level of the sea leading to shore erosion. In the early-years, the operating cost benefits of the location and high productivity of its workforce outweighed the climate risks. A producer of smart watches chooses Oceania as the location for its new regional assembly plant in response to rising costs and increasing geopolitical and trade tensions threatening its existing plants. The capital budget consists of 60% debt and 40% equity, with the latter led by the producer and to be funded primarily by a consortium of international investors. The sponsors will invest in storm-resistant construction and logistics which should limit the impact of all but the most extreme weather events.

2. Debt Transaction

Lenders are sanguine about Oceania' relatively high exposure to extreme storm events given the planned (high winds) storm-resistant infrastructure investments, but have identified the additional risk of storm surges that could result in flooding. As a result, the requirement is made to raise the level of the facility, raise the height of the protective walls, and improve drainage works. The equity resists this demand at first, but acquiesces and the syndication close.

3. Equity Transaction

The original plan did not include the more extensive flood control investments. These raise the capital budget significantly. As a result, the outside equity investors pushes for a lower valuation, which has the effect of diluting the producer's shareholding.

4. Summary

This is an example of lenders being aware of the need for adaptation measures and being in a position to force the equity investors to undertake the requisite investments as a condition for financial completion of the debt syndication. This private sector initiative is observed by the government of Oceania, which decides to support such actions with tax provisions (e.g., credits and accelerated depreciation) to encourage investments in flood protection measures, and these are made retroactive to cover this project.

The Second

1. Background

Provincia is located in the Southern Hemisphere and has become a leading producer of fruits and vegetables for export to the Northern Hemisphere during the northern winters. The most critical production input is water, and over the recent past rain patterns have become more prone to periods of lower-precipitation levels. Water rights have become more costly. Espinosa Family Farms has been in business for several generations and is one of Provincia's most successful agri-business companies. To take advantage of increased demand and higher prices in the Northern Hemisphere markets, Espinosa Family Farms decides to undertake an expansion program by increasing the hectares under cultivation by a third to be used for a variety of crops. Given the strong and profitable legacy of the company, the board attempts to finance the expansion purely with debt. The only debt on the books is short-duration working capital funding of the asset conversion cycle provided by local banks.

2. Debt Transaction

The company's traditional debt providers of short-term working capital balk at the longer-duration capital investment requirements. As a result, the family turns to climate smart agriculture (CSA) funds whose strategies fit the project well. Negotiations result in an agreement in which: (i) technical assistance grants are provided to move into drought resistant varieties of certain of the planned crop-types; (ii) a combination of water rights and irrigation investments are to be undertaken; (iii) the capital budget is adjusted to be

75% debt and 25% equity, based on the strong balance sheet and historical cash flow of the company; and (iv) a series of measures to ensure environmental sustainability.

3. Equity Transaction

Given the agreement with the CSA funds, the family trust invests the 25% equity requirement.

4. Summary

The climate-smart funding solution benefits from the convergence of a strong corporate credit, a highly attractive business opportunity, and a specialized debt fund.

The Third

1. Background

The Federation of Pacific Islands encompasses several dozen islands. Governance is loose, with individual islands running much of their affairs in a decentralized manner. In the Federation, there are three major economic pillars—tourism, fishing, and coconut production. An international hospitality group operates exclusive, boutique hotels on several islands. Post-pandemic, the group invested in a luxury upgrade of their facilities and undertook an ambitious marketing program to attract travelers to the resorts. In time, just over half of the group turnover was attributable to this tropical area, with the remainder coming from European locations. Included in the investments were marine ferries from the Federation's airport to the outer islands. Significant bridge financing from the group LPs and hedge funds funded the investment program, with the aim of refinancing these amounts at a new, regional sub-holding company. In recent years, many of the islands have been experiencing moderate rises in sea levels, increased beach erosion, and progressive reef bleaching. Visitor complaints about the impact of these developments on their holiday experience have contributed to a decline in occupancy rates, and reduced profitability. Additionally, elsewhere in the Pacific region, severe typhoons have destroyed large swaths of the coconut palm plantations. Whilst the Federation has been spared a direct hit of a mega-typhoon, there have been an increasing number of near-misses in recent years. Lastly, reef bleaching has impaired the local, marine ecosystems, and reduced fish stocks. All of these factors combined have caste a pale over the outlook for the Federation.

2. Debt Transaction

The refinancing of the bridge funding at the newly formed regional holding company level hits serious headwinds. The underlying business dynamics, real concerns about growing vulnerability to these climate change risks, and the intermediate-co funding structure frighten off investors. Coincidently, at this time, a powerful typhoon passes through the Federation causing severe damage to the beaches, infrastructure, and palm plantations. Investor confidence in the group is damaged. The design of the refinancing requires a material overhaul. The regional holding company structure is abandoned in favor of a parent-company level transaction. The refinancing is split into two tranches, with the first being third-party investors in medium-term secured notes, and the second dealing with the group LPs (see following).

3. Equity Transaction

Attempts to raise straight equity to take out the LPs flounders, due to valuation expectation mismatches the group LPs are forced to convert their bridge loans into hybrid capital, in the form of redeemable convertible preferred shares, with transfer rights. This move is hotly contested but agreed in the end. In the immediate after market, the notes are priced at a steep discount, but in time, when there is no further bad press about the group's business, the notes trade up, with most of the LPs selling out their positions. Subsequent discussion with investment banks about equity raises does not progress as market concerns persist.

4. Summary

The group's heavy reliance on locations acutely vulnerable to the effects of global warming created a fragile base. In retrospect, the capital used to supercharge occupancy rates in the Federation could have been better invested in diversifying their business footprint. Given the reality of global GHG emission levels and the failure of many countries to take responsible actions to decarbonize, the destruction of the tropical paradise of the Federation becomes a matter of time. The group faces the long-term risk of having stranded assets and material hit to shareholder value.

The Fourth

1. Background

Sierra is a country just to the north of Provincia (from the earlier narrative). Like its neighbor, the economy boasts a strong fruit and vegetable export sector, benefiting from winter-season demand in the Northern Hemisphere. However, Sierra is less well positioned than Provincia. The north and west of the country—formerly fertile growing regions—have become increasingly arid, as rainfall levels have declined and surface temperatures have risen. These developments reflect the impact of global warming. Local ground water resources are constrained. Yield levels in a number of products have slipped and progressively the market share of Sierra has fallen. In this fraught environment, a North American avocado wholesaler purchased a bankrupt avocado producer in the north-central region to increase its captive supply base. The transaction is funded initially with equity and corporate level debt, with the intention of refinancing part of transaction in the local banking market in Sierra, and using these local institutions to fund ongoing working capital and fixed investment needs. The idea of bringing in local, minority shareholders is even mooted. Key to the success of the business is securing access to sufficient water supplies at an economically sustainable cost. Water access is deemed a medium to high risk, even assuming "normal" rainfall levels.

2. Debt Transaction

Two successive years of low rainfall are followed by a drought. Irrigation fails to compensate fully, and per-hectare yields decline to near-record lows for the company. This situation is less acute in the south and east of the country, and combined with Provincia's bumper harvest, prices actually fall marginally. The company's financial performance slips into the red. Access to secured local bank credit to fund working capital requirements is sufficient. Longer-duration debt is not available, and the parent is forced to downstream capital in the form of shareholder loans to over capital expenditures.

3. Equity Transaction

Under these stressed conditions, a local equity raise becomes an impossibility. Under pressure from the local, working capital debt providers, the shareholder loans are first reclassified as PIK subordinated debt and eventually, in order to maintain access to these local debt funds, converted into common equity.

4. Summary

The region in which the company chose to invest is on the road to a likely state of permanent agricultural abandonment due to aridification. Climate change is reducing water availability and soil fertility, making avocado production in particular uneconomic and potentially unsustainable. As a long-term value accretive investment, the move was deeply flawed, and must have been taken on the misguided logic that either the aridification process was a short-term blip, and/or they could succeed in making a killing in the short-run and recoup their investment by capturing a disproportionate quantity of the available water supplies—a failed effort given all the other producers were trying to do the same.

7.6 Closing Remarks

To close this chapter, we will summarize our four narratives. Of the four, the first two have happy endings, the last two, the opposite. The first two see: (i) a smart watch assembly factory benefit from informed and assertive lenders and ultimately a government providing fiscal support to necessary adaptation measures; and (ii) a diversified fruit and vegetable export-oriented producer whose experienced and responsible owners work constructively with a climate smart agriculture fund to fashion a sustainable, long-term solution.

The second two feature managers and investors who resemble the sad figures wandering across the seabed towards the approaching tsunami in the picture that opens this chapter. In the first, we see affirmation that small island nations are the ultimate victim of the reckless energy policies of the industrial economies, in which our fictional resort hotel business is collateral damage. In the second, we see that aridification can be slowed but ultimately is the by-product of forces well outside the control of an individual country, much less a single company.

A View of the King at the Shore - by Richard Marney

From these latter two, we observe a kind of King Canute in reverse. From our childhoods, we recall this myth in which this eleventh century ruler is said to have stood by the shore and commanded the incoming tide to stop. The sea, of course, a force of nature did not stop and soon the water washed up on the bemused king, wetting his feet and showing him that even a king's power has limits.

Keep this in mind—ignore changing climate at your peril—as we navigate the remainder of the book.

Notes

1. *Climate Change 2023: Synthesis Report. Contribution of Working Groups I, II and III to the Sixth Assessment Report of the Intergovernmental Panel on Climate Change. [Core Writing Team, H. Lee and J. Romero (eds.)]. IPCC, Geneva, Switzerland.*
2. Working Groups: I—The Physical Science Basis (2021) IPCC (2021) Climate Change 2021: The Physical Science Basis. Contribution of Working Group I to the Sixth Assessment Report of the Intergovernmental

Panel on Climate Change. [Masson-Delmotte, V. et al. (eds.)]. Cambridge University Press. DOI: 10.1017/9781009157896. II—Impacts, Adaptation and Vulnerability (2022) IPCC (2022) Climate Change 2022: Impacts, Adaptation and Vulnerability. Contribution of Working Group II to the Sixth Assessment Report of the Intergovernmental Panel on Climate Change. [Pörtner, H.-O. et al. (eds.)]. Cambridge University Press. DOI: 10.1017/9781009325844. III—Mitigation of Climate Change (2022) IPCC (2022) Climate Change 2022: Mitigation of Climate Change. Contribution of Working Group III to the Sixth Assessment Report of the Intergovernmental Panel on Climate Change. [Shukla, P.R. et al. (eds.)]. Cambridge University Press. DOI: 10.1017/9781009157926.
3. *Climate Change 2023: Synthesis Report. Contribution of Working Groups I, II and III to the Sixth Assessment Report of the Intergovernmental Panel on Climate Change. [Core Writing Team, H. Lee and J. Romero (eds.)]. IPCC, Geneva, Switzerland.* p. 5.
4. These include: NASA (2024) 'Global Climate Change: Vital Signs of the Planet'. NASA. https://climate.nasa.gov. NOAA (2024) 'Climate.gov'. National Oceanic and Atmospheric Administration. https://www.climate.gov.UK Met Office (2024) 'Hadley Centre Climate Programme'. Met Office. https://www.metoffice.gov.uk. Scripps Institution of Oceanography (2024) 'Climate Change and the Keeling Curve'. https://scripps.ucsd.edu. NSIDC (2024) 'National Snow and Ice Data Center. https://nsidc.org. IEA (2024) 'Global Energy and CO_2 Status Report'. International Energy Agency. https://www.iea.org
5. Intergovernmental Panel on Climate Change (IPCC) (n.d.) IPCC Interactive Atlas. Available at: IPCC Interactive Atlas (Accessed: 16 August 2025).
6. *IPCC (2021) Climate Change 2021: The Physical Science Basis. Contribution of Working Group I to the Sixth Assessment Report of the Intergovernmental Panel on Climate Change. Edited by V. Masson-Delmotte, P. Zhai, A. Pirani* et al. *Cambridge: Cambridge University Press. https://www.ipcc.ch/report/ar6/wg1/*
7. *Buhr, B., 2022. Climate Risks: An Investor's Field Guide to Identification and Assessment. Hoboken, NJ: Wiley Finance Series, John Wiley & Sons, a useful risk taxonomy is developed along these lines.*
8. Janik, R. (2015) *Watch a Senator Throw a Snowball on the Senate Floor.* TIME, 26 February. Available at: https://time.com/3724969/james-inhofe-snowball-senate/ (Accessed: 12 July 2026).
9. University of Notre Dame, 2024. *ND-GAIN Country Index: Methodology.* Notre Dame Global Adaptation Initiative (ND-GAIN). https://gain.nd.edu/our-work/country-index/methodology/

10. University of Notre Dame, 2023. *Notre Dame Global Adaptation Initiative (ND-GAIN) Country Index*. Notre Dame: University of Notre Dame. https://gain.nd.edu
11. Theses include: (1) PVCCI—structural physical vulnerability, https://www.ferdi.fr/en/indicator/physical-vulnerability-to-climate-change-index; (2) CRI—past climate related impacts, https://www.germanwatch.org/en/cri;(3) WRI—exposure and social vulnerability; https://drmkc.jrc.ec.europa.eu/inform-index; (4) INFORM Risk Index—quantifies disaster risks, https://drmkc.jrc.ec.europa.eu/inform-index; and (5) CFVI - To prioritize countries needing concessional climate finance, https://www.rockefellerfoundation.org/report/climate-vulnerability-index
12. *Chen, C., Noble, I., Hellmann, J., Coffee, J., Murillo, M. and Chawla, N., 2015. University of Notre Dame Global Adaptation Index: Country Index Technical Report. Notre Dame, IN: University of Notre Dame.* https://gain.nd.edu/assets/254377/nd_gain_technical_document_2015.pdf
13. https://gain.nd.edu
14. University of Notre Dame, 2023. *Notre Dame Global Adaptation Initiative (ND-GAIN) Country Index Rankings*. Notre Dame: University of Notre Dame. https://gain.nd.edu/our-work/country-index/
15. Moody's Investors Service (2024) *Sector In-Depth—ESG—Global: Share of Rating Actions Citing ESG Factors Greatest for Governments, Companies.*
16. Moody's Investors Service (2024) *ESG—Global 2025 Outlook: Policy and Financing Will Shape Environmental and Social Risks.*
17. S&P Global Ratings (2021) *The Heat Is On: How Climate Change Can Impact Sovereign Ratings.*
18. S&P Global Ratings (2023) *ESG Credit Indicators for Corporates: 2023 Update Highlights Sector-Specific Climate Risk.*
19. Sources include: *Fitch Ratings ESG Credit Quarterly—Q2 2023*; Fitch Ratings (2014). *Climate Change, Vulnerability and Resilience. Fitch Ratings, 18 November; and Fitch Ratings (2024). ESG Credit Trends 2024—Sovereigns. Fitch Ratings.*
20. Klusak, P., Agarwala, M., Burke, M., Kraemer, M. and Mohaddes, K. (2023) *Rising Temperatures, Falling Ratings: The Effect of Climate Change on Sovereign Creditworthiness*. University of Cambridge, Bennett Institute for Public Policy.
21. Sources include*:* J.P. Morgan (2023)—*Climate Change: Economic Implications and Investment Risks;*J.P. Morgan Asset Management (2024) *Climate Change Investment Risks and Opportunities*; J.P. Morgan Asset Management (2025) *2025 Long-Term Capital Market Assumptions: Climate and ESG Integration in Portfolio Construction.*
22. Goldman Sachs Asset Management (2021) *GSAM Sustainable Finance Report—Investing in the Net Zero Transition*; Goldman Sachs Asset Management (2023) *Sustainable Investing: The Climate Change*

Challenge—Risks and Opportunities in the Transition to a Low-Carbon Economy.
23. Cevik, S. and Jalles, J.T. (2020) *This changes everything: Climate shocks and sovereign bonds.* IMF Working Paper No. 20/79. Washington, D.C.: International Monetary Fund.
24. Kling, G., Volz, U., Murinde, V. and Ayas, S. (2021) *The impact of climate vulnerability on firms' cost of capital and access to finance.* World Development, 137, 105131.
25. Buhr, B., Volz, U., Donovan, C., Kling, G., Lo, Y.C., Murinde, V. and Pullin, N., 2018. *Climate change and the cost of capital in developing countries.* London: Imperial College London, School of Oriental and African Studies, and UN Environment.

8

Demographic Transitions om EMDEs: Easing Pressures to Youthquakes

Young people can be a force for growth and development, but they can also be a source of social and political tension if they lack opportunities for productive employment.

—Paraphrase of themes of The World Bank—World Development Report

8.1 Overview

Population dynamics represent a fundamental driver of long-term economic performance and are a central contributor to the risk profile of countries. Their effects are seen on labor supply, productivity, consumption, savings, fiscal sustainability, and social stability. For EMDEs these dynamics have been especially consequential because population growth rates are generally higher, age structures are changing more rapidly, and institutional capacity to manage these transitions is often uneven. While the global population crisis has not fully materialized as feared in the past, the challenge remains.

Population size alone, however, is an incomplete metric. What matters most for economic performance and country risk is demographics—the age structure and characteristics of the population—and how effectively the economy and institutions absorb demographic change. A growing working-age population can support faster growth and rising living standards. This positive outcome arises only when adequate productive employment opportunities are created and human capital is developed at scale. Where this absorption fails, demographic pressure instead manifests as unemployment, fiscal strain, social tension, and, potentially, political instability.

R. Marney, P. Waeber, *The Emerging Markets Investor's Guide to Country Risk*,
https://doi.org/10.1007/978-3-032-26824-2_8

Population growth can be beneficial for businesses in the short run. A larger population expands potential markets, increases labor supply, and may reduce marginal labor costs. Employment growth fuels gains in household incomes and supports an increase in aggregate demand. Over time, however, these advantages depend critically on institutional development and policy design and implementation. Weak labor absorption, skills mismatches, and deteriorating social conditions raise operating risks, disrupt supply chains, and undermine investment returns.

Even when demographic change is managed successfully, longer-term risks remain. Population growth, urbanization, and structural transformation intensify pressure on land, water, air quality, biodiversity, and climate-sensitive sectors. In the absence of effective environmental governance and adaptation, these pressures can erode productivity and reverse earlier gains. This latter risk set becomes more threatening as the impact of climate change intensifies.

This chapter examines how population growth and demographic transitions influence economic performance, political stability, environmental sustainability, and ultimately country risk in EMDEs. It establishes the analytical foundations for understanding why similar demographic profiles can produce sharply different outcomes across countries, and why demographics should be treated as a central—rather than peripheral—input into investment analysis. As will be discussed below, demographic factors play an important role in the Investor's Rutter's evaluation of country risk. We start this discussion in Sect. 8.2.

8.2 Demographic Dynamics and Country Risk

Population growth and changes in age structure are among the most powerful structural forces shaping country risk in EMDEs. Through multiple transmission channels—labor supply and productivity, savings and investment behavior, fiscal balances, political incentives, and pressure on natural resources—demographics influence both growth potential and the stability of the investment environment (Fig. 8.1).

Demographic outcomes are not predetermined. Rapid population growth and a rising share of working-age individuals can generate a demographic dividend, but only where institutions, policies, and labor markets can absorb new entrants productively. Investments in health, education, gender inclusion, and labor market flexibility, combined with a credible investment climate, are necessary conditions for converting demographic change into sustained growth. Where these conditions are absent, the same demographic forces become a source of economic imbalance and political risk.

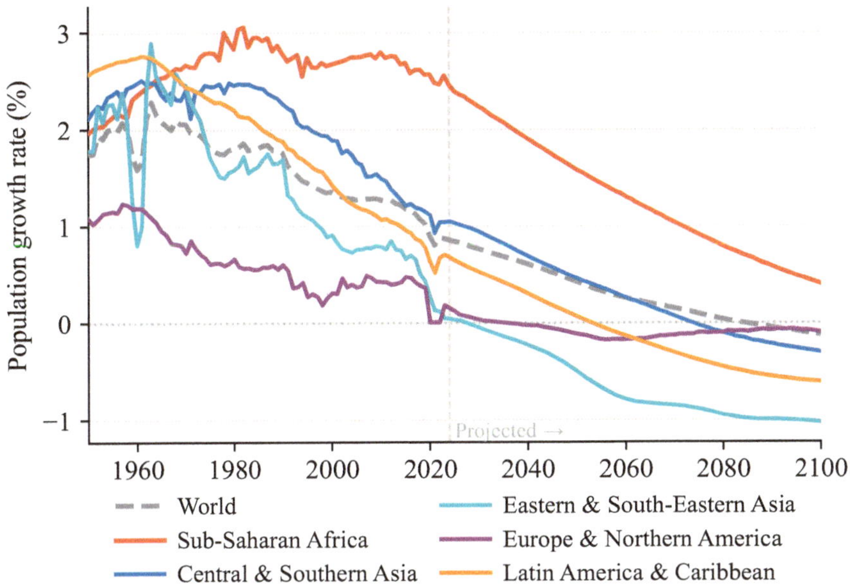

Fig. 8.1 Population growth rates by region, 1950–2100. (Source: United Nations, World Population Prospects 2024 (medium variant). Note: Dashed vertical line marks 2024, after which values are UN projections)

Three core insights follow.

First, population size and age structure must be considered jointly. High fertility and a rising dependency ratio create very different risk profiles than a declining fertility rate accompanied by a growing working-age share. Focusing on population growth alone obscures the dynamics that matter most for productivity, fiscal sustainability, and social cohesion.

Second, institutions and policy effectiveness dominate demographic outcomes. Attempts to manage population growth in isolation are rarely successful. What matters is whether governments can align labor supply and demand in a sustainable and equitable manner—by strengthening human capital, reducing barriers to employment (especially for women), supporting private investment, and maintaining macroeconomic stability.

Third, even successful demographic transitions generate new environmental risks. Rapid urbanization, industrialization, and rising consumption increase pressure on natural resources and climate-sensitive systems. Without integrating environmental sustainability into economic planning, demographic success can undermine long-term growth and stability.

Demographic pressures also interact with other sources of fragility. Where economic opportunities are insufficient, political conditions unstable, or climate vulnerability high, demographic stress can contribute to civil unrest and forced migration. These dynamics impose lasting costs on countries of origin through lost human capital and fiscal strain, while placing political and institutional pressure on receiving countries. Forced migration is therefore not only a humanitarian concern, but a signal of underlying structural weakness with direct implications for country risk.

For investors, demographics are a slow-moving but material risk factor. They shape market size and demand patterns, labor costs and quality, savings behavior, fiscal space, and the resilience of political and social systems. Countries that successfully align demographic change with institutional reform and productive employment creation tend to offer more durable investment opportunities. Where demographic pressures overwhelm absorption capacity, risks accumulate—often gradually, but sometimes abruptly.

8.3 Causes and Effects

This section examines how population growth and changes in demographic structure affect macroeconomic performance, political stability, and environmental sustainability in EMDEs. The analysis proceeds in three steps: the demographic transition, its drivers, and the so-called demographic dividend[1]; observed demographic pressures across EMDEs; and the principal economic, political, and environmental effects.

Demographic Transition

Population growth reflects the interaction of fertility, mortality, and net migration. These variables are shaped by income levels, education, urbanization, cultural norms, public policy, health outcomes, and—increasingly—environmental conditions. While the relative importance of these drivers varies across regions and over time, several broad patterns are evident.

High population growth typically reflects elevated fertility rates combined with declining mortality. This configuration remains common across much of the EMDE cohort, particularly in sub-Saharan Africa, where improvements in health outcomes have reduced mortality more rapidly than fertility has fallen. By contrast, stable or declining populations reflect sustained low fertility and population aging, more characteristic of advanced economies and a small subset of EMDEs (Fig. 8.2).

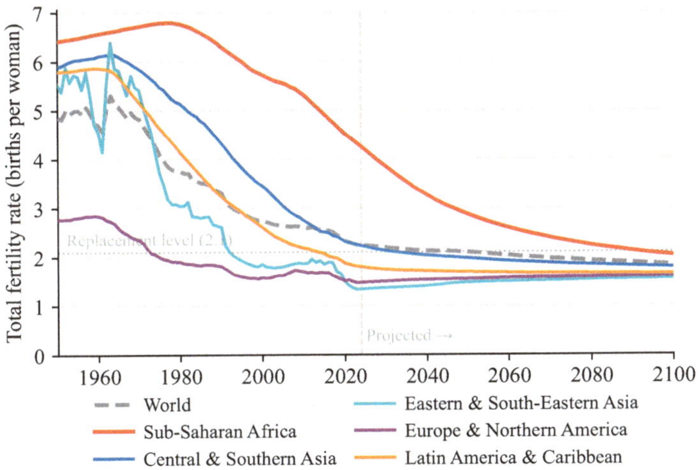

Fig. 8.2 Total fertility rate by region, 1950–2100. (Source: United Nations, World Population Prospects 2024 (medium variant). Note: Dotted horizontal line marks the replacement-level fertility of 2.1 births per woman. Dashed vertical line marks 2024, after which values are UN projections)

Box 8.1: The Demographic Transition and Growth

1. Empirically, the decline in the fertility rate follows the onset of the fall in the mortality rate. As depicted below, in the period between the point at which the mortality rate begins to fall and the point when the fertility (birth) rate follows, we observe a population bulge.

The Demographic Transition and Population Growth over the Course of the Demographic Transition

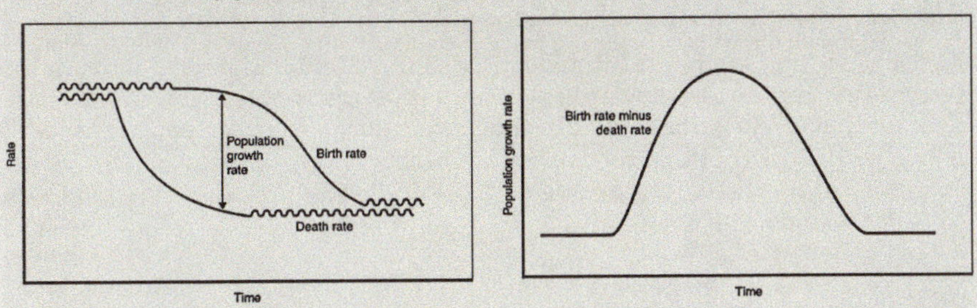

Source: Bloom, D., Canning, D. and Sevilla, J. (2002) The Demographic Dividend, P.31

The expected decrease in the fertility (birth) rate commences, the population curve begins to decline until the assumed flattening and approximate equality trend between the two rates, where growth plateaus.

2. In this transition period, we see the golden effect of the so-called demographic dividend effect.[1] This effect is defined as an episode of strong economic growth when a country experiences a decline in fertility and mortality rates, producing a larger share of working-age population relative to dependents (children and the elderly).
3. The demographic structure of the country influences the level of savings, investment, and capital formation. Innovation and human capital development can benefit from increased populations, assuming investment in health and education, and sound institutional development. The experience of East Asia in the period 1960–1990 is an example of the demographic dividend.
4. Conversely, the failure to achieve some form of sustainable equilibrium between the size and age structure of the population, on the one hand, and the absorption capacity of the labor market and equitable economic opportunities, on the other, can result in economic imbalances, lost potential growth, the specter of civil unrest and political instability, and even forced outward migration. Despite rapid population growth, many African countries struggled to create enough jobs and infrastructure. Fertility rates remained high in the absence of coordinated investments in education, health, and labor markets. Countries like Nigeria and the Democratic Republic of the Congo face youth bulges with limited economic opportunities, chronic underemployment, weak institutions, and growing risks of political and social instability.

Migration affects population dynamics unevenly. While outward migration from EMDEs is substantial in absolute terms, it has generally not altered aggregate population trajectories, given high fertility in many origin countries. Its significance lies instead in its composition: emigration often

Box 8.2: Africa's Youthquake: Demography in the Investor's Rutter

Africa is undergoing one of the most consequential demographic shifts in the twenty-first century. As Edward Paice argues in *Youthquake* (2021), the continent's population—estimated at ~1.4 billion in 2023—is projected to reach ~2.5 billion by 2050, accounting for over half of global population growth (UN DESA). By mid-century, one in four people globally will live in Africa, with around 60% of Africans under the age of 25.

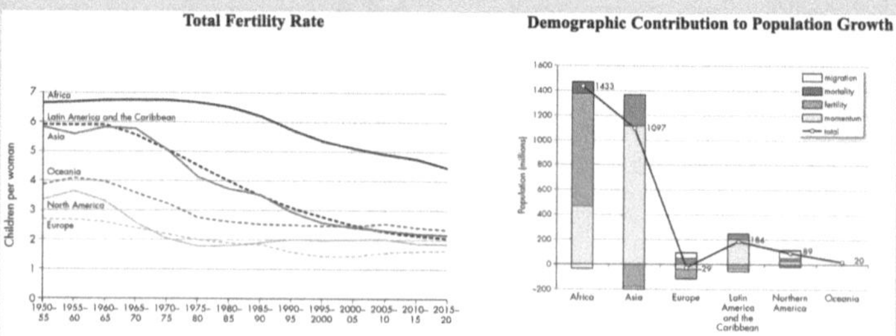

Source: Paice, E. (2021) Youthquake: Why African Demography Should Matter to the World. London: pages 30 and 92
Based on UNDP Data

Within the Investor's Rutter, demography operates as a structural conditioning factor, revealing the depth and effectiveness of institutions rather than determining outcomes in isolation. Each year, 20–22 million young Africans enter the labor force, while formal employment creation remains insufficient (World Bank; ILO). Where institutions can deliver human capital formation, infrastructure, and policy credibility, the youth bulge can reinforce growth and fiscal resilience. Where they are not, demographic pressure amplifies unemployment, social tension, migration pressures, and policy volatility.

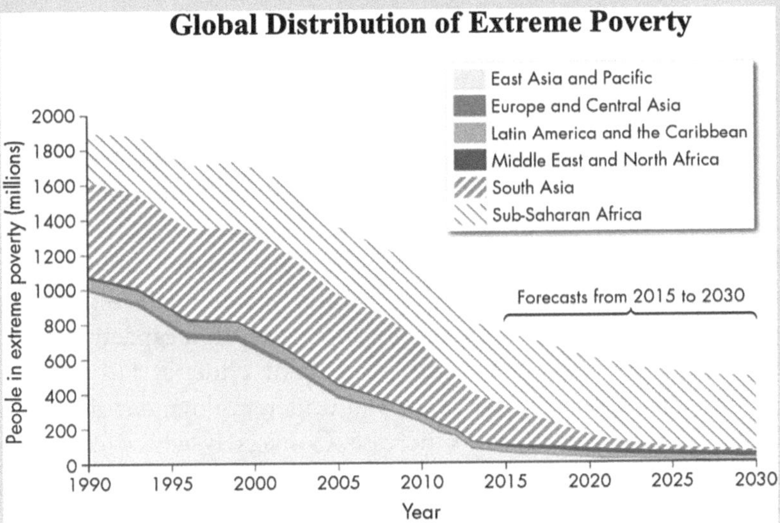

Source: Paice, E. (2021) Youthquake: Why African Demography Should Matter to the World. London: page 278 Based on World Bank Data

Investor takeaway: In Africa, demographic trends function as an institutional stress test, shaping political risk, sovereign credit trajectories, and long-term capital allocation decisions.

disproportionately involves working-age and skilled individuals, contributing to human capital loss and reduced productivity growth. Forced migration imposes long-lasting costs on the countries losing population through lost human capital, potential output, and resultant fiscal strain. At the same time, receiving countries confront political, institutional, and financial pressures as they integrate the displaced populations. Forced migration is not simply a humanitarian issue. The development points to underlying national fragility, with direct implications for growth potential, social cohesion, and country risk.

The demographic transition (see Box 8.1) describes the sequencing of declining mortality followed by declining fertility. Mortality reductions—driven by improvements in health care, sanitation, nutrition, and disease control—tend to precede fertility declines. As fertility responds with a lag, population growth accelerates temporarily, creating a bulge in the working-age population. This phase presents the opportunity for a demographic dividend, if institutions and labor markets can productively absorb new entrants.

Fertility decline is closely linked to structural change. Urbanization raises the cost of childrearing, education becomes more central to economic participation, and female education and labor force participation increase. These forces jointly reduce desired family size and reshape age structures. Where fertility decline is sustained, population growth slows and dependency ratios eventually stabilize.

Demographic Pressures in EMDEs

Across EMDEs, demographic pressures remain highly uneven. Africa stands out as the global epicenter of population growth, driven by persistently high fertility rates and rapidly expanding youth cohorts. In contrast, much of East Asia and parts of Latin America have already passed through the demographic transition, while several EMDEs in Eastern Europe face aging populations and declining workforces.

The central risk in high-growth EMDEs is not population growth per se, but the mismatch between labor supply and absorption capacity. Where education systems, labor markets, and investment climates fail to scale with demographic change, unemployment and underemployment rise, fiscal pressures intensify, and social tensions increase. Conversely, where fertility declines are accompanied by improvements in human capital and job creation, demographic change can support sustained growth.

Forced migration represents an important manifestation of unresolved demographic pressure. Youthful populations combined with weak labor demand, political instability, or climate stress increase outward migration, particularly among educated workers. While this may relieve short-term labor market pressure, it erodes the domestic human capital base and can weaken long-term growth potential. Receiving countries, often EMDEs themselves, face integration, fiscal, and political challenges.

Effects on Economic Performance, Stability, and the Environment

The economic and political effects of demographic change depend critically on whether population growth is absorbed productively.

In low or declining population growth settings, labor shortages may constrain growth unless offset by immigration, productivity-enhancing investment, or technological adaptation. Aging populations raise dependency ratios, increasing pressure on public finances through pensions and health care. While advanced economies generally possess the fiscal capacity to manage these challenges, several EMDEs facing aging dynamics do not.

In high population growth settings, two paths emerge. Where labor demand expands in line with workforce growth, countries can benefit from a demographic dividend through higher productivity, rising incomes, increased savings, and improved fiscal sustainability. Where labor absorption fails, demographic pressure instead amplifies unemployment, fiscal strain, inequality, and political instability. Youth bulges in particular raise the risk of social unrest when economic aspirations are frustrated.

Environmental effects cut across both paths. Population growth, urbanization, and rising incomes intensify pressure on land, water, air quality, biodiversity, and climate-sensitive systems. In low-income, agriculture-dependent economies with weak institutions, these pressures can directly undermine livelihoods and growth. In more successful EMDEs, rapid industrialization and consumption growth can generate environmental degradation that eventually feeds back into economic and political risk.

Consider the following, highly simplified schematic (Fig. 8.3).

The first level node is whether the population growth rate is low or high. Low population growth is defined as where the fertility rate is less than the 2.1 replacement rate, while the high alternative assumes a fertility rate greater than the replacement rate. The former sees a decline in population, while the latter sees an increase over time. Relative population growth rates in AE (low to negative) versus EMDE (high) reflect the respective fertility rates.

In the case of the low alternative, labor shortages may develop and hence be a drag on economic growth, unless immigration, capital-intensive adaptation, and/or innovation can compensate. If not, then a form of secular stagnation sets in. Additionally, in such a case, aging of the population increases the dependency ratio. This development raises pressure on the limited fiscal resources to cover higher retirement and medical outlays to the elderly. This is

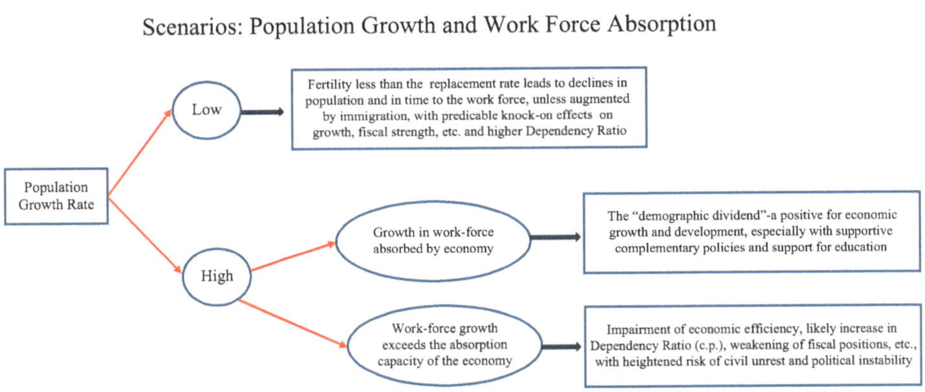

Fig. 8.3 Population growth and labor market outcomes. (Source: The authors)

the now and future for countries such as Japan or (for the most part) the member states of the European Union, which fortunately have the national wealth to manage in such a scenario. This is not necessarily the case for emerging economies in Eastern Europe, Russia, and the former Soviet Union.

In the case of the high growth alternative, the nodes indicate two possible paths. The first—where the labor market can absorb the new workers—is where a country can potentially cash in the so-called demographic dividend to varying degrees. The second—where unemployment and underemployment rise—is where the economy is buffeted by the headwinds of excess population and demographic imbalances, performance slips, and, as a result, the society becomes more vulnerable to civil unrest and political instability. In both cases, there can be higher stress placed on the environment. All things being equal, the financial capacity to engage in effective mitigation measures and adaptation responses is higher in the first case.

We now consider two scenarios:

First

A high growth country with a fertility rate above the replacement level and a large informal sector, where the government has begun to think about policies to create and benefit from a demographic dividend in the future and compare/contrast successful and failed outcomes.

Second

A high growth country that has successfully harnessed the demographic dividend, but confronts looming threat of environmental stress, which it has not begun seriously to address.

Scenario One

At this point, the country reaches a fork in the road. The path followed will be a function of whether the sum of their policies result in an outcome where the future demand for labor equals or exceeds the supply or, alternatively, where the size of the potential work force exceeds the labor requirements of the economy.

In the first case, the country will have succeeded in shifting the age structure to increase the relative size of the workforce by reducing the fertility rate.[2]

To achieve this result, the country requires appropriate institutions (law, governance, etc.) and focused, well-funded and soundly implemented government policies aimed at improving access to quality education and health care.[3] Supported by policy measures to establish sound fiscal and public finance management, incentivize foreign and domestic private investment, strengthen financial intermediation, reduce gender barriers, encourage innovation and risk taking, and the like, the country will realize the benefits of the demographic dividend in the form of increased productivity, household income, savings, etc., driving superior growth and equality outcomes. In the context of higher growth and a lower dependency ratio, the financial stability of pension and other social safety net programs improves. Additionally, the overall strengthening of the fiscal accounts generates additional resources to support human capital development, research and development, and other measures to enhance productivity, hence creating a virtuous circle of sustainable development and equitable growth, civil and political stability, and overall welfare gains.

The opposite macroeconomic effects are present when a country experiences damaging demographic changes—either aging populations or, as is relevant in the EMDE, a youth bulge, to which government is unable to respond effectively, by expanding employment opportunities. In the downside case above, the increase in the dependency ratio strains the fiscal capacity to cover pensions and social safety net outlays, and fund education, health, infrastructure, and other human capital and productivity-enhancing measures, and can contribute to debt sustainability problems. A negative cycle intensifies, adversely affecting macroeconomic performance, social welfare, and political stability.[4] The mismatch between the aspirations of a large youth cohort and the realities of an underperforming economy is tinder for civil unrest and political destabilization.[5]

Scenario Two

As discussed in Chap. 7, the connection between rapid population growth and an increased threat of environmental degradation is clear and compelling. In the current era of global warming and its deleterious impacts on the environment, this risk grows. For poor countries, reliant on agriculture, situated in low-lying areas, with weak institutions/governance, the impact is even greater.[6]

The key insight is that demographic change acts as a risk multiplier.[7] Where institutions, policies, and environmental management are strong, demographic pressures can be absorbed and transformed into growth. Where they are weak, the same pressures accelerate fragility—manifesting in economic underperformance, social tension, forced migration, and environmental stress.

8.4 Implications for Investors

Introduction

As we note above, the absolute size and rate of growth of the population and changes in demographic structure contribute to the level and evolution of a wide variety of business drivers, including: (1) market size; (2) consumption; (3) demand preferences; (4) factor supply and costs; (5) savings and investment capital; (6) resource availability; and (7) environmental sustainability. The local business landscape, today and tomorrow, is a function of the investment climate and this demographic nexus exercises a significant influence on the evolution of its opportunities and risks.

In this section, we use the "Positive Outcome" and "Negative Outcome" country cases employed above. In this, we juxtaposed the two countries: one having positioned itself to benefit from the demographic dividend and the other still confronting the economic damages of a persistently high fertility rate. We present two firms (a "Debt Investor" and an "Equity Investor") each making an investment in the two countries. For the Debt Investor, their counterparty is a local commercial bank, while for the Equity Investor, a corporate in the telecom equipment space.

These short cases are intended to provide examples of the ways in which population growth, the nature of the demographic transition, institutions, and government policy interact to affect the investment environment. These dynamics will be introduced into certain of the case studies in Chaps. 14–17 in Part IV of this book.

The Positive Outcome Country

Country Snapshot (a Ba1-Rated Sovereign)

GDP growth per capita has increased markedly, supported by higher FDI attracted by the notable increase in the quality of human capital and the supply of high value-added labor. This development is the result of significant government investment in teacher training, curriculum development, school physical infrastructure, and student financial aid. Enhanced worker productivity compensates for higher wages and benefits. Corporate operating cash flows and profitability have risen.

Debt Investor Case

The proposed underwriting is a medium-term funding line to a local bank to support portfolio growth, especially in the expanding domestic, high-tech manufacturing and assembly sectors. The institution has a moderate track record in this lending area but has benefited from the build-up of experienced senior executives returning home from overseas and recent graduates from the local technical university. The credit structure and monitoring have been fashioned to comply with best international practice and the establishment of intercreditor arrangements. In analyzing the credit risk of the bank's planned high-tech portfolio, the investment firm has focused on the usual and customary risk elements, but with a special emphasis on the supply side—the availability of technically qualified staff at all levels of the operations to ensure operating efficiency as the companies expand their operations and contend with evolving market conditions and competitive pressures.

Equity Investor Case

The investee is a local corporate historically active as an assembler of handsets for major international technology companies. They are now branching out into the production of proprietary manufacturing. The opportunity is to take a significant minority stake in the company as it undertakes the construction of a plant to manufacture a new brand of handset, using locally developed technology to compete in the budget markets at home and in the neighboring countries. The design and technical features, and the price points for the range of handsets appear to be real winners in the targeted market segment at home and abroad. As in the case above, the Equity Investor gains comfort due to the highly positive capability of the local economy to furnish the necessary quantity and quality of requisite staff, to adopt new technologies, and to innovate.

The Negative Outcome Country

Country Snapshot (a B3-Rated Sovereign)

A stubbornly high fertility rate has fueled a persistently rapid increase in population, to the backdrop of a static mortality rate and heightened outward migration of educated citizens and their families. GDP per capita has progressively declined over the past decade in purchasing power parity terms. FDI and domestic fixed capital investment levels have slipped in real terms, with the available funding going into the low value-added service sector. Youth unemployment/underemployment has drifted upward. Urbanization has increased as climate change and water resource depletion have plagued a struggling agriculture sector. Housing conditions have become overcrowded, and the lack of social/transportation infrastructure investment has reached a critical stage. The crime rate and the incidence of episodes of civil unrest have increased markedly, as have concerns about the country's political stability.

Debt Investor

The country and financial market ratings place the country in the high-risk category. The banking sector consists of two large systemically important and a minor subset of smaller institutions. The investment firm has worked with one of the two systemically important banks for many years and continues to do so. However, the progressive deterioration in country conditions, exacerbated by the demographic pressures, has resulted in a gradual reduction in the amount, a shortening of the duration, and an increase in coupon. At the last investment committee, the decision stipulated that if the sovereign rating is either put on a negative outlook or downgraded from the current B3, no further lending will be approved (necessitating repayment at the next principal payment date).

Equity Investor

The investment firm has been a minority shareholder in a network of retail, consumer product stores for a decade. Under the terms of its original investment agreements, they have the right to put their shares to the majority shareholder under certain conditions and at a fair market valuation at the time. Given the fear that in time the civil/political conditions could degenerate further into a dangerous space, the investment firm exercises its put option. They accepted the unattractive valuation, rather than running the risk of further value destruction.

8.5 Closing Remarks

Population growth and changes in age structure shape economic performance, through multiple channels including labor supply and productivity, savings and investment, fiscal space, political incentives, and resource pressures. Whether these factors result in the positive outcome—a demographic dividend—or the opposite—a demographic burden—depends on institutional quality, policy coherence, and the economy's ability to generate productive employment.

For investors, demographic trends are material considerations. They influence market size, demand characteristics, cost structures, human capital quality, economic duality, and the stability of the operating environment. A growing working-age population paired with improvements in education and policy credibility can expand opportunity and strengthen the investment climate. Conversely, the same demographic profile, combined with weak governance, ineffective policy implementation, or insufficient job creation, raises social risk, political volatility, and operating disruption.

Population size alone tells only part of the story. The real impact comes from the interaction between demographic scale, age structure, and absorption capacity. Countries that have successfully navigated the demographic transition have done so through sustained investment in health and education, labor market reform, gender inclusion, and policies that crowd in private investment. Where high fertility, weak institutions, and limited economic diversification coexist, demographic pressures amplify fiscal strain, erode social cohesion, heighten political risk, and may result in environmental degradation.

Even successful demographic transitions bring new challenges. Rapid urbanization, industrialization, and rising consumption increase pressure on land, water, air quality, biodiversity, and climate-sensitive sectors.[8] In many EMDEs, where regulatory capacity and fiscal buffers are limited, failure to integrate environmental sustainability into economic planning risks undermining productivity, harming public health, and destabilizing politics.

Notes

1. Bloom, D.E., Canning, D. & Sevilla, J., 2003. The Demographic Dividend: A New Perspective on the Economic Consequences of Population Change. Santa Monica: RAND.
2. Various authors have identified this result, including: Kelley, A.C. and Schmidt, R.M., 2009. Economic and demographic change: A synthesis of models, findings, and perspectives. In: D.A. Coleman and R. Düvell, eds. The demographic challenge: A handbook about population issues in Europe. Cheltenham: Edward Elgar, pp. 67–94; Bloom, D., Canning, D. and Sevilla, J. (2002) The Demographic Dividend; and Ahmed, S.A., Cruz, M. and Go, D.S., 2023. How significant is sub-Saharan Africa's demographic dividend for its future growth and poverty reduction? Population, Space and Place, 29(1), e2660.
3. This linkage is discussed in a variety of sources, including: Eastwood, R. and Lipton, M., 2011. Demographic transition in sub-Saharan Africa: How big will the economic dividend be? Population Studies, 65(1), pp. 9–35; Canning, D., Raja, S.; Yazbeck, A.S., 2015. Africa's demographic transition: Dividend or disaster? Washington, DC: World Bank; and Williamson, J.G., 2013. Demographic dividends revisited. Asian Development Review, 30(2), pp. 1–25; and Aiyar, S. and Mody, A., 2011. The demographic dividend: Evidence from the Indian states. IMF Working Paper No. 11/38. Washington, DC: International Monetary Fund.
4. Sources include: Hanushek, E.A. and Woessmann, L., 2008. The role of cognitive skills in economic development. Journal of Economic Literature, 46(3), pp. 607–668; Tyers, R. and Shi, Q., 2007. Global demographic change, policy responses and their effects: A general equilibrium analysis of the Asia-Pacific region. World Economy, 30(11), pp. 1725–1752; Loayza, N., Fajnzylber, P. and Calderón, C., 2005. Economic growth in Latin America and the Caribbean: Stylized facts, explanations, and forecasts. World Bank Policy Research Working Paper No. 3621. Washington, DC: World Bank; Bloom, D., Canning, D. and Sevilla, J. (2002) The Demographic Dividend; and Fox, L. and Kaul, U., 2017. The evidence is in: How should youth employment programs in low-income countries be designed? USAID Policy Research Working Paper No. 9127. Washington, DC.
5. See: Mason, A., Lee, R. and Lee, S.-H., 2021. The demographic dividend: A conceptual and empirical primer. Manila: Asian Development Bank; Bova, E., Carcenac, N. and Guerguil, M., 2014. Fiscal rules and the procyclicality of fiscal policy in the developing world; IMF Working Paper No. 14/122. Washington, DC: International Monetary Fund International Monetary Fund (IMF), 2011. The challenge of public pension reform in advanced and emerging economies. IMF Policy Paper. Washington, DC; International Monetary Fund; Clements, B., Eich, F. and Gupta, S., 2015. Equitable and sustainable

pensions: Challenges and experiences. Washington, DC: International Monetary Fund; Holzmann, R., Hinz, R. and Dorfman, M., 2008. Pension systems and reform conceptual framework. SP Discussion Paper No. 0824. Washington, DC: World Bank.

6. See: Bricker, D. and Ibbitson, J., 2019. Empty planet: The shock of global population decline. New York: Crown Publishing Group; Cincotta, R.P., Engleman, R. and Anastasion, D., 2003. The security demographic: Population and civil conflict after the Cold War. Washington, DC: Population Action International; Urdal, H., 2006. A clash of generations? Youth bulges and political violence. International Studies Quarterly, 50(3), pp. 607–629; Goldstone, J.A., 2010. The new population bomb: The four megatrends that will change the world. Foreign Affairs, 89(1), pp. 31–43.
7. The concept of a "risk multiplier" follows the established "threat multiplier" framework used in development, security, and climate-risk analysis, in which structural conditions amplify the impact of shocks rather than generate risk independently (World Bank 2014; CNA 2007; IMF 2018). The term is adapted here to demographic dynamics.
8. See: Cole, M.A. and Neumayer, E., 2004. Examining the impact of demographic factors on air pollution. Population and Environment, 26(1), pp. 5–21 and Bongaarts, J., 1992. Population growth and global warming. Population and Development Review, 18(2), pp. 299–319.

9

In Search of the Future Growth Model: Promise and Perils of Technology

The winds of change are blowing. The question is not whether they will blow, but how we will set our sails.
A traditional sailing expression.

Technological change has been a key part of modern economic history, typically moving in waves, from mechanization and electrification to automation and digitalization. A precondition for development was not least productivity gains in agriculture—unleashed through mechanization, improved seeds and irrigation—that freed up labor for other activities and lowered food prices. These gains enabled urbanization and industrialization, which have long been considered cornerstones of economic development (Fig. 9.1).

At times, technological shifts have been profound. Numerous are the examples of what the famous Austrian economist Joseph Schumpeter labeled as *creative destruction*, where leading global companies lost much of their dominance due to having missed a major technological shift. Readers might think of Kodak missing the digital photography revolution, Nokia the development of smartphones, and lately some of the traditional car makers the shift toward electric vehicles (EVs).

Historically, industrialization has been the main path to prosperity. Many of the rising Asian economies have successfully followed a manufacturing-led growth model, starting with low value-added production, to gradually move up the value-chain. Globalization, itself enabled by technological progress in transportation and communication, played a vital role in the Asian growth miracle.

R. Marney, P. Waeber, *The Emerging Markets Investor's Guide to Country Risk*,
https://doi.org/10.1007/978-3-032-26824-2_9

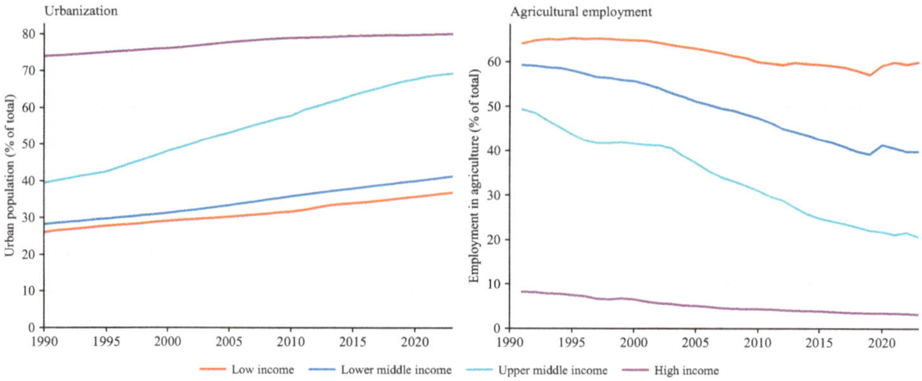

Fig. 9.1 Urbanization and agricultural employment by income group. (*Source: World Bank*)

EMDEs seemed a natural fit to most segments of manufacturing, needing plenty of cheap, unskilled labor, while its output was tradeable and hence not constrained by domestic demand. It was also a sector that demanded hardly any of the resources that were scarce in the developing world, including education, physical capital, and high-quality institutions.[1]

Many researchers worry that this characterization of manufacturing no longer applies, and hence that the standard model for development has run its course. This worry is covered in the first part of this chapter, which explains the concept of premature deindustrialization, how widespread it is, and whether there are regions or countries escaping it. The first Sect. 9.1 also provides an outlook on how automation might change manufacturing in the foreseeable future, drawing a line between technological capacities and actual implementation, while highlighting the key role of incentives. In the big scheme of things, it will become clear that for most EMDEs, manufacturing has ceased to be a well-paved road to prosperity. Could the services sector play that role? That question is addressed in Sect. 9.2. Arguably, services have a reputation for being relatively unproductive and hardly scalable and tradable. However, that view fails to acknowledge the wide variety of services and also how technological change has transformed their potential. Clearly, services trade has been on the rise in recent decades, and EMDEs' stake in it has increasingly grown. That said, some of the most obvious success stories, from India to the Philippines, seem now endangered by advancements in artificial intelligence. It is Sect. 9.3 that looks into how EMDEs are affected by AI, showcasing how they score in AI preparedness and job exposure, to derive the promises and perils of AI for EMDEs. The chapter concludes with the implications of technological change for investors.

9.1 Premature Deindustrialization and Automation

Dani Rodrik, a leading development economist, in his seminal work titled *Premature Deindustrialization* published in 2016 pointed out that in many EMDEs industrialization seems to peak much earlier than it historically did in AEs, in terms of both timing and income levels.[2] The phenomenon is observed since the 1980s in large parts of sub-Saharan Africa and Latin America, while Developing Asia largely escaped. Globally, the phenomenon is well visible in the chart below, showing how the timing of "peak manufacturing" has shifted over decades, with more recent peaks occurring at much lower levels of income and manufacturing employment (Fig. 9.2).

Countries showcasing the phenomenon very well include South Africa and Brazil. In both cases, manufacturing's share in total employment peaked in the 1980s. Compared to many other EMDEs, the employment peak was actually rather elevated, at 17% (Brazil) and 21% (South Africa) respectively. However, it happened at rather low levels of GDP per capita of US$5500–6500 (constant 2015 prices). Ever since, the economic importance of manufacturing has steadily eroded, with both countries reporting less than 10% of total employment in manufacturing as of late.

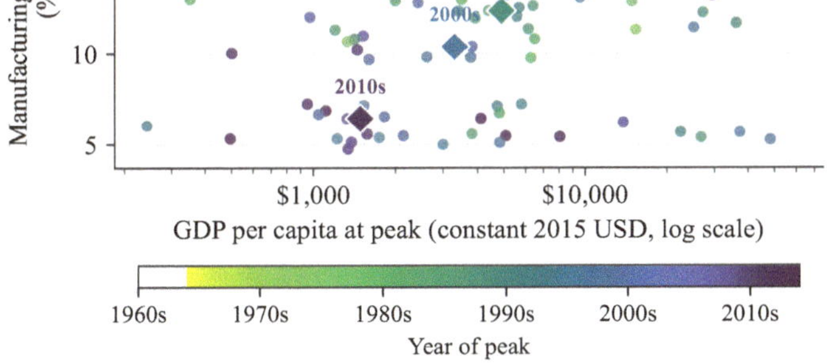

Fig. 9.2 Shifting manufacturing employment peaks over time. (Sources: ILO, World Bank, the authors. Note: Each dot represents one country at the year of its highest manufacturing employment share. Diamonds show median values by decade of peak. Color indicates decade of peak manufacturing employment)

Rodrik attributes premature deindustrialization in EMDEs primarily to trade and globalization and less to technological change. In many instances, EMDEs liberalized their economies and integrated into global markets, without a strong comparative advantage in manufacturing. Consequently, domestic producers suddenly faced intense competition from established exporters, particularly from Asia. Not being competitive, domestic manufacturing sectors quickly recorded losses at the expense of mostly Asian competitors, a pattern that is also evident in two country cases highlighted before, Brazil and South Africa. In both economies, labor-intensive manufacturing segments such as textiles, clothing and basic consumer goods saw a rapid decline once they were exposed to import competition. In addition, both countries suffered periods of real exchange-rate appreciation, associated with large mining sectors and commodity cycles, further eroding the price competitiveness of manufactured goods, and reinforced the decline of domestic producers.

Yet another element highlighted by Rodrik is the relative decline in prices for manufactured products, reflecting stronger productivity gains in manufacturing—not least thanks to automation—compared to other sectors globally. Due to impediments to technology adoption in many EMDEs, such as deficiencies in infrastructure and human capital, for many EMDEs, domestic productivity growth in manufacturing was outpaced by relative price declines for manufactured products, further undermining their competitiveness.

Vietnam stands out as a notable exception to the broader trend of premature deindustrialization. Over the past three decades, it has successfully pursued a manufacturing-led, export-oriented growth model that leveraged its low labor costs and proximity to manufacturing powerhouses such as China, South Korea, and Japan. Deep institutional reforms, including the transition to a market-based economy and the opening up to foreign investment, paired with substantial investment in infrastructure such as ports, roads, and power networks, helped it to attract sizable foreign investment into low-cost manufacturing and integrate into global value chains. For now, though, domestic value added is rather limited, with Vietnam mostly being a final assembly hub. This leaves it very vulnerable to rising wages, automation, and geopolitical shocks (Fig. 9.3).[3]

By only looking at the peak manufacturing, the analysis above misses out on potential trends below it. Since the early 2000s, there has been a modest manufacturing renaissance in several low-income countries, particularly in sub-Saharan Africa. Unlike the large-scale, export-oriented industrialization seen historically, this renaissance is driven by small, informal firms servicing domestic demand for basic goods.[4]

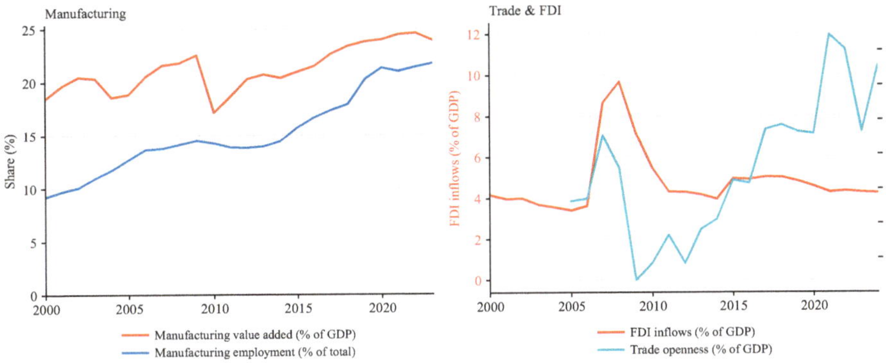

Fig. 9.3 Vietnam's manufacturing depth and trade integration. (Source: World Bank, UNCTAD)

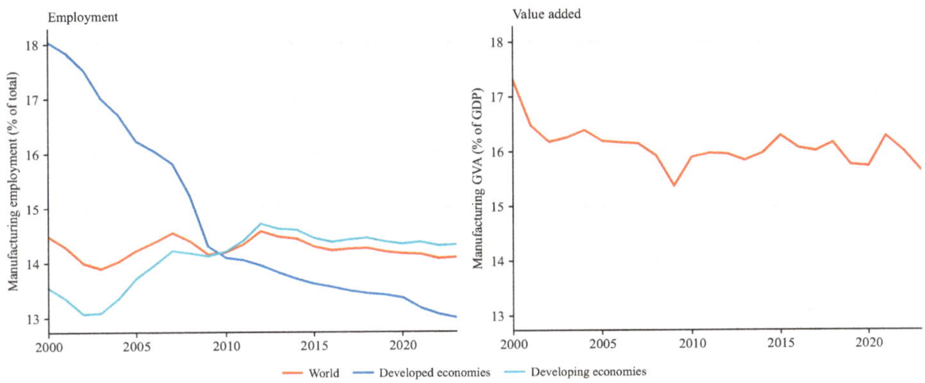

Fig. 9.4 Global manufacturing employment and value added. (Source: World Bank, UNDESA)

It is noteworthy that on a global level, the share of manufacturing employment in total employment has been quite steady since 2000 (marking the start of an aggregate indicator provided by the World Bank—earlier on, the data was rather patchy), hovering around 14%. The year 2010 marked the year when the share of manufacturing employment in EMDEs overtook the one in AEs, following a decade of opposing trends, with the share trending down in AEs while trending up in EMDEs. The uptrend in EMDEs lasted until 2012, since when the ratio has stabilized. Also the share of manufacturing value added in global output has been relatively stable since the early 2000s (Fig. 9.4). Taken together, these global indicators do not point toward automation having—at least so far—destroyed lots of manufacturing jobs at the global level.

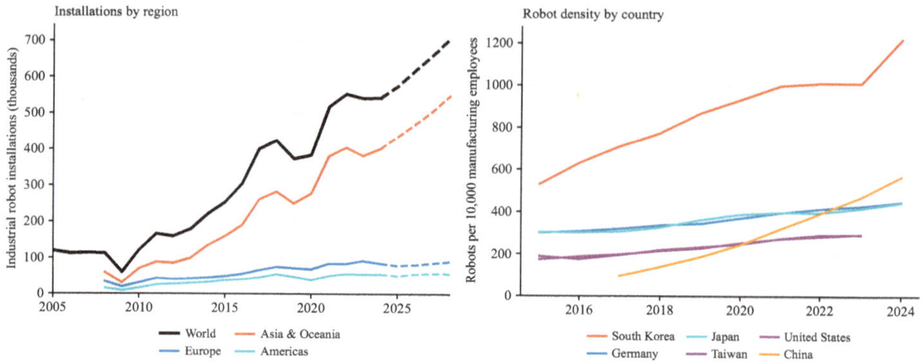

Fig. 9.5 Industrial robot installations and density in manufacturing. (Source: International Federation of Robotics, via Macrobond)

Again, the aggregate picture might hide underlying differences. Particularly in electronics and automotive manufacturing, automation has increased meaningfully since 2010, with vast deployment of industrial robots (Fig. 9.5). That said, in EMDE, automation and industrial robots are above all a story of China, which has made meaningful progress within little time. A notable feature of China's deployment of industrial robots is that these are increasingly made in China.[5] Furthermore, despite the mass deployment of industrial robots, employment in manufacturing of automobiles and electronics has steadily trended up in recent years in China, as it has globally.

In the end, automation has the potential to replace routine, repetitive tasks in labor-intensive industries. Instructive in this regard are the textile, apparel, and footwear industries, which have historically been an entry point into global manufacturing, requiring lots of unskilled, cheap labor. While these industries have certainly evolved, adopting laser cutting, automating knitting, and 3D printing of shoe soles, the bulk of manual work is in sewing, where automation challenges remain. Furthermore, by itself, the potential for automation is a necessary but not sufficient condition for it to actually happen. As long as there are few incentives for automation, it is unlikely to happen. With regard to the garment sector, incentives seem limited due to an abundance of cheap labor in EMDE, large investment requirements for automation, and concerns about skill shortages for new job profiles under an automated production approach. As such, for the time being, "today's factories typically resemble those of the early twentieth century with each worker operating a stand-alone sewing machine."[6]

For now, we conclude that there are important doubts about the future of the main development model of the past given widespread premature deindustrialization. That said, there are countries where the manufacturing-led and export-oriented growth model is still implemented successfully, supported by investment in solid infrastructure and a favorable investment climate. Furthermore, in some places, there is a moderate renaissance of manufacturing, which by itself though hardly provides the employment opportunities widely needed in EMDE. Lastly, we take some comfort from automation so far not having led to sizable job losses in manufacturing, and that this is unlikely to change in the near future amid a lack of incentives to deploy automation at much bigger scale.

Taken together, there are clear indications that the traditional manufacturing-led path to development is narrowing for most EMDEs. For investors, this has important implications. Investments related to the manufacturing sector need careful evaluations of structural risks. What is a company's growth potential in its market segment? Are there downside risks from the dominance of China, supply-chain recalibration, or automation? These questions arise everywhere, even in Emerging Asia, i.e., the region where manufacturing has flourished the most. Beyond sector-specific exposure, investments sensitive to overall economic dynamism, such as longer-term investments in financial institutions or sovereign debt, may be significantly influenced by the future course of the manufacturing sector. That said, for such investments, not least the question of whether there is an alternative engine of growth for many EMDEs is of critical importance. The next section explores whether services could play that role.

9.2 Is there a Services-Led Development Model?

As outlined earlier, with its high demand for unskilled labor and tradability, manufacturing seemed a natural fit for EMDE. For services, at least at first sight, the fit is less obvious. Particularly the perception of limited tradability ultimately poses a major constraint, capping demand by moderate domestic income levels. Furthermore, services are widely perceived as being comparably unproductive, suggesting that a services-led growth model would hardly allow EMDEs to narrow their income gaps with AEs.

Luckily, reality is more nuanced. Services are a very broad category, encompassing subsectors with vastly different characteristics, not least in terms of tradability, scalability, and innovation. At one end of the spectrum, there are services that meet widespread perceptions about low productivity and tradability, such as retail and personal services. A hairdresser, for instance, serves a local clientele and offers little potential for scaling and productivity gains.

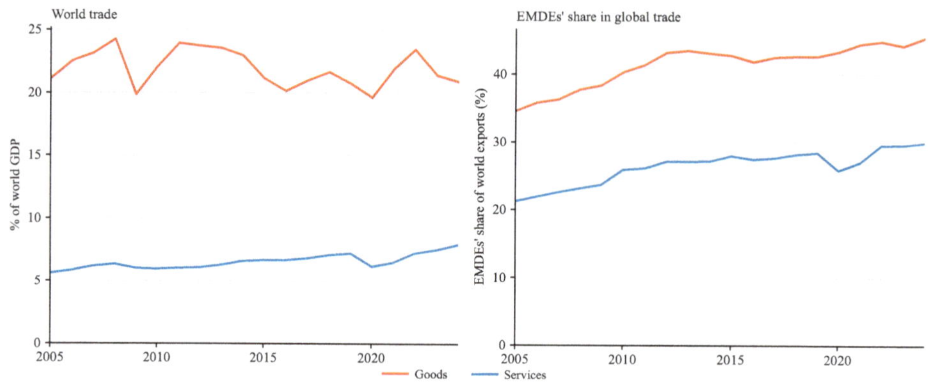

Fig. 9.6 World trade in goods and services. (*Sources: UNCTAD, the authors*)

At the other end of the spectrum is what the World Bank calls "Global Innovator Services", such as information and communication technology (ICT), finance, and professional services. These services are highly productive, skill-intensive, and tradable.

Between the two poles lie two other categories: First, low-skill tradable services such as transportation and accommodation might offer limited scope for innovation, but have significant employment potential and contribute positively to connectivity and tourism. Second, there are skill-intensive social services such as education and health, which are less tradable, but play a vital role in the development of human capital and in enabling people to perform more demanding and higher-productivity jobs.[7]

This typology of services highlights the diversity within this vast category. That services are not necessarily low productivity is also confirmed by the fact that over the past three decades, in many countries, productivity growth in services at least matched that of manufacturing, if it did not exceed it. Technological change such as digitalization and advances in information technology have transformed many services, making them increasingly tradable and scalable. Services have been a growing export business in recent decades, globally, and even more so in EMDEs, which were able to grow their share to 30% of global services trade as of late (Fig. 9.6).

Two countries and industries stand out as poster children of this development. One is India and its IT services, leveraging a large pool of skilled, English-speaking labor, significant cost advantages, and well-developed digital infrastructure. The other example is the Philippines and its business process outsourcing (BPO) industry, which started with voice-based call center operations and eventually upgraded into nonvoice procedures and back-office operations. Several factors supported this rise, including again a large pool of relatively well-educated and English-speaking labor, affordable telecommunications (thanks to early liberalization), and effective policies such as export processing zones and tax incentives.[8] In both countries, services exports now account for roughly 10% of GDP (as of 2024), underscoring the transformative role of technology in making services tradable.

There are success stories on other continents as well. Kenya has emerged as a digital services hub with a growing tech ecosystem, referred to as "Silicon Savannah". Meanwhile, Rwanda's digital transformation is a story in the making, the government's ambition to become a digital leader underpinned by sizable investment in ICT infrastructure, regulatory reforms, education and digital skills, as well as innovation hubs such as the Kigali Innovation City.[9] In Latin America, Costa Rica and its high-value IT and shared services stand out, with a strong education system, political stability, and early investment in digital infrastructure playing a critical role. Another example is Colombia and its growing BPO sector, which has benefited from government incentives and improvements in connectivity.[10]

The role of services though goes beyond their direct employment potential. Increasingly they play a role as enablers for other sectors, with, for instance, logistics, finance, and ICT services underpinning competitiveness in agriculture and manufacturing. One example is Ethiopia's cut flower industry, which tremendously benefited from improvements in transportation services. Still nascent in the late 1990s, the industry leveraged the country's fertile soil, cheap labor, and proximity to Europe, to generate 15% of Ethiopia's total export proceeds by 2022. There is also a trend toward "servicification", with manufacturing firms increasingly selling services and blurring the line between manufacturing and services. Some argue that the increased services intensity of manufacturers creates measurement issues that likely lead to an underestimation of the growth- and productivity-enhancing role of services.[11]

So is there potential in a services-led development model, stepping in to play the role the manufacturing-led model has played in the past? The answer seems "yes", not least thanks to technological change having made some services tradable and scalable. Global innovator services have shown their potential to generate export revenues, attract foreign investment, and drive innovation.[12] That said, for now, their scale is relatively limited in most EMDEs, accounting for only a small fraction of GDP and employment.

Moreover, the interconnectedness of services with agriculture and manufacturing implies that services-led growth does not entail abandoning other sectors. Rather, it is a more complex and integrated growth model where services play a central role.

To unlock the potential and the promise of a services-led growth model, EMDEs must overcome important structural impediments such as informality, skill gaps, and uneven access to technology. Countries that invest in digital infrastructure and human capital, and reduce regulatory barriers, are better positioned to grow high-value services and unlock services' full potential as a driver of growth.[13]

To assess countries and regions' readiness for the services-led growth model, UNCTAD's Productive Capacity Index (PCI) provides useful insights. The index builds on the assessment of productive resources, entrepreneurial capabilities, and production linkages, to determine countries' capacities to produce goods and services, and ultimately to grow and develop.[14] It distinguishes between eight categories, of which some are more relevant for the services-led development model than others. In particular, the accessibility and integration of communication systems as measured by the ICT component, human capital, institutions, and private sector development are most relevant for the Global Innovator Services, while the transport infrastructure and energy components matter for other tradable services like logistics and tourism. Of interest is also the structural change component, which strives to measure countries' ability to shift resources into higher-productivity activities.

Overall, PCI scores are heavily correlated with income levels, with higher incomes being associated with better scores, except for the endowment with natural resources (Fig. 9.7). The gap with high-income countries in many instances remains large, highlighting that the many demands of the services-led growth model might not yet be met by most EMDEs. There are exceptions though, with particularly China and Vietnam standing out, but also India and the Philippines doing comparatively well.

Another angle to look at countries' potential in services-led growth is to check how their services exports performed in the past. Looking at the size and growth dynamics of services exports, there are several countries that stand out, many of which are hardly present on global investors' portfolios. Some are primarily trade and logistics stories, notably Djibouti, Kyrgyzstan, and Panama, where transport and transit-related services dominate. Others are focused on tourism, such as Tunisia, and to a lesser extent Georgia, with travel exports over the past decade having driven both growth and volatility. Yet another group of countries show strength in financial and fintech-related services, including Ghana, while IT and other commercial services have driven services exports growth in Armenia and Serbia. There are several countries where multiple parts of services exports have thrived, with Georgia standing out, seeing tourism, transport, and higher-value commercial services grow (Fig. 9.8).

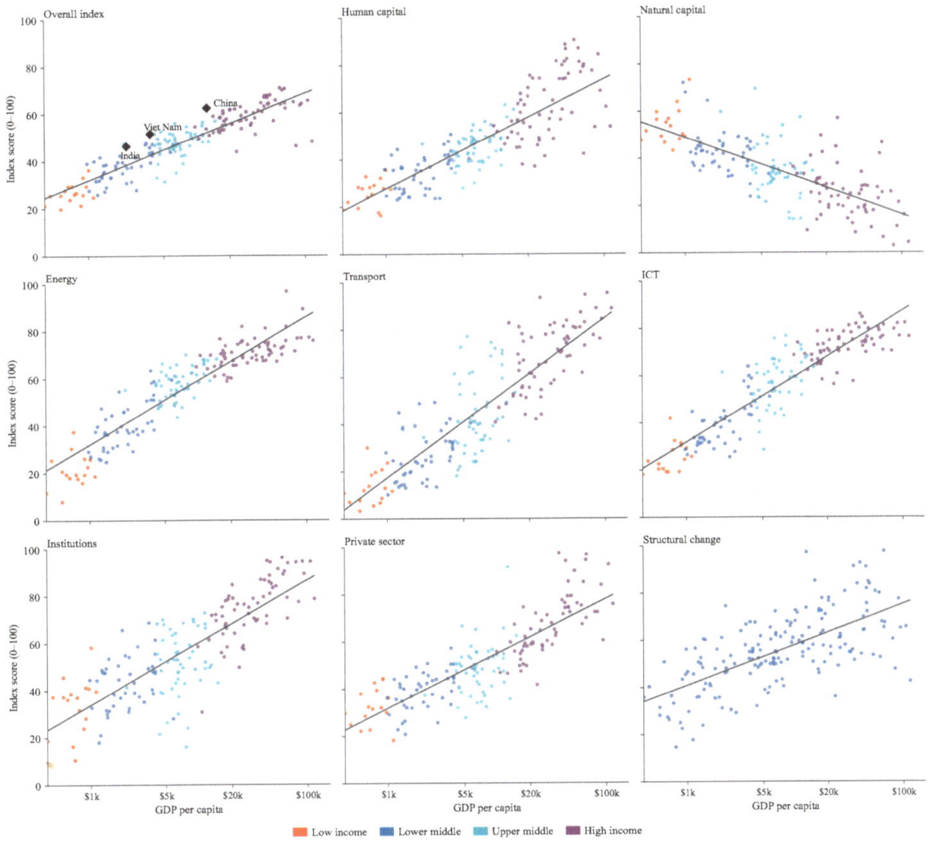

Fig. 9.7 UNCTAD Productive Capacities Index by income group, 2024. (*Source: UNCTAD*)

At the regional level, Emerging Asia is most advanced in exports of skill-intensive commercial services, whereas Africa's services exports remain predominantly related to lower value-added tourism and transport. Latin America sits in between, with commercial services having stagnated for most of the 2010s, and only since the pandemic regained some growth momentum.

In sum, we have learned that services are a very broad category, of which some are increasingly tradable and scalable, thanks to digitalization and advances in information technology. Global innovator services such as ICT, finance, and professional services have great appeal, but still mostly play a minor role in EMDEs. There are though important success stories, such as India's IT services and the Philippines business process outsourcing services. Furthermore, services are enablers of other sectors, implying that overall, countries' future success likely lies in a more complex and integrated growth model, in which services play a central role. Preconditions are strong digital

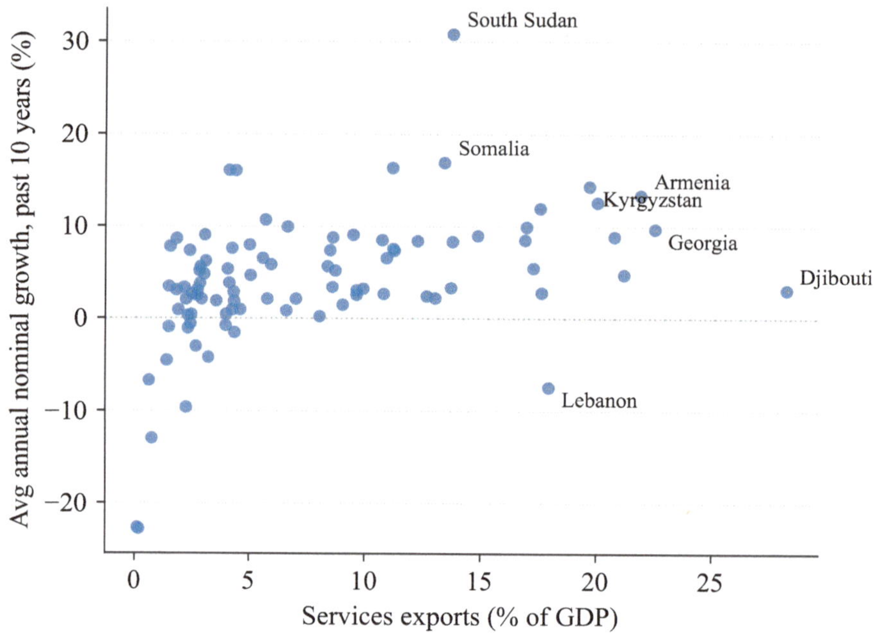

Fig. 9.8 Services exports (2024) and growth performance across countries. (Source: UNCTAD, the authors)

infrastructure and skills, with success though not being automatic, even in countries with seemingly favorable starting conditions. Latin America's stagnation of other commercial services is illustrative in this regard, with other regions having shown stronger services momentum in the 2010s despite seemingly worse digital infrastructure and skill. Furthermore, global innovator services' demand for infrastructure is ever increasing amid surging data volumes, requiring high-capacity, reliable, and affordable connectivity.

9.3 The Promise and Perils of AI

An important question is whether services sector's potential as a growth and export engine is affected by the rise of artificial intelligence (AI). This section addresses it, laying out what AI is and where its potential lies, to then analyze both how prepared (for adoption) and exposed EMDEs are to this technology, and to finally conclude with what AI possibly means for the potential of services exports going forward.

Ever since the launch of ChatGPT in 2022, AI has become a hot topic. Equity markets boomed, investment in data centers surged, and trade

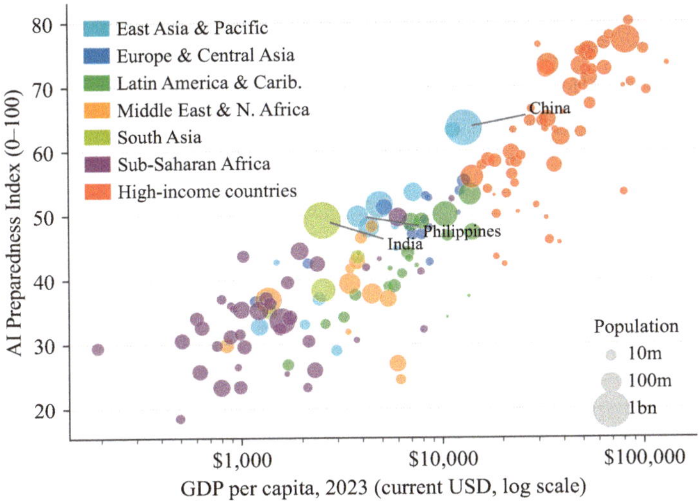

Fig. 9.9 AI preparedness and economic development, 2023. (*Sources: IMF, WB, the authors*)

tensions between the US and China escalated once more, not least accentuating in the field of advanced semiconductors needed to train and power large language models.

AI is widely considered a so-called general-purpose technology, i.e., a technology that fundamentally reshapes economies, as it can be embedded across many different industries, keeps improving, and enables many other innovations, thereby lifting productivity across the spectrum.[15] In recent years, the capabilities of AI have rapidly improved, with AI systems today surpassing human-level performance in many domains, including reading comprehension, image recognition, language understanding, handwriting recognition, and speech recognition.[16]

However, its diffusion and impact have been highly uneven, reflecting disparities in infrastructure, talent, and capital. With the exception of China, AI adaptation has mostly focused on AEs. That primarily AEs fulfill the prerequisites of AI, and that generally these factor endowments are above all a function of income levels, is well visible in the IMF's AI Preparedness Index, which builds on four dimensions: digital infrastructure, human capital and labor market policies, innovation and economic integration, and regulatory and ethical framework (Fig. 9.9).

EMDEs feature a combination of weaker AI readiness and lower occupational exposure to AI.[17] The latter comes through their occupational structures, with employment in areas that are less exposed to AI, such as agriculture, informal services, and low-skill manufacturing. Consequently, on the one hand, EMDEs are less exposed to short-term disruptions and job displacements due to AI than AEs, where clerical and professional roles play a more important role and are more exposed to AI.[18] On the other hand, EMDEs also risk missing out on the productivity gains that AI promises, thereby potentially widening income gaps and slowing convergence toward high-income countries.[19]

There is though some occupational exposure even in EMDE. When we previously touched on the services-led growth model, we highlighted the successes of India and the Philippines in services exports. However, it is exactly their tradeable services that face heightened exposure to AI-related automation risks.[20] Business process outsourcing and IT services involve tasks like customer support, coding, and document processing, which all are activities that generative AI can increasingly perform. AI hence risks eroding the comparative advantage of EMDEs in some tradeable services.[21]

That said, where there is a risk, there is often also an opportunity. Here, the opportunity lies in the early adoption and integration of AI into workflows, allowing these economies to move up the value chain by offering higher-value services. To capture this opportunity, countries, though, need to invest in skill and infrastructure.[22]

Yet other opportunities lie in "Small AI", i.e., context-specific, resource-light applications that address specific, local challenges. Unlike "Big AI", which works with massive datasets, high computing power, and sophisticated infrastructure, "Small AI" builds on minimal resources and the existing infrastructure to deliver practical solutions. There are already a number of promising applications in different sectors, from agriculture to health and education. In agriculture, there are several small AI tools that help farmers in several African countries with diagnosing crop diseases, estimating water needs, and providing hyper-local weather forecasts, all of which in the end boost farmers' output. In health care, small AI can help people where doctors are out of reach or where language barriers exist. Lastly, in education, small AI can bridge gaps, with AI tutoring systems extending personalized learning to remote areas, and generally making knowledge more accessible. Together, these examples illustrate that AI is a powerful technology for EMDEs as well, carrying the opportunity to boost output, human capital, and resilience.[23]

Taken together, we have learned that AI is a general-purpose technology, which is likely to reshape economies fundamentally. Its capabilities have been improving rapidly in the recent past and now surpass human-level performance in many domains. The diffusion and impact of AI will be uneven, with AEs generally better prepared, thanks to better digital infrastructure, skills, innovative capacity, and regulation. The lower occupational exposure of EMDEs to AI means on the one hand lesser risk of economic disruption, but on the other hand entails the risk of missing out on a productivity boost. Furthermore, also in EMDEs, some jobs might be affected, with AI threatening to erode EMDEs' comparative advantage in some tradable services. Meanwhile AI also poses opportunities for EMDEs, not least in the form of context-specific and resource-light applications in agriculture, health, and education.

9.4 Implications for Investors

The preceding analysis has shown that the traditional manufacturing-led growth model might have run its course, as showcased by the widespread phenomena of premature deindustrialization, of which Brazil and South Africa are pronounced examples. That said, there are countries, most notably in Asia, that even in the recent past managed to grow their manufacturing sectors, above all Vietnam, and ongoing geopolitical shifts and global supply chain recalibration might offer new opportunities, not least Vietnam, Mexico, and Poland. Further, there is potential in services, some of which have become more tradable and scalable thanks to digitalization and advancements in ICT. Services trade has steadily grown over the past two decades, with EMDEs capturing an increasingly large share. Poster children are India's IT services and the Philippines BPO industry. The emerging new growth model might less be a services-led one, but a more of an integrated one, with services increasingly interconnected with agriculture and manufacturing. Hence, there seems lots of potential that countries can tap into, but therefore need to invest in digital infrastructure and skills, among others. Lastly, AI might undermine some of EMDEs' comparative advantage in tradable services, with EMDEs, though, generally showing lesser occupational exposure to AI than AEs, which reduces both job displacement risks and economic opportunities.

The implications of technological change and shifting development models in EMDEs are manifold. For one, the implications certainly differ between debt and equity investors, as big shifts due to technological change usually take time.

Many EMDEs continue to benefit from demographic tailwinds, policy reforms, and incremental improvements in infrastructure. As a result, cash flows in established sectors should remain resilient in the near-term, especially where macroeconomic management is sound and where external vulnerabilities are contained, creating great appeal for debt investors.

Equity investors, on the other side, clearly need to worry about potentially larger, ongoing shifts. For them, the risk of disruption, due to automation, changing global value chains, and the rise of new technologies like AI, is more pronounced. It is the adaptability of companies and countries in the face of technological change that provides equity investors comfort.

What should investors look for? The experience of India and the Philippines in services exports is instructive, as in both cases, supportive policies and investment in (digital) infrastructure played a vital role in giving rise to large services export sectors. As such, countries with high policy effectiveness and credibility, and some basic infrastructure are certainly better placed to capitalize on rising economic opportunities.

When we look at the different sectors, manufacturing is heavily dominated by China. However, with rising labor costs and the country moving up the value chain, China above all seems to pose risks to manufacturing sectors in AEs, while there might be new opportunities arising for other EMDEs. Examples are Bangladesh and Cambodia, which have both found their place in garment production, building on their cost advantage. Also geopolitical tensions likely pose opportunities for manufacturing in some EMDEs, as outlined in Chap. 6, including Vietnam, Poland, and Mexico. What about the risk of automation? For now, we conclude that it is likely overstated, given a lack of incentives to actually implement automation in contexts of abundant cheap labor.

For services, the outlook seems more nuanced. On the one hand, technological change has made services more tradable and scalable. Countries with a combination of digital infrastructure, human capital, and sound policies are best positioned to capitalize on that change. On the other hand, the success stories of services exports suddenly look shaky in the context of rapidly evolving AI capabilities. The threat through AI underscores the need for ongoing investment in skills and digital infrastructure.

Ultimately, for debt and equity investors alike, the most attractive investment opportunities might arise in countries and sectors that combine foundational strengths in infrastructure, education, and policy effectiveness, together with adaptability to technological change.

Notes

1. Rodrik, D. & Sandhu, R. (2024) *Servicing Development: Productive Upgrading of Labor-Absorbing Services in Developing Economies.* NBER Working Paper 32738.

2. Rodrik, D. (2016) *Premature deindustrialization.* Journal of Economic Growth, 21(1), pp. 1–33.
3. World Bank (2024) *Vietnam 2045: Trading Up in a Changing World—Pathways to a High-Income Future.* Washington, DC: World Bank Group.
4. Kruse, I., Timmer, M.P. & de Vries, G.J. (2022) *A manufacturing renaissance? Industrialization in the developing world since 2000.* Journal of Economic Perspectives, 36(2), pp. 83–108.
5. International Federation of Robotics (2025) *World Robotics 2025 Report.* Frankfurt am Main: IFR. Available at: https://ifr.org/worldrobotics (Accessed: 30 November 2025).
6. Bárcia de Mattos, F., Eisenbraun, J., Kucera, D. & Rossi, A. (2021) 'Disruption in the apparel industry? Automation, employment and reshoring', International Labour Review, 160(4), pp. 521–538. © International Labour Organization.
7. Nayyar, G., Hallward-Driemeier, M. & Davies, E., 2021. *At Your Service? The Promise of Services-Led Development.* Washington, DC: World Bank.
8. World Bank & WTO (2023). Trade in Services for Development: Fostering Sustainable Growth and Economic Diversification. Geneva: WTO; Washington, DC: World Bank.
9. World Bank. (2024). *Pathways to Sustainable and Inclusive Growth in Rwanda: Country Economic Memorandum.* Washington, DC: World Bank.
10. Rodrik, D. & Sandhu, R. (2024); World Bank & WTO (2023).
11. See Bárcia de Mattos et al. (2021).
12. Nayyar et al. (2021).
13. World Bank & WTO (2023).
14. UNCTAD (2020) *UNCTAD Productive Capacities Index: Focus on Landlocked Developing Countries.* Geneva: United Nations Conference on Trade and Development.
15. OECD (2025) *Is generative AI a general-purpose technology? Implications for productivity and policy.* OECD Artificial Intelligence Papers, No. 40, OECD Publishing, Paris.
16. Kiela, D., Thrush, T., Ethayarajh, K. & Singh, A. (2023) 'Plotting Progress in AI', Contextual AI Blog, 31 July. Available at: https://contextual.ai/blog/plotting-progress-in-ai (Accessed: 13 December 2025).
17. International Monetary Fund (2024) *Gen-AI: Artificial Intelligence and the Future of Work.* IMF Staff Discussion Note. Washington, D.C.: International Monetary Fund.
18. Demombynes, G., Langbein, J. and Weber, M. (2025) *The Exposure of Workers to Artificial Intelligence in Low- and Middle-Income Countries.* Policy Research Working Paper 11,057. Washington, D.C.: World Bank.
19. International Monetary Fund (2025) *The Global Impact of AI: Mind the Gap.* IMF Working Paper. Washington, D.C.: International Monetary Fund.
20. International Monetary Fund (2024).

21. Citi (2025) *Is Generative AI Impacting Services Offshoring in India and the Philippines?* Citi Global Perspectives & Solutions Report. New York: Citigroup.
22. Demombynes et al. (2025).
23. World Bank (2025) *Small AI, Big Impact: Harnessing Artificial Intelligence for Development.* Available at: https://blogs.worldbank.org/en/voices/small-ai-big-impact-harnessing-artificial-intelligence-for-development (Accessed: 14 December 2025).

10

A View of the Future

He who lives by the crystal ball will eat shattered glass.
Paraphrase of themes of Ray Dalio.

For over three decades, the global environment has been quite supportive to EMDEs. This period has been characterized by deepening trade integration and facilitated by technological advancements in ICT and transportation. Ever since the fall of the Berlin wall, there was no longer a disruptive geopolitical rivalry, and the US played the policeman safeguarding the rule-based order. Outside sub-Saharan Africa (SSA), demographic pressures moderated, and large parts of the population were active. Climate change did not yet cause that many interruptions, but was widely recognized, with collective efforts striving to reduce global emissions.

Clearly, the world has been changing in recent years.

Globalization has stalled since the Global Financial Crisis, and free trade is no longer the ruling dogma of our time. The impact of climate change is increasingly felt, while collective efforts have failed to keep the world on a +1.5 °C path. Meanwhile, geopolitical rivalry resurfaced, and tensions escalated, with Russia emerging as a pariah state. Lastly, the rapid advancements and spread of AI have given rise to speculation about how this general-purpose technology will change the world.

While these topics have been around for some time, their importance in economic life has risen in the recent past. Furthermore, in the view of the authors, it is the interaction between these forceful trends that makes the current juncture a decisive one. Clearly, some countries are better positioned to

R. Marney, P. Waeber, *The Emerging Markets Investor's Guide to Country Risk*,
https://doi.org/10.1007/978-3-032-26824-2_10

benefit, partially by luck, but also importantly by their institutional capabilities helping them to translate risks into opportunities.

The previous four chapters examined these changes and trends, striving to assess what they mean for EMDEs' future path. After having analyzed them individually, the aim of this chapter is to assess them collectively, by looking at the different regions. While such a high-level view provides valuable insights, for investors, it does certainly not replace a more detailed assessment on an investment level.

10.1 Emerging and Developing Asia

Emerging and Developing Asia has been the rising star of the global economy over recent decades. Its share of global output, measured in purchasing-power parity terms, increased from roughly 12% in 1990 to 35% in 2025. China accounts for a large part of this shift, its weight increasing from 4% to 20% over the same period. But many other economies in the region performed relatively well too.

Looking ahead, the region faces a less supportive external environment. Tailwinds that supported its rise—notably strong population growth and deepening globalization that supported manufacturing-led development—are weakening. While globalization has likely passed its peak, the region remains very competitive and has continued to gain market share in global merchandise and services exports. Solid productive capacities in large economies such as China, Vietnam, India, and the Philippines position the region well to seize further opportunities, including in tradeable services.

Asia though is far from homogeneous, with risks varying substantially between countries.

Geopolitics represent a major fault line. For China, its rivalry with the US poses an important headwind to its growth potential in sectors of strategic importance. For other countries in the region, this rivalry creates opportunities, with trade diversion for instance already having benefited Vietnam in recent years. That said, it is a delicate balancing act that countries in the region need to perform, particularly vis-à-vis the US, which closely monitors transshipments. In particular, countries must avoid being seen as a transit point for Chinese products to avoid US tariffs.

Climate change constitutes another major source of risk, with the frequency and severity of natural disasters set to increase further. Recent experience illustrates the scale of potential disruptions, examples ranging from severe droughts in Vietnam (causing electricity shortages) to cyclones and heavy rains causing floodings and landslides in Pakistan and Sri Lanka. Arguably the most climate-vulnerable country in the region, and one of the most vulnerable globally, is Bangladesh, with sea-level rise and heavy rains risk causing major floodings.

Not only risks but also the capacity to deal effectively with these risks varies across countries. The largest economies in the region display decent coping capacity, featuring a combination of solid institutions and fiscal space. China and India furthermore feature an attribute that is rare in EMDEs: they have a large pool of domestic savings, limiting their reliance on foreign funding. However, there are also weak spots and vulnerabilities. In particular, public debt sustainability is under strain in countries such as Pakistan and Sri Lanka (even after the recent sovereign debt restructuring), while private-sector leverage is elevated in China, Vietnam, and Thailand.

Asia is therefore neither risk-free nor homogeneous but will most likely continue increasing its weight in the global economy over the coming decade, thereby offering important investment opportunities to international investors.

10.2 Eastern Europe and Central Asia

While initially struggling after the collapse of the Soviet Union, Eastern Europe, the Caucasus, and Central Asia (EECCA) have seen rapid improvements in living conditions over the past two decades. Eastern Europe in particular had some manufacturing success stories, with parts of the region becoming closely integrated into Western European supply chains. Furthermore, the ambition of joining the EU has provided a strong policy anchor and led to widespread institutional improvements. Meanwhile, the Caucasus and Central Asia have boomed in recent years, ever since Russia's assault on Ukraine triggered inflows of migrants and capital, alongside a surge in trade.

With respect to the risks outlined in earlier chapters, EECCA stands out as the EMDE region with the highest geopolitical risk. Russia is likely to continue exploiting opportunities to exacerbate internal divisions in Europe and to cause occasional operational disruptions. For countries in the Caucasus and Central Asia, Western sanctions against Russia have created risks of secondary sanctions. For some countries, orienting themselves toward the West has strained relations with Russia, most notably Georgia and Armenia. Also there, Russia will likely continue to interfere in democratic election processes, to influence outcomes in its favor. Elevated geopolitical risk is likely to weigh on investment spending and thereby constrain the region's growth potential.

For most countries, particularly in Eastern Europe, the growth potential is also constrained by adverse demographics. Despite rising income levels, emigration has remained high, especially among younger cohorts. Over the coming decade, with the exception of Central Asia, the working-age population is expected to decline across most countries, which will weigh on economies' production capacity.

Shifts in global supply chains toward greater resilience and near-shoring offer some upside potential for manufacturing in Eastern Europe, which generally benefits from decent infrastructure. At the same time, a number of countries are increasingly exporting services, with notable success stories including Poland's business process outsourcing industry and emerging ICT sectors in the Caucasus. Overall, Eastern Europe is better positioned than Central Asia in terms of productive capacities and AI preparedness, although like other EMDE regions it remains some distance to the global frontier.

Lastly, in terms of climate change, EECCA is the least affected EMDE region overall. Nevertheless, there are also risks there, not least stemming from heatwaves, droughts, and localized floodings.

A key factor that mitigates risks is comparably good institutions and some fiscal space, translating into better coping capacity which ultimately enhances resilience.

10.3 Latin America

If there is one region that has so far been notably absent in this book, it is Latin America. For much of the post-war period, it was the EMDE region with the highest per capita income, despite a lost decade in the 1980s. Then, in the early 2010s, it was overtaken by East Asia, and soon Eastern Europe and Central Asia (excl. High-income countries) might follow. Latin America's growth performance since the 1950s has been quite poor, despite a comparably good starting position, reflecting at least in parts the limited success of the region's dominant development models from the 1950s to 1970s, notably import-substituting industrialization and state-led development.

The region has been largely absent from earlier chapters because it does not score particularly high or low across the dimensions covered in this book. The highest risk to the region comes from climate change, with vulnerabilities varying greatly between countries. Central America is highly exposed to droughts and water stress, and so are parts of South America, where additionally irregular rainfall will cause challenges. Climate change will above all affect agricultural production, reduce the reliability of hydropower generation, and periodically disrupt transport infrastructure. The Caribbean in turn faces an increasing threat from hurricanes, which through climate change are expected to become stronger. It is a risk exemplified by Hurricane Melissa that hit Jamaica in late October 2025 and caused enormous damage, the reconstruction effort alone potentially costing up to 40% of GDP.

The US capture of Venezuelan President Nicolas Maduro in January 2026 has brought geopolitical risks to the fore. It emphasized the US' ambition to keep the western hemisphere "free of hostile foreign incursions" and showcased that the current administration in the US shies back neither from using military force nor from violating international laws. Going forward, there is less of a risk of direct military confrontation, but of US actions amplifying domestic political risks. Trump's interference in Honduras' presidential elections in late 2025 is exemplary in this regard, threatening to cut US aid if his favorite candidate did not win, further suggesting that Honduran election officials tried to rig the election. Similarly, Brazil suffered important US import tariffs in response to what Trump called a "witch hunt" against former president Bolsonaro, while effectively Brazil's judiciary was prosecuting Bolsonaro for an alleged coup attempt. In the near-term, the risk of such US interference is likely to be highest in Latin American countries with left-leaning or non-aligned governments that do only moderate effort to curb drug trafficking and illegal migration.

While Latin America has suffered from premature deindustrialization in the past, the ongoing recalibration of global supply chains will offer some opportunities, particularly for Mexico. Beyond manufacturing, there have been some success stories in services exports, ranging from IT, shared services, and business process outsourcing, with countries such as Costa Rica and Colombia standing out. The region offers decent infrastructure and has seen a vibrant digital economy expanding vastly. Several countries score reasonably well in terms of AI preparedness, suggesting that the region could benefit to some extent from this new technology.

The demographic transition is largely complete. Going forward, demographic pressures will be rather contained, with the working-age population growth further slowing on a relatively low level, and the working-age population peaking in the late 2030s or early 2040s. Country profiles, though, differ meaningfully, with Brazil, Chile, and Costa Rica barely seeing their working-age population grow over the coming decade, while parts of Central America continue to experience demographic pressure which may translate into continued migration pressures in the absence of sufficient job creation.

Institutional quality and fiscal buffers vary substantially across the region. Corruption remains a widespread issue and has contributed to an erosion of popular trust in public institutions. Political fragmentation has increased, at times translating into governability challenges. Taken together, these factors weigh on the region's adaptive capacity and risk hindering some economies from capture opportunities and others from addressing emerging risks from a changing world effectively.

10.4 Middle East and North Africa

The Middle East and North Africa (MENA) is a very heterogeneous region. Given the focus of this book, the analysis excludes high-income countries, including the hydrocarbon-rich Gulf states as well as Israel. Instead, the focus is on the low- and middle-income countries of the region, whose growth performance in recent decades has been quite constrained. About half of the countries in the region are officially labeled as countries in fragile and conflict-affected situations (FCS), where instability and weak institutions are hindering development. The Arab Spring marked a defining moment in the recent past, but in many instances ultimately failed to yield lasting improvements in governance and living conditions.

To the authors, MENA is the region with the highest geopolitical risks, with the region featuring protracted conflicts, regional rivalries, and an involvement of external powers. In the past, escalations have repeatedly caused operational disruptions and protracted security concerns posing risks to tourism and inducing a rerouting of global maritime trade. Also climate change poses a major threat to the region. Much of the region already suffers from severe water scarcity, with global warming increasing water stress.

Demographics yet add another layer of risk. Population growth remains relatively strong across the region, but countries struggle to create sufficient employment opportunities for the young. Economies are mostly import-dependent and lack major export industries, Morocco being the major, positive exception.

Finally, weak institutions and strained fiscal positions constrain the region's adaptive capacity, which amplifies vulnerabilities to adverse external and domestic developments. Taken together, non-high income MENA features a combination of high risks and low coping capacity. As such, the region will hardly perform better than in the past going forward.

10.5 Sub-Saharan Africa

Sub-Saharan Africa remains the poorest region globally. Its catch-up process has been uneven, with lost decades in the 1980s and 1990s, a boom on the back of a commodity super-cycle in the 2000s, and treading water over the last ten years (2016–2025). Internal conflicts and divisions paired with weak governance have held the region back. The region failed to capitalize on opportunities offered by globalization. Parts of its industrial base have even suffered from premature deindustrialization as economies opened up to foreign trade. The reliance on commodity exports further constrained development, with many countries suffering from the Dutch disease and the resource curse.

Prospects for a material improvement remain limited. As discussed in Chap. 8, much of Africa—with a few exceptions in northern and southern parts—faces a "youthquake". Continuously high fertility rates translate into substantial population growth. Year after year, many young people will enter the labor market. As such, the continent will desperately need to create employment opportunities, to avoid rising unemployment and social tensions.

Worst positioned to deliver on that need are countries in fragile and conflict-affected situations (FCS), as instability and weak institutions hinder development. The 2025 list of FCS featured 20 countries in SSA, which are home to close to 60% of the region's population. In several of these countries, Russia has rapidly expanded its presence over the past decade, often exchanging regime protection against access to natural resources, thereby entrenching existing fragilities.

Climate change adds another burden. Sub-Saharan Africa is the most vulnerable region to climate change globally, featuring a combination of high vulnerability and lower adaptive capacity. The vulnerability stems from frequent droughts and heat stress, alongside a reliance on rain-fed agriculture.

While the region has seen a modest manufacturing revival since 2000, the sector mostly serves domestic demand for basic goods, rather than external demand. With Asian economies remaining highly competitive, and global supply chains increasingly focused on resilience, it is doubtful that sub-Saharan Africa will see a manufacturing miracle in the foreseeable future. Productive capacities also remain weak, constraining the expansion of services exports beyond low-skill tradable services such as transport and accommodation.

Overall, sub-Saharan Africa faces substantial structural challenges. At the same time, the region's coping capacity remains rather limited, with many countries featuring a combination of weak institutions and limited fiscal space.

10.6 Closing Remarks

The regional summaries provided very high-level views while acknowledging intra-region differences. The chart below summarizes the shared views (Fig. 10.1).

Looking ahead, the "great convergence" is likely passé, with paths of EMDEs again showing divergence. Shocks and setbacks are going to become more frequent, with risks reinforcing each other. Institutional strength will determine how well countries will navigate these choppy waters.

When analyzing a particular investment, the analysis must go deeper. Countries are not uniformly affected by certain trends. Particularly the impact of climate change might vary importantly across regions within a country, especially in larger countries. And even there, the micro location might still matter, on whether a company's assets and operations are exposed, for example, to flooding risks. Other risks vary substantially between sectors. As part of geopolitical risks, state-sponsored cyberattacks, for instance, are more likely

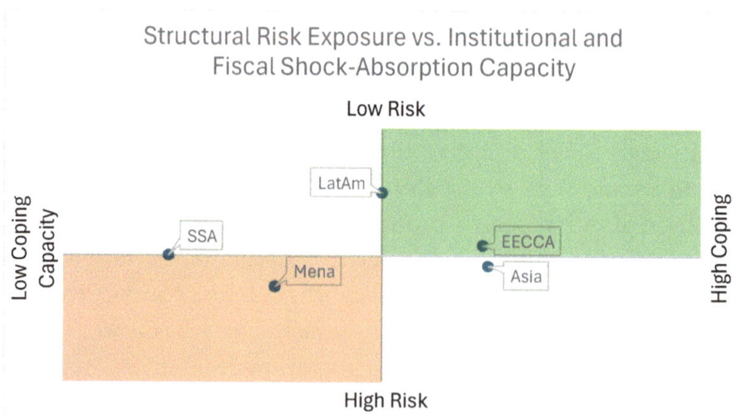

Fig. 10.1 Structural risk exposure and shock-absorption capacity across regions. (Source: The authors)

to hit industries like energy, finance, and communications. Similarly, risks and opportunities from technological change vary by sectors (and countries).

Ultimately, for debt and equity investors alike, the most attractive investment opportunities will likely arise in countries and sectors that combine muted exposure to risks with strong institutions.

Part III

Investor's Rutter

Sailing by Richard Marney

11

The Investor's Rutter

You cannot direct the wind, but you can adjust your sails.
Anonymous.

11.1 From the Investment Climate to the Investor's Rutter

In Chap. 5, we used the concept of the "investment climate" to offer a simplified structure and flow diagram depicting the country risk drivers influencing economic and ultimately investment performance. From the bottom up, the drivers were:

(i) Endowment

A country's climate, natural capital, and other fundamental characteristics, such as population and demography

(ii) Enablers

The institutional framework of a country that shapes the rules by which social, political, legal, commercial, and financial interactions play out

(iii) Context

Supported by these institutions, the structure of a country's markets and macroeconomy and how they perform

R. Marney, P. Waeber, *The Emerging Markets Investor's Guide to Country Risk*,
https://doi.org/10.1007/978-3-032-26824-2_11

In the same chapter, we placed the investment climate into a simplified investment underwriting process to depict how country risk factors interact with:

(i) global markets (i.e., capital, FX, trade, etc.)
(ii) economic sector/industry or business group of the investment (e.g., mining, agribusiness, telecom, etc.)
(iii) financial condition, operational performance and business outlook of the investee
(iv) structure of the investment (i.e., place in the capital structure, and transaction terms and conditions)

to arrive at an investment underwriting decision. Our portrayal of the investment climate was predominantly static in nature, with a limited focus on process.

Now we move from the static investment climate presentation to a dynamic, process-focused approach, which we call the "Investor's Rutter". This general approach is inspired by R. Marney and T. Stubbs 2021, *Corporate Debt Restructuring in the Emerging Markets* (Palgrave Macmillan).

Below appears (Fig. 11.1) depicting the progression from the Investment Climate to the Investor's Rutter:

Keep this diagram of the transition from the Investment Climate to Investor's Rutter in mind.

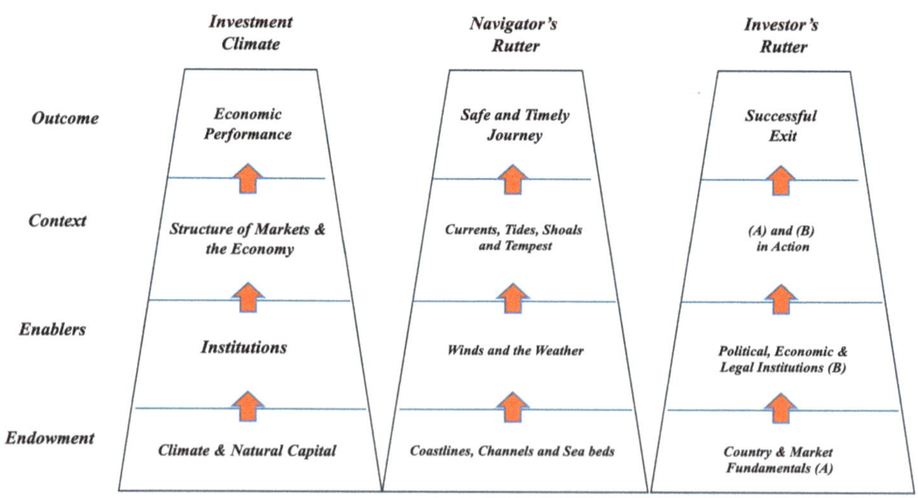

Fig. 11.1 Transition from investment climate to the Investor's Rutter. (*Source: The authors*)

11.2 The Investor's Rutter

Box 1 - The Investor's Rutter and Four Authors

Sources:

Acemoglu, D. and Robinson, J.A., 2012. *Why nations fail: The origins of power, prosperity and poverty*. New York: Crown Business.

Frey, C.B., 2019. *How progress ends: Technology, innovation, and the fate of nations*. Princeton, NJ: Princeton University Press

Norberg, J., 2023. *Peak human: What we can learn from the rise and fall of golden ages*. London: Atlantic Books.

Smil, V., 2021. *Grand transitions: How the modern world was made*. Oxford: Oxford University Press

Background

Readers will recall (at least from the history books) that before the modern era with GPS, accurate maps, instant communications, and the like, safety on the seas depended on the navigator's experiences, personal notes, and drawings. These handwritten materials codified his knowledge and the collective memory drawn from other pilots on how to navigate specific, often treacherous, coastlines, and described directions, landmarks, coastal profiles, timing of tides, trajectory and strength of currents, depth soundings, harbors, and various other hazards. Their value was not purely descriptive. Their paramount importance was to depict process—how to get there, where to turn, what to avoid, when to travel or not given seasonal tempests, where to berth and provision. These notes and drawings were contained in a "rutter". The word was drawn from the French, "routier" or route, and entered the lexicon in the fourteenth to fifteenth century, as the Age of Discovery dawned. Often, rutter and rudder are confused, but are relevance for each other. The latter refers to the flat, movable surface used to steer a vessel. The best way to think of the rutter, as described above and used throughout this book, is a kind of intellectual rudder.

Marney and Stubbs applied the concept to debt restructurings. This chosen approach reflected the reality that by their nature, restructurings don't conform to an Ikea-like guide to assembling a dresser for your child's bedroom. Instead, the constituent parts of every workout are different. To provide relevant and actionable advice, the authors focused on the "process" (think: the mariner's journey), and they populated this "restructuring rutter" with a set of principles and mileposts, touching on workout structure, order, and timing prerequisites, spiced with observations on negotiator personality traits, legal and documentary challenges, major transaction pitfalls, and the like (think: distances, geography, sea characteristics, climate, etc.).

For our purposes here, we employ the concept of an "Investor's Rutter". The objective is to share our compiled, practical knowledge on how to navigate country risks to arrive at a satisfactory return outcome.

Imagine in a hypothetical case of the Republic of Oceania a globally known brand of organic, heathy snack foods looks to establish a manufacturing plant and develop a wholesale distribution network. An investor needs to understand and incorporate into their investment decision-making realistic views of the capacity of local institutions to ensure the fulfillment of the legal actions to support and protect branding, and the organic certifications central to their business. These will include strong patent law, an effective judiciary, and stable policy making. As the plant will be dependent on reliable power, water, and transportation infrastructure, there must be confidence that the government's public finances are sound. Lastly, the investor must be able to rely on the government to honor agreements on taxes and import regulations.

The definitions of each are simple and clear, the descriptive data or evidence (formal or anecdotal) usually easy enough to collect, and basic interactions intuitive in many cases. What is lacking is the overlay that distinguished the rutter as an essential tool of navigation—the linking of definitions, descriptions, and basic interactions into a useful methodological (process) guide that translates into effective transaction selection, analysis, structuring, monitoring, and when necessary "reworking" (restructuring and/or recapitalization). As noted above, for our potential investor in Oceania, the local government's fulfillment of commitments to develop port and roadway infrastructure, and to adhere to negotiated tax incentives is essential to the underlying investment thesis, as is access to an efficient, transparent, and unbiased judicial system to ensure contract enforcement.

The Investment Rutter aims to assist in the investment analysis by helping navigate through these issues, which include a view of the questions:

(i) Does the government have sufficient resources and the policy continuity to see the infrastructure build to its end?
(ii) Given politics in the country, how resilient are the tax incentives in the event of a change in administration or policy priorities?
(iii) How secure is the ability of a foreign litigant to enforce their rights in the local courts and within a reasonable period of time?

Does the investment's viability survive the failure of one or more of these requirements? Are there other actions/structural elements that can be introduced to mitigate these risks? Let's assume that the evaluation and identification of mitigates exercise adequately addresses the risks and the investment proceeds. The journey is not yet over. The same (and arguably a larger analytic) exercise is maintained until the successful exit is achieved. The investor's rutter aims at taking us through to this point, the successful return to port. In the next section, keep the Oceania example in mind.

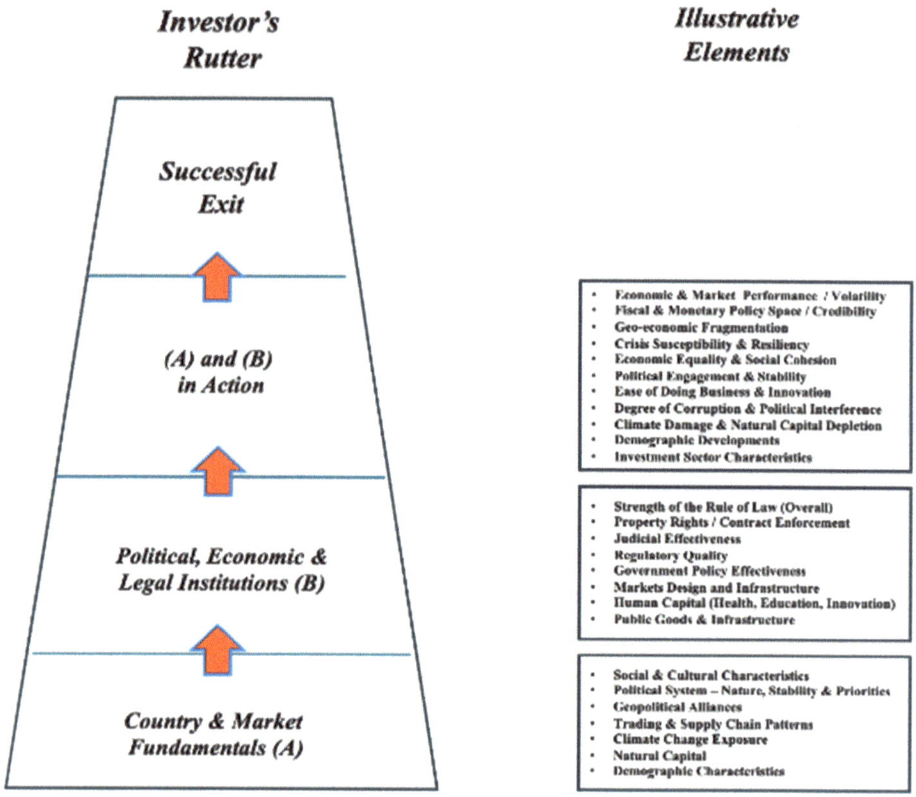

Fig. 11.2 Investor's Rutter: illustrative elements. (*Source: The authors*)

How the Rutter Operates

How does the Rutter operate? Consider the following graphic (Fig. 11.2):

At its base, we expand the concept of "Endowment" from the Investment Climate Roadmap to encompass a wider range of "Country & Market Fundamentals". These foundational elements—*the playing field—include* social and cultural characteristics, the political system—nature, stability and priorities, geopolitics, trading and supply chain patterns, in addition to the elements of the investment climate. Resting on this base are the "Political, Economic and Legal Institutions", the country's institutional framework—*the rules of the game*. The Illustrative Elements are a selection that mirrors those in the Investment Climate Roadmap. On the next level, "In Action", we focus on how the identified country fundamentals and institutions translate into action in the social, political, economic, and legal arenas—how *the game plays out on the pitch*. These also mirror the Investment Climate Roadmap.

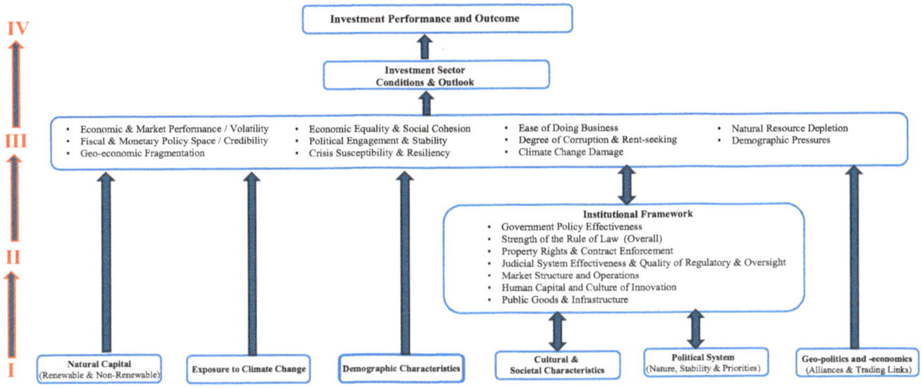

Fig. 11.3 Investor's Rutter Mind Map (IRMM). (*Source: The authors*)

A key point, already noted but worthy of repetition (again), is that the Rutter is about process, a flow. Consider the following "Mind Map" (Fig. 11.3):

This is intentionally over-simplified to emphasize the flow of the three levels. A more complete picture would include the other elements of the investment underwriting process, not to mention the entire post-approval to exit lifespan of the investment. We will include these elements in the discussion below in this chapter, as well as in detailed case studies in Part IV.

11.3 Illustrative Cases

To demonstrate how the Investor's Rutter operates in practice, we present three high-level cases—a white goods manufacturer/distributor, a fruit producer/exporter, and a telecom equipment final assembly company. For each, we present an upside and downside alternative as proxies for a stronger and weaker country situation (see Fig. 11.4–11.9 below). The cases are stripped-down to focus on country and market risks and exclude transaction structure, detailed economics, investor/investee backgrounds, etc., as well as their lifespan post disbursement through their retirement.

- Case 1: White Goods Production and Sales

Upside

Assume a middle-income country in the "demographic dividend" phase, with a cohesive and stable social and political environment. Institutional development in the country is well advanced for its peer group, reflecting the

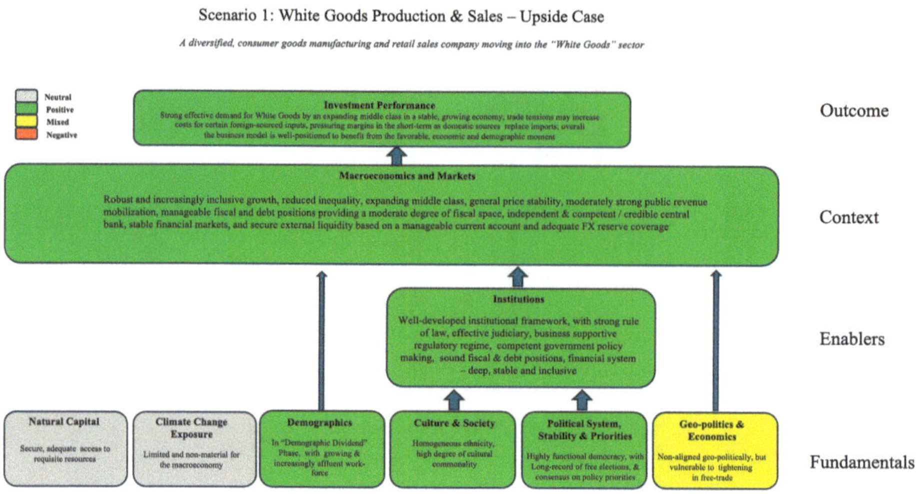

Fig. 11.4 Scenario 1 upside case (IRMM)

political class' commitment to supporting a sustainable economic trajectory. The economy's performance is characterized by solid, balanced, and inclusive growth. Income and wealth inequality has declined, and employment and returns to labor have increased. The country's middle class has expanded in this positive macroeconomic climate.

In response to a rise in effective demand on the part of increasingly affluent households for modern, energy-efficient white goods, a diversified domestic consumer goods manufacturer and retail sales company decide to expand into the white goods segment and begin to explore funding sources. The decision is taken to establish a contractual arrangement with a leading foreign manufacturer to produce and distribute their products under license. External funding will be in the form of debt to complement a rights issue by the existing shareholders. The obvious question arises: how will foreign debt investors view this new market for the company, the relevant country risk considerations, and their impact on the viability of the investment?

An in-depth analysis is undertaken by the potential external debt provider. The results are (Fig. 11.4):

The outcome of the analysis is positive. Strong country, foundational elements, supportive institutions, and constructive economic and market characteristics reinforce the view that the business opportunity is real. The only material risk, albeit moderate in nature, is a tightening global trading environment that could affect imported component costs and weigh on economic activity.

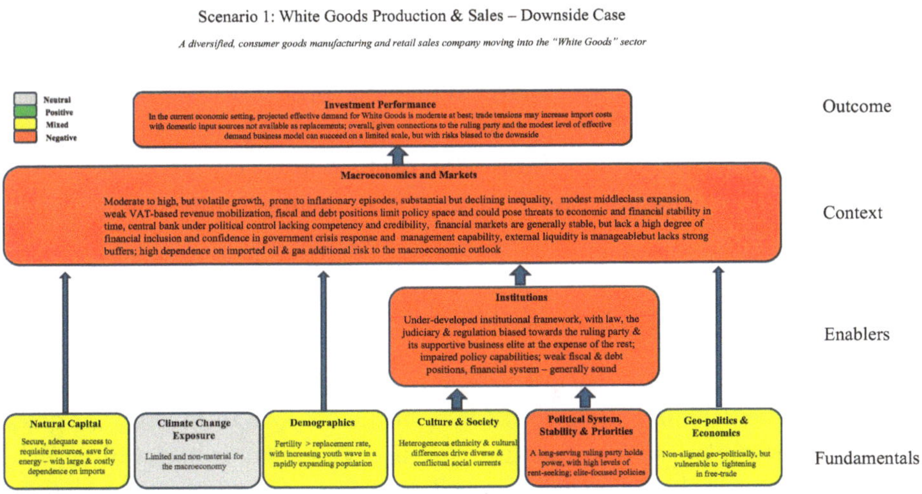

Fig. 11.5 Scenario 1 downside case (IRMM)

Downside

This second country is a low-middle-income sovereign and confronts a challenging and uncertain future. The institutional framework is underdeveloped and provides a weak base for sustainable and balanced economic growth over the longer term. An increasingly unpopular single party regime has used government for self-enrichment, which has discouraged private investment, save for pet projects of the regime, through the failure to: (i) design/implement coherent policy; (ii) respect the rule of law/regulation; and (iii) control pervasive corruption. In this crony-capital economy, growth has been high, yet volatile, with most domestic and external macroeconomic metrics in the fair to poor range. There is a modest yet expanding middle class. A local consumer goods manufacturing and sales company with strong connections to the government is considering the establishment of a white goods production and sales division and has approached the same foreign company to negotiate a licensing agreement as in the upside case (above). A similar set of discussions have been conducted with external debt providers. The local company has indicated that the government is prepared to provide generous tax and other forms of support to the new venture. How does foreign debt investor view the country risk? (Fig. 11.5).

The outcome of the evaluation is not positive. The proffered government support compensates in part for the marginal demand outlook, and while not as compelling an investment profile as in the other country case, the projected returns do exceed the minimum corporate return hurdle. Despite this return green light, the foreign lender declines the opportunity. Their decision reflects unease with the reliance on the current political regime and the ties of the local partner with these politicians. While the probability-adjusted risk of immediate regime change and possible financial backlash from a new government is deemed low, it is not zero. Moreover, serious concerns were voiced about potential reputation damage arising from being connected, even indirectly, to a deeply unpopular and undemocratic regime.

- Case 2: Fruit Production and Export

Upside

This Southern Hemisphere country is on the cusp of an investment grade rating. While the population is ethnically diverse, society is harmonious. The political system is characterized as a well-functioning, representative democracy with a generalized consensus among the parties on most significant policy issues. The institutional framework is advanced, with a strong rule of law, a highly efficient judicial system, and an effective regulatory regime. Infrastructure development—ports, roads, water distribution, electricity generation and distribution, etc.—has been a long-standing public priority and is well placed to support economic activity. The country's domestic and external macroeconomic metrics depict a positive trajectory. The risk-outlook is stable.

The country is a major exporter of fruits into the winter market in the Northern Hemisphere. An investor is considering a large-ticket, long-term subordinated debt investment in one of the leading producers and exporting companies (Fig. 11.6).

The country-level analysis undertaken by the prospective investor resulted in a very positive rating. The one risk identified relates to flooding. Historically, given the country's extensive river network and topography, there have been episodes of floods. With recent changes in rain patterns, believed to be the result of global warming, the incidence of such episodes has risen. As a precaution for the future, the government has been supporting a portfolio of investments to conserve water, manage extremes, protect ecosystems, empower citizens with data, and create flexible economic systems. Given the government's proactive policy stance, the actual economic damage from flooding has been moderate.

Downside

The country, enterprise, and transaction details of this case are broadly identical with the upside alternative (above) save for the topic of water

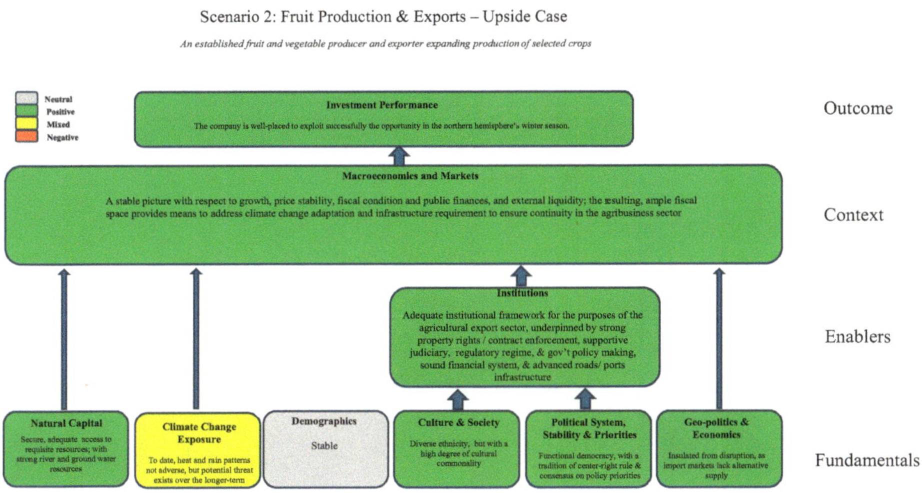

Fig. 11.6 Scenario 2 upside case (IRMM)

security. The country is more exposed to climate change's impact on rain patterns. Given its location and topography, the country has already begun to experience enormous volatility in precipitation patterns, with several years of lower rainfall volumes, even drought-like conditions, followed by excessive precipitation and flooding. Their natural water resources are materially weaker. There is only one significant river, which the country shares with a neighbor, and water levels have been declining during the country's distinct dry season. Drought has been a reoccurring problem in sections of the country. Agriculture is highly dependent on rain-fed water supplies in local reservoirs. Government investments can only mitigate the impact to a limited degree, and market participants recognize that further mitigation measures fall to individual companies. A similar investment is under consideration (Fig. 11.7).

The investor's risk analysis identified the two extremes: too much and too little water depending on the year as a medium-to-high threat to the business. Increased investments in water rights, development of drought-resistant crop varieties, strengthened post-harvest loss reduction measures, and the like were identified as necessary. The incorporation of the combination of the cost of these investments and the potential for lower crop yields pointed to the need for increased equity in the business. As a result, the financial leverage covenant was lowered, with the shareholders agreeing to invest new common equity capital to complement the subordinated debt issue.

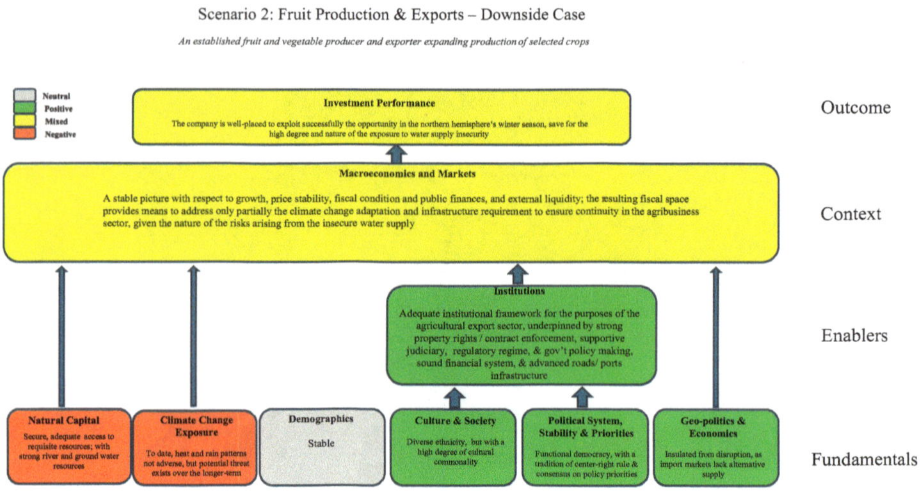

Fig. 11.7 Scenario 2 downside case (IRMM)

- Case 3: Telecom Equipment Assembly

A leading global telecom brand has decided to relocate the assembly facility for a product line. This decision has been based on rising costs in the current location and the threat of tariffs from a major importing country. Two countries have been evaluated.

Upside

In the first country, the government is a single-party-run, highly centralized regime, with pervasive and tight controls on civic and economic life. Their export-focused economy has been very successful. The government has controlled labor and other costs, invested in requisite infrastructure, and established supportive regulations and tax provisions. Additionally, investments in education and the country's culture of a strong work ethic have created a stable, qualified, cost-competitive workforce that has successfully attracted foreign investment. As a result, an increasing number of foreign companies are considering the country as an assembly location.

As a first step, the telecom company evaluated the prospective location's country risk characteristics. The results (Fig. 11.8):

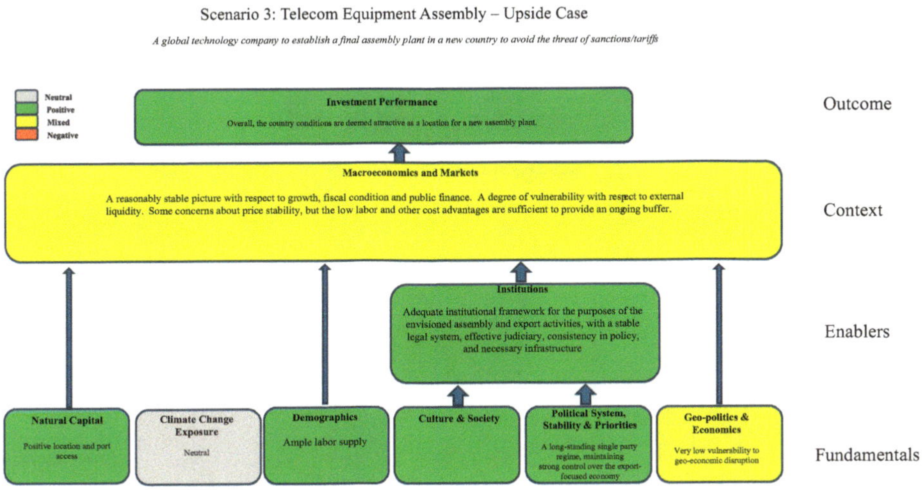

Fig. 11.8 Scenario 3 upside case (IRMM)

The evaluation identified certain low to moderate risks—some cost pressures have begun to surface and the unpredictable nature of global trade relations—but the overall report card was positive. In this case, the telecom company and the government had held preliminary discussions on the arrangements to be established. These confirmed, inter alia, the availability of the necessary infrastructure, the details of tax, import/export, supply, labor provisions to apply to the business, and the like. Most importantly, given the nature of the government and its track record, the telecom company recognized that they would be able to rely on agreements reached with the government and on their policy continuity. Notwithstanding, the investor has been considering political risk insurance (PRI). On this basis, the project was greenlighted.

Downside

The second country represents a stark contrast and was dropped from consideration. As depicted below, unstable politics, weaker institutions, shortages in trained labor, higher vulnerability to secondary sanctions, and a less stable macroeconomy with the greater risk of rising labor and other costs made the relative case against the country clear and simple. The geographic location and the quality of the port facilities are lower. PRI is not available for the country (Fig. 11.9).

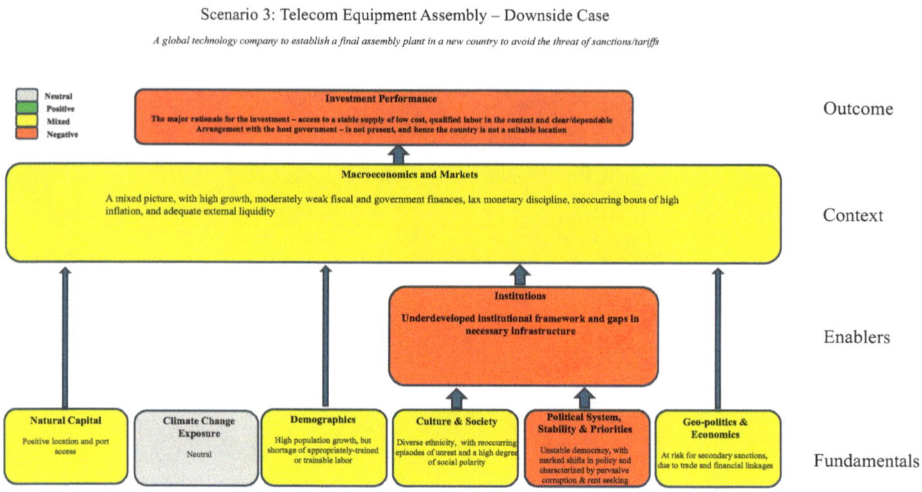

Fig. 11.9 Scenario 3 downside case (IRMM)

11.4 Closing: Key Learnings

The upside and downside cases presented are a form of caricature. We admit real life is rarely so simple. The upside cases portray a clear, positive view of the impact of country risk on the investment decision, and the downside cases the opposite, all things being equal. In our cases, we saw that the differences between the two outcomes reflected:

(i) White Goods

Growth and income distribution

(ii) Fruit Exports

Natural capital endowment (water) and exposure to climate change (rain patterns)

(iii) Telecom Product Assembly

Predictability of supportive government policy creating a conducive operating environment

Real life is more nuanced and the outcomes never so clear and simple. And most importantly, country risk, the investee's idiosyncratic characteristics, and the transaction structure exist as parts of a larger, analytic whole at one moment, and with the passage of time as the economy, the market, the investee's business evolve, the outcome changes.

Hence the Investor's Rutter is a tool that must be used in this larger context, and then again and again over the life of the investment to ensure the picture, its interpretation and any necessary, remedial actions by both the investee and the investor must be updated.

In the next two chapters, we will do this. We will develop the three illustrative cases into more detailed scenarios, encompassing the trifecta of the country risk, investee characteristics, and transaction structure. We walk through the full life span of the investments in each and apply the Rutter to the changing environment. Once done, we will present certain counterfactuals to highlight the learnings.

12

Transaction Lives

A good sailor likes a stiff wind—it challenges her seamanship, but she knows it's what ultimately fills her sails and drives her home.
Inspired by traditional seafaring sayings.

12.1 Introduction

In this chapter, we develop further the three cases introduced in Chap. 11—the white goods company, the fruit export company, and the global tech company. We presented in that chapter brief synopses for each. We divide the cases between upside and downside alternatives for the purpose of demonstrating the application of the Investor's Rutter. Here for the three upside cases (labeled the "base cases") we will:

Deepen the analysis to include relevant commentary on prevailing global market and business sector conditions at the time of investment and elements of the original transaction structure.

Monitor each of the three investments through its life cycle, as the investees navigate evolving global and domestic political, macroeconomic, and market conditions. Throughout their expanded narratives, we will reference the Investor's Rutter to identify changes in key elements and their impact on investment outcomes. For this chapter, we suggest the reader print out the Investor's Rutters presented in Chap. 11 for each case for use as helpful notes.

R. Marney, P. Waeber, *The Emerging Markets Investor's Guide to Country Risk*,
https://doi.org/10.1007/978-3-032-26824-2_12

12.2 Background: The Base Cases

General Goods Company

Country

The Green Republic is a middle-income country in the demographic dividend phase, with a cohesive and stable social and political environment. Institutional development in the country is well advanced for its peer group, reflecting the political class' commitment to supporting a sustainable economic trajectory characterized by solid, balanced, and inclusive growth. GDP and exports are well diversified, as are exports, with competitive presences in agriculture, mining, and manufacturing. The key macroeconomic metrics are solid. Growth has been consistently in the 3–4% p.a. range, inflation low at around 3%, the fiscal account at near balance, a current account deficit of less than 1%, low to moderate public and external debt levels, with comfortable debt service capacity, and FX reserve coverage ample at 7 months of imports. Income and wealth inequality has declined as the country's middle class has expanded in this positive macroeconomic climate.

Recall the Investor's Rutter presented in Chap. 11 (Fig. 12.1).

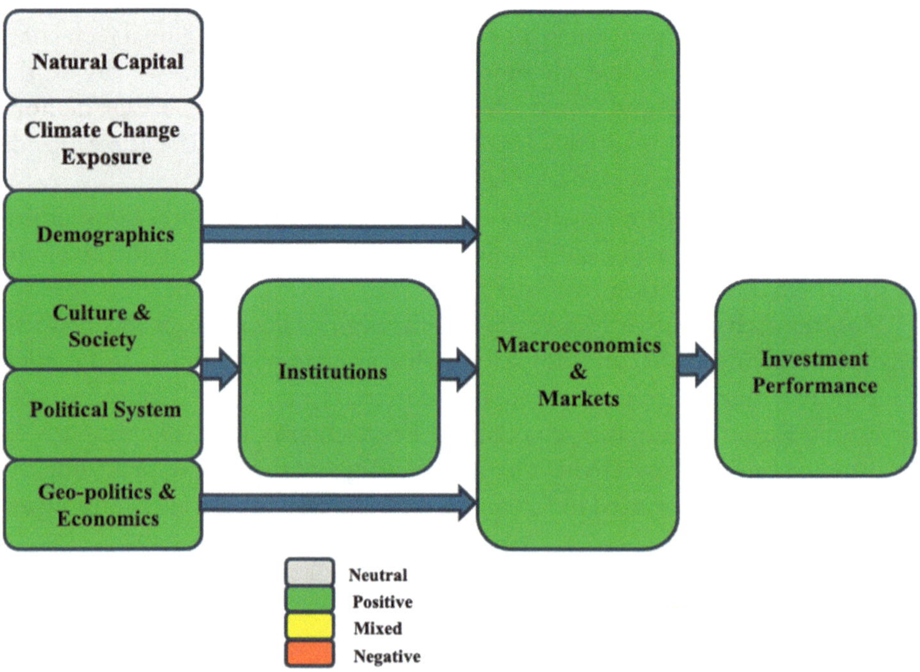

Fig. 12.1 Green Republic Investor's Rutter

As promised above, we now insert into the discussion the relevant global market, sectoral, and transactional background facts.

Global Markets

Markets are enjoying a Goldilocks moment. The global economy is in its fifth year of a sustained recovery. Interest rates have been stable. Equity markets have rallied strongly over this period, and while for some analysts valuations are becoming stretched, investor sentiment remains supportive. In the EMDE space, the story is positive. Major sovereigns, like the Green Republic, have maintained fiscal and monetary discipline, and there is keen investor interest in these growing economies across asset classes.

Sector

The rising incomes in the Green Republic's expanding middle class are fueling heightened demand for a variety of household goods. Consumer preferences have moved, in particular, toward a higher quality level of household white goods and ones that are more energy efficient than are available from domestic production. Imports have increased to address this market demand, but the high cost of these foreign-sourced products have limited sales. As a result, overseas manufactures have pursued one of two avenues to onshore production: (i) a direct investment in a local manufacturing plant or (ii) licensing a local partner to establish a manufacturing facility.

Transaction

The Business

General Goods reaches a licensing agreement with a foreign manufacturer. To operate the business, a new division is established within the company. This business line required the construction of a new plant with a significant capex budget. To exploit a perceived market opening, the board decides to choose a "big bang" option, under which the initial capex budget will be sufficient to accommodate long-term growth and a broad product mix. Operating expenses and working capital requirements are projected to rise.

Overall company profitability is expected to decline during the initial year or two, but remain in the black, before increasing as sales of white goods picked up. Cash flow from operations is expected to fall into deficit initially, before returning to surplus over the next few years.

Investment

The capital budget is 60% debt/40% equity. General Goods has engaged International Banking Corp. (IBC) to raise a debt facility to complement the rights issue agreed by General Goods' three shareholders (each holding one third of the equity). The debt issuance will have two elements: (i) a seven-year term tranche to cover capex and (ii) a four-year term revolving working capital tranche. The capex facility allows for prepayment beginning in year 5 (with a prepayment penalty). The facility is structured as a senior secured, with a first security interest in the project's fixed assets, and floating lien on identified inventory and receivables, a debt service reserve account held in trust, restrictions on new indebtedness, and a series of financial covenants. The two points of contention in the negotiations have been: (i) the lack of prepayment in years 1–4 and most notably (ii) restrictions on new indebtedness. In the end, the company has acquiesced despite its view that the expected success of the new business should allow them to refinance the IBC-arranged debt before the end of year 4.

Family Fruits Ltd.

Country

The country, Agricola, is located in the southern hemisphere. Originally, an agriculture- and mining-based community, the government has successfully diversified the economy to reduce dependence on these cyclical activities. While the population is ethnically diverse, society is harmonious. The political system is characterized as a well-functioning, representative democracy with a generalized consensus among the parties on significant policy issues. The institutional framework is advanced, boasting a strong rule of law, a highly efficient judicial system, and an effective regulatory regime. Infrastructure development—ports, roads, water distribution, electricity generation and distribution, etc.—has been a long-standing public priority and is well placed to support economic activity. The country's domestic and

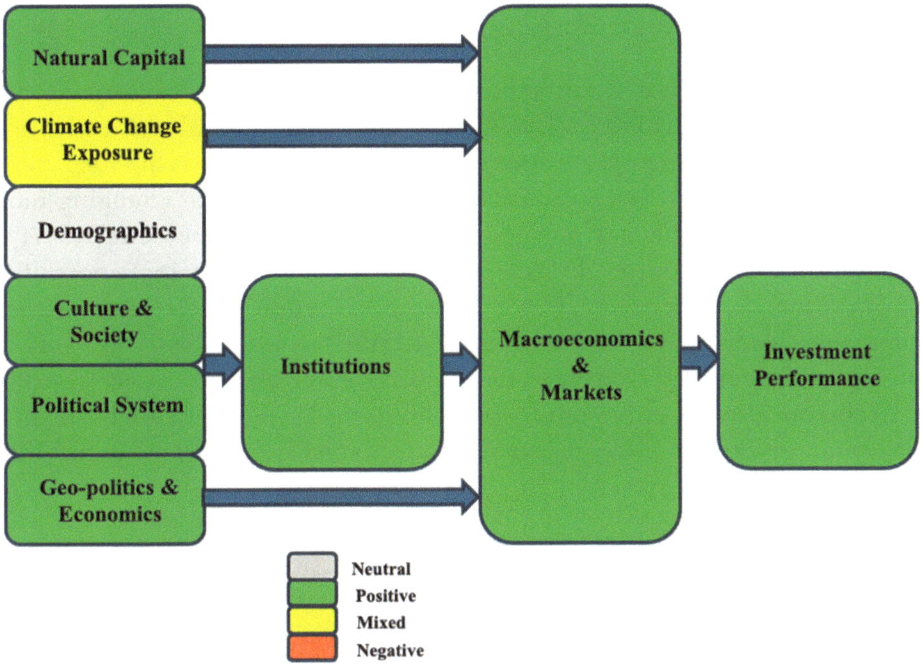

Fig. 12.2 Agricola Investor's Rutter

external macroeconomic metrics depict a positive trajectory. The risk outlook is positive, and many analysts believe the country is on the cusp of investment grade.

Recall the Investor's Rutter that was presented in Chap. 11 (Fig. 12.2).

Global Markets

The global markets environment resembles the Goldilocks state described in the white goods case, above, with one exception. The new administration of Xenith, an economic superpower, has begun to use trade as both an economic and a geopolitical tool of national policy. To date, Agricola has not been affected. Relations between Agricola and Xenith have remained cordial due to personal ties between the two chief executives, and given the importance of Agricola's exports in the Northern Hemisphere winter to keeping fresh fruit on the country's tables, officials in Agricola recognize that this protection could evaporate given the mercurial nature of trade policy in Xenith.

Sector

As noted, Agricola is a major exporter of fruits into the winter market in the Northern Hemisphere. The quality and reliability of the country's exports has made Agricola a valued supplier. Sectoral analysis has identified the risk of long-term water security. To date, the impact of changing rain patterns in the region has not had a material effect on the country. As a precaution for the future, the government has been supporting a portfolio of investments to conserve water, manage extremes, protect ecosystems, empower citizens with data, and create flexible economic systems. This is on top of the country's ample water resources from a broad network of rivers. Historically, excessive rainfall and flooding have represented a bigger risk, and government has invested in mechanisms to guard against this long-standing risk.

Transaction

The Business

Family Fruits has remained a Lopez family-held since being established over 75 years ago. The operation has grown in hectares under cultivation and the variety of its crops, becoming one of Agricola's major exporters. Their products are sold as premium selection. Save for a scattering of episodes where either excessive rain or a disease outbreak has had a material adverse effect on production, the company has been consistently cash flow positive and profitable business. The company has invested over the years in developing biological assets to establish a long-term, high-yielding production base that ensures consistent quality and supply for lucrative markets. Recently, the company has been given the opportunity to purchase a long-abandoned plantation. When the land is fully productive, the purchase would result in roughly a 30% increase in the top line.

Investment

Meridien Agricultural Capital Partners (Meridien), a leading capital provider to the agribusiness sector, has agreed with the company to underwrite a secured facility to cover the 75% debt component of the project budget. The proceeds will be used to acquire and prepare the land, purchase and develop the plants, contract water rights, construct processing and packaging facilities, and contribute to covering operating losses during the pre-breakeven phase. The facility will have an eight-year term, amortized on an increasing scale, with prepayments permitted in the fourth year. During this period, there is a Payment in Kind (PIK) option, with amounts capitalized to be amortized over a subsequent three-year term. There is a revenue participation provision. The facility will be secured by first liens on, inter alia, the purchased land, processing and packaging facilities, selected biological assets, irrigation, and other equipment on the purchased land, all determined sets of inventories and receivables, and water rights. The secured assets are placed in a form of trust.

NG Technology

Country

Veridia is lower-middle-income country. Its government is a single-party-run, highly centralized regime, with pervasive and tight controls on civic and economic life. Civil and political liberties are limited. The export-focused economy has been very successful. The government has controlled labor and other costs, invested in requisite infrastructure, and established supportive regulations and tax provisions. Additionally, investments in education and the country's culture of a strong work ethic have attracted foreign investment. An increasing number of foreign companies are considering the country as an assembly location.

Recall the Investor's Rutter that was presented in Chap. 11 (Fig. 12.3).

Global Markets

An escalating trade war between the economic superpowers of Xenith and Pacifia has severely disrupted the intricate global supply chains for smartphones, which were heavily reliant on Pacifia's manufacturing ecosystem. In response, global electronics firms—including NG Technology—are urgently evaluating Veridia, a developing nation, as an alternative.

Sector

The near-term outlook for the global smartphone industry is positive. Growth is projected to continue but at lower rates than in the past. Demand is being

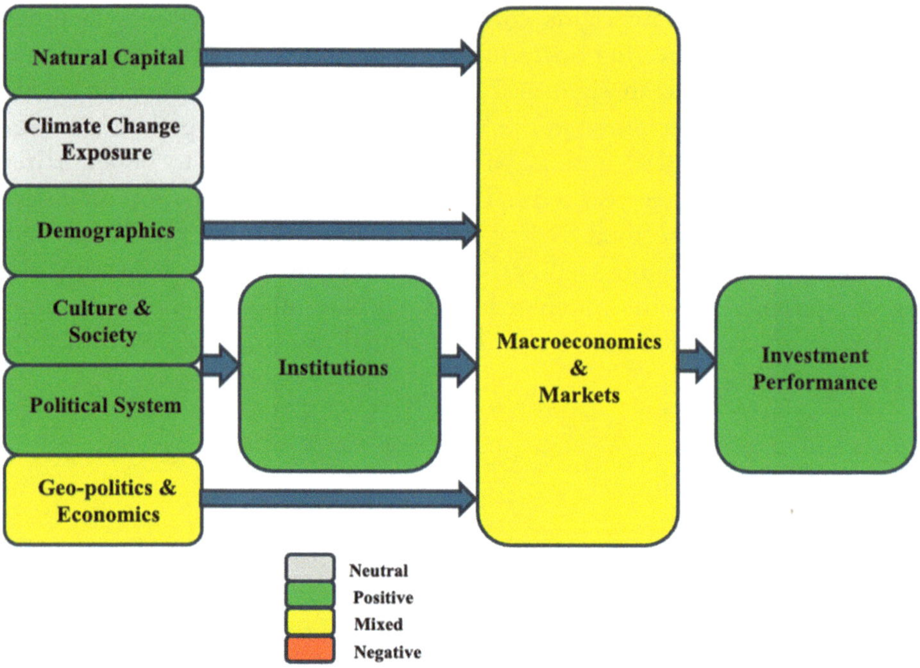

Fig. 12.3 Veridia Investor's Rutter

constrained by lengthening replacement cycles, as incremental hardware improvements no longer provide a compelling upgrade case for many consumers, particularly in mature markets. On the supply side, manufacturers remain exposed to fragile and highly concentrated supply chains, with geopolitical tensions adding uncertainty around component sourcing, trade restrictions, and production costs.

Transaction

The Business

NG Technology is one of the leading, global manufacturers of smartphones. The company is highly profitable and can fund its operations from internal cash flow, if it chooses. Debt markets are accessed when opportune for tax, cost of capital, and other reasons.

Investment

In this case, the requisite funding for the new assembly facility will come from NG Technology's cash reserves. The decision to invest will be predicated on: (i) an analysis of the capabilities of the proposed plant to source the inputs, assemble the units on a timely and technically compliant basis, and within budget; (ii) an evaluation of the country's political, social, institutional, and macroeconomic characteristics, deemed necessary to ensure secure and stable supply; and (iii) a view on the potential for adverse trade and other actions taken by the government of Xenith.

12.3 Investment Life

In this section, we will present two alternative "lives" (scenarios) for each investment. The first is the "looks too good to be true" version, in which everything goes according to plan, if not better. The second depicts a more realistic storyline where there are speedbumps, with the outcome dependent on the nature of the events and the reaction capability of the players, given the environment and the structure of the investment. In both scenarios, changes in the Investor's Rutter will be noted.

General Goods Company

First Scenario

1. Demand Overperformance

The new, GG energy-efficient appliances become a status symbol for the Green Republic's expanding middle class. Sales volumes beat projections by year 3, allowing the company to achieve profitability and positive cash flow from operations ahead of schedule.

2. Supportive Market and Macroeconomic Conditions

The "Goldilocks" global market continues. The Green Republic's stable economy attracts more foreign investment, strengthening its currency. This reduces the cost of any imported components General Goods needs, improving margins, and lowering the effective cost of debt service. Strong growth has driven robust job creation and wage increases. In response to a marked increase in tax revenue, the government lowers marginal income tax and selected value added tax rates. The effect of these developments fuels a sustained rise in household disposable incomes. Financial institutions increase the availability of buyer financing as consumers' creditworthiness strengthens.

3. Successful Early Refinancing

Due to the business's strong performance, a local bank offers to refinance the IBC debt in year 4 at a lower interest rate and without the restrictive pre-payment penalties. IBC agrees to waive the prepayment penalty, saving the company significant capital, in return for other financing mandates.

In the Investor's Rutter (Fig. 12.4).

We note the positive macroeconomics and markets changes (continued economic growth and a rise in disposable income driving increased demand, supported by greater availability of buyer finance). The remaining elements exhibit no change.

The outcome validates the "big bang" decision.

As noted in (3) earlier, a successful early refinancing validates the initial analysis. General Goods' entry into this segment appears to be a winner, and

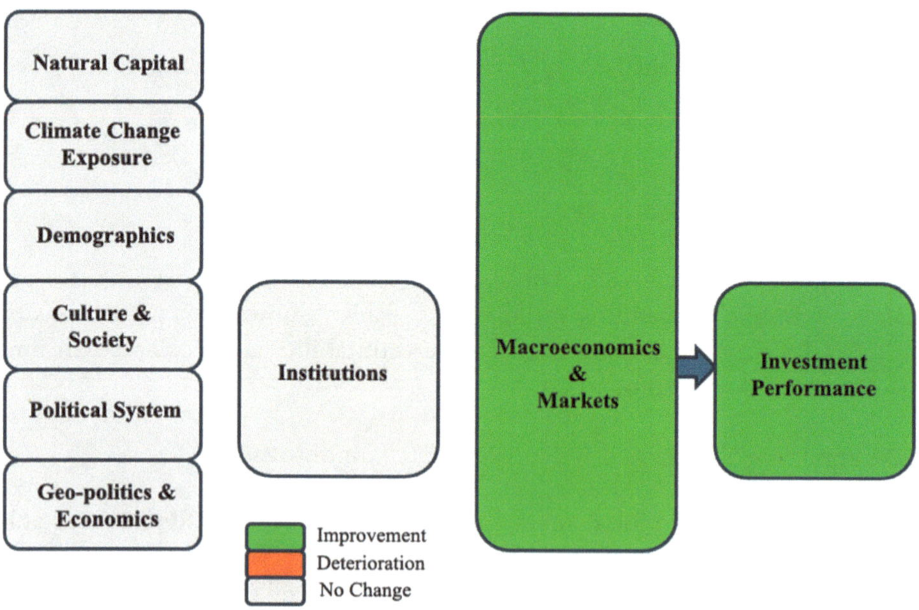

Fig. 12.4 General Goods Investor's Rutter

its choice of the IBC facility a sound decision. IBC comes out well under the circumstances, having achieved its return objectives up to the refinancing point, and its decision to waive the prepayment fee positions it for future business.

Second Scenario

1. Construction Delays and Cost Overruns

The construction of the new plant faced delays due to permitting issues, unprecedented strikes at the country's major ports—that successfully thwarted a government attempt to weaken the powers of the union—that required alternative and more costly sourcing, and frivolous legal challenges to the licensing agreement by local competitors that drag on in the courts. These developments pushed back the production start date and increased the project cost. The period of negative cash flow was extended.

2. Macroeconomic and Market Headwinds

The global "Goldilocks" period ended. In the global markets, a risk-off episode developed in response to a combination of a major EMDE sovereign declaring a moratorium on its external debt and the onset of monetary tightening in a major advanced economy. Non-resident funds began to flow out of the country and pressure built up on the exchange rate. In response, the Green Republic's central bank hiked local interest rates. This step weighed on economic activity and eventually the country entered a recession. Consumer demand slumped, exacerbated by more costly equipment financing just as the new plant came fully online.

3. Heightened Competition

A direct competitor, the foreign manufacturer that chose the "direct investment" path, opened a larger, more automated plant. They engaged in a price war, forcing General Goods to lower prices and accept slimmer margins, further weakening their ability to service debt.

The developments outlined in (1)–(3) above resulted in General Goods' revenue and EBITDA widely missing plan. Net income slips into the red. The company breaches several of the financial covenants in the IBC facility, most notably the debt service coverage ratio.

In the Investor's Rutter (Fig. 12.5):

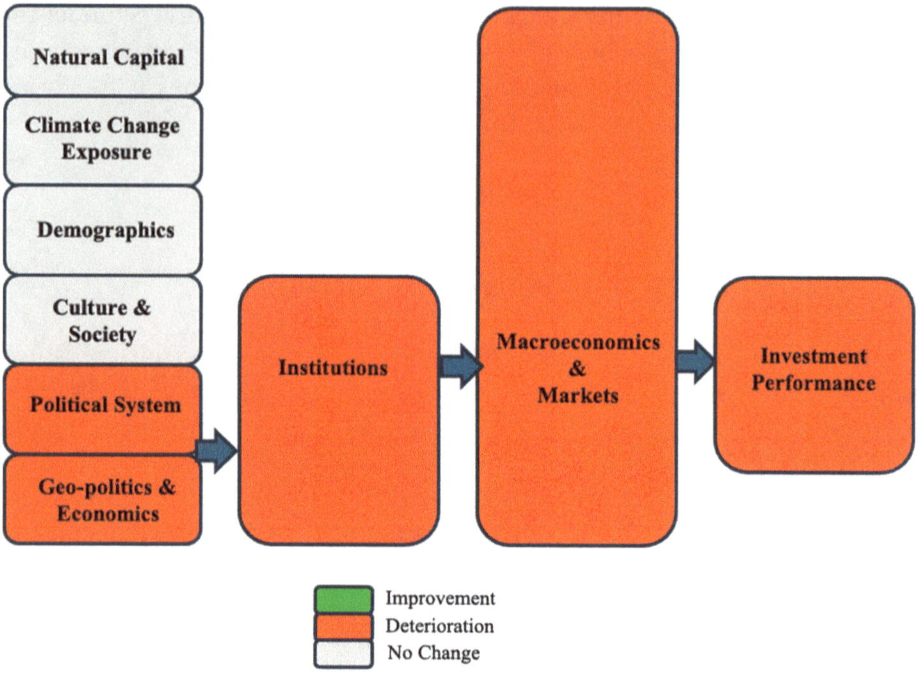

Fig. 12.5 General Goods (downside) Investor's Rutter

On the right in "Fundamentals", two elements have changed adversely. The *first*, the political system, has witnessed an ill-advised attempt on the part of the government to curtail the powers of the unions. The port strike was the response. This event marked an unprecedented movement in the political history of the Green Republic where left-leaning parties supported organized labor to challenge the national consensus. The implications for political stability and policy making are thought to be profound. The immediate effect was that the ruling administration reined back orthodox economic policies aimed at addressing the macroeconomic challenges developing in the country, due to concerns that these would exacerbate these political risks. In the *second*, geo-politics and economics, the deterioration reflects the impact of the risk-off episode and the global monetary tightening. These developments drove adverse knock-on effects—rise in domestic interest rates, reduced credit availability—on the level of economic activity, employment, household incomes, and consumer demand for durable goods. In this context, General Goods' operational performance and financial condition suffered. As a result, the company breached the financial covenants of the IBC credit facility.

In response, the parties negotiate a restructuring of the debt. They recognize that there are both structural (increased competition) and cyclical (the recession) drivers. Therefore, the agreement addresses both. The smaller, potential market share, reduced profitability, and lower cash flow generation meant that the current leverage is excessive. The shareholders agree to complete a rights issue to pay down a portion of the debt. For the new principal amount, the duration was extended and the financial ratios recalibrated to match better the base case projections.

Family Fruits Ltd.

First Scenario

1. Growing Conditions

The new plantation benefits from perfect weather. The yield and quality of the fruit are exceptional. The first harvest coincides with a supply shortage in the Northern Hemisphere, most notably in Xenith, allowing Family Fruits to sell its premium produce at record prices, generating surplus cash.

2. Xenith Trade Relations

The personal rapport between the countries' leaders holds, blocking any adverse action against Agricola. Subsequently, legal actions in Xenith result in invalidating the trade tariffs, removing a major cloud of uncertainty, and solidifying market access.

3. Timing of First Harvest

The new plantation becomes productive faster than anticipated. This triggers the revenue participation clause for Meridien much earlier, but the sheer volume of cash flow allows Family Fruits to easily make these payments and consider an early prepayment of the PIK debt, reducing overall leverage.

In the Investor's Rutter (Fig. 12.6).

As noted above, the company's operations outperformed. To the backdrop of Family Fruits' strengthened financial condition and more robust cash flow, the management enters into discussions with Meridien to refinance the debt. The proposed terms will be more relaxed than in the original structure reflecting the company's improved creditworthiness.

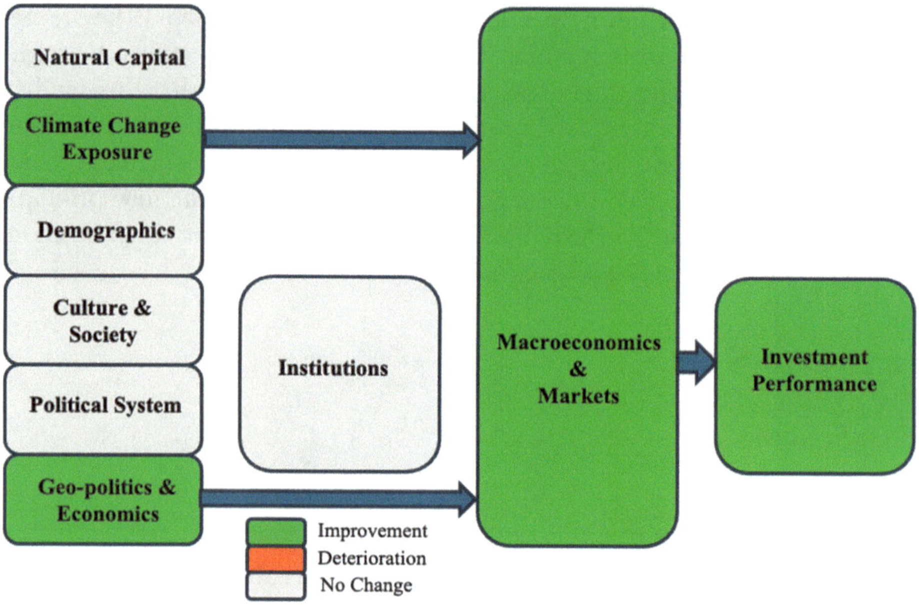

Fig. 12.6 Family Fruits Investor's Rutter

We note again that the "big bang" strategy pays off.

Second Scenario

1. Tariff Action

The mercurial Xenith administration suddenly imposes punitive tariffs on all fruit imports from Agricola, citing "national economic security". Competing exporting countries operating free of tariffs are able to seize market share causing revenues to decline.

2. Climate Crisis

A period of unusually heavy rainfall produces flooding throughout the company's growing areas, reducing yields, and resulting in an outbreak of disease.

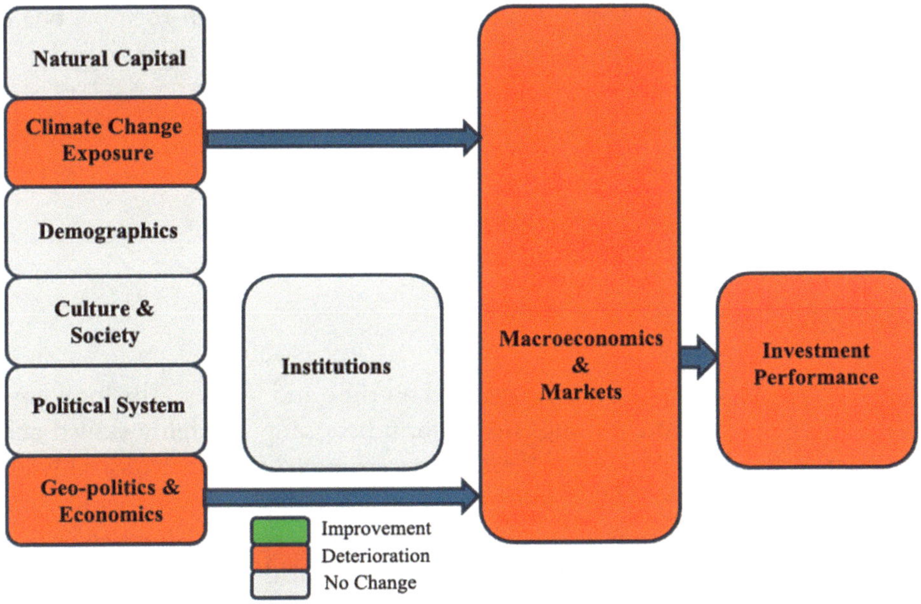

Fig. 12.7 Family Fruits (downside) Investor's Rutter

3. Disease Outbreak

In the aftermath of the flooding, there is an outbreak of Phytophthora Root Rot. This pathogen spreads in the pools of water that build up in the fields. The estimate of the damage places the loss of plants in the range of 15–20%.

In the Investor's Rutter (Fig. 12.7).

The Xenith tariff action and the damaging rainfall affecting yields and destroying biological assets hurt conditions in the macroeconomy, but even more the business of Family Fruits. The impact of the loss of up to 20% of the plants. To replace the lost plants will require a significant capital infusion and multiple years to realize cash flow from this investment.

In the meantime, orderly debt service even with the PIK arrangement becomes problematic. As a result, the company and Meridien negotiate a transaction, which combines: (i) new funding in the form of a convertible preferred note; (ii) a conversion of a portion of the existing Meridien debt into this convertible preferred note; and (iii) a restructuring of the remaining Meridien debt. At the same time, the company reaches an agreement with local banks under which it commits to maintain its working capital credit lines. In the event of full conversion of the preferred notes, Meriden would acquire roughly a third of the common equity of Family Fruits. In the interim,

Meridien is granted two representatives on the expanded seven-member board of directors of the company. After many years, the family has lost control of the company.

NG Technology

First Scenario

1. Plant Operation

The new assembly facility is completed on time and budget. The local government fulfills its undertakings up to commissioning. A highly skilled and productive workforce is hired. Veridia's government, eager for more investment, provides additional tax incentives and enhances relevant civil infrastructure in the area of the plant. The facility becomes a crucial, reliable node in NG's post-Pacifia supply chain, protecting its global market share.

2. Global Trade

Xenith increases tariffs on smartphones assembled in Pacifia, making NG's competitors' products more expensive. NG's foresight in moving assembly to Veridia gives it a significant competitive advantage and cost leadership, leading to increased global market share and profitability.

3. Institutional Framework

The centralized, single-party regime in Veridia continues to provide a stable, low-cost operating environment with no labor unrest or political upheaval, proving the company's country-risk analysis correct.

In the Investor's Rutter (Fig. 12.8).

Continued social and political stability within the country's single-party system underpins the maintenance of supportive institutions for Veridia's value-added export economic model. The country's positive economic performance and strengthened public finances allow the government to provide additional tax incentives and fund ongoing infrastructure investments. These factors contribute to a stable operating base for NG in the country. Further, Xenith's ongoing trade war works to Veridia's and NG's benefit as the company's global sales and hence assembly requirements in Veridia increase.

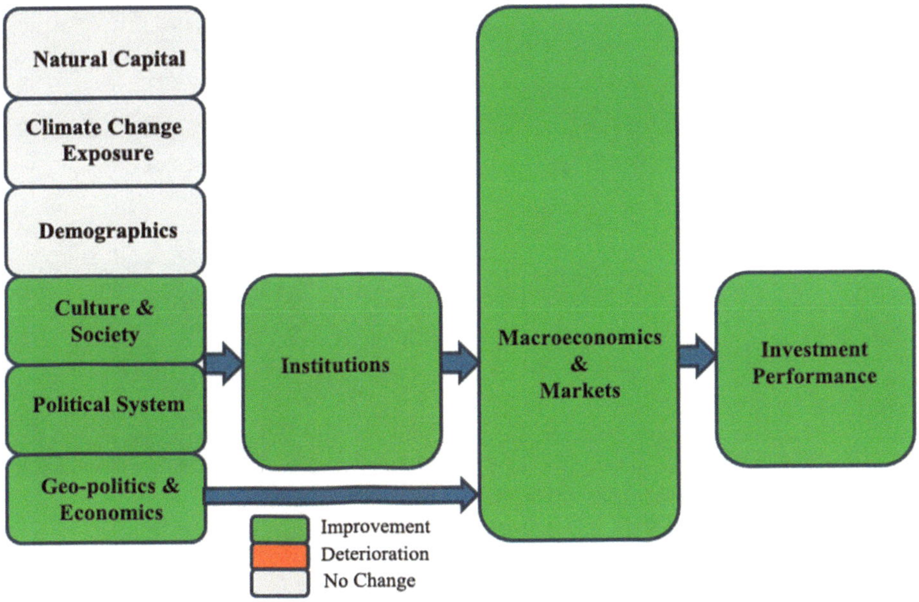

Fig. 12.8 NG Technology Investor's Rutter

Second Scenario

Geopolitics.

The trade war expands, and Xenith decides to extend high tariffs to Veridia due to its diplomatic, financial, and commercial ties to Pacifia. NG's new facility is suddenly caught in the crossfire, and its products are heavily tariffed in its most important market (Xenith).

In the Investor's Rutter (Fig. 12.9).

The elimination or at least the lessening of the tariffs becomes a matter of critical national economic policy for Veridia. At the NG company level, this turn of events transforms a valuable, strategic investment into potentially a material liability. This alignment of interests forges a joint effort to reach a *modus vivendi* with Xenith. After protracted discussions—in which NG played an important role—the two governments agree to a number of concessions to promote Xenith investments and exports in Veridia. In return, the new tariffs are rolled back. However, NG recognizes the threat of Xenith reimposing tariffs and therefore concludes a longer-term solution is necessary.

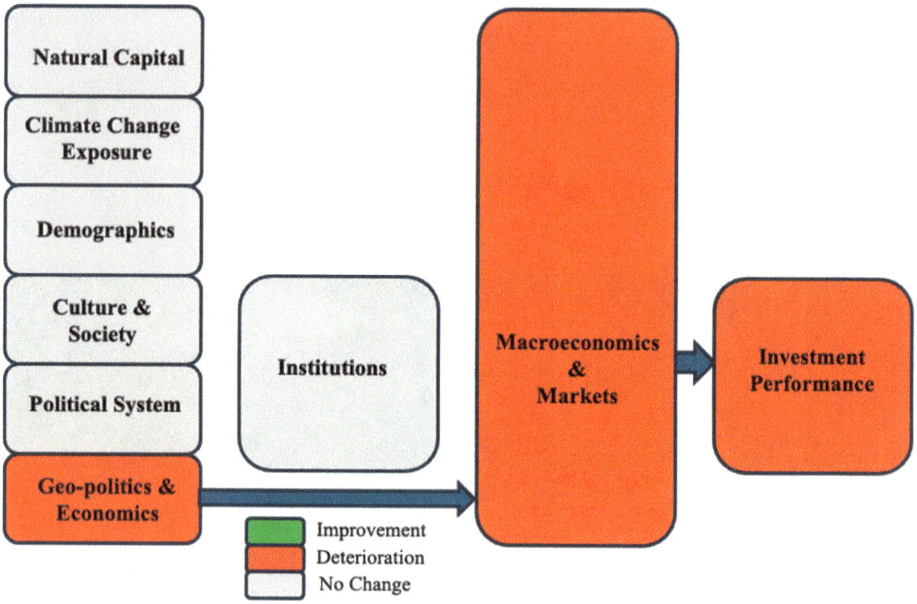

Fig. 12.9 NG Technology (downside) Investor's Rutter

12.4 Summary

General Goods Company

The three core macro-level success factors were:

1. Increasing middle-class disposable income translating into higher demand for white goods in a market segment characterized by weak competition
2. A benign global markets environment conducive to capital flows into the EMDE space and the maintenance of low interest rates
3. A sound institutional framework supporting the requirements of the commissioning of the production plant and operating the new business line

In the downside scenario, there are two major adverse changes related to: (i) a deterioration of political stability and its impact on policy making and (ii) the effects of a global risk-off episode and monetary tightening on domestic monetary and real sectors of the economy, and in turn on the private credit supply. As noted above, fearful of exacerbating political divisions, the government opted for a weaker policy response than warranted. Ultimately, the policy was ineffective. In this weakened economic environment, General Goods' business suffered.

Could this script have been anticipated and preventive steps taken? Your homework assignment is to answer these two questions (suggested responses are in the appendix to this chapter).

Family Fruits Ltd.

The two core macro-level success factors were:

1. A climatic environment supporting the company's harvest yields and quality necessary for profitable operations, specifically in this case—not too much rain!
2. Freedom to export to the countries in the Northern Hemisphere, most notably the company's major customer-country, Xenith

In the downside scenario, the two major adverse changes were: (i) exceptionally heavy rains that caused flooding, resulting in harvest loss and disease-induced biological asset destruction, and (ii) Xenith's imposition of tariffs.

As in the above, could this script have been anticipated and preventive steps taken? Your homework assignment is to answer these two questions (suggested responses are in the appendix to this chapter).

NG Technology

The two core macro-level success factors were:

1. A supportive institutional environment to facilitate plant commissioning and operations
2. Insulation from Xenith's trade war

In the downside scenario, the second factor gives way to an initially debilitating development. The net of Xenith's tariff actions captures Veridia and threatens the country's value-added export model. Subsequently, the country negotiates a compromise that reestablishes the economics of projects like NG, but does raise the specter of a repeat.

As in the above, could this script have been anticipated and protective steps taken? Your homework assignment is to answer these two questions (suggested responses are in the appendix to this chapter)!

Appendix: Suggested Answers to Questions in Section 15.3

General Goods Company

Cyclicality is a standard feature of the macroeconomy. The drivers of economic downturns vary over time and by country context. The drivers this time originated in the global markets. Specifically, for the Green Republic—a small, open economy—the government's ability to insulate the monetary and financial sectors of the country from the contractionary impact of the risk-off episode and the generalized monetary tightening was limited. Should the company and the IBC have predicted the situation? Not precisely. That is, it would have been reasonable to assume that, over the period before the new business line matured and generated sufficient cash flow to repay the debt, there would be an episode of some kind that would negatively affect sales of these big-ticket durable household goods. The exact drivers? Not so easy to predict. Given the likelihood of a downturn over time, a prudent course for the company might have been to phase in the capex and other fixed costs of the new line, rather than—as they did—invest in capacity that might only be fully employed over the medium term. Had they done this, their debt burden would have been less, and they would likely have been able to navigate the downturn without a restructuring. In fairness, however, this falls into the "20/20 perfect hindsight" category of analysis. Had there not been a downturn, they could have been criticized for not investing in more productive capacity right out of the blocks and so leaving space for competitors to seize market share.

Family Fruits

Too much rain and capriciously imposed tariffs are the gremlins in this case. What should the company have done? For the rain and flooding, we had noted above that government had been investing in water management and flood control measures. Clearly, given the story line, this was not sufficient for the company. Let's assume a case where the rains were heavy but not materially beyond what has been observed in the past. In that case, again in retrospect, the lenders should have required more investment by the company to protect the fields against this risk. Climate change–driven damages are arguably tail risks, until they happen. For the second gremlin, before the tariffs were imposed, who would have imagined such a reckless policy stance? Once this has happened, the Xenith market needs to be viewed as high risk. Going forward, for the company the answer is straight from risk management 101—diversify away from Xenith as an export destination and in the interim hope that the government can negotiate as best as can be to reduce or eliminate the tariffs.

NG Technology

As in the case of Family Fruits, it is arguably not reasonable to criticize NG Technology's failure to anticipate Xenith's tariff action. While the tensions between Xenith and Pacifia were long-standing, the trade measures imposed against Pacifia by Xenith were not something many would have predicted. Their extension to Veridia would have been even less probable. The idea of onshoring the assembly work to Xenith is not viable commercially, and there are a limited number of jurisdictions like Veridia. Therefore, what actually happened strikes one as the best that could be done, given the capricious nature of the Xenith government.

13

Counterfactuals

It is not down in any map; true places never are.
Paraphrased from Herman Melville, Moby-Dick.

In this chapter, we take the "upside case" version of the Investment Rutter for each of the three cases presented in Chap. 12 and then the "second scenario" (the not so great outcome) depicting the transaction life for each, and ask ourselves the question, *"Given these facts, what could the parties have done differently to keep the car on the road when forced to confront these treacherous driving conditions?"* For each case, we will review briefly the relevant "factual" background facts from the preceding two chapters and then suggest an alternative approach, the "counterfactual", to the investment and the rationale, with the latter representing a mix of the benefits and risks. This approach will reinforce a core message that while the Investor's Rutter does dictate the maritime conditions in which a pilot navigates her ship, the outcome is not preordained. For our purposes, the investor's reaction to market conditions and events, and the skill with which she fashions and executes a response can be game changers. That is, within a wide range, the Rutter guides, but the pilot drives the outcome.

R. Marney, P. Waeber, *The Emerging Markets Investor's Guide to Country Risk*,
https://doi.org/10.1007/978-3-032-26824-2_13

13.1 General Goods

The Factual

Below appear the summary diagrams for the IR for the upside case (on the left) and the diagram showing the second scenario, the one where challenging conditions arise to influence the investment outcome (on the right) (Fig. 13.1).

We repeat here the summary of adverse changes that occurred in the factual case:

1. Construction Delays and Cost Overruns

The construction of the new plant faced delays due to permitting issues, unprecedented strikes at the country's major ports (that successfully thwarted a government attempt to weaken the powers of the union) that required alternative and more costly sourcing, and frivolous legal challenges to the licensing agreement by local competitors that dragged on in the courts. These developments pushed back the production start date and increased the project cost. The period of negative cash flow was extended.

2. Macroeconomic and Market Headwinds

The global "Goldilocks" period ended. In the global markets, a risk-off episode developed in response to a combination of a major EMDE sovereign declaring a moratorium on its external debt and the onset of monetary tightening in a major advanced economy. Non-resident funds began to flow out of

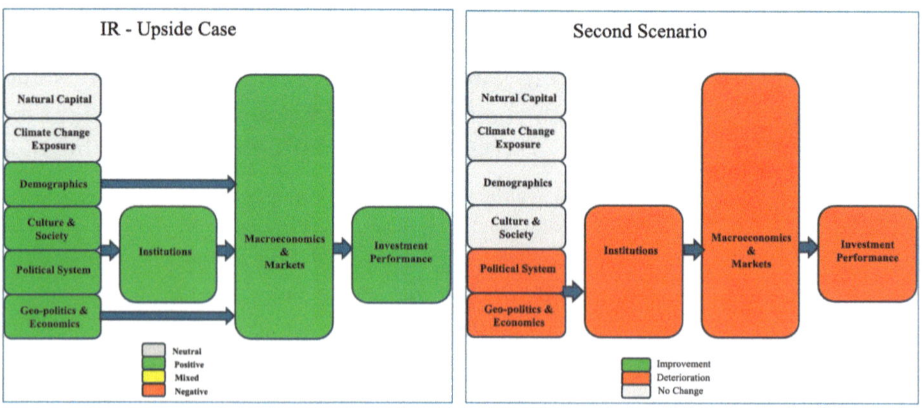

Fig. 13.1 General Goods: the factual

the country and pressure built up on the exchange rate. In response, the Green Republic's central bank hiked local interest rates. This step weighed on economic activity and eventually the country entered a recession. Consumer demand slumped, exacerbated by more costly equipment financing, just as the new plant came fully online.

3. Heightened Competition

A direct competitor, the foreign manufacturer that chose the "direct investment" path, opened a larger, more automated plant. They engaged in a price war, forcing General Goods to lower prices and accept slimmer margins, further weakening their ability to service debt.

1. The developments outlined in (1)–(3) above resulted in General Goods' revenue and EBITDA widely missing plan. Net income slipped into the red. The company breached several of the financial covenants in the IBC facility, most notably the debt service coverage ratio.

The Counterfactual

In the factual case, the company invests in the productive capacity for a full range of white goods and for volumes expected to be reached only years into the future. The rationale is:

1. To achieve a first-to-market position in each of the major product groups (e.g., washers, dryers, dishwashers, refrigerators) and quality and size segments
2. To have the manufacturing flexibility to increase output of any one or more "hot sellers" without having to construct the plant and purchase the equipment to accommodate such growth

This flexibility comes at a price. The sunk capital may rest underutilized in situations if the level and nature of demand fails to correspond to plans. The expanded investment size requires more funding, and the higher leverage carries increased costs. Operating results and cash flow generation may suffer. In such cases, the capability to raise new debt may become constrained or even blocked in the future. If there are other adverse developments such as those outlined in the factual case, then things can get even more challenging.

Let's assume that this "big bang" approach is replaced with a more "phased-in" approach. In such a case, the company identifies a smaller set of products that balance higher margins and likely stronger consumer uptake. The fixed investment in property, plant, and equipment is sufficient for a moderate degree of growth in the medium term, but does not bet on the outlook assumed in the big bang. Leverage is lower, with the obvious benefits for financial resiliency in the event that the storm clouds appear.

Outcome of the Counterfactual

The company is protected against the risks of slower growth in overall and/or specific product demand or other adverse macroeconomic or market developments. The lower, past capital commitment and leverage provide the flexibility to react to changing market conditions by channeling investment capital into developing, higher growth areas.

When comparing the factual to the counterfactual, there is the obvious benefit of the phased-in approach—the company doesn't confront the need (and the risk) to restructure its debt. There is a risk of course. We noted that a major foreign white goods manufacturing company has elected to invest directly in the Green Republic. If the market takes off, then this competitor could secure market share at the expense of General Goods.

13.2 Family Fruits

The Factual

Below appear the summary diagrams for the IR for the upside case (on the left) and the diagram showing the second scenario, the one where challenging conditions arise to influence the investment outcome (on the right) (Fig. 13.2).

We repeat here the summary of adverse changes that occurred in the factual case:

1. Tariff Action

The mercurial Xenith administration suddenly imposes punitive tariffs on all fruit imports from Agricola, citing "national economic security". Competing exporting countries operating free of tariffs are able to seize market share causing revenues to decline.

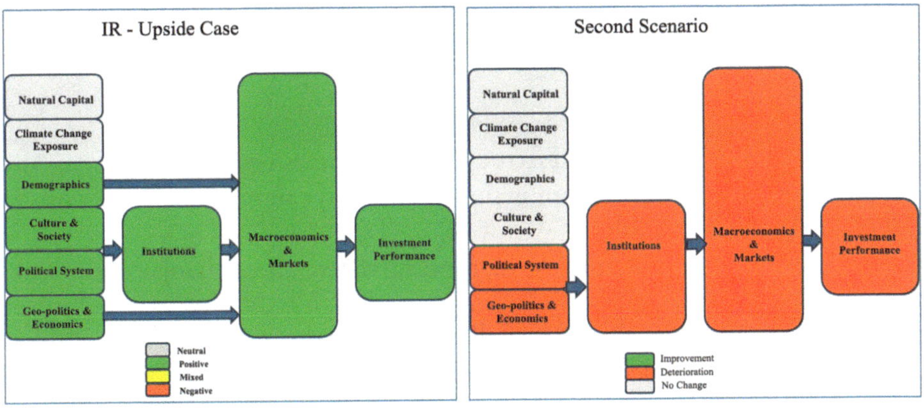

Fig. 13.2 Family Fruits: the factual

2. Climate Crisis

A period of unusually heavy rainfall produces flooding throughout the company's growing areas, reducing yields, and resulting in an outbreak of disease.

3. Disease Outbreak

In the aftermath of the flooding, there is an outbreak of Phytophthora Root Rot. This pathogen spreads in the pools of water that build up in the fields. The estimate of the damage places the loss of plants in the range of 15–20%.

The Counterfactual

In the factual case, production growth is prioritized. As a result, the full amount is devoted to the purchase of the land and the biological assets, and financing land preparation works. Climate change–related and global trade–related risks are deemed as high impact, but very low probability events and hence are discounted. In this counterfactual, these risks are given greater prominence in the investment analysis. As a result, the company follows an alternative approach, under which:

1. The planting of bushes/certain land preparation works will be undertaken once adequate progress is made on elements (2) and (3), below.
2. Enhanced flood control infrastructure will be designed and constructed for the full plantation.

3. Several sales promotion offices will be established in promising, but still underdeveloped markets to support efforts to achieve greater diversification.

Once the flood control infrastructure is commissioned by engineers and the sales diversification program is showing positive signs, then the actions in (1) will be started.

The amounts and structure of the funding reflect these changed priorities:

1. The overall amount of funding will be lower, as the reduction in the project budget due to the delay in the expenditures on biological assets and land improvements being greater than the increased outlays for (2) and (3).
2. For this decreased budget, the shareholders have agreed to increase the proportion of equity
3. The lower quantum of debt is structured to facilitate a subsequent refinancing when the company moves to the execution stage for the planting of the expanded plantation.

Outcome of the Counterfactual

Let's assume that at a point in the future, the company has completed the flood control infrastructure and succeeded in reducing the participation of buyers from Xenith in its sales from roughly 35% down to less than 10%. The first debt facility with Meridien is refinanced with a higher amount and the biological assets are purchased, and the land preparations completed. Thereafter, after production from the new plans comes on line, two events occur:

1. There is a protracted period of heavy rainfall, which results in severe flooding in the region of the company's plantations. However, given the efficacy of the flood control infrastructure, biological asset losses are minimal, thus validating the company's decision to treat this climate change threat as a routine business risk warranting active management, rather than as some tail risk for which effective adaptation is not financially viable.
2. A new administration in Xenith imposes tariffs on all exports from Agricola. The impact on the company is a decline of sales amounting to a few percentage points, which is easily absorbed by other markets.

13.3 NG Technology

The Factual

Below appear the summary diagrams for the IR for the upside case (on the left) and the diagram showing the second scenario, the one where challenging conditions arise to influence the investment outcome (on the right) (Fig. 13.3).

We repeat here the summary of the adverse development that occurred in the factual case, "The trade war expands, and Xenith decides to extend high tariffs to Veridia due to its diplomatic, financial, and commercial ties to Pacifia. NG's new facility is suddenly caught in the crossfire, and its products are heavily tariffed in its most important market (Xenith)." With this development, NG's investment in Veridia has been transformed from a valuable contributor to the company's global business into a liability. In the second scenario, we inserted an interim solution under which the government (supported by NG) negotiates a compromise with Xenith to open the country to investment and trade in return for tariff relief. Given the nature of trade policy making in Xenith, NG recognizes the gossamer-like nature of the current arrangement.

The Counterfactual

In this case, let us assume that the agreement between the governments of Veridia and Xenith has been reached during NG's evaluation of alternative country locations. Given the compelling economics and (otherwise) stable operating environment in Veridia, NG's management maintains their

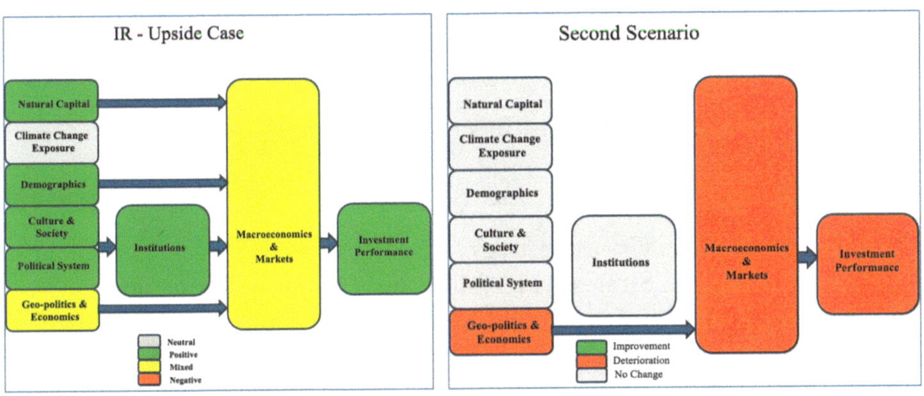

Fig. 13.3 NG Technology: the factual

recommendation for Veridia, but adds the further recommendation that a second location also be chosen for the establishment of an additional facility.

To economize, the board dictates that rather than NG creating a wholly owned subsidiary in each of these two new locations, management should pursue joint ventures with local partners.

This decision creates diversification of product assembly locations to protect NG against a novel risk type, the so-called Xenith Risk. With this decision, NG will have assembly production capability in three countries. When Xenith modifies once again its tariffs, NG can smoothly shift a significant portion of the production quota to other countries not yet targeted or where the economics are more attractive.

This risk mitigation comes with a cost. The initial investment is higher due to duplicated overhead, compensated in part by each facility being smaller and more flexible. The premium for redundant, diversified manufacturing capacity is a direct cost of geopolitical risk management, in this case against Xenith Risk.

Outcome of the Counterfactual

With Pacifia still in Xenith's crosshairs, and Veridia benefiting from what could prove only a temporary truce, NG's establishment of a third location protects the company's business. In the future, should more sense and stability return to international trade affairs, then NG is well positioned for growth.

13.4 Closing

Summary

We present three counterfactuals. In summary form, these appeared:

1. General Goods: Phased Investment
    - Altered Variable: Capex Strategy
    - Key Motivation: Strategic Flexibility and Downside Protection
    - Investor Rutter Message: Build Resilience to Demand Downturns
    - Outcome: Near-Term Survival and Opportunity for Future Growth

2. Family Fruits: Export Market Diversification and Flood Protection
   - Altered Variables: Export Strategy and Capex Timing and Strategy
   - Key Motivations: Export Market Diversification and Protection Against Climate Risks
   - Investor Rutter Messages: Treat Tail Risks as Real Threats
   - Outcome: Avoidance of Financial Crisis and Loss of Control

3. NG Technology: Multi-country Strategy
   - Altered Variable: Operational Footprint
   - Key Motivations: Building Supply Chain Resilience
   - Investor Rutter Message: Diversify Geopolitical and Economic Risks
   - Outcome: Production Flexibility

Closing Remarks

Strong Winds Along the Coast—Richard Marney

The foregoing cases validate the maxim that true strategic value lies not in the projected base-case returns, but in preserving the right to change course, when evolving circumstances warrant. Each counterfactual explores an investment in such flexibility—phased capex, market diversification, multi-country operations—actions that may lower the ideal upside but unquestionably improve the downside.

The imagery of the mariner reinforces this view. Trimming sails and seeking shelter to ride out tempest may delay a journey but could prove the difference between reaching port and floundering. For our pilot, familiarity with the timing of the storm seasons, ability to read the clouds and winds for danger signs, and knowledge of the location of protected bays along the coast provide (downside) protection indeed likely allow the ship and its sailors to survive.

Similarly, experienced investors can read the clouds and the winds of their markets and, having built into their business operating and financial flexibility, can balance upside returns with downside protection. When warranted and within reasonable bounds, a moderate reduction in the IRR of investment serves well the long-term interests of all stakeholders.

Part IV

Case Studies

Rural and Village Scenes by Richard Marney

You can't cross the sea merely by standing and staring at the water.
Rabindranath Tagore

In the Preface, we identified the Investor's Rutter as the book's central country risk analysis methodology/tool. Up to this point, we have surveyed in Parts I and II several topics that provide necessary background for the Rutter's constituent elements. In Part I, we covered macroeconomics, institutions, the financial system, and financial crises, and thereafter in Part II, four, forward-looking/evolving issues—geopolitics, climate change, demographics, and artificial intelligence.

Having established this foundation, we introduced the Investor's Rutter in Part III. To reinforce the understanding of the structure, flow, and interpretation of the Rutter, we walked the reader through several short base narratives and counterfactuals. These cases were very high level and focused on getting a grasp of the Rutter's use.

In this section, we aim to deepen the reader's understanding of the Rutter. We approach this task by presenting four, more detailed case studies. Consistent with the country-risk focused nature of the book, the analysis is centered on the impact of macroeconomic, political, institutional, and market risks on investment viability. For the most part, we avoid digging into the corporate finance numbers and instead limit ourselves to describing the operational and performance characteristics of the parties in general terms. Additionally, we portray the impact of one or more country risk effects on current operating cash flow, leverage, projected sales, operating margins, and the like, with descriptive adjectives, which denote their nature, force, and direction. For example, all things being equal, when observing expansionary fiscal policy in the context of sound public finances and low inflationary pressures, we assume a boost to sales and profitability. The greater the increase in aggregate demand, the higher the top line expansion. Or, when faced with foreign capital outflows and FX reserve depletion, the government abandons a fixed exchange rate peg, then counterparties with short, open FX positions will be adversely affected. The higher the open currency position, the more severe the impact. This "simplifying approach" has been chosen to enhance the clarity of the analysis of the nature of the impact of country risks on investment performance. The exception to this treatment is Enterprise Bank in Chap. 16. In this case, we employ summary financial data to portray the asset quality, solvency, and liquidity metrics of the bank.

In the four cases, we sketch out diverse landscapes. The sovereign ratings will vary, with the narratives playing out in economies ranging from a vibrant BBB country to a Ca jurisdiction, mired in a debt default/country. The nature of the business will be different in each case. We cover a green energy company, an infant nutritional product manufacturer, a commercial bank, and a coffee and tea producer, processor, and exporter. The position in the capital structure will range from senior secured debt to equity. Lastly, each investment decision will play out in the face of different challenges: for our green energy company, a strategic pivot for a tech company; a market-entry decision for the global infant nutrition company; a bank debt refinancing at a problematic time; and an overseas, vertical integration for an agribusiness company to the backdrop of a severe financial crisis in its home market. Together, while differing significantly, the four collectively underscore a unified truth—country risk is not a peripheral concern but a central determinant of investment success or failure.

In Part III, the reader encountered the "Investor's Rutter Mind Map". We suggest readers print out the blank template that appears on the next page. When proceeding through the cases, the reader should populate the template with the observations that reflect their characterizations of the endowment, enabling, and contextual elements that lead to an overall evaluation of the country risk situation and its impact on the investment in question. This will assist in the navigation of the cases that follow. Based on this work, readers should feel free to challenge the investment decision/outcome. In Chap. 18, Summary Lessons, we offer our markup of the Investor's Rutter for each case.

Given the nature and objectives of the cases, we omit the customary abstract and keywords.

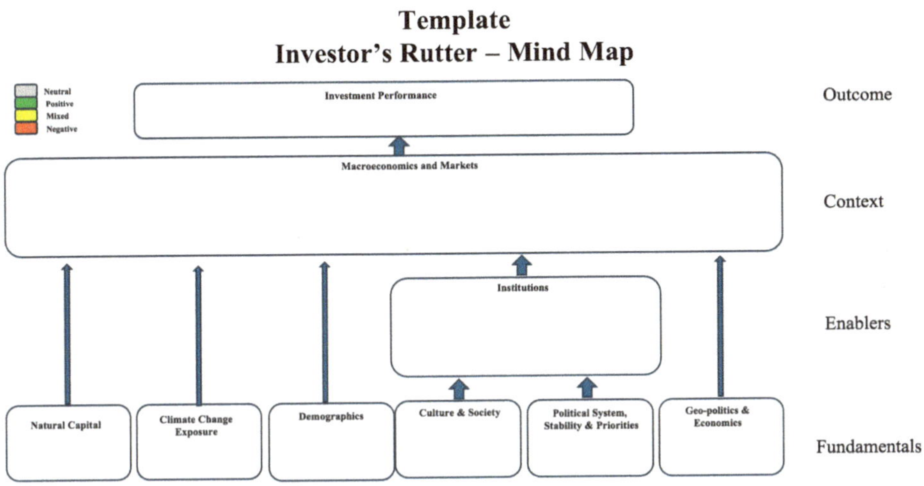

Template Investor's Rutter – Mind Map

14

Case Study 1

14.1 Country: Marcadia

In this chapter, we meet a successful company—Tomorrow's Energy (TE), operating in the electric vehicle (EV) space. The company is headquartered in Marcadia, an emerging market economy that recently achieved investment grade status. The company was established by three friends, all engineering PhD graduates of the leading local university. TE began as a battery producer before developing a battery swapping service and then in a defensive move buying their major customer, a two- and three-wheeler vehicle producer. Along the way, a private equity firm, Global Tech Investors (GTI) has acted as the sole institutional investor and the lead advisor on strategic investments for TE. The company is now in the process of a strategic review in which two distinct and transformational investments are being considered: (i) a hybrid/EV passenger car and truck manufacturing JV with the country's major traditional car and truck company, National Motors; and (ii) solar storage, either as a pure equipment supplier or as a solar generation/distribution operator. The process comes at a pivotal time for the group. The operating environment is increasingly fraught, yet the opportunities are vast. GTI and the founders are challenged by (i) volatile government policy and regulations toward the green economy and (ii) geoeconomic headwinds in the context of war and the rise of mercantilist policies on the part of one great power that could (a) adversely affect economic growth in Marcadia and (b) limit or even block access to key EV and battery components. Yet, two untapped market areas await. Marcadia has no domestic producer of electric passenger cars and trucks. Despite a reliance on imported oil and gas for almost 100% of its

R. Marney, P. Waeber, *The Emerging Markets Investor's Guide to Country Risk*,
https://doi.org/10.1007/978-3-032-26824-2_14

domestic power requirements, the development of the renewable energy sector is underdeveloped. This case study focuses on the domestic institutional, market, and macroeconomic conditions, and the current array of volatile geo-economic drivers in the international sphere that will underpin the board's evaluation of strategic alternatives for the next step in the evolution of TE's business.

Endowment

The country rests between 1°S and 10°N. Average temperatures range between 25 °C and 30 °C, but with a distinct rising trend and increased frequency of extreme heat events. Vulnerability to climate change is moderate to high. Rainfall is generally evenly distributed throughout the year, but with the northernmost parts of the country experiencing a more pronounced dry season. Marcadia's major river system, on which the country depends for much of its water supply, has demonstrated a marked decline in volume. Two severe drought events have occurred in the decades. In the urban areas, the country's traffic jams are legendary, and the resulting air pollution is an increasing threat to public health.

Marcadia has realized the demographic dividend. At present, the fertility rate is approximately at the replacement rate. A youth bulge drives an expansion in the available workforce, which is being well accommodated by the robust growth in the economy. Marcadia's location, highly educated workforce, and investor-friendly regulatory climate have acted as a magnet for foreign tech companies.

Marcadia is fully dependent on imports of oil and gas. Solar and wind-power generation capabilities are underdeveloped. The country's mineral resources are limited. Only copper and iron ore are mined and exported. Relevant for the green economy, there are no domestic origin supplies of lithium, nickel, magnesium, cobalt, graphite, silicon, and rare earths.

History

An Economic Success Story

The country has transformed itself from a low-income, primary sector dependent economy (agriculture, mining, fishing) to a high-middle-income economy boasting a mix of manufacturing and services. The country's development has been fueled by the government's concerted focus on: (i) institution building, (ii) the strengthening of human capital, through investments in secondary and tertiary education, and financial support for gifted students to pursue tertiary/graduate education at home and abroad in STEM topics, and (iii) encouraging FDI in export- and high-tech industries.

Increasing Political Polarization

The form of Marcadia's government is a parliamentary democracy. Politics are characterized by multiple parties, spread across the political spectrum. For much of Marcadia's history, a collection of centrist parties maintained a working majority in the parliament. Political life has recently become more polarized. The old coalition has dissolved, replaced by a sequence of center-left, center-right alliances, and more frequent elections.

Policy focuses have diverged. The center-left's aim has been to strengthen the role of government in society and the economy to ensure equitable, sustainable development and respect for diversity, while the center-right's platform has highlighted smaller government, deregulation, and maintenance of traditional social values. As will figure prominently in this case study, the two sides have adopted opposing policies on the green economy. The center-left sees renewable energy as an important element in the country's climate change adaptation strategy, while the rightist parties view climate change as somewhat of a hoax and investments in clean energy unnecessary.

Institutional Framework

From the outset, the government recognized the positive connection between the development of an appropriate institutional framework and sustainable economic growth. There has been a significant commitment to policies that: (i) strengthen the rule of law; (ii) safeguard civil and economic freedoms; (iii) create and sustain a representative democracy, supported by an effective system of checks and balances and administered by qualified officials; and (iv) invest in human capital (education and health) and physical infrastructure.

The government succeeded on the whole.

However, as often observed, "*there are differences between the story we tell and the reality we see on the ground.*" Two major differences (institutional failings)—relevant to our tale—are:

First

The structure of the judiciary was well designed. However, certain processes were flawed, with the result that the timely adjudication of cases became increasingly rare. Simply stated, the courts were slow. Delays in reaching a verdict, exacerbated by the absence of injunctive relief, resulted in an increased perception by some that the court system could be employed as a tool, for example, to weaken intellectual property protection.

Second

In the context of rapid economic growth and the increased polarization of politics, the investment in physical infrastructure sometimes lagged the requirements of newly developed areas in the country. The electrical grid was a prime example. The result was that in selected new-build townships and commercial/industrial areas, power availability was constrained.

On the positive side, the investment in human capital was exceptionally successful. Literacy, secondary school completion, tertiary enrollment rates, and STEM test results rose to levels that equaled or even exceeded those of advanced economies. Several local universities rose into the top 25 of global rankings, and the saying developed that "MIT" stood for the "Marcadia Institute of Technology" and not *that other school*. A culture of intellectual curiosity and innovation developed. As we will see in the field of electric vehicles, below, Arcadia's young women and men are becoming pioneers in the development of more efficient lithium-ion batteries and may well lead the world in solid-state battery technology in the future.

Lastly, while the changes in the political arena did result in more rapid turnover in administrations and as will become more evident, shifts in policy, the country can still boast a resilient democracy. The legitimacy of election results has never been questioned, and the country's constitution is seen as sacrosanct by all. Hence, the fundamental institutional landscape is secure.

Macroeconomy

The performance of the economy has been spectacular. See Fig. 14.1 below for selected macroeconomic highlights. Since independence, growth has averaged well north of 5% per annum in real terms, inflation has rested in the low single-digit range for most of the time, the twin deficits (fiscal and current account) have remained within a very manageable range, and debt sustainability is unquestioned (see Fig. 14.1 below for selected macroeconomic highlights).

A significant boost to growth has come from international technology companies locating production and assembly facilities, and R&D centers in

	Y-3	Y-2	Y-1	Y
GDP (% Change)	5.6	5.1	5.3	5.2
Inflation (%)	3.8	2.4	2.2	2.5
Fiscal Balance (%GDP)	(1.6)	(2.5)	(2.0)	(2.8)
Government Debt (%GDP)	39	41	40	41
Government Interest Pmts (%GDP)	14.8	15.8	15.2	15.6
Current Account (%GDP)	(0.1)	(0.5)	(0.8)	(0.9)
External Debt/CA Receipts	131	129	128	118
EVI	53	54	51	51

EVI: (Short-Term External Debt + Currently Maturing Long-Term External Debt + Total Nonresident Deposits Over One Year)/Official Foreign Exchange Reserves

Fig. 14.1 Macro data. (*Source: The authors*)

the country. This success reflects the long-term commitment to building effective institutions and the implementation of specific investment incentives for targeted companies. In return for generous tax benefits (corporate levies and import duties), access to subsidized government credits, and profit repatriation provisions, the foreign investors commit to transfer technology, hire/promote local staff, and to contribute to certain community development programs. Inputs are imported, processing occurs, and the output exported. Overall export growth, the share of higher value-added items in the mix, and the size of the trade surplus have increased. This model has benefited from globalization, but as discussed below, the darkening skies and rising headwinds of the global trade environment carry great risk for Marcadia.

Financial System

Marcadia's financial system is broad and deep, with strong fundamentals. The system is well-regulated/supervised. The central bank operates with the mandates of price stability, full employment, and financial stability and enjoys independence from the government. The execution of monetary policy is highly professional. Within the banking sector, institutions are diversified, well-capitalized, and operate with high levels of liquidity and solid asset quality.

Capital markets are deep and liquid. The stock exchange has grown impressively over the last decade and has seen domestic companies increasingly listing there as an alternative to overseas exchanges. Local government and private sector bond issuance is active and the secondary markets robust. Overall, the financial system acts as a positive impetus to economic growth and a bulwark against instability.

Recent Events

In the recent past, two major events have significantly changed the geoeconomic environment.

First, a major producer of oil and gas ("Sustov") invaded a neighbor. As a result, Sustov has been sanctioned in an international campaign led by the "Powerhouse Republic" (PR)—the dominant global economic and political power—and purchases of Sustov's exports have been proscribed. Notwithstanding, in "underground markets" facilitated by "ghost" freighters the sale of Sustov's oil and gas continued. Buyers defying the sanctions have been threatened with secondary sanctions, tariffs, and other measures by the PR.

Second, the new administration in the PR instituted a series of high tariffs that touch on most countries in the world. This rash action contributed to tit-for-tat responses in the areas of trade and finance. These geoeconomic tensions have become acute with Aurelis, whose fast-growing economy competes with the PR for global dominance. In addition to tariffs based (loosely) on commercial considerations, PR has singled out Aurelis for harsher treatment due to its refusal to cut economic ties to Sustov. Selected sanctions have been placed on Aurelis, with the threat of high tariffs and even secondary sanctions on countries that defy the PR actions against Aurelis.

This geoeconomic environment has introduced novel threats to Marcadia: tariffs, embargoes, and sanctions. As background, the country was a founding member of the non-aligned movement and has fastidiously avoided "playing sides" in the geopolitical arena. Indeed, on occasion, their neutral posture has permitted the country to act as constructive intermediary between belligerents. All the while, the country built an economy with strong linkages with suppliers and export customers across the globe. Recent events have placed Marcadia in an increasingly challenging position. The country is fully dependent on imported oil and gas and sources roughly a third from Sustov. In the field of the green economy, save for copper, Marcadia imports 100% of the necessary minerals and rare earths for electric batteries. Most come from either Aurelis or mining companies in third countries owned by Aurelian investors.

Due to Arcadia's continued purchases from these sanctioned countries, the PR is threatening to impose secondary trade and investment sanctions on Arcadia. To cease imports from the "other side" to escape these secondary sanctions would carry a heavy economic cost, and there are many in Marcadia who would object to forsaking Aurelis, a long-standing friend. In certain cases, the impact would be to raise costs—accessing more expensive alternative sources—while in others—EV inputs from Aurelis—the complete cessation of supply would immobilize production altogether, as alternative supplies are not available at all. Marcadia chose to continue, with an indication to the PR that an attempt would be made to diversify away from the two countries overtime. In response, the government of the PR opted to use tariffs in place of secondary sanctions. An initial across-the-board tariff of 35% was soon replaced with a graduated scale of between 10% and 50% on a range of consumer durables, most notably computers and smart phones. Discussions with the PR have continued. Marcadia has countered with: (i) reiteration of the diversification pledge; (ii) investment concessions, which would open sectors of the economy to selected private investors from the PR, and (ii) in cooperation with the foreign electronic end-product producers to source, when possible, inputs from countries the PR feels are friendlier (i.e., not Aurelis). The Marcadia-Aurelis commercial ties are mutually beneficial and in truth are unlikely to change materially over the long term, despite the policies of the current PR administration.

A local economist has estimated that the impact of these measures could shave between 0.5% and 1.5% of GDP, depending on the level and duration of the PR actions. Purchases of large-ticket items such as vehicles are projected to decline noticeably, as lower aggregate demand pushes up unemployment and lowers household incomes.

As discussed below, these developments will become quite relevant for TE, with respect to demand for their EV production and the cost/availability of essential inputs for lithium-ion batteries.

14.2 The Investee: Tomorrow's Energy (TE)

History

Following graduation two decades ago, a recently minted PhD from the electrical engineering doctoral program of the Marcadia Institute of Technology took a research position at a leading, global consumer products manufacturing company.

Several years later, upon returning home to Marcadia for the holidays, he met up with two MIT batchmates. Over a few beers, he commented that when he bought a few batteries for home appliances for his mother earlier that day he was struck by how expensive they were, almost twice what he had seen outside of the country. There were no tariffs involved, just plain old discriminatory pricing, he concluded. This was the thought that would eventually lead to the birth of TE. The three pooled their limited financial resources and pulled in some funding from GTI, the country's leading PE firm. Marcadia Battery Ltd. (MBL) was created.

Within four years, MBL had grown significantly, with operations expanding into multiple segments of consumer appliances in their home market and in selected overseas locations. Then, the three struck gold in the form of a contract to provide batteries to a start-up domestic producer of 3G mobile cellular handsets.

The true, transformational event came several years later when a fellow MIT alum, now the co-owner of a small but growing two- and three-wheel vehicle manufacturer approached the group with a proposition—let's develop a local battery for my new electric vehicle division, and we can staff the R&D team by bringing back all the brilliant MIT graduates working overseas. The idea was enthusiastically received. TE was created to house this effort and the foray into the green economy began in earnest.

Fortuitously, the ruling government coalition at the time had begun to support such investments as a means of lowering the bill for imported oil, attenuating the force of reoccurring, debilitating heat waves, and lessening the stifling air pollution in the cities. TE greatly benefited from low-cost loans, tax credits, and accelerated depreciation.

Their R&D team succeeded in developing a proprietary model of lithium-ion battery for vehicles, which was lighter-weight and cheaper. This product undercut the imports and fueled rapid sales growth. Additionally, TE created a subsidiary to operate a related business in battery swapping for drivers of these two- and three-wheel vehicles. In this activity, a driver enters a swapping station where their low-charge battery is replaced with a fully charged one in minutes. This business grew with great success, with coverage soon extending to the major metropolitan areas in the country. At this point, the founders of the two- and three-wheel vehicle production company announced their intention to sell the business. When it appeared likely that a foreign group with its own battery manufacturing unit might buy the company, TE swooped in to block the deal and acquired the business.

Along the way, GTI continued to support TE's growth. By the beginning of year T, Tomorrow's Energy was looking into the next phase of its growth.

Structure and Ownership

As of year T, the corporate structure of the group appeared as depicted in Fig. 14.2:

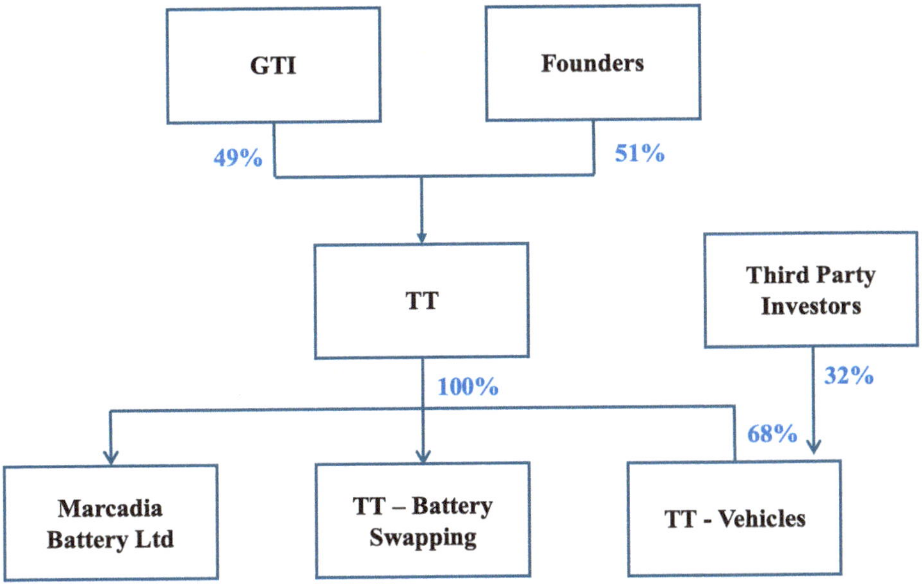

Fig. 14.2 Corporate structure

The Business

Roughly 95% of TE's sales are currently to the domestic market. The legacy business of MBL is now a small portion of the group turnover, and of that, all is sold to local buyers, primarily for use in the domestic market. TE-Vehicles (the two- and three-wheelers) produces only for the national market, and the service business of TE-Battery Swapping is for local use. TE's EV battery business does export. With the development of their newest generation Lithium-ion battery, the company has come onto the radar screen of foreign EV manufacturers and EV fleet operators, even in Aurelis, the global leader in EV technology and production. Today, while foreign sales account for just under 5% of total revenue, this export potential represents a significant future growth opportunity for TE.

Overall, TT is cash flow positive and has registered consistent ROIs in the low to mid-teens. Leverage is low.

Government and Green Energy

As noted above, Marcadia's political life has been changing. A stable center-right coalition-dominated landscape has given way to a more volatile environment. Opposing coalitions of the right and the left have begun recently to trade the gavel with an unprecedented frequency in the country's history. Policy differences are many. With respect to energy, the left-leaning coalition has continued the previous centrists' support for an ambitious green energy agenda, while the right-leaning parties have moved to reverse many of the regulatory, fiscal, and other policies enacted in the past.

As background, at the high-water mark of public support for green energy, measures included:

- *Regulatory*: mandated carbon reduction goals, streamlined permitting approvals, green energy building code requirements.
- *Fiscal: investment and production tax credits, allowance for accelerated depreciation, reduction/elimination of import duties, VAT rebates for consumers.*
- Finance: Ministry of Commerce green energy direct funding and loan guarantees, mandated minimum bank portfolio commitment to green energy projects.
- Public-Private Partnerships: feasibility studies related to: (i) grid expansion and modernization and (ii) a nationwide EV charging station network.
- Innovation: financial support for a green energy research and development center at MIT.
- Public Awareness: education around energy conservation, decarbonization, green energy choices.
- *TE's businesses benefited directly from these policies in various ways; in particular, a lower cost of debt capital, the availability of tax credits, and decreased input costs. Indirect boosts came from the demand side where increased public awareness of the means and benefits of green energy, and VAT rebates have combined to strengthen* interest in renewable alternatives.

Since that time, the rightist parties have weakened or even eliminated certain regulatory and policy initiatives during their time in office, only to have the succeeding administration reverse the actions. As a result of this policy instability, renewable energy represents a minor part of Marcadia's power generation. One small crack in the reactionary wall has begun to show, as geopolitics threatened access to cheap oil and gas supplies.

For companies in the sector like TE, this policy volatility has created a predictable atmosphere of uncertainty that has slowed new investments and weighed on top-line growth, with a further, adverse knock-on effect in the form of a higher, marginal cost of capital. Notwithstanding, TE's business has continued to grow profitably, albeit less than would have been expected without the shifts in policy.

In two areas, the impact has been felt more for TE. *First,* plans for an IPO have been mothballed for the time being at the recommendation of GTI. *Second,* discussion of a move into EV production has been delayed. The challenge of unpredictable and volatile government policy will be redoubled by the arrival of the storm clouds of sanctions, counter-sanctions, tariffs, and more!

Oil, Sanctions, and Counter-Sanctions

In the aftermath of Sustov's invasion of its neighbor, oil prices spiked temporarily from the low 60 s (USD per barrel) to as high as 120 before falling into the 80 s range. Since that time, prices have trended downward into the mid to low 60 s. This period of benign energy prices reflected, in part, an ambivalence on the part of the PR administration on the question of effective measures to halt Sustov's oil and gas exports. Shell companies, ghost freighters, and murky bank transfers were clearly in play. Yet, exports continued as the PR turned a blind eye, save for the opportunistic use of these oil purchases as a justification for punishing "today's target" with higher tariffs, much like Captain Renaud using the discovery of gambling in Rick's Cafe as a pretext for closing the nightclub, as he pocketed his roulette table winnings in the 1940s movie *Casablanca.*

Finally, exhausted by Sustov's refusal to enter good faith negotiations to halt the war, the PR announced a set of directed sanctions against the energy sector in Sustov. Time will tell if these are just words. If not, then upward pressure on prices should follow.

For TE, oil price uncertainty or renewed price spikes are a double-edged sword. On the positive side, public (even the conservative parties traditionally opposed to the green economy) and private support for renewable energy development will increase. On the negative side, a slowdown in economic growth could hurt product demand, and increase the energy component of production costs. Net, net? TE's management has come out on the "positive" side.

Tariffs and More

As discussed above, Marcadia dodged the bullet of secondary sanctions, but has been hit by tariffs on its sales of computers and smart phones to the PR. For TE, the situation is manageable. The tariffs' impact on domestic economic activity of slowing exports will of course weigh on the company's top line. However, directly the PR's actions less so. In the last fiscal year, TE's sales to the RP amounted to only a low single-digit percentage of total turnover.

A subsequent private "accommodation" between the CEO of the importer of TE's advanced batteries—the country's largest producer of EVs—and the PR's administration resulted in a drastic reduction in the battery tariff rate. Further, despite the PR government's official lack of support for green energy, the importer's orders look to rise, given the attraction of TE's battery's superior characteristics.

Strategic Alternatives

In discussing TE's strategic alternatives, consider:

Existing

(1) TE

This EV Battery production business represents TE's growth engine. The development of their advanced lithium-ion battery has caught the attention of foreign electric vehicle manufacturers. Additionally, TE and the MIT's R&D work on future battery technologies such as solid-state and nickel-based batteries has received great praise in technical, industry journals. The recent increased order from the RP's largest EV manufacturer and conversations with Aurelis companies bode well, if geoeconomic headwinds don't rise too much. Overall, the future performance does depend on a consistent, supportive policy stance on the part of the government of Marcadia and benign external markets. Despite significant R&D expenditures, the company is profitable on a standalone basis.

(2) MBL

This small, and only marginally profitable, legacy business is on the sales block and will be exited. Several buyers are in the data room.

(3) TE-Vehicles: Two- and Three-Wheelers

This moderately but consistently profitable business can be scaled successfully, especially given TE's advantage in batteries. Advances in batteries and vehicle design distinguish the company and bode well for growth and increased profitability. The future performance does depend on a consistent, supportive policy stance on the part of the government. The existing plant has some additional capacity but over the longer term, a larger and more modern facility will be necessary. However, there are nagging reservations about this business, as it deviates from the pure focus on batteries and battery swapping, preferred by two of the founders.

(4) TE-Battery Swapping

The existing business has recently broken even. Projected usage volumes and improvements in charging efficiency are expected to support increased profitability. The grid's long-term structural dependency on oil-fired power plants in an environment of higher oil prices could weigh on profitability. The expansion of this business to new geographies will require significant capital investment, but can be justified, especially should government invest appropriately in the expansion/modernization of the electrical grid. The future performance does depend on a consistent, supportive policy stance on the part of the government.

Future

(1) EV: Cars and Trucks

EV passenger cars and trucks represent the future in transportation. A move into this area might seem an obvious next step for TE. Indeed, the domestic traditional car and truck company—National Motors—has indicated interest in buying TE's battery business, and failing this, to form a JV to collaborate on hybrid and EV production. TE's pedigree is compelling in several respects. The company is the clear market leader in batteries, with innovative designs that offer superior cost efficiency, power, durability characteristics. Despite the opportunistic and defensive purchase of the business, their franchise in two- and three-wheelers has been highly successful. This fact demonstrates the capacity to manage vehicle manufacturing at scale and to improve designs that significantly reduce the weight of the vehicles. The experience in building and operating the swapping infrastructure has also equipped it with relevant operating skills and assets for EV charging. Notwithstanding, a move into EV car and truck manufacturing represents a very big and potentially risky step forward. The capital requirements and the stress that these could place on TE's operational and financial resources cannot be underestimated. EV businesses have absorbed an immense amount of capital, with cash flow-breakeven and profitability elusive. The leading EV manufacturer in the PR took ten years to reach breakeven, and many other start-ups have yet to do so. Legacy car and truck producers have benefited from their existing infrastructure, processes, and human capital, have spent vast amounts, and still have not shown consistent profitability for their EV divisions. At GTI's insistence, TE's board did reluctantly agree to undertake a formal analysis of this alternative, but with the understanding that three fundamental assumptions would be in play: *first,* government policy would need to be clearly supportive of electric vehicles and that such regulation and programs would not be subject to change; *second,* some form of joint venture with the country's internal combustion engine-based car and truck manufacturer, with strict protections for TE's battery IP; and *third,* there would be stability of supply of key inputs for battery production, likely in the form of a long-term contract or other arrangement with Aurelis.

(2) Solar Power: Batteries

A classmate of the founders is the current Minister of Commerce in the ruling, conservative coalition. As noted, this coalition has been a long-time foe of renewable energy. The Minister has indicated there is growing support within the government for a push into renewable energy, primarily solar. Even to the traditionalists in the parliament, there is no avoiding the fact that Marcadia is highly vulnerable in terms of energy supply. As noted above, the country has no domestic oil, gas, or coal resources; 100% of its hydrocarbon supply must be imported. Despite having regions with high solar insolation, the country has very limited solar generation and storage resources. This situation reflects the failure of successive administrations to coalesce around, execute and maintain a renewable energy policy in Marcadia. The most recent "oil crisis", stifling pollution, and clear signs of global warming, have convinced officials on both sides of the political divide in the country of the need to move aggressively into renewable energy. In the cabinet, TE is recognized as a world-class designer and producer of lithium-ion batteries. The Minister has made it clear that a move by TE into the solar storage space or even into a role as solar power generation and distribution company would be well received. As a result, TE is considering moving into the solar storage space.

The board of TE instructed management to evaluate the strategic alternative in this area.

14.3 A Strategic Decision

In this section, we will review together the summary minutes taken by the GTI managing partner of the board's deliberations to review the management's subsequent presentation of strategic alternatives. The reader can imagine there being in-depth discussion of pages and pages and pages of supporting analysis and data that filled the daylong session.

The use of the summary minutes aims at highlighting the key drivers of the board's decision-making.

I. Four alternative paths were outlined: (1) an EV joint venture with National Motors; (2) a new subsidiary in Solar Storage; (3) a solar generation and distribution JV; and (4) the status quo.

II. The discussion of the EV alternative presented a mix of pros and cons. On the positive side: (i) a large potential market; (2) a compelling energy story; (3) TE's mastery of the essential battery component of the EV; (4) vertical integration in the vehicle segment that could replicate the company's success in the two- and three-wheeler space. However, significant negatives were also identified, including: (1) the high capital requirements, which risk escalating over the expected long period of time before breakeven; (2) the policy uncertainty/volatility in Marcadia; (3) TE's concerns about the control of their battery IP; (4) the uncertainty around supply of battery inputs; and (5) the non-core nature of vehicle production. The biggest concern was the potential price tag of the investment at a time of geoeconomic instability that could affect battery costs. For TE's legacy businesses, such a development could dampen returns, but for a high-stakes foray into the EV business at a time of policy uncertainty, the outcome could be catastrophic. All were highly skeptical.

III. The high-level case for solar is compelling. The country's energy supply is vulnerable to adverse, global forces outside of the government's control. The potential macroeconomic threats of rising oil and gas prices or, at worst, inadequate supply are serious. Renewable sources could mitigate these risks. The private conversations with the government indicate that the politicians on both sides of the parliamentary divide are finally coming around to the need to develop solar and wind power in the country. That TE could play a role is evident. The question is in what form?

IV. Two business models for solar were presented. The first (#2 above) would see TE "stick to batteries". The business would build on its current expertise on lithium-ion batteries and develop batteries for solar storage. TE would act as supplier of these specialized batteries to solar power generation and distribution companies. Given the company's R&D and production strength, this activity would be highly successful, and we could create a dominant position in this sector over the long-term. The second option (#3 above) is a vertical integration strategy, in which TE will create a joint venture with a leading international solar power developer. This alternative carries a higher capital price tag and higher financial risks, has greater policy/regulation exposure, and may be affected more by external trade issues (solar panels in addition to the battery components) but potentially could generate higher returns.

V. Prior to the board vote, the discussion was summarized:

EV Versus Solar

Aspect	EV	Solar
Market growth potential	Significant and rapid	Significant and steady
Alignment for TE	An extension from two- and three-wheelers, but with significant design and production challenges	For the storage segment, great alignment, while for the generation/distribution segment, the need to rely on the JV partner
R&D	Significant	Moderate
Policy and regulation exposure	High	Moderate to high
Capital requirements	Very high	For the storage segment, low while for the generation/distribution segment, moderate
Time to breakeven	Long	For the storage segment, short while for the generation/distribution segment, medium
Financial risk	High	For the storage segment, low while for the generation/distribution segment, low to moderate
Competitive edge	Moderate	For the storage segment, very high while for the generation/distribution segment, moderate to high

A clear consensus emerged against the EV alternative. The group agreed the project faces high regulatory, technical, operating, and especially financial risks. The capital requirement is very high, with much of the amount having to go in upfront. The necessary quantum would be more than TE's current capitalization and would result in significant dilution for the existing shareholders. Under the best of circumstances, breakeven is expected to require many years, up to a decade based on global peers, raising the specter of additional capital calls. For these international companies, the electric car and truck business has required nerves of steel and a seemingly bottomless bank account. Any one of three "gremlins" could drag down the business further. *First*, supportive government policy and regulations for the green economy are necessary. Given history, there is a risk that this may prove elusive. *Second*, should geoeconomic tensions rise and access to essential raw materials be adversely impacted, cost of goods sold would rise at a minimum and the outcome could be even worse, were supplies to be cut-off. *Third*, the threat of imported EVs is present. Today, imported cars and trucks are subject to 25% tariffs. This protection has been crucial to National Motors, as it would be for the EV JV. In an increasingly mercantilist trading world, Marcadia might be forced to lower or even eliminate such levies, hence opening the domestic market to EV imports, as a concession to avoid hefty tariffs on its exports. The PR has shown a willingness recently to employ this tactic. The CEO of the leading EV manufacturer in the PR is well connected with the administration and may attempt to influence tariff policy against Marcadia to help gain access to the country's EV market. Such a development would constrain the topline and squeeze margins. Given the size of the financial bet and the expected leverage to drive the EV business, the gremlin driven, downside results could become an existential threat quite easily. Further, the financial stresses could spill over into TE's crown jewels—the battery businesses. Key to the continued success is R&D, especially as the industry moves into new technologies. A "car wreck" in the EV JV could imperil this effort and drag down the core battery business, an area of great sentimental value to the three founders. Lastly, there is suspicion that National Motors is just after TE's intellectual property in batteries and that a JV agreement and the country's ineffective IP laws would not protect TE against any skullduggery should the JV flounder. Overall, the potential downside for TE did not appear to be justified by the base case's return prospects.

For the solar alternative, especially the solar storage element, the view was much more positive. Regulatory exposure is less acute. The technical requirements of the battery business are well within TE's capabilities. The solar generation and distribution requirements are standardized. The capital requirement is low to moderate, and the amounts can be phased calibrated to the evolution of the business. Cash flow and net profitability breakeven are achieved earlier in the base case scenario. Even in the downside case where access to raw materials and imported equipment are affected by geoeconomic events, the financial impact is more manageable given the stronger financial buffers. Hence, the overall residual financial risk is satisfactory. Given TE's strong position in battery production and innovation track record, the competitive edge in solar storage area is arguably unequaled and would be substantial in the generation and distribution space for the foreseeable future.

The question then arose, having dismissed the EV project in order to focus on solar, what's more attractive, storage or generation/distribution?

Solar Storage Versus Solar Generation/Distribution

Aspect	Solar storage	Solar generation and distribution
Revenue model	Battery sales	Battery sales and periodic service payments
R&D	Low to moderate	Moderate
Policy and regulation Exposure	Low	Moderate to high
Capital requirements	Low	Moderate
Time to breakeven	Short-term	Medium term
Financial risk	Low	Low to moderate
Competitive edge	Very high	Moderate to high

The board's view quickly coalesced around the Solar Storage alternative. Such an investment aligns well with TE's core battery business focus and builds on the company's superior technology and outstanding innovation track record. The capital requirement will be much lower and can be partially funded by internal cash flow. Solar storage is an adjacent space for TE and hence implementation and operational risks are low. Time to cash flow breakeven and profitability can be expected to be short, and the return on investment high and stable. Additionally, the product suite could find market demand across a wide range of energy sectors. The downside risks of changing government policies, access to raw materials, and import competition remain. However, as a market-leading battery producer, TE can better navigate these shocks. Overall, the board's unanimous preference was to "stick to our knitting". Solar generation and distribution are arguably an adjacent space. However, the opportunity in batteries alone is enough for the group and doesn't come with the risks of a new business line and the vagaries of a JV, at a time of great uncertainty and volatility on the global stage.

VI. The board approved a project budget to explore further the solar storage business opportunity.

14.4 Closing: Role of Country Risk

There are two levels to be examined: macro and the firm. The macro-level encompasses the economy and society, and the firm-level pertains to the individual enterprise. Political, economic, and financial characteristics and ongoing developments in Marcadia, both positive and negative in nature, influence the country's macroeconomic and market performance. In turn, TE's evaluation of these drivers influences the company's investment decisions.

In our narrative, the relevant, macro-level elements are:

Positive

- Solid macroeconomic fundamentals
- Well-developed institutions
- Robust financial system
- Strong human capital and innovation culture
- Cooperative foreign relationships

Negative

- Growing political polarization, leading to a degree of policy dysfunction (relevant for TE relates to policy and regulation on the green economy, which has resulted in severe underdevelopment of renewable energy in the country)
- No domestic oil and gas reserves, hence 100% dependence on imports
- Exposure to an international trading system growing increasingly fragmented and protectionist, with a rogue power imposing tariffs capriciously
- Reliance on key minerals and other imports for key sectors of the economy

From the "negative", we identified disruptions in the global trading system—PR's tariff actions—as the paramount external risk, leading to a slowdown in domestic economic activity. Given the sound fundamentals at the macro level, this development does not result in serious damage or, given the robust financial system, any financial contagion.

However, at the firm level, this slowdown could weigh on capital goods purchases, a potential negative for TE today and in the future. The PR tariffs on TE's exports are relevant, but don't have a material impact on TE's performance and financial condition given the company's small volume of such sales at present. There are indications of interest in TE's advanced lithium-ion batteries on the part of PR's major EV producer. Given politics in the PR, there is a real possibility that the CEO of the PR company would succeed in negotiating a private deal to reduce or even eliminate import duties. Such a backroom deal would facilitate this sales channel despite the generalized move to increased protectionism.

Any potential disruption of supply of rare earths and essential minerals represents a serious threat to TE's business, given the complete dependence on imports. Aurelis is the major supplier. Relations between Aurelis and Marcadia have been historically "respectful and constructive", and on this basis, supply should be secure. The geoeconomic rivalry between the PR and Aurelis, and the Sustov oil and gas sanctions/secondary sanctions dangers, could have threatened this supply security. However, clever diplomacy on the part of Marcadia has appeared to defuse the brewing crisis. Taken together, these considerations lead to a view that the current business outlook for TE is favorable.

The discussion of strategic alternatives for expansion into new businesses assumed that the economy would continue to perform well, tariffs be manageable, and essential imports be available. For TE, the major question is the stance of the government toward the green economy. Political polarization, with one side supportive, one not, combined with more rapid turnover in administrations has constrained the growth of electric vehicles and the development of renewable energy, most notably, solar. Recent "green shoots" of interest on the part of the conservative coalition in solar power have encouraged TE to study solar storage in the next phase in their development. Their decision to pursue solar storage, rather than solar power generation/distribution or even the jump into hyper-space that an EV JV would represent, is idiosyncratic—batteries being their core competency and requiring a manageable quantum of capital—and not principally a function of macro-level factors. That having been said, one assumes that the board's ultimate decision will incorporate the nature of the government's commitment to green energy and the degree of policy reliability.

15

Case Study 2

In this chapter, we examine the case of Global Nutrition—a leading, global producer of infant formula and early-childhood enriched milk powder, and nutritional supplements—which is considering an investment in the Republic of Solera, a BB (positive outlook)-rated country.

Until recently, Solera was ruled by a conservative government. Inequality was (and continues) high, and vested interest in this primarily agricultural economy succeeded in limiting FDI from companies like Global Nutrition. The new, center-left government has prioritized reducing wealth and income inequality, lowering a serious nutrition deficit in the poorer classes, and encouraging FDI to address certain social priorities and the chronic and widening current account deficit that poses a long-term threat to economic stability. These policies stand in strong contrast to the former conservative administration. Solera has represented an important export market for Global Nutrition, and their management has agreed to study the possible establishment of the production facility in the country. This investment has a defensive aspect, as the government is considering tariff and other measures to encourage foreign companies such as Global Nutrition to invest in Solera and help develop the great, but untapped potential in the dairy sector. This process takes place against the backdrop of some discontent on the part of middle- and upper-class voters, who have been affected by the new government's more assertive tax audit and collection practices, and among landowners to a land reform agenda aimed at unlocking the agricultural potential of the vast quantity of idle lands. The next, nationwide elections take place in just under two years, and current polls point to a very tight race.

R. Marney, P. Waeber, *The Emerging Markets Investor's Guide to Country Risk*,
https://doi.org/10.1007/978-3-032-26824-2_15

15.1 Country: Republic of Solera

Endowment

Solera is situated between 12° and 22° North. The country consists of low-lying plains along the coast that give way to extensive, rolling highlands with elevations up to 2000 meters. The climate is temperate in these areas, with temperatures averaging around 15–20 °C. The country has distinct wet and dry seasons. In the wet season, the lowlands experience heavy rainfall due to the regional monsoon, while the annual patterns in the highlands see a more even distribution. A series of microclimates is present in these higher elevations.

The country is already feeling the impact of climate change. In the coastal plains and lower highlands, more frequent and intense heatwaves are being observed, with faster warming rates registered in the highlands that threaten certain of the microclimates. In the recent past, rain patterns have demonstrated a degree of change. Previously rare, prolonged dry spells and even drought have been occurring with increasing frequency. These changes in temperature and rainfall have reduced yields of temperature-sensitive crops and native pastures and increased the range of pests and pathogens affecting both crops and livestock.

Solera is in the early stages of its demographic transition. The fertility rate is declining and approaching the replacement level. This downward trend has just begun. The country confronts two dependent cohorts: high numbers between the ages 0 and 14 and a second, older youth bulge in the 15–24 age range, which is beginning to join the working-age population.

Land-owning patterns are highly concentrated, with much land lying idle. Imagining a kind of "Gini Coefficient for Land", the figure peaked in the upper 80 s (versus an overall Gini Coefficient in the mid to high 50 s). The estimated idle and/or underutilized land may be as high as 50% of the total.

Institutional Framework

Solera inherited generally strong institutions upon independence. The rule of law, the judicial system, regulation in business and finance, and infrastructure are superior to the country's rating cohort.

However, since independence, increasing wealth and income inequality have plagued society. Until recently, the government has been dominated by the country's landed and commercial elite. Policy has not focused on the challenges of stagnant, real household incomes, remedying underdevelopment of available health and education resources, and resolving a distressing degree of undernourishment present for much of the population.

A few years ago, an electoral shock occurred. The long-serving right-of-center party—the National Democratic Front (NDF)—lost to the center-left United Peoples Party (UPP). The overall focus of the government's policy has been to address these economic and social inequalities.

A centerpiece of the program has been childhood nutrition. Two elements of this policy initiative have been to increase access to infant formula/milk, enriched cereals, and other food products, and to develop local production as a means of reducing dependence on costly and often insecure imports. For the latter, the government has encouraged leading global companies, who currently supply the imports, to invest in the establishment of production capacity in the country. Such investments would attract a series of government fiscal and financial incentives tied to the achievement of impact goals.

Macroeconomy

Solera boasts a balanced economy, with agriculture and agro-processing figuring as significant contributors to both national income and exports. The extensive highlands support high-value crops requiring cooler temperatures, including coffee, tea, horticultural products (flowers, berries, vegetables), and certain fruits (apples and pears). The presence of microclimates allows for a diverse range of specialty products. Dairy farming in the highlands has grown noticeably in recent years, but has been constrained by land-owning patterns that have resulted in large tracts held by absentee owners resting inactive.

The UPP inherited a generally healthy economy as depicted in Fig. 15.1.

Despite its redistributive policies, the new administration has adopted a measured approach intended not to destabilize the favorable macroeconomic situation by excessive, debt-funded fiscal spending or reckless monetary

	Y-3	Y-2	Y-1	Y
GDP (real, % YoY)	4.7	5.1	4.9	5.0
Inflation (% YoY)	2.1	2.4	2.3	2.8
Fiscal Balance (% GDP)	(2.1)	(1.9)	(2.0)	(2.4)
Revenue/GDP (% GDP)	17.0	18.3	19.8	21.1
Current Account (% GDP)	(1.7)	(1.8)	(1.7)	(2.0)
Debt/GDP (% GDP)	58.0	57.0	59.0	62.0
Debt/Revenue (% rev)	208.0	198.0	205.0	214.0
Debt Service/Revenue (% rev)	52.0	49.5	51.3	53.5
External Debt / CA Recipts	45.7	47.1	46.9	49.5
Gini Coefficient	55.0	54.0	53.0	51.0

Fig. 15.1 Macro data. (*Source: The authors*)

expansion. Instead, the focus has been on supporting government investment by increasing the efficiency of tax collections. This latter action has "ruffled some feathers" in the high-net-worth and local corporate communities, long used to laxity on the part of the national revenue authority. Revenue to GDP has risen from 17% to 21%. This success has kept the debt service burden materially unchanged, with the total government debt service to revenue ratio only edging up from 52 to 53.5, and external debt to CA receipts from 45.7 to 49.5.

The external liquidity position represents a potential source of vulnerability. The current account has been persistently in deficit, resting in the 1.7–2.0% of GDP range. Solera is highly dependent on agricultural exports. As a result, the country is exposed to the threat of (i) supply disruptions at home due to drought or disease and (ii) overall terms of trade shocks in volatile, global markets. At present, FX reserve coverage amounts to seven months imports and the government's managed float regime has succeeded in maintaining the REER (Real Effective Exchange Rate: inflation adjusted, trade-weighted exchange rate) within a plus/minus range of a few percentage points for much of the last five years. However, the liquidity buffer could prove to be a gossamer band if the current account deficit were to widen materially.

The risk scenarios are many, but most likely would take the form of waterfall of events: (i) starting with some material shock in the agricultural sector that materially widens the current account deficit; (ii) morphing into a currency crisis, as FX reserves are depleted and the government is forced to abandon the managed float in favor of strong devaluation; and (iii) knock-on effects to the financial system, as the impact of FX translation-losses combine with increased NPLs and heightened provisions pressure systemic solvency.

The recognition of these risks has prompted the new government to consider steps to incentivize increased foreign direct investment. Historically, vested, domestic interests working with past, conservative administrations succeeded in limiting the involvement of foreign capital in the economy. The new government has controversially reversed these past impediments. The developments in the infant and childhood nutrition space are an example of this policy reorientation.

The Government's "Family and Food Program"

As noted above, a key plank in the government's platform is the improvement in infant and childhood nutrition. The Ministry of Health has highlighted the need to increase the availability and lower the cost of a range of products, including infant formula and enriched dairy products. Disadvantaged families would receive government financial aid to support their access to these products.

To ensure supply, imports alone are not a viable solution given the consideration of cost and the impact on the country's balance of payments. Several international companies, including Global Nutrition, have been identified as prime candidates for onshoring production. To encourage foreign brands like Global Nutrition to set up local production plants and reduce imports, the Solera government looks to implement a multi-faceted strategy.

First, the government will phase in a series of measures aimed at reducing imports. These include rising import tariffs on imported formula and powdered milk (after a suitable lag to permit new domestic consumption to fill the gap) and a local content requirement or "Made in Solera" labeling campaigns that appeal to consumer patriotism.

Second, to incentivize foreign investors, the government has approved several measures, including (i) tax and subsidy investment incentives; (ii) supportive regulatory and policy changes; and (iii) infrastructure and ecosystem development. Additionally, the domestic supply of milk needs to be increased. Given the rich, untapped potential for dairy farming in the highlands, the government has been exploring measures to incentivize the owners of the vast tracts of idle land to cooperate in this national priority. For landowners who refuse, the government is prepared to force the sale of the land.

Financial System

Solera's financial system is exclusively bank-based, save for the government bond market, where the direct buyers are the banks and a diverse set of domestic and international institutional investors, and the banks exercise the role of market makers.

The Bank of Solera acts as both a central bank under a dual mandate in its monetary policy role and the financial system supervisory authority. The quality of supervision is fair to good.

Overall systemic health is good, with solvency, profitability, asset quality, and liquidity metrics above regulatory minima. One area of potential vulnerability is the open currency positions (short FX) carried by most banks. Overall, the net, open currency position amounts to roughly 20% of consolidated banking system equity. To date, given the effective management of the exchange rate, this risk has not exercised an adverse effect on systemic solvency.

Lending policies are conservative throughout the industry, with low loan-to-value ceilings and demanding credit standards. The result is that asset quality has remained high over the cycle, with limited impact of cost of risk on profitability. However, the negative side of this credit approach is that debt capital is constrained in several sectors. For our purposes here, the development of dairy farming by small-to-medium operators has been hampered by this fact, as land as collateral is subjected to a severe haircut from already low valuations.

Recent Events

Elections for the Presidency and the Legislative Assembly are held every six years. Just over four years ago, the center-left opposition party—UPP—unexpectedly won the Presidency and swept to a margin of 57 seats in the 300-seat Assembly.

This outcome was due to widespread unhappiness with the government's handling of the pandemic. Since that time, support for the UPP has slipped in the polls. Part is the usual criticism of the incumbent party, but much is the result of: (i) the government's aggressive tax audit and collection efforts aimed at increasing revenue to fund increased fiscal outlays, while minimizing incremental debt, and (ii) the threat of forced land sales to support the expansion of dairy and other farming in central highlands.

The latest poll placed the two parties in a dead heat, were the elections to be held today. The significance of a return of the rightist NDF party to power for this case is the threat to the key elements in the government's Family and Food program. The leadership of the NDF in the Assembly has indicated opposition to the increase in food subsidies to the poor, the investment incentives being offered to foreign investors, and the forced land sales.

15.2 The Investment

Exploratory Diligence Team Report/Recommendation

1. **Summary and Recommendation**

We view this opportunity favorably and recommend we continue to the next phase to negotiate a term sheet. We stress that this is a high-risk, high-reward strategic investment for our company. The opportunity is being created by a unique and potentially fleeting political alignment in Solera. We can secure a dominant, first-mover position in a large, underserved market with strong government support. However, this entire opportunity is contingent on the current government's policies remaining in place, which is a significant risk given the upcoming election.

2. **Opportunities**

   (A) **Securing Market Access and Defensive Investment**

   (i) The Solera government is explicitly planning to implement protectionist measures (tariffs, local content requirements) to encourage local production. Investing now allows us to get ahead of these changes.
   (ii) Instead of facing rising costs and barriers as an exporter, we can become a local producer, protecting and likely expanding its market share in a strategically important country.

   (B) **First-Mover Advantage in an Untapped Market**

   (i) Solera has a significant, government-identified nutrition deficit, especially among infants and children. This represents a large, latent demand for our products.
   (ii) By being one of the first major international companies to invest, we can establish brand dominance, secure government partnerships, and build a distribution network that will be difficult for competitors to replicate later.

   (C) **Strong and Aligned Government Incentives**

   (i) The government's "Family and Food Program" is a core policy priority. Our objectives of selling nutritional products are perfectly aligned with the government's social goals (improving childhood nutrition).
   (ii) This alignment translates into tangible incentives: tax breaks, subsidies, and supportive regulatory changes, which can significantly improve the project's financial returns and lower the initial investment burden.

   (D) **Potential for Backward Integration and Supply Chain Control**

   (i) The government is keen to develop the local dairy sector, which is currently constrained by idle land. This presents a future opportunity for us to source raw materials (milk) locally, reducing costs, FX exposure, and supply chain risks associated with imports.

(ii) We could eventually partner with or incentivize local dairy farmers, creating a more resilient and cost-effective supply chain.

(E) **Favorable Current Macroeconomic Fundamentals**

(i) The government is pursuing its social goals without reckless fiscal or monetary expansion. Key metrics like debt service ratios are stable.
(ii) We deem the institutional framework to be strong, which reduces operational risks related to contract enforcement and regulation.

3. **Risks**

(A) **Significant Political and Regulatory Risk**

(i) The next election is in two years, and the race is a "dead heat". The opposition party NDF has explicitly stated it opposes the key policies underpinning our possible investment: food subsidies, foreign investor incentives, and forced land sales.
(ii) If the NDF wins, we could find our incentives revoked, tariffs not implemented (removing its competitive advantage), and its entire business case undermined. This is an existential risk to the investment.
(iii) Alternatively, the policy rollback by the NDF could be partial or phased-in slowly, and agreements/contracts renegotiated. Hence, the impact of an NDF victory is not necessarily as severe.

(B) **Social Unrest and Implementation Risk**

(i) The government's policies (aggressive tax audits, threat of forced land sales) are creating discontent among the wealthy, landowners, and middle–/upper-class voters.
(ii) This could lead to social unrest or legal challenges that delay the government's agenda, including the development of the dairy sector and the rollout of its nutrition program, thus delaying the payoff for our investment.

(C) **FX and Macroeconomic Vulnerabilities**

(i) Solera has a persistent current account deficit and is highly dependent on volatile agricultural exports.
(ii) A climate-related shock (drought) could trigger a "waterfall" crisis: a widening deficit -> depletion of FX reserves -> currency devaluation.

(iii) For us, a sharp devaluation could have a material adverse impact through a reduction in the book value of the investment (translation loss), could weigh on earnings through an increase in the cost of any imported equipment or raw materials, and lastly could potentially cause a banking crisis, complicating access to local financing.

(D) **Land Reform and Supply Chain Uncertainty**

- The success of the local dairy sector—and thus our potential for adequate local sourcing—hinges on the controversial and politically charged process of unlocking idle land.
- If land reform is slow, blocked, or reversed after an election, local milk supply may remain scarce and expensive; then this would force us to continue relying on costly imports for raw materials, negating a key cost advantage.

(E) **Financial System Constraints**

- While the banking system is stable, it is conservative. This could make it difficult for potential local dairy farmers to get the loans needed to start or expand operations, constraining the growth of the local supply ecosystem. This could constrain domestic supply availability for us.

(F) **Climate Change Impact**

- Solera is already experiencing climate change effects: heatwaves, droughts, and changing rain patterns. These directly threaten agricultural output, including the dairy and crop production that our supply chain would depend on, adding a long-term operational risk.

4. **Subsequent Diligence: Risk Mitigation**

(A) We must conduct rigorous political risk analysis**.** This analysis is extremely important. We should seek meetings with both the ruling UPP and the opposition NDF to understand their positions and negotiate potential safeguards. Based on these conversations, we must model various election outcomes and their impact.

(B) To address these political risks, we will need to negotiate strong investment protections. Our investment agreement with the Solera government should include clauses like stabilization agreements (locking in current incentives) and clear dispute resolution mechanisms (e.g., international arbitration). Additionally, we might consider political risk insurance to cover the eventuality that such an investment agreement is abrogated or materially violated by a future government.

(C) We could also consider a joint venture with a reputable local partner, able to provide political protection against a possible NDF victory. This could help navigate the fraught landscape that could ensue. This consideration is above and beyond the other possible benefits of such a partnership.

(D) We could consider a phased investment approach: Instead of one large lump-sum investment, structure it in phases. The initial phase could be a smaller-scale production facility to serve the market and build relationships. Further expansion would be contingent on the political landscape post-election and the successful development of the local dairy supply chain.

Results of the Subsequent Diligence

Conversations with local politicians provided a degree of comfort that the NDF would respect core elements of any investment agreements signed during the previous administration. However, the risk of changes occurring cannot be dismissed entirely.

As a result, the decision was taken to explore a possible JV arrangement with a local partner who would, of course, be value-accretive for the business, but also who might help mitigate the political risk inherent in the electoral landscape of the country. Such a partner would be of a stature in the country that would make it less likely that any administration would take actions that would be materially prejudicial for the JV in which they are a shareholder. A very short-list of possible JV partners has been prepared and will be explored in the next phase.

While such a suitable, local JV partner could provide crucial on-the-ground political leverage and negotiation power, the risk remains that they would be unable to prevent a future government changing policies to the detriment of the JV. To create a financial backstop, the recommendation is to take out a political risk insurance (PRI) policy. Such an approach directly addresses the primary risk, which is not expropriation in the strict sense, but a "creeping" or "disguised" expropriation whereunder a subsequent government nullifies the investment agreement, removes the tariff protections, and revokes the incentives, rendering the investment commercially unviable. The investment's viability is contingent on the government's "Family and Food

Program". PRI would provide a financial payout if this foundation is pulled away.

15.3 Closing: Role of Country Risk

Often (most of the time?), country risk analysis is centered on economic and market fundamentals. Is the economy growing fast enough? Can the government roll over its debts? What's happening to the exchange rate? An evaluation of Global Nutrition's investment would focus on the macroeconomic drivers of effective demand for baby formula and enriched dairy products (GDP growth, subsidies, etc.), milk supply (investment, tariffs, etc.), and margins (inflation, taxes, interest rates, etc.). Indeed, the requisite analysis of investment returns will be predicated on these factors.

In this case, however, the first step must focus on political risk. For Global Nutrition, the success of the investment will depend significantly on the continuation of supportive government policies and the sanctity of signed investment agreements, even in the event of a conservative return to power. Hence, a positive investment decision will be less a bet on Solera's economic fundamentals and more a calculated wager on its political future.

In the spirit of the story of the rancher who once said, "decide first whether you want to buy the cow, then argue over the price", Global Nutrition must first decide whether it is possible to mitigate this political risk sufficiently to justify moving from a historically profitable export strategy to a local production and distribution model. This is the decision to buy the cow.

The assessment of the political risk bet's handicap requires the development of a sophisticated mitigation strategy. Above, we saw two layers of protection identified: *first,* a JV with a reputable partner whose stature in Solera's political world could be expected to protect the JV against a future government taking action to abrogate past investment and business agreements; and *second,* as a financial backstop, the belt and braces approach so to speak, taking out a political risk policy to protect the investment against creeping expropriation.

Once these mitigation measures are known, Global Nutrition can move onto the detailed business and financial planning underpinning the investment analysis, establishment of the JV, negotiations with the government, and eventual transaction closure. This is deciding the price of the cow.

16

Case Study 3

In this chapter, we examine a debt refinancing transaction for Enterprise Bank (EB), a B2-rated commercial bank located in the B1-rated Aurora Republic. Aurora's economy is highly dependent on copper exports and tourism. Our investor, the EM Finco Debt Fund (EM Finco), is the largest lender to EB. Their exposure is in the form of a one-year term, senior unsecured loan used to fund the Bank's loan portfolio. A multilateral development institution, the Global Development Bank (GDB), has been mandated to arrange a syndicated A-B form facility whose purpose is to extend the average duration of EB's funding to match more closely the roughly three-and-a-half-year average life of its loan portfolio. In this case study, we examine EM Finco's analysis of the transaction and their feedback to the syndicate agent GDB.

16.1 Country: Aurora Republic

Endowment

Aurora boasts two great natural resources: *first*, along its coast and on the nearby island of Aetheria are found some of the most beautiful beaches in the world; and *second*, in its hill country in the hinterland, rich and easily accessed deposits of high-quality copper ore.

These resources have proven a mixed blessing. On the one hand, mineral exports and, since the beginning of the era of easy and affordable air travel, a flux of vacationers to the country's picturesque resorts have supported the economy. On the other hand, these "low-lying fruit", to use this expression, have

R. Marney, P. Waeber, *The Emerging Markets Investor's Guide to Country Risk*,
https://doi.org/10.1007/978-3-032-26824-2_16

contributed to the mix of factors holding back the diversification of the economy, with negative spillovers to political, social, and human capital development.

Two other facts warrant mention.

First, the predominant agricultural production area between the coast and the hill country is low lying and crisscrossed by waterways. These fields are vulnerable to flooding. During the annual typhoon season, these areas and the beach resorts are periodically negatively affected by these extreme weather events. By global measures of vulnerability to climate change, the country ranks in the top third.

Second, a high fertility rate drives a rapid rate of population growth. This has resulted in a youth bulge, which presents potential challenges for the economy and civil/political stability. This risk arises from the insufficient availability of high value-added jobs in the economy and the weak social safety net in the country, which together have contributed to acute and worsening inequality and poor human welfare outcomes for much of society.

Institutional Framework

Aurora ranks at the lower end of various international indicators of political, legal, and economic institutional development and effectiveness. At its base rests a highly unequal society, reflecting the historical antecedents of an agricultural and mining-based economy.

In this setting, the country's elite has no incentive to undertake the requisite, structural reforms to develop, inter alia: (i) an independent, meritocratic central bank; (ii) strong rule of law and a fair and efficient judiciary, with necessary areas of technical specialization (e.g., insolvency, IP protections, etc.); (iii) high-quality and universally accessible health, education, and social services; (iv) effective regulation and other measures to facilitate enterprise creation; and (v) financial regulation and, in particular, supervision/enforcement is underdeveloped.

With particular relevance to this case study, there have been concerns voiced about: (i) the lack of independence of the central bank, leading to impaired capabilities in the fields of monetary policy and foreign exchange management; (ii) the timeliness and strict adherence to the law in commercial disputes involving foreign investors, and in a notorious case foreign creditors were treated disadvantageously in a bankruptcy case as compared to their domestic counterparts; and (iii) while the capabilities of the financial sector regulatory and supervisory regime have improved in recent years, two areas of weakness remain: (a) the control of portfolio concentrations and (b) limitations on related party/insider lending.

Macroeconomy

Mining and tourism have historically been the twin pillars of the macroeconomy.

Recently, with government tax incentives and subsidies, the construction sector has exhibited strong growth. Structurally, the economy appears: primary sector (1/3) and the tertiary sector (1/2), with the remainder in a small secondary sector.

Until just recently, GDP growth has averaged more than 5%, in the context of moderately high inflation, a manageable fiscal deficit, and low and sustainable domestic and external debt levels. Raw copper ore accounts for the lion's-share of exports (roughly ¾), followed by tourism receipts. GDP per capita is low, as is domestic savings. Investments in both the mining and tourism sectors have been sourced predominantly from offshore interests, with the government (in mining) and powerful, private individuals (in the major hotels) as local partners. The capital-intensive mining industry contributes little to high valued-added job creation, and within the resort hotels, locals are limited to low-level service jobs.

Government revenue mobilization is dependent on levies on copper operations and value-added sales taxes. Corporate taxes in the hospitality sector yield little due to generous investment incentives granted to global hotel chains to attract these companies to Aurora. Individual income tax payments are resting at de minimis levels due to corruption and under-investment in collection and auditing capacity. Historically, the fiscal and primary balances have been moderately negative, with government debt volumes and service obligation resting in a manageable range, and the country's current account has been maintained in a modest surplus, supporting adequate reserve coverage.

The country maintains a currency peg, where the national currency, the Cuprum (C$) is linked to the US Dollar, a legacy of a previous currency crisis. Thereafter, government and business circles were plagued by a deeply held "fear of floating". The REER has appreciated over time. In part due to this FX market distortion, the country's current account surplus has weakened recently. FX reserve coverage slipped into the inadequate range.

The most recent rating B-1, with a stable outlook, done at time T-1 appeared (Fig. 16.1):

Economic Strength	B+
Institutional and. Governance Strength	B -
Economic Resilience	B
Fiscal Strength	B
Government Financial Strength	B
Susceptibility to Event Risk	B-
Rating	B-

Fig. 16.1 Credit rating. (*Source: The authors and the generic approach of Moody's Investor Services*)

Financial System

The financial system is exclusively bank-based. The sector consists of one large state-owned bank (the State Bank of Aurora, or "SBA"), with roughly a 40% market share (focus—SOE, copper production and exports, and other public sector financings) and one foreign bank, with a 20% market share, and a group of local, private banks accounting for the remaining 40%. This latter segment has been the fastest growing, having more than trebled in the last five years, with the expectation that this trajectory should continue, albeit at a lower rate. The banks in this group are fast growing, profitable, good asset quality, liquidity, but as discussed below with growing currency and duration mismatches. EB is one of the leading players in this private banking cohort and ranks in the upper tier.

There are potential vulnerabilities among these private banks.

First, during the last IMF Financial System Stability Assessment in Year "Y-1", all met minimum regulatory capital ratios, but stress tests revealed capital shortfalls versus the regulatory minimum solvency of 12% in severe macro-financial shock scenarios. The major factor cited was a deterioration in asset quality, with exchange rate translation losses for certain institutions with larger Open Currency Positions (OCP).

Second, the rising level of purchases of short-term government securities increasingly exposes the banks to government fiscal sustainability risk.

Third and last, the banks have increased the role of short-duration (typically 12-month renewable), foreign currency senior debt to fund their portfolios. This development has resulted in the creation of duration mismatches for a number of the institutions. In most cases, banks have matched the FX liabilities with FX-denominated credits extended to companies with natural hedges, thus keeping open currency positions OCP within a manageable range. On the assumption that the natural hedges hold, should the currency peg break, the impact on solvency would be limited. However, should external debt capital flows reverse, then the duration mismatch could produce a systemic liquidity crisis. These risks are present in a regulatory and supervisory regime which has been strengthened over the last decade but still requires further work. The central bank's liquidity support capacity, macro-prudential tools, and systemic risk monitoring capabilities are still in an underdeveloped state. Bank resolution tools are not yet operational, and the authorities have yet to manage a large bank failure.

Recent Events

Aurora Macro highlights.

First, a rise in global inflation has resulted in a generalized tightening of monetary policy across the DM space. This development has resulted in: (i) a reduction in fixed investment and hence demand for industrial metals, and declines in export volumes and prices on world markets; (ii) portfolio reallocation into DM capital markets from the EMDE; and (iii) a widening of the current account deficit of, and the onset of capital flow reversals from, economies like Aurora. The central bank's reaction to these developments was slow and when rates were raised initially muted. Over time, subsequent rate hikes took the reference rate to 10%, still negative in real terms. Aurora's FX reserve levels declined as capital flowed out, with the result of increasing pressure on the currency peg as depicted in Fig. 16.2.

Second, in Aurora the combination of the increase in domestic interest rates, the slowing economy, and overbuilding in the residential property market has weakened demand in the property market, which has weighed on the operating cash flows of construction and development companies. NPL levels have begun to edge up across the sector.

	Y-3	Y-2	Y-1	Y
GDP (% Change)	5.2	7.6	6.8	3.3
Inflation (%)	6.1	8.7	8.9	11.5
Fiscal Balance (%GDP)	(1.4)	(1.5)	(1.7)	(2.8)
Primary Balance (%GDP)	(0.9)	(1.1)	(1.4)	(1.9)
Government Debt (%GDP)	19	19	21	24
Government Interest Pmts (%GDP)	4.1	4.0	4.4	7.5
Current Account (%GDP)	1.6	1.3	0.9	0.2
External Debt/CA Receipts	29	35	51	55
Reserve Coverage (months)	7	5	5	4

Fig. 16.2 Macro data. (*Source: The authors*)

16.2 The Investee: Enterprise Bank ("EB")

History

EB was founded a decade ago by the Mark Family (see below) following the government's financial sector liberalization program. This initiative was designed and supported by multilateral institutions, including the GDB. The program was aimed at creating private sector banks in a market dominated by one state-owned institution, with the objectives of fostering competition in the financial sector and stimulating capital investment in small and medium enterprises.

Group Structure and Ownership

The group structure appears as depicted in Fig. 16.3.

The shareholders of EB were: (i) the Marks, a prominent local family; (ii) their flagship commercial enterprise, NH Development, an engineering, construction, and property management group ("NHDG"), funneled through a related, offshore investment vehicle; and (iii) a group of private investors, reportedly well-connected local parties. Their principal motivation was to lessen their dependence on the SBA in the financing of their group companies and the group's customers in the commercial and residential property development sector.

The Mark Family is among the country's wealthiest, having made their fortune in the two central pillars of the local economy. They are well respected

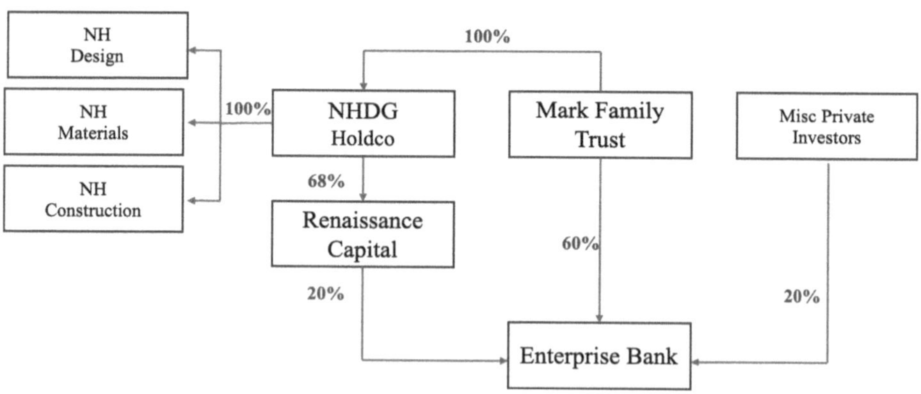

Fig. 16.3 Corporate structure

in the country as successful and responsible businesspeople. In addition to their domestic businesses, the Family has substantial overseas investments in technology, financial services, and agribusiness. The Family and the Group have constructive ties to the political class but have fastidiously avoided the appearance of partisanship (i.e., taking sides) that could backfire during changes in administration. As noted, market sources suspect that well-connected parties from across the domestic business and political spectrum have been granted equity in EB.

The Board is controlled by representatives of the Mark Family. The private investors have one member, a former finance minister, and governor of the central bank. There are no independent directors. The long-time auditors are a local accounting firm.

Business Model

The business strategy of EB has been centered on the commercial and residential property development sector. In executing this strategy, the shareholders were very clear from the outset that lending to the NHDG (which is shown earlier in the text), their suppliers and buyers would figure prominently in the portfolio. As shown in 16.2.4, this credit strategy has played out according to plan. The average life of the loan book has averaged in the range of 3.75 years. The bank has pursued a wholesale funding strategy, which over time, has used increasingly foreign-sourced debt capital, which has flowed into the country, supported by the stable currency peg. The term of these FX funds has been generally limited to 12 months, however, with the overall duration of EB's debt funding book in the range of 1.75 years. This mismatch reflects a conscious strategy aimed at limiting funding costs. The bank has maintained a disciplined and conservative approach to FX risk. FX-denominated lending has been limited to creditworthy borrowers, whose businesses generate foreign currency revenues in dependable volumes. That is, they have natural hedges.

With respect to the maturity gap, a consensus has arisen that the degree of mismatch needs to be reduced. Over time, the board has come around to this position. The global market context was becoming increasingly volatile and, as a bank operating with this mismatch in a small, open economy, the risk of a capital flow reversal was deemed unacceptable, hence the discussions with GDB on the longer-duration syndication, below.

Financial Summary

Selected, summary financial data, and metrics appear (Fig. 16.4):

	Y-3	Y-2	Y-1	Y
Cash & Marketable Securities	10	20	59	90
Loans and Advances	80	150	200	275
Non-Current Assets	10	15	20	25
Total Assets	100	185	279	390
Short-term Notes Payable	30	67	111	167
Long-term Notes Payable	30	70	110	152
Total Liabilities	60	137	221	319
Capital	40	48	58	71
Total Liabilities and Capital	100	185	279	390
ROCE	18%	21%	20%	23%
Solvency (Capital to Total Assets)	40%	26%	21%	18%

	Y-3	Y-2	Y-1	Y
Funding Duration (% Total Liabilities)				
Short-term (< 360 days)	50%	49%	50%	52%
Long-term (>360 Days)	50%	51%	50%	48%
Average Duration (Years)				
GLP	3.50	3.75	3.60	3.80
Notes Payable	1.75	1.85	1.70	1.65
Gap	(1.75)	(1.90)	(1.90)	(2.15)
Currency - FX %				
Assets	38.0	80.0	86.0	98.0
Liabilities and Capital	35.0	77.0	87.0	100.0
Open Currency Position	3.00	3.00	(1.00)	(2.00)
OCP as % of Capital	7.5%	6.2%	-1.7%	-2.8%
Asset Quality				
NPLs	1.6	3.6	4.5	9.6
(% GLP)	*2.0%*	*3.0%*	*3.5%*	*4.3%*
LLR	1.6	3.6	4.4	9.5
Coverage Ratio	100%	100%	98%	99%
Related Party Lending (% GLP)	12%	15%	15%	18%
Property Sector Exposure (% GLP)	16%	21%	26%	29%
Cash and Marketable Securities				
Cash	5	7	7	6
Government Securities	5	13	52	84
Government Securities to Capital	13%	27%	90%	118%
Liquidity Coverage				
Cash and Marketable Securities	10	20	59	90
75% of GLP cashflow in next 30 days	1	3	3	5
Total	11	23	62	95
Installments - Notes Payable in next 30 days	4	9	15	22
Coverage Ratio	2.7	2.4	4.1	4.2
Coverage Ratio (ex-Government Securities)	***1.5***	***1.0***	***0.7***	***0.5***

Fig. 16.4 Financials. (Note: Amounts in C$ million unless otherwise noted

Risk Considerations

Credit Rating

EB's last foreign currency rating in Time Y-1 was B2, with a stable outlook.

Summary Analysis

- Risk: Asset Quality.

NPLs have increased from 2% of GLP in year Y-3 to 3.5% of year Y-1, before reaching 4.3% in year Y. This progressive rise reflects the impact of the general economic slowdown. The pick-up in NPLs for EB has been spread throughout its portfolio, with non-group property sector loans moderately higher. The bank has followed a conservative loan loss provisioning policy, with the Risk Coverage Ratio (loan loss reserve to NPLs) at close to 100%, even though under their credit policy collateral coverage levels are high, especially in the property sector book.

Mitigant 1: Earnings.

Despite challenging market conditions and higher loan loss provisioning, EB succeeded in increasing profitability. ROCE rose from 20% to 23%. This positive result reflected portfolio growth, higher yields, effective treasury management, and expense controls.

Mitigant 2: Solvency.

Solvency weakened from 40% in year Y-3 to 21% in year Y, and then to 18% in year Y, but remained well above the regulatory minimum of 12%. This slippage was due to the bank's aggressive loan portfolio growth. This development has been noted by the rating agencies, which have indicated the bank does need to consider a capital raise to counter the decline in the capital adequacy ratio. EB's board has taken this recommendation into its future planning, and a rights issue will be an element in the upcoming fundraising. The rating agency commentary did comment on the possibility of an adjustment in the currency peg but gave EB a high grade for their conservative approach to FX risk.

- Risk: Liquidity.

Overall, EB's liquidity position represents its greatest potential weakness. To date, its strong franchise, sound financial metrics, and capable shareholding has ensured sufficient access to requisite funding to maintain adequate liquidity. As discussed below, vulnerabilities exist.

Funding Structure.

EB is wholly dependent on wholesale funding. An increasing proportion of these liabilities is denominated in FX sourced from overseas investors. The OCP risk is minimal. Given the duration mismatch, EB is highly vulnerable to a reversal in external capital flows. The average maturity mismatch has increased from 1.75 years in year T-3 to 1.90 years in year T-1, before rising further to 2.15 in year T. As noted above, EB's risk management identified this risk as requiring remedial action, hence the approach to the GDB.

Liquidity Coverage.

Liquidity coverage (liquid assets to liabilities due over the next thirty days) is strong when including cash and government securities (4.2x). However, the volume of the bank's holdings of government securities has increased markedly over the past several years, reaching 84% of capital in the last year. The government's fiscal deficit (2.8% of GDP) and debt position (24% of GDP) still rest within a manageable range. However, were conditions to change, then the liquidity (and solvency) impact could be a serious threat to the bank (liquidity coverage 0.5x).

Other Considerations

Governance: The tightly knit Mark Family controls the board. While their business acumen is unquestioned, there are risks in an institutional environment where regulation is weak and supervision tends toward a very light touch approach, especially with respect to the "well connected". These include (i) excessive exposure to group companies and external commercial stakeholders and (ii) lack of transparency around the application of accounting standards.

Shareholder Support: The substantial, financial means of the Mark Family and their long-standing record of being responsible stewards of their business interests, even in difficult times, translate into a very high likelihood that solvency and/or liquidity support would be forthcoming should circumstances require.

16.3 Transaction

Background

The IMF's most recent FSAP identified a growing systemic maturity mismatch as a structural weakness. The rating agencies also highlighted this threat for EB as a factor that could lead to a downgrade. Based on this, the management of EB reached out to the GDB to request a syndication that would consolidate a number of bilateral, foreign currency short-term credits into a longer duration credit.

The plan is to refinance all C$100 million of the foreign-sourced short-term loans into a single 5-year final maturity, amortizing (30-month grace, 6 equal, consecutive, semi-annual installments, 3.75 years average life),

The syndication would be structured as a so-called A-B Loan. Such a structure consists of two parts: (i) the "A-loan" in which the GDB acts as the sole lender of record and (ii) the "B-loan" in which banks or other eligible institutional investors (such as EB) "lend" via a funded participation agreement with GDB, not a direct loan agreement with the borrower. Such a structure has several benefits, most notably, the preferred-creditor status "pass-through", in which, because the GDB is the lender of record, B-loan participants benefit indirectly from the GDB's de-facto preferred creditor treatment in many EMDEs, and so reduce perceived sovereign or transfer risk. The motivation for this structure was to strengthen the argument to the foreign lenders for approval.

Prior to the formal launch of the syndication, the GDB reached out to EM Finco. As EB's largest lender with C$20 million in exposure, the GDB wanted to test the proposed structure with EM Finco and, were changes warranted, clear them with EB prior to launch.

EM Finco Credit Process

Analysis

In the analysis of EB's financials, the risk team pointed out several areas of concern in addition to the duration gap:

First, at an 18%, EB's capital adequacy ratio (CAR) remains well above the regulatory minimum of 12%. The solvency measure has weakened however in recent years. Given market conditions and the outlook, their recommendation was to consider an equity raise to bring the CAR back to a minimum of 20%. As there had been recent talk of a rights issue, but this was not included as a condition precedent (CP) in the draft term sheet. EM Finco's risk team included an equity raise CP of C$30 million. This equity infusion would raise the pro-forma solvency ratio to 24%. This level combined with the strong shareholder support capacity of the Mark Family will assure investors of the strength of the institution's capitalization.

Second, despite the fairly strong performance to date, the high exposure to the property sector and related companies represents a threat to solvency. Consideration should be given to steps to reduce this concentration and to maintain the highly conservative Loan Loss Reserve coverage practice.

Third, given global market conditions and recent macroeconomic developments at home, any material increase in EB's (short) OCP could leave EB vulnerable to a loosening of the currency peg and a subsequent devaluation of the currency. EM Finco's risk team established the requirement to maintain a (short) OCP open currency position of no more than 5% of capital.

Fourth, EM Finco's risk team noted the GDB's recommendation to EB to change their external auditor from the local firm they have been using for much of the last decade to an international firm. To ensure that financial reporting, most notably the application of IFRS 9 to loan loss provisioning, is accurate, EM Finco's risk team required this action to become a legally binding commitment of EB under the loan documentation.

Base Case

Based on this analysis, EM Finco elaborated a base case that included the following major assumptions:

(i) A C$30 million rights issue (as a CP).

(ii) The C$100 million syndication reduces the short-term notes payable from C$167 million to C$67 million, and subsequent domestic refinancings lower this further (ex-current portion long-term notes payable), which significantly reduces the maturity mismatch.
(iii) The continuation of the disciplines' approach to managing FX risk.
(iv) Given the continued fraught macroeconomic conditions, a moderate increase in NPLS, but with a continued policy of 100% risk coverage.
(v) A moderate rise from the 23% ROCE to 25%.
(vi) Based on the foregoing, an increase in solvency from 23% in the post-money financials to 25% at the end of the forecast period (*n*).

The summary projections appeared (Fig. 16.5):

Downside Case

In constructing a set of stress cases, the EM Finco risk team assumed certain major developments.

First, Aurora's external position would deteriorate.

(i) The copper market conditions to weaken materially over the near term, due to: *first*, medium-term global macroeconomic growth prospects—and hence overall growth in demand for copper—are subdued. *Second*, inventory levels in most major importing markets are at record high levels. This build-up reflects the hangover from (i) a period of strong economic growth and (ii) a recent supply disruption in which a major exporter was at risk of being out of the market for a protracted period due to a domestic crisis and importers created large precautionary balances. *Third*, the exporter noted in (ii) is now back in the market and is dumping supply to make up for lost sales.
(ii) Bookings for Aurora's tourist attractions have fallen due to a combination of: first, storm damage from last year's historically severe typhoon that closed a number of resorts; second, coral bleaching has begun to damage the marine ecosystem along the coast, with negative fallout on tourists' experiences; third, recent episodes of protest, sometimes spilling into violence, against the government by unlicensed shopkeepers and taxi drivers; and fourth, a well-publicized murder of a foreign tourist and his spouse. Analysts project that the country will need several years to return to previous booking levels in the most optimistic

	Y	Y Pro-Forma	Y+n (Base)
Cash & Marketable Securities	90	120	100
Loans and Advances	275	275	375
Non-Current Assets	25	25	30
Total Assets	390	420	505
Short-term Notes Payable	167	67	30
Long-term Notes Payable	152	252	289
Total Liabilities	319	319	319
Capital	71	101	126
Total Liabilities and Capital	390	420	445
ROCE	23%	nm	25%
Solvency (Capital to Total Assets)	18%	24%	25%

	Y	Y Pro-Forma	Y+n (Base)
Funding Duration (% Total Liabilities)			
Short-term (< 360 days)	52%	21%	9%
Long-term (>360 Days)	48%	79%	91%
Average Duration (Years)			
GLP	3.80	3.80	3.25
Notes Payable	1.65	3.45	3.15
Gap	(2.15)	(0.35)	(0.10)
Currency - FX %			
Assets	98	98	283
Liabilities and Capital	100	100	286
Open Currency Position	(2)	(2)	(3)
OCP as % of Capital	-2.8%	-2.0%	-2.5%
Asset Quality			
NPLs	9.6	9.6	18
(% GLP)	4.3%	4.3%	*4.8%*
LLR	9.5	9.5	18
Coverage Ratio	99%	99%	100%
Related Party Lending (% GLP)	18%	18%	20%
Property Sector Exposure (% GLP)	29%	29%	25%
Cash and Marketable Securities			
Cash	6	6	8
Government Securities	84	114	92
Government Securities to Capital	118%	113%	73%
Liquidity Coverage			
Cash and Marketable Securities	90	120	100
75% of GLP cashflow in next 30 days	5	5	8
Total	95	125	108
Installments - Notes Payable in next 30 days	22	22	3
Coverage Ratio (x)	4.2	5.6	36.0
Coverage Ratio (ex-Government Securities)	***0.5***	***0.5***	*5.3*

Fig. 16.5 Projections. (Note: Amounts in C$ million unless otherwise noted)

(iii) The drivers of capital flows from the EMDE to the AEs would continue, thus reducing the supply of foreign inflows.

Based on these factors, EM Finco's chief economist argued that there is a medium probability that Aurora could see:

(i) The current account slipping into deficit territory
(ii) A period of net foreign capital outflows
(iii) FX reserve depletion to a dangerously low level
(iv) The abandonment of the C$/US$ peg

In such a scenario, the subsequent decline in the value of the Cuprum could reach as high as 25%, if based on current estimates of the currency's divergence from fair market value.

Second is the impact of higher interest rates and a slowing economy on asset quality.

The GDB had conducted an in-depth review of EB's loan portfolio (an asset quality review or AQR), first to validate the most recent IFRS 9 provisioning exercise, and second to construct stress tests on the portfolio. The EM Finco risk team was given access to this work. The results placed the potential increase in NPLs in a downside macroeconomic scenario and hence the increase in provisions in the range of 5–15% of the loan book, assuming 100% provisioning.

Based on this work, the EM Finco risk team ran a series of downside or "Bear" scenarios.

First: FX.

Assuming in one case (Bear 1) a 25% devaluation at the current OCP level, and a 75% devaluation at a higher OCP level in a second (Bear 2) (Fig. 16.6):

For EB, the direct impact of the abandonment of the currency peg ranges from immaterial in Bear 1, a less than 1% decline in the solvency ratio, to more meaningful, but not a material threat in Bear 2, where the decrease is

	Bear 1	Bear 2
Foreign Exchange (FX)		
OCP (in $)	(7)	(35)
% Devaluation	*25%*	*75%*
FX Impact	(2)	(26)
Solvency post-FX Impact	**24.6%**	**19.8%**

Fig. 16.6 FX analysis. (Note: Amounts in C$ million unless otherwise noted)

roughly 5%, although still markedly above the regulatory minimum. The assumptions in a further scenario to take solvency down to this minimum level were not plausible.

Second: Asset Quality.

Assuming in one case (Bear 1) a 10-percentage-point (%) increase in the ratio of NPLs to Gross Loan Portfolio (GLP), and a second (Bear 2) of 18 percentage points, where in each case 100% provisioning is assumed (Fig. 16.7):

The impact is meaningful but can be absorbed in Bear 1 where solvency ratio drops to 18%, which still provides an adequate buffer to the regulatory minimum. Such a development would place the increase in the mid-range of the GDB AQR. In Bear 2, a degree of deterioration of 18 percentage points is assumed, a figure outside the GDB range. In this scenario, the increased cost of risk (provisioning) takes EB down to the regulatory minimum (Fig. 16.8).

Third: A Combination of the Two.

In Bear 1, solvency drops to 17%, a scenario in which EB remains in regulatory compliance, with a reduced but still adequate capital buffer. The more extreme Bear 2 case results in a material breach of the 12% regulatory capitalization requirement, with the solvency ratio declining to 7%.

	Bear 1	Bear 2
Asset Quality (AQ)		
% Increase in NPLs to GLP	*10%*	*18%*
Incremental Provisioning Impat	(38)	(66)
Solvency post-FX Impact	**18%**	**12%**

Fig. 16.7 AQ analysis. (Note: Amounts in C$ million unless otherwise noted)

	Bear 1	Bear 2
Dual Case - FX and AQ		
FX Impact	(2)	(26)
Incremental Provisioning Impact	(38)	(66)
Solvency Post-Dual Csse Impacts	**17%**	**7%**

Fig. 16.8 Combined FX and AQ analysis. (Note: Amounts in C$ million unless otherwise noted)

Based on this analysis, EM Finco's risk team reinforced the need for the C$30 million rights issue as a CP. Additionally, they argued that a downside case in which macroeconomic conditions do result in a more pronounced deterioration in asset quality cannot be dismissed and some further downside protection should be built into the structure. The investment committee responded to this recommendation by establishing the requirement that a legally binding shareholder commitment be included in the structure, under which EB's shareholders would have a joint and several obligation to invest additional Tier 1 capital to maintain a solvency ratio of 20% within 90 days of a breach of this level. If this element were to be included in the transaction structure, then the investment committee was prepared to proceed.

As the final step in the EM Finco's approval process, the proposed transaction was submitted to Portfolio Management (PM) for consideration. The amount for the country (the B1-rated Aurora), sector (financial institutions) and the borrower (B2-rated EB) was deemed acceptable. The proposed longer duration resulted in debate. PM acknowledged the risk management rationale of extending the duration from the perspective of EB. However, in PM's opinion, the longer duration necessitated a higher coupon. A minimum increase of 50 basis points, with a target of 75 was agreed.

Based on the foregoing analysis, EM Finco proposed to the GDP two significant revisions to the draft term sheet, namely, *first*, the shareholder capital backstop requirement and, second, an increase of 75 basis points in the proposed pricing. Following consultations between GDB and EB, and lengthy discussions between the board of GDB and the shareholders, both elements were agreed.

Term Sheet

The term sheet for the syndicated contained the usual and customary provisions for such a transaction. Highlighted elements relevant to the discussion above included:

First, a CP of a Tier I equity raise of 30.

Second, by Time Y+n, covenants for:

(i) The Open Currency Position of no greater than 10% of net worth
(ii) Related party lending of now more than 17.5% of GLP
(iii) Property sector lending of no more than 20% of GLP
(iv) A defined maturity gap limitation to conform with the status quo post syndication

Third, a legally binding joint and several commitment on the part of the shareholders to invest sufficient additional capital to maintain the CAR at a level of no less than 20%, within 90 days of the reporting date on which a breach occurred.

Fourth, a provision to be included stipulating that for the fiscal year beginning in 202x, the selection of the auditor will be subject to the prior written approval of the Lenders.

16.4 Closing: Role of Country Risk

There is a saying in financial institutions banking that goes something along the lines of the following: "*a bad bank in a good country is a better credit risk than a good bank in a bad country*." This tart aphorism does carry an important message.

The message is that country (i.e., sovereign) risk dominates idiosyncratic bank risk. Even well-managed and profitable banks with strong liquidity and capital buffers can be pulled down if their home jurisdiction is unstable, while even mediocre banks benefit from the support of their home country's well-developed institutional framework, strong macroeconomic fundamentals, and ample financial resources.

For example, consider the impact of country characteristics on asset quality and cost of risk. The empirical evidence that macro-level (sovereign) risks are more responsible for non-performing loan (NPLs) than institutional level (idiosyncratic) risks is robust, and in Marney, R. and Stubbs, T. (2024) *Emerging Markets Debt Restructuring: Effectively Navigating Local Institutional Frameworks,* we see the role of appropriate institutions in shaping effective out-of-court and judicial restructurings contributing to limiting loss given defaults. Similarly, high savings rates, well-developed financial intermediaries, and strong rule of law contribute to stable access to funding, limiting liquidity risk. Profitability, asset-liability management, portfolio planning, and, for that matter, various critical enterprise risk management outcomes all benefit or are prejudiced by the environment in which the bank operates. And when there are headwinds, or worse, strong and competent systemic support can help avoid a descent into crisis territory.

A bank's standalone credit strength is heavily influenced by the creditworthiness of its home government. A core rating agency principle attests to this fact. All three major agencies have established that, in the absence of unquestioned external support from a higher-rated third party, a bank cannot be rated higher than the sovereign in whose jurisdiction it operates. That is, banks are constrained by their respective "sovereign ceiling".

In closing, let's consider again the case of EB and the downside stress scenario. What are the fundamental threats confronting the bank? Excessive export (and growth in general) dependence on a single commodity for one. Vulnerability to a reversal of external capital flows and pressure on a rigid exchange rate peg potentially resulting in external and domestic illiquidity and a severe decline in the value of the currency for another. Given EB's conservative approach to FX risk management, this latter threat has been largely eliminated. The knock-on effects of these and other macro-level factors on bank-level asset quality, profitability, solvency, and liquidity were discussed above and are easy to understand. In the case of EB, there is no denying that the fairly high portfolio concentration in the property sector and the duration mismatch create vulnerabilities to external shocks. However, what is indisputable is that the severity/impact of these external shocks should be greater in a single B- than in a triple B- or for that matter a double A-rated sovereign.

The suggested takeaways from this case are three-fold:

First, recognize the material impact of the institutions and macro-environment of the jurisdiction in which the bank operates and, where possible, take steps to address concomitant risks. The use of GDB A-B loan structure was intended to mitigate certain of these risks present in Aurora.

Second, identify the nature, sources, timing, power, and likely transmission channels of these resulting shocks that can affect the performance and financial condition of the bank. For EB, the reliance on short-duration, foreign funding when pressures were building on the country's external liquidity position created a potentially dire liquidity threat, and hence the approach to the GDB was made to mitigate such a risk.

Third, once these are cataloged, use this knowledge to be selective in portfolio construction and creative in building greater resilience into the credit structure and risk-adjusted pricing of the selected transactions. EM Finco's PM group evaluated GDB's proposed pricing as inadequate and required an increase as a result.

17

Case Study 4

In this chapter, we examine a privately owned and vertically integrated, coffee and tea production, processing, and distribution company—Emporium Ltd. The company is headquartered in a B2-rated country—the Republic of Chaffee—from whose rich and fertile soil their superior quality coffee and tea come. The business is over 100 years old. Internationally, the Emporium name is synonymous with the country. Recently, the company's new CEO decided to move beyond the legacy business of exporting green coffee and raw tea into processed products—roasted coffee and fermented tea—and is poised to enter the fast-growing specialty coffee and tea markets. Overall, the operating performance and financial condition are satisfactory, and creditors view the company as a very solid credit risk.

The case study covers the launch of the next phase in Emporium's development. In this campaign, the company will begin to market directly in their export markets a range of specialty coffees and teas to grocery chains, coffee and tea store networks, and other wholesale buyers. A network of regional sales and distribution subsidiaries will be created, funded by equity from the parent company. External debt financing will be raised in these geographies to finance working capital. With Emporium's long-standing presence in the global coffee and tea markets, and a well-earned reputation for reliable delivery of products of great quality, industry analysts are highly bullish on the company's prospects.

Emporium's "Achilles Heel" is an increasingly unstable "home". Chaffee's foundational political and economic weaknesses are threatening to morph into a debt and/or currency crisis. The fundraising discussions take place as this latter threat becomes more real.

R. Marney, P. Waeber, *The Emerging Markets Investor's Guide to Country Risk*,
https://doi.org/10.1007/978-3-032-26824-2_17

17.1 Country: Republic of Chaffee

Endowment

Chaffee sits at latitude 10°N. The country's topography is characterized by a combination of low-lying coastal areas and a hilly central region with elevations rising to 3500 feet. The climate is warm and consistent with temperatures in the range of 20 °C and 30 °C.

The hill country is crisscrossed with river valleys creating a series of secluded areas, with distinct micro-climates. For the country, there is relatively high humidity and consistent rainfall, with distinct wet and dry seasons. Heavy rainfall and slightly cooler temperatures are observed in the wet season, with lower precipitation levels and slightly warmer temperatures for the rest of the year. The soil is generally fertile, loamy, and well-drained, with a slightly acidic pH. Recently, the country has experienced at rise in temperatures during the dry season, whose duration has lengthened in some years. The impact has been a modest decline in the tea and coffee harvests, especially in varieties produced at lower altitudes.

The rate of population growth is moderate but uneven across the demographic spectrum. Two observations are key. *First*, the percentage of the population under the age of 25 has risen markedly. *Second*, the descendants of the colonial settlers have declined to a point where for the first time in the country's history this group is in the minority, giving way to the original indigenous groups and the offspring of forced labor imported into the country years before to work in the plantations.

History: Society and Politics

Colonial Legacy

Chaffee was first colonized in the sixteenth century. From the beginning the new arrivals seized fertile agricultural lands and displaced the indigenous people in the process. These natives were variously incorporated into the colonial economy as cheap, semi-free labor or driven into the hilly, central regions of the country, where they became small-holder farmers, known as "Hillsiders". For the country, a thriving farming economy developed.

Over time, coffee and tea production became the major cash, export crops. To expand the cultivation, farmers began to take over even more land in the hill country, often at the expense of the Hillsiders. Sporadic incidents of violence occurred but were quickly repressed. In the mid-nineteenth century, the colony became independent as the Republic of Chaffee. In the period that followed, the economy thrived for the land-owning elite. However, an underclass made up of the Hillsiders and the descendants of former slaves brought into the country long ago to work in the fields grew on the margins of the community. In effect, this produced a fragile society of two nations inside one set of borders. Income and wealth inequality became extreme. In particular, the marginalized groups came to believe they would never have any meaningful involvement in the lawful, political management of the country, and hence their fight for economic welfare might have to be through armed struggle.

Failed Rebellion

Global demand for Chaffee's cash crops—coffee and tea—grew dramatically over the years.

This expansion of production created a need for more land. These fields lay in the hill country and were occupied by the displaced locals. When the plantation owners moved in, they exploited the displaced local's lack of legal title to the land. Large tracks were seized. This trend accelerated to the point where Hillsiders fought back. The rebels' weak organization and sparse financial resources meant the uprising was short-lived and unsuccessful. Many Hillsiders, including innocent bystanders, were killed, their homes burned, and their economic wherewithal destroyed. The two sides were now in a sometime cold, sometimes hot war.

Simmering Tensions

Until the present day, this divide persists. An informal liberation movement has engaged in sporadic episodes of violence against government officials and infrastructure. In response to these actions and, at great expense, the government established a form of martial law and imposed tight security on the affected regions. Social spending was increased modestly to address health and education needs, and infrastructure projects were undertaken to improve the provision of clean water and electricity.

Despite these measures, the situation has not fully stabilized. Over time, coffee and tea growers expanded their land holdings further in these hill regions, spurred on by growing overseas demand, especially for varieties that benefit from higher altitudes and cooler temperatures.

Institutional Framework

Since independence, Chaffee's politics have been dominated by a rich, landed elite. These parties and their allies control the levers of political power, the courts, and the commercial and financial activities of the formal economy. A right-of-center coalition known as the National Front (NF) has controlled the parliament and placed its adherents throughout the government. Institutions and public policy are designed to support the business interests of the elite and the NF's political agenda and not to provide for the welfare of the society as a whole. The establishment of experienced and highly competent staff in the finance, economics, and central banking functions within the government has been a priority. Spending on public goods and social welfare programs is low. Human capital development lags, with access to quality education and health services limited to the upper classes.

The judiciary is well-developed and efficient, although there has been criticism that judgments are sometimes biased toward the rich and well connected.

Revenue mobilization is reliant on regressive sales taxes and other charges. The national budget has been in chronic deficit, with a widening trend as necessary outlays to counter security threats in the affected areas of the country mount. Attempts by technocrats in the Ministry of Finance—led by a former senior IMF economist and renowned academic—to reform the individual and corporate tax regimes, have floundered in the parliament given NF opposition. As a result, there has been a progressive accretion in the level of government debt to a point where long-term debt sustainability is imperiled.

The NF's majority has narrowed in recent years reflecting the country's demographic changes, namely, greater numbers of displaced locals and more generally young people throughout the country. Unemployment and underemployment in these cohorts have risen, exacerbating the country's severe income inequality and disparity in human development outcomes. Elections are not truly free, reflecting the repressive effect of gerrymandering and registration obstacles that dilute the non-NF vote, and arguably stifle the popular will. Recognition of this fact is a source of resentment and has fueled increasing unrest. New measures to protect the NF's monopoly of power have safeguarded the majority for the present but have redoubled growing resentment toward the government.

The rating agencies have noted these trends. As recently as a decade ago, the country's sovereign rating rested at BB/Ba2. The impact of these economic and political developments has resulted in three rounds of downgrades to the current level of B2, with a negative outlook.

Macroeconomy

The structure of the economy consists of: (i) a large primary sector accounting for roughly 35% of national income, which is dominated by the coffee and tea production and export; (ii) a modest secondary sector, c.20% of GDP, made up of businesses providing inputs to the dominant agriculture sector, and various small manufacturers of non-tradable goods; and (iii) a low value-added service sector. The informal economy is reportedly quite large, with estimates placing its share of employment at well over half the population, and the output around a third of GDP.

The country's FX regime is a managed float that has resulted in a generally accurate fair-market valuation of its currency, the peso (P$).

The economy is dependent on the export of coffee and tea and hence is vulnerable to global market cycles in these commodities, as well to the effects of climate and disease. The development of the café culture throughout the advanced economies, and an increasing consumer demand for the Chaffee's specialty coffees and teas, has sustained a moderate and stable level of economic activity until recently (Fig. 17.1).

This positive picture has come under pressure, due to a combination of: (i) the damaging impact of the security situation on investment sentiment; (ii) the weight of the worsening fiscal situation and debt burden; and (iii) increased global supply competition as multiple countries' producers of specialty coffees and teas have aggressively entered the market space of local companies like Emporium. In year "Y-1", the economy slipped into recession.

	Y-3	Y-2	Y-1	Y
GDP (real, % YoY)	2.7	1.2	(0.5)	(0.9)
Inflation (% YoY)	10.5	11.5	13.7	7.5
Fiscal Balance (% GDP)	(4.8)	(5.7)	(6.3)	(6.5)
Revenue/GDP (% GDP)	15.0	14.5	14.0	13.5
Current Account (% GDP)	(2.7)	(3.2)	(4.4)	(6.7)
Debt/GDP (% GDP)	89	96	104	106
Debt/Revenue (% rev)	593	662	743	785
Debt Service/Revenue (% rev)	51	66	78	84
Interest/Revenue (% rev)	20	24	28	32
Interest/GDP (% GDP)	3.0	3.5	5.7	7.1
Primary Balance (% GDP)	(1.8)	(2.2)	(2.4)	(2.2)
Gross DS/GDP (% GDP) *(interest+amort.)*	7.7	9.6	10.9	11.3
Implied avg. interest rate *(Interest/Debt)*	3.4%	3.6%	5.5%	6.7%

Fig. 17.1 Macro data. (*Source: The authors*)

The fiscal balance has long been in a structural deficit but has widened alarmingly in recent years—from 4.8% of GDP in year "Y-3" to a precarious level of greater than 6% in year "Y". The failure of tax reform in the parliament has hamstrung efforts to increase government revenue at a time of increased expenditures. As a result, the government indebtedness increased further. Debt to GDP now sits 106% of GDP, a level at which debt service absorbs 84% of government revenue.

Market access continued, but with the worrying trend of greater dependence on short-duration, foreign currency-denominated debt at increasingly higher rates of interest. With news reports of increased opposition to the NF amidst the simmering security situation filter and the stagnating economy filling the international press, signs of a capital reversal become unmistakable. Increasingly, the country began to draw down on foreign exchange reserves to cover debt service. A weakening trade performance further lowered FX reserve coverage to just below three months imports and increased pressure on the peso. In response, the government instituted several measures to conserve dwindling FX reserves and maintain orderly debt service. *First*, the Central Bank (CB) required banks to purchase CB-issued foreign currency–denominated notes using their FX holdings, the proceeds of which they repassed to the national treasury. This had the result of reducing the government's funding requirements and increasing the government's access to foreign exchange. *Second*, exporters (like Emporium) were required to sell their foreign exchange sales proceeds to the CB within 90 days of receipt. *Third*, strict limits were established on new foreign remittances for commercial and financial purposes. Central bank policy has attempted to balance the competing considerations of export competitiveness and the cost of external debt service and, according to market experts, has succeeded in keeping the exchange rate close to a reasonable value, albeit slightly over-valued. While helpful in the short term, the Central Bank recognized the country's increasing vulnerability to external liquidity shocks. As a result, with the assistance of IMF staff, a toolkit of crisis management measures was developed and where necessary, the government obtained requisite parliamentary approvals. These measures would permit a rapid and effective response, should circumstances require. Additionally, two currency swap facilities were negotiated with neighboring central banks.

Financial System

The financial system is bank-based. The sector consists of about a dozen, small private banks, with mixed local and foreign ownership. The CB acts as the supervisory authority. The quality of its professional staff is high, with senior officials having been educated at leading global universities and having worked in the international financial institution space.

According to the IMF and the GDB analyses, and a dated rating agency report, the effectiveness of the CB in its supervisory role receives high marks. Industry analysts are confident about the reliability of the asset quality and solvency figures throughout the sector.

The recent requirement imposed on the banks to buy CB notes to help fund the fiscal deficit has been controversial, but there is agreement that overall systemic liquidity and solvency has not been threatened.

Recent Events

A trifecta of bad news triggered the crisis.

First, a single B sovereign not unlike Chaffee declared a payments moratorium on its foreign debt. In reaction, global markets traded out of the EMDE space, a "risk-off" episode ensued.

Second, a security force official was killed in what many felt was an act of petty crime. However, the local officials reacted in a heavy-handed and unfortunate manner, which inflamed emotions within the Hillsider community and precipitated a series of increasingly violent confrontations with the government. These events received widespread, international press coverage.

Third, in a local, special election, an opposition candidate lost to an NF loyalist. The count was widely suspected of being fraudulent in order to ensure a government victory.

In response to these events, and despite the CB controls and monetary policy tightening, capital began to flow out of the country. The exchange rate depreciated rapidly. The price of Chaffee sovereign bonds collapsed in the secondary market. International and domestic market access evaporated. A scheduled sale of CB notes in the local market met bank resistance and had to be abandoned. The markets were set for a free-fall.

17.2 The Investee: Emporium Coffee and Tea ("ECT")

History

Emporium dates to the colonial era, when the Jansen family settled in the area, now Chaffee. Building on their tradition in their original homeland, they established a successful farming business. In time, their cash crop became tea, to be followed later by coffee, when they bought out a failed coffee plantation.

The Emporium moniker was adopted during the period when the family used contacts in Europe to develop a robust sales channel for green coffee beans and raw tea in these markets. Almost the entire harvest was destined for these overseas buyers.

Over the years, Emporium expanded the size of their proprietary landholdings, becoming a leader in acquiring choice sites in the hill country, and also became a buyer from independent, small-holder growers—including unique microclimate producers. This has permitted the company to diversify the varieties under cultivation and increase the available supply. Their disciplined commitment to maintaining quality and ensuring customer satisfaction translated into Emporium the leading exporter of these unprocessed products from the country.

Group Structure and Ownership

The Jansen family through a foundation holds 100% of the equity of this private, limited company—Emporium. The financial resources of the family and the foundation are substantial, and they have shown willingness to support the business when circumstances have warranted such action. The various plantations are owned by the company and appear as fixed assets on the balance sheet.

The Business

Until recently, the Emporium's business was to supply green coffee beans, both Robusta and Arabica, and raw green and black unfermented teas to overseas traders. When the current chairman assumed her position after the death of her father, a change in strategy was adopted. She recognized correctly that

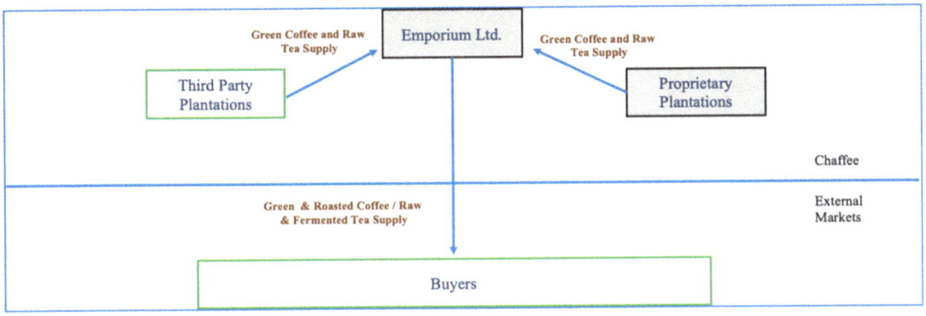

Fig. 17.2 Corporate structure I

the company was leaving significant money on the table by operating only in the lower gross margin segments. To bolster margins and hence profitability, Emporium began to process its raw output in country and, to the extent practical, moved to disintermediate the global market traders and sell directly to wholesale buyers. The organization appeared (Fig. 17.2).

The cash conversion cycle has averaged variously in the 90–120-day range. Working capital financing is sourced predominantly from local banks on a secured basis. As Emporium's business grew, foreign financing was increasingly tapped to the point where the mix was roughly 2/3 local and 1/3 foreign.

Given global market trends, consumers were expected to put a premium on the quality and diverse characteristics of the finished coffee and tea that Emporium's varied growing areas and conditions would permit. The CEO recognized the opportunity and acted. She mandated the investment of significant financial and human capital resources to develop specialty coffee and teas products.

The question arose—how best to market these higher value-added products? The board-approved business plan for this new segment envisioned the establishment of three wholly owned, regional, operating subsidiaries, appearing as (Fig. 17.3).

Each subsidiary would purchase white-label specialty coffee and teas from Emporium for resale to local wholesale buyers. As warranted by the opportunities in the future, individual regional subsidiaries might establish one or more distribution centers in their geographies. Thought was also given to a move into the branded space where products could be sold in group owned-operated retail stores, but this initiative was deferred. Each regional subsidiary would be capitalized by Emporium but otherwise will operate on an arm's length basis. Working capital financing will be raised from international lenders at the subsidiary level. Initial research indicated the cash conversion cycle could be as long as 150 days. This estimate reflected the combination of the

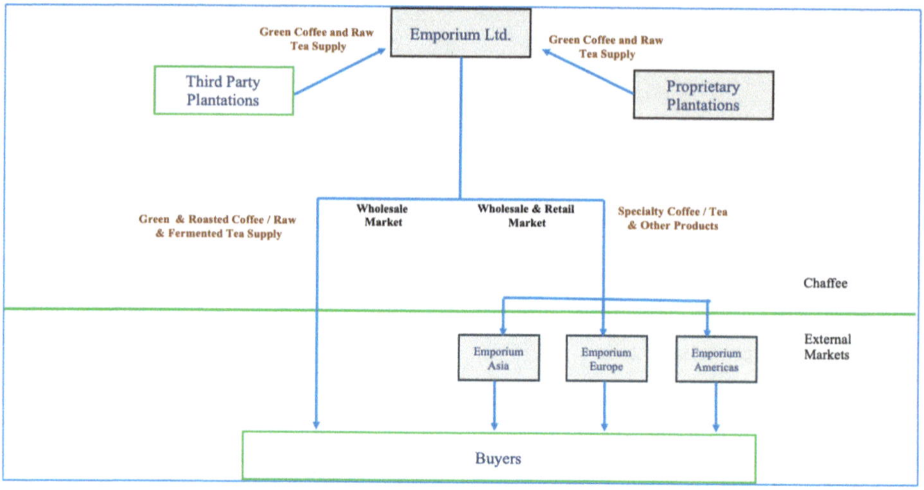

Fig. 17.3 Corporate structure II

necessity of building up stocks to permit efficient fulfillment of orders and the expectation that competitive pressures might require more generous deferred payment terms.

Preliminary discussions with working capital financiers indicated that terms would likely include a ceiling on gearing of up to 2.0x and a minimum collateral coverage ratio of 1.25x. Based on Emporium's market projections and this research, the requisite total working capital funding for the three subsidiaries was estimated to be in the \$75 mm to \$85 mm range by the end of year 2.

In anticipation of this debt fund-raising (the "Transaction", below), Emporium completed the various steps to establish/operationalize the subsidiaries and to invest the equity capital. Trial sales began, with promising market reactions.

17.3 Transaction

Preliminaries

Emporium engaged an international bank—AgroFinco Europa (AFT)—to underwrite a term working capital finance facility. AFT is a market leader in agricultural commodity financing, with an accomplished track record of arranging syndicated and club-style credit facilities such as required by Emporium.

The requested parameters included: (i) a multi-borrower, revolving credit arrangement, with a minimum draw amount; (ii) a committed amount of US$100 mm; (iii) a three-year availability period, with a final repayment at four years, with determined incurrence and maintenance covenants; and (iv) a senior, secured (inventory and receivables) structure with a minimum collateral coverage ratio of 1.25x.

AFT's (retained amount US$20 mm) book-building exercise resulted in an oversubscription of US$30 mm. The deal was circled at US$100 mm with a total of eight participants. Work on documentation began.

Crisis Outbreak

As the lawyers drafted away, Chaffee's financial crisis erupted. Given recent events, the government was left with no alternative but to declare a temporary moratorium on selected international bond payments. Additionally, the CB instituted a forced roll-over of all the outstanding CB notes, a de facto moratorium, and the Treasury froze payments of interest and principal on domestic government bonds. In response to these developments, the rating agencies downgraded Chaffee from B2 to Ca/RD/SD.

AFT immediately hit the brakes on the Emporium syndication. While AFT's three bankers had sold the Emporium facility to the market as a "self-liquidating working capital facility", for the "premier global purveyor of specialty coffee and tea products", featuring a structure with "largely insulated from material, sovereign risks of Chaffee", they recognized that to proceed now, before the dust settled, would be imprudent. The syndicate members supported this view. In particular, all parties agreed that a minimum requirement must be an agreement with the IMF—which they understood the government intended to pursue—and the bondholders.

The government reacted quickly to the crisis, benefiting from its earlier preparatory work. *First,* the Finance Ministry approached the IMF to begin urgent consultations, with the intention of following this with discussions with bondholders. *Second,* the Central Bank activated a pre-arranged standby currency swap arrangement, providing several additional months of foreign exchange coverage. *Third,* from the previously prepared "toolkit", the government authorized a series of measures to insulate the domestic economy against the knock-on effects of the crisis on investment, credit intermediation, production, employment, and consumption, knowing that without such circuit breakers the financial disturbance could set in motion a downward spiral from which the country could struggle to recover.

Deal Repair

The credit evaluation of the transaction contained in AFT placement memorandum supported a strong, positive recommendation. The analysis did identify certain threats tied to the sovereign risk of Chaffee and even discussed a low-probability scenario in which a crisis not dissimilar to the actual event breaks out. In retrospect, they got it wrong.

A meeting takes place with the syndicate members. AFT's risk management and macroeconomic research teams presented the following risk matrix:

	Risk element	Mitigants	Residual risk level
1	Domestic security issues interfering with the cultivation, harvesting, processing, and export of the company's products	The company has been operating for decades in this fraught security context, with no material impact on its business. Were the financial conditions to become dire and long-lasting, then the economic situation could deteriorate significantly, with adverse effects on social stability throughout the country and, in particular in the Hillsiders' areas. Even should this happen, the company feels itself to be well-placed. Over the years, emporium has been a responsible employer and a supportive neighbor to the local Hillsider communities, both of which have earned it enormous goodwill. Additionally, management has developed rigorous business continuity plans.	**Low**

(continued)

(continued)

	Risk element	Mitigants	Residual risk level
2	Adverse developments in the domestic economy and banking markets that might reduce the availability of working capital to the company to fund its business	The risk here is that two developments—No new external funding and a long-term restructuring of the CB notes held by local banks—Could lead to moderately, reduced, systemic credit availability. For emporium, this could result in local banks declining to renew short-term W/C lines of credit, which are important to the business. Analysis indicates that these developments could result in a worst-case scenario in a slowing of growth in credit availability and, possibly, a decline. For emporium, the impact would likely be muted for three principal reasons. First, emporium is a stellar credit in the domestic market and would likely continue to enjoy local bank support in any reasonable downside scenario. Second, initial feedback from the government points to the conclusion that unless the situation really gets bad, trade-related short-term lines will be exempted from any restructuring and/or exchange controls. Third, bank holdings of CB notes have not constrained noticeably credit growth to date. However, combined with the potential for no or limited external capital inflows, this risk of a decline in private credit supply exists. In the worst case, the Jansen Foundation has the capacity to provide liquidity support and has shown itself willing to do so in the past	**Medium**

(*continued*)

(continued)

Risk element	Mitigants	Residual risk level
3 Exchange controls blocking the future remittance of equity capital and/or shareholder loans as may be necessary to support the offshore subsidiary borrowers	Temporary capital controls have been put in place to conserve the country's limited foreign exchange reserves. Their scope and duration will depend on future progress in the negotiations with the IMF and bondholders and the efficacy of structural reforms. Emporium's management believes that were they to approach the government with an application to provide new equity and/or shareholder loans to their overseas subsidiaries, they would receive a positive response, given the company's important contribution to Chaffee's export balances. Additionally, the parent could lengthen the duration of deferred payment terms on the sales to the subsidiaries (creating AP and hence reducing the requisite volume of bank-sourced working capital financing).	**Medium**
4 Government mandated measures that affect adversely the economics of the commercial transactions between emporium and the offshore subsidiary borrowers	Government could take fiscal or regulatory actions that would squeeze the subsidiaries margins (increase the cost of the exported coffee/tea), limit deferred payment terms, and/or mandate minimum dividend remittances from the subsidiaries to the parent as means to increase the inflow of foreign exchange. Management discounted this risk, as it would represent a dramatic change in government practice and could hurt a business that contributes significantly to reserve accumulation of the country over time. Their conclusion is that government would be unlikely to take such actions	**Low**

Based on this matrix, the syndicate discussed whether and under what circumstances the transaction could proceed. All agreed with the need for clarity around the IMF and bondholders as a strict condition precedent. Additionally, the parties agreed on four major changes to the term sheet. These were:

1. The Jansen family foundation would commit to invest additional equity capital in Emporium to provide both a liquidity (against the risk of a decline in the availability of working capital finance) and solvency buffer (against a variety of risk events that could result in a reduction of profitability).

2. Emporium to undertake to increase the duration of deferred payment terms, as may be necessary in the future, to compensate for any adverse liquidity events at the subsidiary level.
3. The collateral coverage ratio to be increased from 1.25 to 1.40x.
4. The pricing on the transaction to be modified—commitment fee to be increased by 25 basis points and the coupon by 100 basis points to maintain the necessary risk-return characteristics.

These terms were reaffirmed with Emporium and the documentation finalized.

Outcome

To reach the point of compliance with the condition precedent concerning the government agreement with the IMF/bondholders took several months. A 36-month Extended Fund Facility (EFF) was approved by the IMF. The bondholder agreement followed. The structural reforms were subsequently approved by the parliament in which the EF worked constructively with the opposition to fashion the legislation. While the long-standing grievances of the Hillsider population were not fixed overnight, the cooperation in parliament, the implementation of new social support programs, and the lifting of the more draconian security measures did improve the political climate.

During this time, bilateral credit—mostly export related—slowly resumed to the country, albeit in modest amounts. Reserve levels and the currency stabilized. Importantly, the measures to insulate the real economy from the damaging effects of the financial crisis were largely effective. While growth remained in negative territory for the next year, the green shoots of economic recovery soon appeared.

Building on the successful trials, Emporium did not wait to begin the full commercialization of its line of specialty coffees and teas. A combination of account payable financing from the parent and the subsidiaries' equity capital supported the business. Sales exceeded projections, as major grocery chains, food and beverage companies, and coffee/tea house groups were attracted to Emporium's fresh product offering in the specialty trade. With these events in the "rear view mirror", the AFT syndication went live.

17.4 Closing: Role of Country Risk

To highlight the role of country risks in the case study, we present a counterfactual narrative, with a less happy ending. Consider this more extreme case:

The same crisis build-up occurs as in the first case. Where events diverge is the policy reaction and capabilities of the government. Recall the three major actions taken:

1. A pre-arranged facility, the currency swap is executed.
2. The government commences serious and good faith discussions with the IMF.
3. From a previously prepared "toolkit", a series of policy actions is rapidly implemented with the objective of limiting the negative impact of the crisis on the real economy and society.

The common themes were competence, realism, and preparation. The government had its faults and made mistakes. These led to the economic imbalances and social tensions, which had contributed over time to a fall from a BB-level sovereign rating. But fortunately, the competent and clear-thinking men and women recruited into key positions within the Central Bank and the Ministry of Finance had understood the potential threats and prepared standby measures, just in case.

In this alternative (counterfactual) reality, no such crisis preparation had been undertaken. Additionally, in the above case, once the storm was upon the country, the political class accepted the need to act and put no obstacles in the way, indeed cooperated across the political and social spectrum to approve the IMF SBA. This time, the opposite happens. Finger-pointing and scrambling for self-protection block constructive responses. In the absence of competence, realism, and preparation, the external financial crisis spills into the real economy like a powerful tsunami smashing onto the shore. Investment, consumption, and employment decline sharply, deepening the recession. Imported foodstuffs and other essential imports such as fuel and medicine become scarcer. The rise in their prices affects the poorer segments of the population heavily, their welfare further exacerbated by job losses and a marked fall in government social spending. NPLs spike, bank solvency comes under pressure, liquidity tightens, and heightened risk aversion leads to a near breakdown in financial intermediation in the system. The incidence and severity of civil violence increase. The popular legitimacy of the NF government is increasingly called into question, even by some traditional supporters. Parliament is unable to coalesce around a constructive dialogue with the IMF and the country's external creditors. Reserve levels decline and the currency, greatly depreciated, becomes inconvertible. Dollars begin to replace the peso as legal tender in the economy. Strike actions, especially in the logistics field (ground transport and shipping), spread. Meanwhile, security measures are intensified. A vicious cycle of violence, repression, and more violence ensues. The NF government's hold on power becomes untenable; the PM resigns, and a coalition is formed, to be soon replaced with another, and another. All the while, the economy drifts downward.

Emporium's business feels the effects. The overseas expansion program and the launch of the specialty coffee and tea lines are delayed indefinitely. Overall production continues at pre-crisis levels, but the increase in costs and a special export tax squeeze margins in local currency terms. Management compensates for a decline in available bank credit by drawing on emergency funding from the Jansen family foundation, but the bigger challenge is in the form of disruptions in domestic transport and shipping through the port. The marked reduction in export volume is only partially compensated by the FX gains due to the dollar denomination of the company's export sales. Conversations with external lenders with which receivable discount facilities are agreed, giving some relief to the company's tight liquidity situation. Traditional buyers fearful of supply disruptions have begun to diversify their sourcing, and Emporium's top line slips moderately. Overall, given Emporium's long tradition in the global coffee and tea markets, and structure of its export-oriented business, the company muddles through, but for the moment, the overseas expansion program remains a shattered dream.

Two years in, the economic and social welfare costs are grave. At last, a broad-based reformist coalition takes power. Beyond certain immediate local imperatives, their first priorities are to reestablish access to external markets and undertake requisite structural reforms. The government reaches out to the IMF. A Standby Arrangement (SBA) is put in place, while longer-term arrangements are discussed with bondholders.

What distinguishes the two cases? Not the structure of the economy and Chaffee's financial markets, nor the country's macroeconomic data in year "Y" or the market reaction to the trifecta of crisis triggers. But the reader knows, because like a poor storyteller, we already spilled the beans! There were two significant differences, which we repeat here.

> *First*:
> Competent and clear-thinking men and women in key positions within the Central Bank and the Ministry of Finance had understood the potential threats and prepared standby measures, just in case.
> *Second*:
> Once the storm was upon the country, the political class accepted the need to act and put no obstacles in the way.

These two observations figure as part of the same phylum, if you will, the institutional framework of the country. Recall that Chaffee's institutions did not deserve an overall high grade. However, noted was the government's focus on supporting the business interests of the agricultural, commercial, and financial elite, admittedly at the expense of many other functions of public policy. As a result, the Central Bank and the Ministry of Finance were staffed with well-educated and qualified officials and operated according to high standards of professionalism. The preparation of crisis response arrangements such as the currency swap line and a tool kit with "circuit breaker" policy measures to mitigate the impact of the financial crisis on the real economy were examples of the benefits of an institutional framework that supports a high degree of professionalism in these organizations.

What should an analyst of a potential debt capital investment in Emporium sitting back in time a few years before the crisis have concluded about the impact of country risks on expected loss. If their crystal ball were focused on our base case, the evaluation would have identified weaknesses/threats around the festering security problems, the growing fiscal imbalance, and serious questions related to the debt structure/trajectory and ultimately debt sustainability. Additionally, however, the positive of the quality of crisis management should have been recognized and credited. A degree of confidence is justified that even if the country encounters headwinds, the crisis management capabilities should soften the impact of such a disturbance, all things being equal. Given these conclusions, a good analyst would have counseled her colleagues in the portfolio and risk management functions to focus on medium-term exposure to companies with strong financial foundations (of course), and most importantly, solid export businesses, where the generation of foreign-currency cash flow would generate hard currency funds for debt service, provide natural FX hedging, and represent a source of such foreign exchange resources for the government and benefit the "don't kill the goose that lays the golden eggs" rule, where support and/or a lack of foolish interference from the authorities for the business would be most likely. In other words, she would have supported exposure to Emporium!!! Other folders on her desk—long dated capital to non-export sector borrowers—for example, or subordinated debt to a local bank for another, would have been viewed with greater skepticism.

Alternatively, had the analyst been faced with a Chaffee lacking the competence, realism and preparation within the Central Bank and Ministry of Finance, that is our alternative narrative, would she have still supported the Emporium proposal? A fair question. Given our confidence in her, let's assume she would have counseled for a smaller amount and shorter duration, but would have still recommended approval. Why do we surmise this? Given Emporium's characteristics, the company's resilience to a crisis environment is high. Only in a total meltdown and with a subsequent long-term stagnation in the country, would Emporium's inherent strengths be threatened to a point where credit impairment becomes highly probable.

This observation brings us to the most important (and admittedly obvious) takeaway—the key in country risk analysis lies in how a specific set of economic and political risk drivers affects the specific investee and the structure in which the capital is provided. Much of the time, the force of the sovereign environment overwhelms the idiosyncratic characteristics of the investee on a standalone basis. But not always. Transaction structure enhancing the strengths of the investee, as in the case of our Emporium deal, can leave the residual risk of a transaction in a place where the probability-adjusted risk-return outcome is satisfactory even when the "boat is navigating troubled waters!"

18

Summary Learnings

Scenes from the Four Case Studies by Richard Marney

18.1 Summary

In the proceeding chapters, we presented four case studies. Each was designed to illuminate distinct facets of country risk and its critical role in emerging market investment analysis. To achieve this goal, we sketched out diverse landscapes:

R. Marney, P. Waeber, *The Emerging Markets Investor's Guide to Country Risk*,
https://doi.org/10.1007/978-3-032-26824-2_18

1. The sovereign ratings varied, with the narratives playing out in economies ranging from a vibrant BBB country to a Ca jurisdiction, mired in a debt default/country.
2. The nature of the business was different in each case. We covered a green energy company, an infant nutritional product manufacturer, a commercial bank, and a coffee and tea producer, processer, and exporter.
3. The position in the capital structure extended from senior secured debt to equity.
4. Lastly, each investment decision played out in the face of different challenges: (i) for our green energy company, a strategic pivot for a tech company; (ii) a market-entry decision for the global infant nutrition company; (iii) a bank debt refinancing at a problematic time; and (iv) an overseas, vertical integration for an agribusiness company to the backdrop of a severe financial crisis in its home market.

Together, while differing significantly, the four collectively underscore a unified truth—country risk is not a peripheral concern but a central determinant of investment success or failure.

Below, we touch on a three key themes.

1. The Macro-Firm Nexus

The central lesson from all four cases is that investment analysis must operate on two interconnected levels: the macro (country) and the micro (firm). A brilliant business plan can be rendered unviable by a hostile macro environment, while a country's strengths can amplify a company's prospects. And well-positioned and managed companies can thrive despite adverse macroeconomic or political environments.

Our Cases:

Case Study 1: Tomorrow's Energy

The company's technological prowess and market position were strong, but the ultimate strategic decision was dictated by macro factors: political polarization causing policy volatility and geoeconomic tensions threatening supply chains.

Case Study 2: Global Nutrition

The investment's entire viability was a bet on the country's political future. The analysis began not with financial projections but with an assessment of political risk and the efficacy of mitigation strategies (JV partners, political risk insurance).

Case Study 3: Enterprise Bank

The bank's standalone metrics were sound, but its fate was inextricably linked to sovereign risk. The refinancing structure was heavily influenced by stress-testing scenarios based on potential macroeconomic shocks (currency devaluation, asset quality deterioration). The quality of management and the financial resilience/commitment of the shareholders acted as underlying strengths.

Case Study 4: Emporium

Emporium's outstanding global brand and idiosyncratic financial resilience reflected its export-oriented, hard-currency-generating business model. However, investor perceptions could not be entirely divorced from the company's home market. Chaffee's foundational political and economic weaknesses morph into a debt crisis, just as an important fundraising approaches closure, and threaten to derail the effort. However, sound crisis management capabilities within the government stabilize this situation sufficiently to put the transaction back on track.

2. A Multidimensional and Dynamic Risk Taxonomy

Country risk is not monolithic or static. Country characteristics are interrelated and the risk elements thereunder and dynamic and at times unpredictable. The use of the concept of the Investor's Rutter allows us to appreciate more easily the imagery of surging winds and the rise and fall of waves as the mariner navigates his ship toward the home port, as an investor navigates changing economic, political, and market conditions during an investment's life. In this spirit, the cases demonstrate the need to analyze a spectrum of interlocking and evolving risks. These include:

- Political and Regulatory Risk: Shifting government policies (Tomorrow's Energy), election cycles (Global Nutrition), and institutional effectiveness (Enterprise Bank, Emporium)

- Macroeconomic and Financial Risk: Fiscal health, debt sustainability, FX regime stability, and vulnerability to external shocks (all cases)
- Sovereign and Transfer Risk: The risk of default on sovereign debt and the imposition of capital controls that block fund transfers (Enterprise Bank, Emporium)
- Legal and Governance Risk: Rule of law, contract enforcement, intellectual property protection, and corporate governance standards (Tomorrow's Energy, Enterprise Bank)
- Geoeconomic Risk: The impact of global tensions, sanctions, tariffs, and supply chain fragmentation (TE, Emporium)
- Environmental and Social Risk: Climate change vulnerability (all cases) and social inequality leading to instability (Chaffee)

3. Active Risk Mitigation

The interrelated and dynamic nature of country risk requires active risk mitigation for successful investing. As the counterfactuals reinforce, building flexibility into transaction structure and timing as well can make the difference between positive and highly negative outcomes. Consider a few examples:

- Structural: Using instruments like A-B loans (Enterprise Bank) to benefit from preferred creditor status
- Financial: Adjusting pricing (Enterprise Bank, Emporium), requiring capital buffers (Enterprise Bank), and securing political risk insurance (Global Nutrition)
- Strategic: Choosing joint ventures with local partners (Global Nutrition), phasing investments, and selecting business models that align with core competencies and minimize exposure (Tomorrow's Energy's choice of solar storage over EV manufacturing)
- Contractual: Negotiating investment agreements with stabilization clauses and international arbitration provisions (Global Nutrition)

In conclusion, an emerging market investor must be both a financial analyst and a student of political economy, not to mention having fluency in non-traditional, but increasingly important risk areas such as climate change. The cases of Tomorrow's Energy, Global Nutrition, Enterprise Bank, and Emporium illustrate that the most successful investments are those where a deep understanding of country-specific risks is seamlessly integrated into every stage of the investment process—from initial screening and due diligence to structuring, pricing, and ongoing portfolio management.

The Investor Rutter's focus on process reminds us of the ongoing imperative to monitor and react to evolving macroeconomic, market, institutional, political, social, environmental, and geopolitical developments throughout the investment's life.

18.2 Application of the Investor's Rutter

As promised above, we present here one point of view on the application of the Investor's Rutter to the four cases. As with many questions, there is no single right answer.

Case Study 1: Tomorrow's Energy

A suggested result appears in (Fig. 18.1):

Marcadia's fundamentals are generally quite strong. The country benefits from a demographic dividend, boasts a highly educated workforce, and has experienced robust economic growth and a deep financial system. However, the playing field is increasingly fraught with geoeconomic headwinds (threat of tariffs/sanctions) and complete dependence on imported energy and

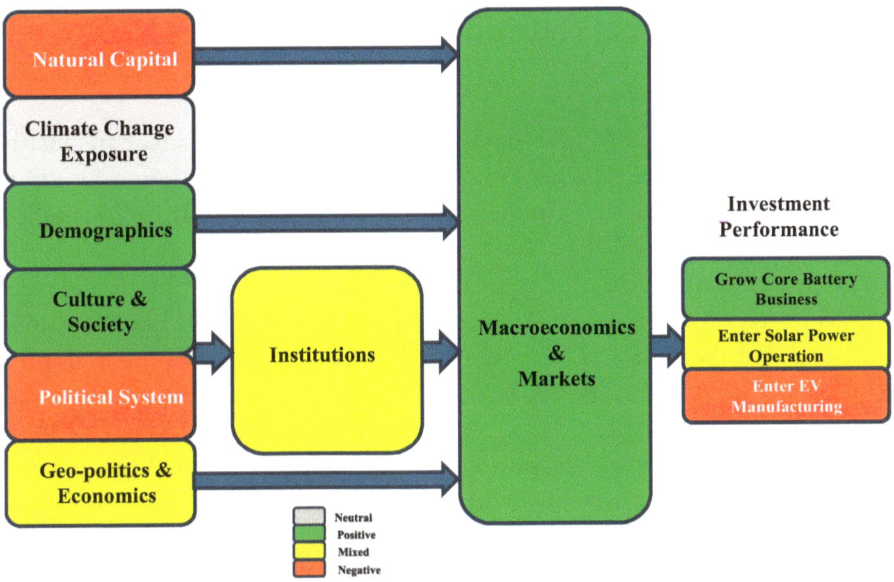

Fig. 18.1 Case Study 1—suggested IR result

critical minerals. The country's institutional framework is strong but has begun to display cracks. The "rules" are becoming unstable due to heightened political polarization, leading to volatile and unpredictable policy with respect to the green economy. The judiciary, while respected, is slow, creating enforcement risk.

The company's initial success has been built on leveraging Marcadia's strong and innovation-focused human capital and benefiting from periods of supportive government policy. The Investor's Rutter analysis has highlighted the convergence of political policy risk and external geoeconomic risk as a major hazard, especially for a capital-intensive, long-gestation project like an EV JV. Tomorrow's Energy's board used the Rutter process to stress-test the strategic alternatives against the volatile "rules of the game". The EV JV, while aligned with market opportunity, was dangerously exposed to these hazards. The solar storage option, by contrast, was closer to TE's core competency, required less capital, had a shorter breakeven time, and was benefiting from a nascent cross-party consensus on energy security.

The Rutter dictated a strategic pivot away from the riskier, headline-grabbing opportunity and toward the more defensible, adjacent opportunity that better navigated the prevailing country risks. The decision was a direct result of interpreting evolving signals (political fragmentation, sanctions) rather than relying on Marcadia's otherwise strong static fundamentals.

Case Study 2: Global Nutrition

A suggested result (Fig. 18.2):

Solera has moderate fundamentals: balanced economy, adequate institutions, but high inequality, a persistent current account deficit, and an underutilized agricultural sector. The key fundamental is a recent political shock (election of the UPP).

The institutions are in a state of active, deliberate flux. The new government is rewriting them to address social inequity, using tools like investment incentives and the threat of land reform. The critical hazard is the high probability that these new rules could be rewritten again after the next election (political/regulatory risk).

The investment case is compelling but exists solely because of the new government's policies. The Investor's Rutter makes clear that this is not a typical macroeconomic bet but a pure political risk bet. The primary hazard is the opposition NDF winning the next election and dismantling the supportive policies.

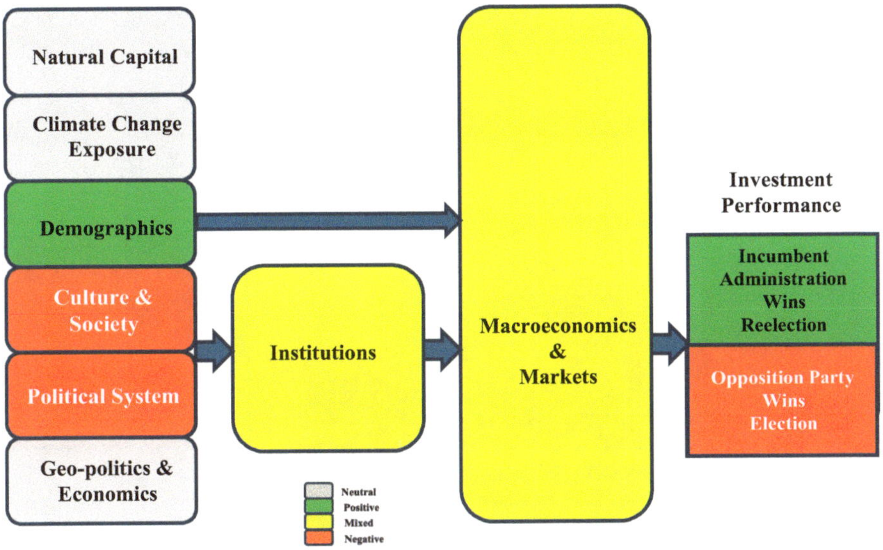

Fig. 18.2 Case Study 2—suggested IR result

The Investor's Rutter process forces the investor to focus first on mitigating the paramount political risk before arguing over financial price. Navigation required building layers of defense: (1) structural (JV with a powerful local partner for political insulation), (2) financial (political risk insurance to cover "creeping expropriation"), and (3) process (phased investment contingent on the political landscape).

The Investor's Rutter framed the entire decision. The question was not "Is this NPV positive?" but "Can we sufficiently mitigate the political risk to make this bet?" The investment process was navigated in reverse—mitigation strategy first, and financial modeling second.

Case Study 3

A suggested result (Fig. 18.3):

Aurora's fundamentals are weak and deteriorating. Its economy is undiversified (reliant on copper/tourism), its institutions are weak, and it suffers from governance issues (related-party lending, light-touch supervision). The playing field is vulnerable to external shocks.

The role of the institutional framework in the economy and markets is impaired. The central bank lacks independence, the judiciary is seen as biased, and financial regulation is underdeveloped. This creates an environment

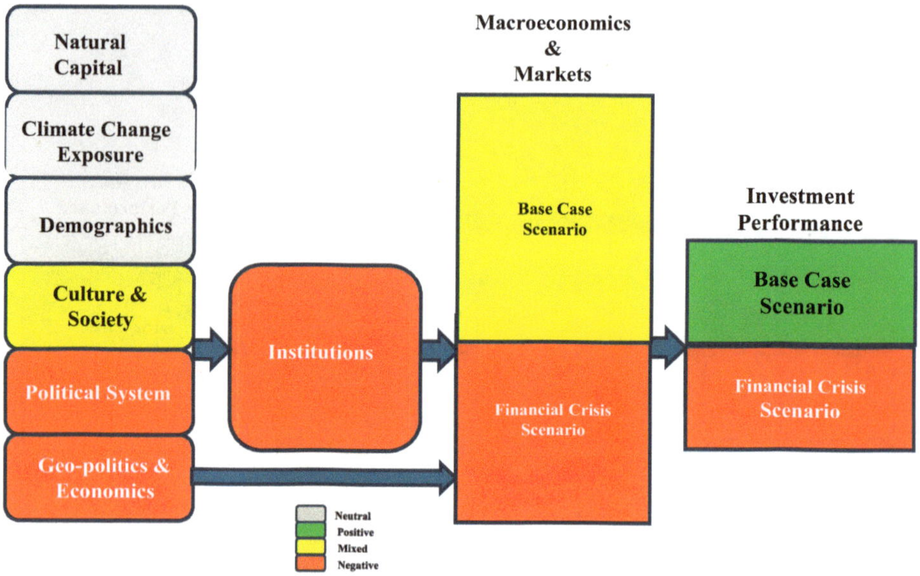

Fig. 18.3 Case Study 3—suggested IR result

where idiosyncratic bank strengths can be overwhelmed by sovereign weaknesses. Enterprise Bank is a well-managed financial institution, with competent management and strong shareholders. The bank's operating results and key financial metrics are solid. Overall, Enterprise Bank is an example of a "good bank in a bad country".

The Investor's Rutter analysis highlights that Enterprise Bank's fate is tied to Aurora's. The hazards are sovereign-driven: a break in the currency peg, a macroeconomic shock hurting asset quality, and a capital flow reversal causing a liquidity crisis. The prospective lender—EM Finco—used the Rutter to rigorously stress-test EB's balance sheet against sovereign-level shocks (FX devaluation, NPL spikes). This proved that even a "good bank" can be broken by a "bad country".

The navigation response was to engineer resilience into the transaction structure: (1) an equity raise to create a solvency buffer, (2) stricter covenants on OCP and concentrations, (3) a shareholder capital backstop promise, and (4) increased pricing to compensate for the sovereign risk that couldn't be fully mitigated. The Investor's Rutter enforced the principle of the "sovereign ceiling". It forced the investor to look past the bank's standalone metrics and navigate based on the treacherous sovereign waters in which the bank sailed, leading to a heavily fortified transaction structure.

Case Study 4

A suggested result (Fig. 18.4):

Chaffee faces poor fundamentals. The country is characterized by deep social fractures, extreme inequality, dangerously high public debt, and a corrupt political system. The playing field is primed for a crisis.

This case highlights a contrast. The formal rules are bad. However, the Rutter focuses on how institutions act in a crisis. Here, the competence and preparedness of key institutions (the Central Bank and Ministry of Finance) were the differentiating factor. Benefiting from staff that had worked in global, public, and multilateral organizations and private financial institutions, they had a "toolkit" ready (currency swaps, circuit-breaker policies). Their responses greatly lessened the fallout from the financial crisis. The Investor's Rutter analysis would distinguish between the static risk (which was high) and the dynamic response. The key signal to interpret was not the debt-to-GDP ratio, but the quality of crisis management.

In this context sat Emporium. A respected global brand, the company's resilient, export-oriented business model able to generate precious hard currency insulates them greatly from the country's liquidity stresses and positions them well in the eyes of global market investors. Notwithstanding these positive characteristics, Emporium could not exit entirely the shadow of the

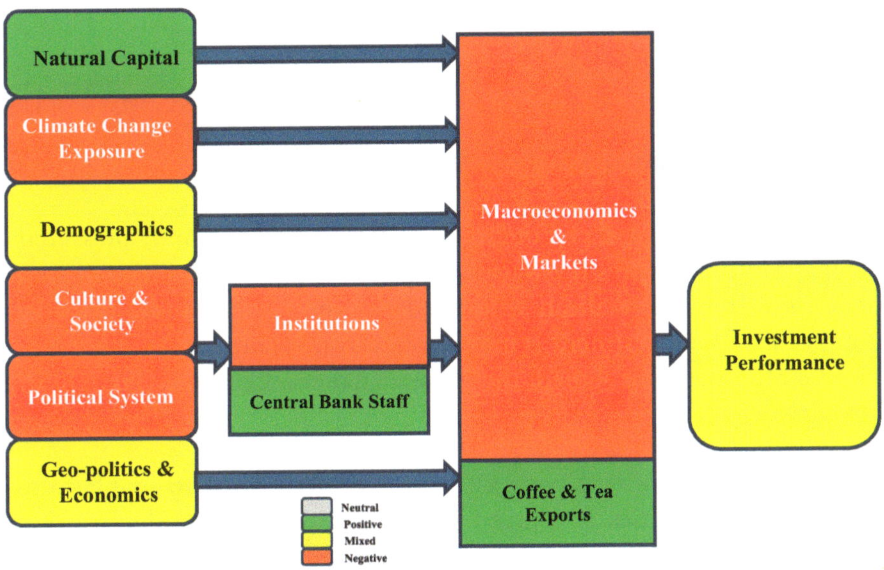

Fig. 18.4 Case Study 4—suggested IR result

country's sovereign default, currency collapse, capital controls, and social unrest. Lenders still adjusted their terms (higher fees, better collateral coverage) to account for the residual risk, but they did not abandon the journey because they trusted the "captains" (competent technocrats within the government and Emporium's managers/shareholders) to navigate the storm.

The Investor's Rutter showed that even in the worst-playing field, the quality of institutional action can be a more important navigational signal than the static fundamentals. It taught investors to look for evidence of preparedness and competence, which can create pockets of safe investing even in a high-risk country.

18.3 Counterfactuals

In Part III, we presented a series of counterfactuals. In that set, the cases worked off the original, unfavorable outcomes, to show how flexibility with respect to amount, structure, use of proceeds, and timing could strengthen the investment's fundamentals to deliver a superior result. Here we will follow the opposite track, by taking the four Part IV cases and showing how decisions and circumstances can convert their favorable into impaired investment outcomes.

Readers should consider whether any modification in the above graphic depictions of the Investor's Rutter or their own versions to accommodate the new facts are necessary.

We offer our views below.

Case Study 1: Tomorrow's Energy

The board sees the market potential of electric vehicles and, pressured by National Motors, ignores the warning signs of political volatility and geoeconomic risk. They move ahead with the EV joint venture under the original assumptions. The investment is massive and front-loaded.

A year after the JV is signed, the picture changes. Consider (Fig. 18.5):

Events are:

1. A center-right coalition wins a surprise election. True to its platform, it cancels EV subsidies and green energy tax credits. Simultaneously, the "Powerhouse Republic" (PR) imposes secondary sanctions on Marcadia for its ties to Aurelis, blocking access to critical battery minerals.

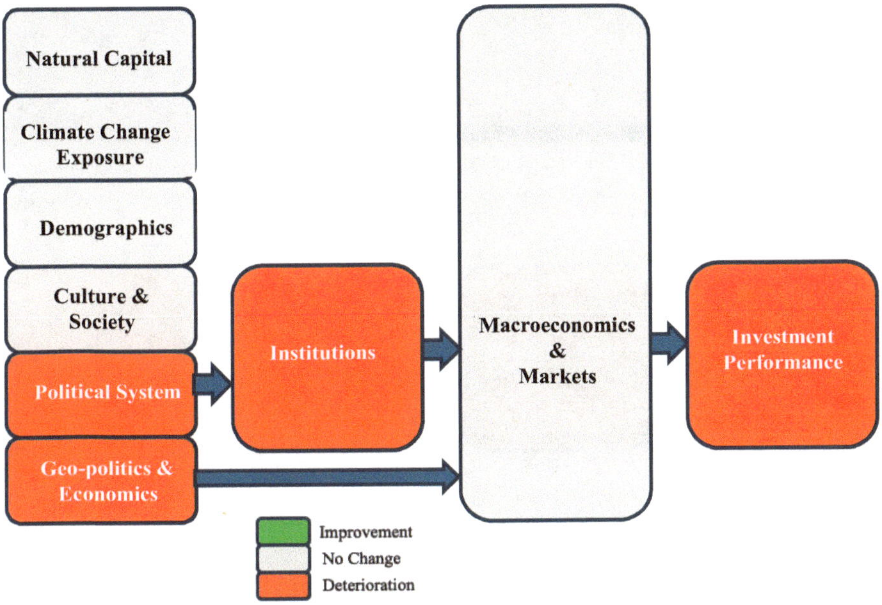

Fig. 18.5 Case Study 1 counterfactual—suggested IR result

2. Tomorrow's Energy is trapped. The JV is bleeding cash due to evaporated demand and soaring input costs. National Motors, itself struggling, is accused of misappropriating TE's battery IP. The slow judicial system offers no recourse. Tomorrow's Energy's core, profitable battery business is dragged down by the financial drain of the JV, requiring a painful bailout from GTI. Shareholder value is destroyed.

Again, the crucial importance of flexibility is demonstrated. The timing was wrong for a transformative, policy-dependent bet. The structure (a deep, complex JV with a local player) was inappropriate for a climate of institutional uncertainty. Flexibility meant pivoting to a smaller, less politically exposed, and core-adjacent opportunity (solar storage) that could weather the storm.

Case Study 2: Global Nutrition

Eager to secure first-mover advantage, Global Nutrition dismisses the political risk as temporary noise. It forgoes the lengthy process of finding a local JV partner and negotiating PRI. It makes a full, upfront investment to build a

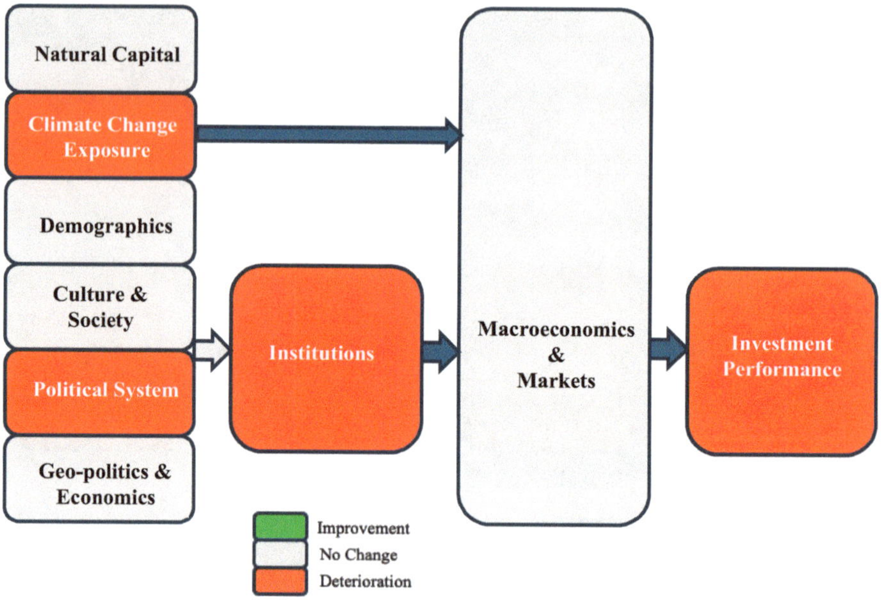

Fig. 18.6 Case Study 2 counterfactual—suggested IR result

large-scale production facility, betting the current government will last. Their bet turns out badly (Fig. 18.6).

Events are:

1. Eighteen months later, the opposition NDF wins the election. Citing fiscal responsibility and nationalism, it immediately rolls back the "Family and Food Program", cancels all foreign investor incentives, and labels the previous government's deals as "corrupt giveaways".
2. At the same time, severe drought ravages the domestic dairy sector. To remedy local shortages in supply, the government refuses to implement the promised tariff protections on imported formula and is forced to provide subsidies on these foreign products to ensure availability.
3. Global Nutrition is left with a state-of-the-art facility that it cannot run profitably. It faces a flood of cheaper imported product and receives no government support. Its investment is stranded. The legal battle to seek compensation is expected to take a decade in Solera's courts. The massive write-down cripples Global Nutrition's regional strategy.

The lesson in flexibility—the amount of capital deployed—was reckless without mitigation. Flexibility meant structuring the investment in phases. A smaller initial phase could have proven the concept and built relationships without overexposure. The flexibility to form a JV and purchase PRI were not just checkboxes; they were essential shields against a predictable political cycle.

Case Study 3: Enterprise Bank

The "It's Just a Refi" Approach EM Finco's portfolio management team, under pressure to deploy capital, overrules the risk team's stringent requirements. They argue the A-B loan structure with the GDB is mitigation enough. They approve the refinancing without the equity raise CP and the shareholder capital backstop, accepting only a modest price increase. Storm clouds arrive (Fig. 18.7).

Events are:

1. The predicted macro-financial shock occurs. Copper prices crash, triggering a currency crisis. The peg breaks, and the Cuprum devalues by 40%. EB's "naturally hedged" borrowers cannot service their foreign currency debts as their local currency earnings collapse. NPLs spike to 25%.

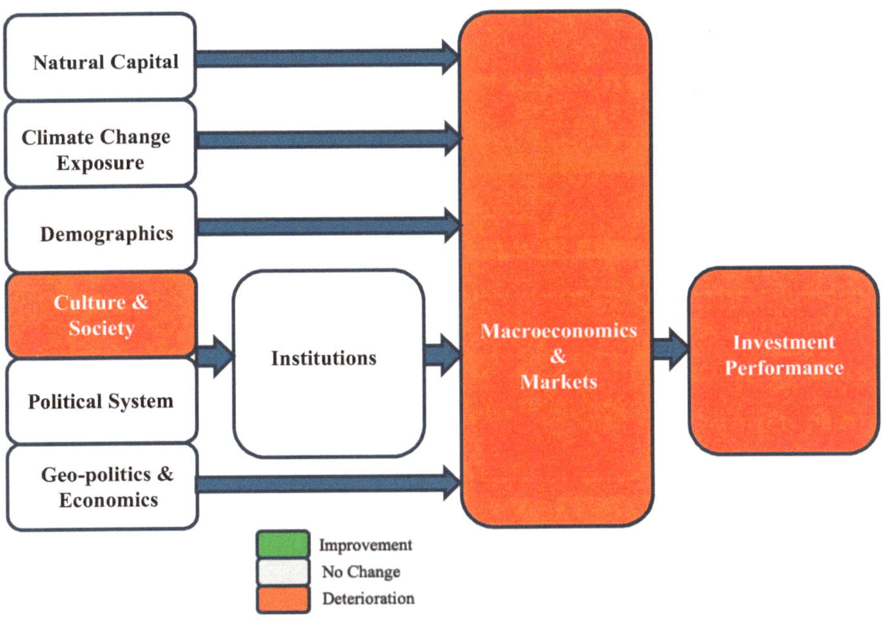

Fig. 18.7 Case Study 3 counterfactual—suggested IR result

2. Enterprise Bank's capital is wiped out by provisioning requirements. The Mark family, facing losses across their portfolio, refuses to inject new capital. The bank breaches regulatory capital limits. The GDB-led restructuring is chaotic and painful for all creditors, including EM Finco, which faces significant losses on what was supposed to be a senior loan. The lack of a pre-agreed equity backstop turned a crisis into a catastrophe.

There is another lesson in flexibility. Flexibility here meant the ability to walk away or to dictate terms. EM Finco's power as the largest existing lender allowed it to force structural changes that improved the credit's resilience. Flexibility meant understanding that in a weak sovereign, a strong covenant package and capital buffers are not optional; they are the only lifeboats.

Case Study 4: Emporium

Confident in Emporium's standalone strength, the syndicate lead ignores the building macroeconomic storm clouds. They rush to close the facility before the government's crisis erupts, using the original terms. The deal closes. Their mistake soon becomes evident (Fig. 18.8).

Events are:

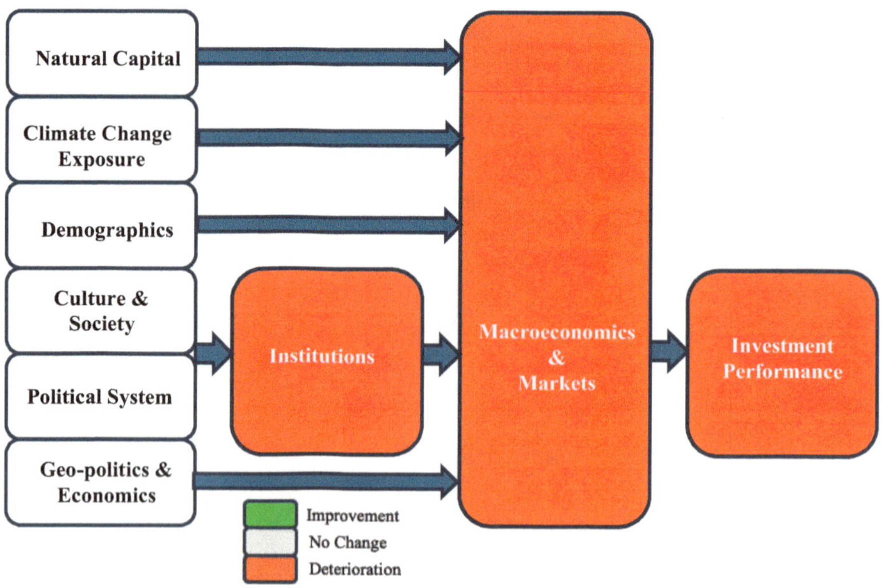

Fig. 18.8 Case Study 4 counterfactual—suggested IR result

1. Soon thereafter, Emporium senses that the government may soon be forced to declares a debt moratorium and impose strict capital controls, which would likely extend to export proceeds, requiring Emporium to repatriate the foreign currency directly to the Central Bank. To ensure liquidity, Emporium draws down the new facilities immediately to fund operations.
2. Two weeks later, the government acts as Emporium suspected. Chaffee declares a debt moratorium and imposes strict capital controls affecting Emporium. The lenders are now dependent on the successful outcome of a sovereign debt restructuring.

Again, we have another lesson in flexibility: the critical flexibility was in timing. AFT's decision to hit "pause" was the most important risk mitigation tool available. It would have allowed them to wait for clarity, assess the government's crisis response (a key part of the Rutter), and then re-make a call on whether to disburse at all. Sometimes, the most appropriate action is a deliberate delay.

18.4 Closing: The Investor's Imperative

The journey through these four cases leads to one inescapable conclusion: in emerging markets, country risk is not a variable to be modeled—it is the environment in which investing takes place. To ignore it is to sail a ship without charts.

The successful investor, therefore, must adopt a dual discipline: first, the rigorous, quantitative analysis of the firm, its cash flows, and its competitive moat; and second, and just as rigorously, the qualitative, dynamic analysis of the sovereign, its institutions, and its political economy. As these cases demonstrate, the second discipline does not merely inform the first; it often dictates its very terms.

The ultimate tool is not a spreadsheet formula, but a process—the ongoing, active navigation embodied by the Investor's Rutter. It demands humility to recognize that even the best-laid financial plans can be overturned by a change in government, a shift in global alliances, or a sudden crisis. And it demands creativity to build the structural, financial, and strategic mitigants that provide resilience. Underlying this creativity is a range of competencies—not just as a financier, but as a strategist, a diplomat, and a student of history. The greatest returns in emerging markets will always flow to those who understand the country as deeply as they understand the company.

19

Closing: Charting Risky Waters

Here we summarize the central learnings of the book.

We undertake this task through the telling of fictional tales of two mariners. Each is an experienced sailor. On the same day, both will start a journey halfway around the world from Fragrant Harbor to Caledonia. Both carry the same valuable cargo. Timeliness is important for the commercial success of their voyages. The first to arrive will command a far higher price.

In this chapter, we *first* present each tale and then map the action of these tales against the Investor's Rutter's four levels of endowment, institutions, context, and the economic and, ultimately, investment outcomes; and *second*, based on the tales' messages, we close with key reflections.

R. Marney, P. Waeber, *The Emerging Markets Investor's Guide to Country Risk*,
https://doi.org/10.1007/978-3-032-26824-2_19

19.1 The Tales

Departing the Port by Richard Marney

The First Tale

Captain Emma of the Steadfast plots her journey to follow a longer but well-charted route. She has navigated this course many times in the past. The itinerary has predictable monsoon patterns, known currents, and a few hidden shoals. There have been no pirate predations in memory. She knows she will encounter storms, but they are expected to be manageable at this time of the year. Along the route, there are friendly city-states and established ports of call. There, she can reliably acquire fresh water, and provisions, and, if necessary, repair her ship. Over the years, the local rulers have always received peaceful travelers well. Their charges for docking and provisioning have been reasonable. Even when crew have misbehaved in port, the local laws have been clear and fairly enforced. In these locations, the harbor masters share information on any new hazards along the route that might be known.

In the days leading up to her departure, Emma has examined carefully the hull, deck, masts, sails, and riggings of the Steadfast. In addition, she has ensured that the crew is all present and rested. Despite her many years on the seas and her choice of a well-known homeward route, she recognizes that the

Steadfast and her crew are the essential preconditions for her voyage along her chosen course.

The Steadfast sails the next day on the tide.

Emma arrives in Caledonia only a week after the estimated time. The journey was arduous—there were storms—but without major catastrophe. The hold is full, the crew healthy, and the voyage very profitable.

The Second Tale

Captain Don of the Swift Return looks to arrive first to sell his cargo before Emma and so maximize his profits. He opts for a theoretically shorter route, which appears tempting on a map. This choice is made, despite the need to passage through the "Dragon's Claw", a treacherous strait through which he has never journeyed. His first mate counsels against this route. He knows it well. There are unpredictable, violent squalls, especially in the area around the Dragon's Claw. The weather itself will be a merciless adversary. In many places, there are perilous, swirling currents. He warns of unmapped reefs and shoals. What worries him most are the long stretches of desolate shores, where it would be difficult to anchor safely and along which there is the constant threat of piracy. Where there are settlements, the locals cannot be trusted. The ports are extractive, charging exorbitant fees for foul water and poor supplies. In each, there is the risk of arbitrary confiscation of cargo by the local warlord. Information is scarce and unreliable.

In the days leading up to his departure, Don and a few of his crew have enjoyed the saloons and the ladies of the Fragrant Harbor. The night before departure, on his return to the ship, he learns from his first mate that the repairs have been completed, although not to the first mate's full satisfaction. Additionally, a number of the crew have deserted. Don's response is the Swift Return sails on the morning tide, as he exudes confidence in his ability to overcome any challenges and reminds the first mate that his share of the profits will be lower if Emma arrives in Caledonia before them.

Captain Don and Swift Return indeed sail on the morning tide.

During the voyage through the Dragon's Claw, the Swift Return is battered by monstrous waves and treacherous currents. The ship eventually exits the straits, only to confront a powerful storm. To take shelter, they approach an unknown shore, where the ship runs aground on a hidden reef. While making emergency repairs, they are attacked by pirates. After a violent fight, his crew drives them off. Thereafter, they enter a port for provisioning and more-lasting repairs. At the hands of the local chief, Don is forced to trade away most of his remaining cargo. Months later, he arrives in Caledonia. His ship is heavily damaged, his hold nearly empty, and his venture a financial disaster.

Mapping

	Mariner – Positive (Emma)	Investor - Positive	Mariner – Negative (Don)	Investor - Negative
Endowment	• Well maintained vessel • Fully-rostered, veteran crew • Longer, but familiar, safe route chosen	• Low climate change exposure • Strong/resilience natural capital • Robust human capital • Stable politics / civil society • Underdeveloped infrastructure	• Poorly maintained vessel • Lasr minute additions to crew • Shorter, but unfamiliar and potentially dangerous route selected	• High climate change exposure • Waak/fragile natural capital • Deficient human capital • Unstable politics / civile society • Underdeveloped infrastructure
Enablers	• Climate and sea conditions are generally accommodative • Friendly ports for provisioning and repairs • No piracy or similar threats	• Strong institutional framework, with solid rule of law, effective judiciary, and competent regulatory capabilities • Effective and credible policy-making	• Potentially very challenging sailing conditions, due to winds, currents, and tempest • Long stretches of coast line without safe harbor • Few ports for provisioning and repairs, and the few are controlled by bad actors • Parts of the route are known for pirate attacks	• Impaired institutional framework, with weak rule of lar, ineffective judiciary, and inconsistent regulatory capabilities • Ineffective policy-making, with weak market credibility
Context	A few storms, but these are easily navigated	• Strong macro-economic metrics • Financial system – well-performing and highly supportive of sustainable economic growth • Overall – highly positive investment climate	• Storm forces emergency repairs • Crew suffers pirate attack • A stop at a port for provisioning and repairs results in loss of most of the cargo	• Weak macro-economic metrics • Financial system adversely affected by domestic and external imbalances • Overall – weak investment climate
Outcome	The journey is completed nearly on time, the crew is safe, and the voyage is a great commercial success	Country conditions act to enhance investment performance	• Months later, the ship arrives in Caledonia. • The ship is heavily damaged, his hold nearly empty • The venture a financial disaster.	Country conditions act to weaken investment performance

Source: The authors.

The reader recalls from Chap. 11 the depiction of the progression of the investment climate to the navigator's Rutter and then finally to the Investor's Rutter. Above, we borrow from this depiction for a map of the characteristics of Emma's and Don's voyages against the four levels of the two Rutters. On each level, we also populate verticals for positive and negative characteristics of the Investor's Rutter.

As shown earlier, differences in endowment lay the predicate for the outcome for both the mariners (primarily the route to be followed, but also the ship and the crew) and investment in the country (political and civil orientation and stability, natural and human capital, etc.). Enablers—climate and sea conditions, availability of friendly reports, and the like for the mariners, and institutions for investors—evolve from these foundations and determine the context and outcome for both a ship navigating the seas and an investor the investment life cycle.

The differences between the positive and negative scenarios are intentionally stark, to underscore the cumulative impact of institutional quality and context on long-term outcomes.

19.2 Summary and Reflections

Summary of the Tales

As our two captains experienced, itinerary ***(investment jurisdiction, deal, and structure)*** selection is not just about distance and timing ***(investment return potential)***, but about the quality of the route ***(investment risks and mitigants)***. Along this route, the prevailing conditions ***(enabling institutions and the macroeconomic/market context)*** materially influence the outcome of the journey—manageable seas versus treacherous waters, safe versus threatening harbors, and the like. Shorter routes through hostile waters ***(challenging country, market, and sector)*** can offer higher headline returns yet be value-destructive despite apparent efficiency. Throughout the voyage, skilled and experienced mariners will be constantly on guard for changes in winds and tides ***(investor monitoring of macroeconomic, market, political, and environmental conditions)*** every-ready to respond and safeguard the ship and crew ***(preemptive restructuring, recapitalization, and the like).***

Emma proved herself to be a seasoned, methodical navigator. She valued safety, reliable intelligence, and sustainable progress over explosive but risky gains. For our purposes, she represents the disciplined, long-term institutional investor.

In contrast, there was Don. He was the bold, ambitious mariner driven by the promise of quick riches and the belief that his skill can overcome any obstacle. He represents the speculative, return-chasing investor, often underestimating systemic risks.

In summary, consider:

1. Sound Fundamentals

The crew ***(the various stakeholders)***, ship (***the investee***), cargo ***(the transaction)***, and the route and its sailing conditions (the sovereign and institutional environment over the length of the investment life cycle) are the core, foundational elements. Of the four, the route—the investment climate by another name—is paramount. As our mariners know well and we observed in the brief tales, this conclusion echoes the book's finding that the investment climate is a primary determinant of long-term investment outcomes. Clearly, Emma's fundamentals were stronger. In the absence of a freak storm or rogue wave or fire on board (fraud or systemic tail risk), her success and Don's struggles did not come as a surprise.

2. Risk Versus Return

Don's shorter route promised a faster journey and hence greater profit (***higher investment returns***). Had he been successful, Emma's likely slower course would have translated into a lower profit ***(lower investment return).*** The outlook ***(risk profiles)*** of each differed. But risk is said to be like beauty "in the eye of the beholder", and we have to assume that Don really believed the risks he and his crew of the Swift Return confronted were manageable. However, a more measured view would undoubtedly be that Don's was significantly higher than Emma's. On a risk-return basis? *Ex ante,* the comparison is debatable, but most informed observers would have ranked Emma's projected risk-adjusted return as superior. Indeed, with the benefit of hindsight, Don appears reckless (and a responsible ***investment committee*** would have likely turned him down).

3. Mitigation

Don believed his skill could overcome the environment—navigate treacherous seas, tempest, and pirates ***(investment country context).*** The story argues that some environments are so hostile that no amount of financial engineering or contractual safeguards (***equity back-up funds, risk insurance,*** **etc.**) can fully protect you. Sometimes, the only wise strategy is avoidance. Don should have copied Emma with respect to her approach to the fundamental elements of her voyage, most notably the route (**the country of the investee**).

4. Institutions and the "Virtuous Circle"

Emma's friendly ports and the ecosystem which they support represent nations with virtuous feedback loops (the benefits of ***strong institutions***) beget stability and prosperity, which in turn further strengthen institutions. Don's hostile coasts represent vicious cycles—extractive institutions lead to poverty and instability, which reinforce those same bad institutions. Even had Emma confronted more severe tempests, she would have likely had access to a safe retreat or repairs ***(restructuring or recapitalization)*** and been able to continue her journey. Despite a slight delay in such a case, she would still have had a successful voyage. In investment practice, this is why reform trajectories matter more than headline growth rates in EMDEs.

Box 19.1 The Institutional Roots of Country Risk

Why Nations Fail (Acemoglu and Robinson) *and How Progress Ends* (Frey).

This chapter's mariners' tales echo messages from these two seminal works—why some countries achieve sustained prosperity while others stagnate (*Why Nations Fail*) and even successful societies can regress when institutional balances erode (*How Progress Ends*)—and together help interpret Emma's and Don's fates and reinforce the use of the Investor's Rutter.

Why Nations Fail.

The central thesis is that inclusive political and economic institutions that ensure rule of law, protect competition, encourage investment, and constrain arbitrary power are preconditions for sustained and balanced prosperity for society, while the opposite—extractive institutions—concentrate power and rents within an economic and political elite and stunt economic welfare and development.

How Progress Ends.

The central thesis is progress is not irreversible. Success is fragile. Progress and success depend on a society's ability to manage a delicate balance between two institutional modes: exploration (chaotic, decentralized experimentation for new ideas) and exploitation (controlled, bureaucratic scaling of proven technologies). When institutions become rigid, fail to adapt to technological change, or allow incumbents to block new entrants, progress stalls and stagnation follows. Even countries with inclusive institutions can slide into oligarchy, polarization, and institutional decay when checks and balances weaken, inequality entrenches, or technology and political capture outpace governance.

Mapping to Emma's and Don's Tales.

Emma's world is not static. Storms still come even along a route which she knows well to be generally safe. The difference for her is institutional resilience—safe harbors, friendly ports, available repair yards, trusted harbor masters, reasonable fees, reliable provisioning, fair enforcement, and information sharing. These represent adaptive capacity: courts that function in crises, regulators that respond, and policy frameworks that correct course. These are the *enablers* that convert endowments into positive context and outcome.

Don's environment lacks buffers. When shocks hit (storms, pirates, groundings), there is no credible refuge or remediation—only further extraction. The hostile coasts are extractive institutions. Arbitrary confiscation, extortionate charges, and unreliable information correspond to weak property rights, corruption, and predation—vicious cycles that undermine returns.

Overall, for the Rutter, route quality (the investment climate) dominates distance (headline return potential). Inclusive institutions reduce tail risk, lower transaction costs, and support compounding. Extractive settings promise speed but destroy value. This is the institutional foundation of Emma's success and Don's failure.

Investor Takeaway.

Do not treat institutional quality as a fixed score. The Investor's Rutter must track **trajectories**, not just levels. Reform momentum, political competition, media freedom, and constraint on executive power matter as much as current growth. This is why reform paths outweigh headline GDP prints.

Reflections

1. High Risks but High Rewards

Just as a ship is designed to sail oceans—not remain docked—investments are meant to grow, not just preserve capital. EMDEs carry higher risks (political instability, macroeconomic volatility, weak institutions), but they also offer significantly higher growth potential compared to developed markets. Staying in the "safe harbor" of mature markets may protect you from storms, but it also means missing out on the transformative returns that emerging economies can deliver. Emma understood and managed the risks confronting her ship and succeeded in achieving great profits, while Don didn't. The message is simple and clear: EMDE risks are a reality to be managed and exploited with courage and acumen.

2. Risk and Volatility as Opportunity

A ship and its pilot face storms, waves, and uncertainty—but that's where they prove their worth. Similarly, EMDE investments are risky and volatile. This reality contains opportunity and justifies higher returns. Investors must recognize that not every transaction will be a low maintenance, "home run". That transactions may require remedial work (restructurings, recapitalizations, enforcement and forced sales, etc.) should not be interpreted as anything more than what a mariner confronts (repairs and provisioning) during their voyages.

3. Long-Term Perspective

Ships aren't built for short, cautious trips—they're crafted for long journeys. Investing in EMDEs requires a long-term perspective and perseverance. Short-term setbacks (e.g., market corrections, financial crises, political shifts) are inevitable, but patient investors who focus on structural growth stories—like strong institutions, rising middle-class consumption, or renewable energy transitions—are often rewarded.

4. Flexibility

When a ship sails, even into known waters, the pilot must be prepared for changing seas, as investors in EMDEs must stay agile and be prepared to act boldly. These markets evolve rapidly—the macroeconomic conditions change, regulations shift, new industries emerge, and consumer behavior changes. Staying informed, using local insights, and embracing innovation is key to success. Bold actions to "double down" or simply persevere in working with a troubled asset become necessary, even in the face of risk management hesitation or short-term concerns about investment returns. Equally, decisions to walk away from a transaction pre-investment or to "pull the plug" and confront losses must be entertained, despite internal criticism and negative publicity.

Key thoughts to commit to memory? We suggest the following seven:

1. Recognize country risk is process not a static matrix
2. Develop the means and acumen to read the evolving situation
3. Be realistic around the risks and volatility to be confronted
4. Be confident about achieving returns
5. Adhere to a long-term view
6. When situations warrant, demonstrate boldness, even in the face of immediate internal/external pressures
7. Remember Emma and Don—and choose your route accordingly

Glossary of Key Terms

Adaptive Capacity The ability of a system, institution, or community to adjust to potential damage, take advantage of opportunities, or respond to consequences from climate change, economic shocks, or other external stressors.

See also: Climate Resilience, Climate Risk

Age Structure The distribution of a population by age groups (e.g., youth, working-age, elderly), influencing labor supply, savings, and the potential for a demographic dividend or burden.

See also: Demographic Dividend, Demographic Burden

Artificial Intelligence (AI) Computer systems capable of tasks requiring human intelligence—such as visual perception, decision-making, or natural language processing—used in automation, productivity growth, and technological transformation.

See also: Technological Change

Banking Crisis A situation in which banks experience widespread failures or withdrawals, leading to credit contraction and economic disruption.

See also: Financial Crises, Non-Performing Loans

Capital Flow Management (CFM) Policy measures designed to moderate the volatility of cross-border capital flows, including restrictions on inflows or outflows, to protect financial stability in EMDEs.

See also: Sudden Stops, External Vulnerability.

Climate Resilience The capacity of social, economic, and environmental systems to maintain essential functions during and after climate-related shocks or trends.

See also: Adaptive Capacity, Climate Risk.

Climate Risk The potential for negative financial, social, or environmental consequences from climate change, including **physical risks**(e.g., extreme weather) and **transition risks** (e.g., regulatory shifts toward a low-carbon economy).

R. Marney, P. Waeber, *The Emerging Markets Investor's Guide to Country Risk*,
https://doi.org/10.1007/978-3-032-26824-2

Commodity Curse The paradox in which countries rich in natural resources experience slower economic growth due to volatility, rent-seeking behavior, or poor institutional quality.
See also: Resource Pressures, Institutional Quality

Contagion The spread of financial or economic crises from one country or market to others through trade, financial interconnections, or investor sentiment.

Counterfactual Analysis A method for evaluating decisions by comparing actual outcomes with plausible alternative scenarios, often used for investment strategy and risk assessment.

Country Risk Analysis The assessment of political, economic, financial, and sovereign risks affecting the performance and returns of investments in a country.
See also: Sovereign Risk, Investment Climate

Creative Destruction The process by which innovation and technological change disrupt existing industries and economic structures, creating new growth opportunities while displacing older ones.

Credit Bubbles Rapid increases in lending that drive asset prices beyond sustainable levels, often followed by sharp corrections or crises.
See also: Financial Crises, Non-Performing Loans

Crisis Life Cycle The progression of a financial crisis through phases: pre-crisis buildup, trigger, acute crisis, and recovery/resolution.

Debt Restructuring Negotiation or reorganization of a debtor's obligations to restore liquidity and solvency, applied to sovereigns or corporations.
See also: Sovereign Debt, Sovereign Risk.

Demographic Dividend Economic growth that arises when a population has a relatively large working-age share, assuming productive employment opportunities.
See also: Age Structure, Human Capital Development.

Demographic Burden The economic pressures caused by a high dependency ratio, often due to a large youth or elderly population relative to working-age adults.
See also: Demographic Dividend, Fiscal Space

Development Bargain The implicit trade-off between state-led economic growth and citizen rights, emphasizing the institutional arrangements needed to foster investment and mass prosperity.
See also: Institutional Quality, Mass Flourishing

Downside Risk The potential for an investment or portfolio to incur losses, with a focus on magnitude and probability of adverse outcomes.

Early Warning Systems Frameworks that monitor economic, financial, and political indicators to signal rising probabilities of crises, enabling preventive action.

Economic Nationalism Policies prioritizing domestic industries, capital, and labor through tariffs, trade restrictions, subsidies, or investment screening, often at the expense of global integration.
See also: Geoeconomic Fragmentation, Strategic Autonomy.

Emerging Markets and Developing Economies (EMDEs) Countries undergoing rapid industrialization and economic growth, characterized by high growth potential alongside elevated political, financial, and structural risks.
See also: Country Risk Analysis, Investment Climate

Exchange Rate Regimes The systems by which a country manages its currency relative to others, ranging from free-floating to hard pegs.
See also: Fear of Floating, External Vulnerability

Extractive Institutions Political and economic institutions designed to concentrate wealth or power in the hands of a few, inhibiting broad-based economic growth.
See also: Inclusive Institutions, Institutional Quality.

External Vulnerability Susceptibility of an economy to external shocks, such as volatile capital flows, commodity prices, or global financial crises.
See also: Capital Flow Management, Sudden Stops.

Fear of Floating A reluctance of central banks to allow their currency to fluctuate freely due to concerns about capital flows or inflation.
See also: Exchange Rate Regimes.

Financial Crises Episodes of severe disruptions in financial markets, including banking, currency, and sovereign debt crises, often with systemic economic impacts.

Financial Inclusion Efforts to make financial services accessible and affordable to all segments of society, promoting economic participation and growth.

Financial Stability A condition where the financial system can withstand shocks, allocate resources efficiently, and support sustainable economic activity.

Fintech Technologies that improve financial services delivery, access, and efficiency, including digital payments, lending platforms, and blockchain applications.

Foreign Direct Investment (FDI) Investment by a foreign entity that establishes a controlling interest in a company or asset in another country, often bringing capital, technology, and skills.

Geoeconomic Fragmentation The process by which global economic integration is reduced through competing regional blocs, trade restrictions, investment screening, and fractured supply chains.
See also: Economic Nationalism, Strategic Autonomy.

Geopolitical Risk The potential for political events, conflicts, or tensions to disrupt markets, supply chains, and investment outcomes.

Global Value Chains The international distribution of production processes, with stages located across multiple countries to optimize efficiency and cost.

Governance The traditions and institutions through which authority is exercised, including policy formulation, enforcement, and accountability.

Great Convergence The narrowing of income and productivity gaps between advanced economies and rapidly developing EMDEs.

Human Capital Development The accumulation of skills, education, and health that enhance worker productivity and economic potential.
See also: Demographic Dividend, Technological Change.

Inclusive Institutions Institutions that allow broad participation in economic and political life, fostering innovation, productivity, and equitable growth.

Informal Economy Economic activities not monitored, regulated, or taxed by the government, including small unregistered businesses and self-employment.

Institutional Change The evolution of formal and informal rules, norms, and enforcement mechanisms that shape economic and social behavior.

Institutional Quality The effectiveness, stability, transparency, and fairness of a country's institutions, including legal systems and governance.

Investment Climate The overall environment—including policies, regulations, and institutions—that shapes the risks and returns of investing in a country.

Investment Lifecycle The stages an investment undergoes: initial screening, deal structuring, monitoring, and exit or restructuring.

Investor Behaviour The study of psychological and behavioral factors that influence investment decisions, including biases, heuristics, and market reactions.

Investment Screening Government evaluation of foreign investments for strategic, economic, or national security purposes.

Macroprudential Policies Regulatory measures aimed at reducing systemic financial risk, such as capital buffers, lending restrictions, or stress tests.

Mass Flourishing Widespread innovation, entrepreneurship, and productivity gains that lead to broad-based increases in living standards.

Middle-Income Trap When a country achieves middle-income status but fails to advance to high-income levels due to structural, institutional, or productivity constraints.

Near-Shoring Relocating business operations to nearby countries to reduce supply chain risks and costs.

Non-Performing Loans (NPLs) Loans in default or near-default, often used as a measure of banking sector health.

Optionality The strategic value of retaining the right—but not the obligation—to take future actions under uncertain conditions.

Phased Investment Committing capital in stages, allowing assessment of performance and risk before further commitment.

Political Instability The risk of abrupt changes in government, policies, or social order due to unrest, violence, or institutional failure.

Premature Deindustrialization The early transition of an economy to a services-led structure before fully industrializing, potentially limiting productivity growth.

Procyclical Fiscal Policy Government spending and taxation policies that amplify economic fluctuations, spending more in booms and cutting in recessions.

Property Rights Legally recognized ownership of assets and resources, enforceable by law, essential for market functioning.

Rule of Law The principle that laws apply equally to all, are publicly known, and enforced independently and fairly.

Sovereign-Bank Nexus Interdependence between a government's fiscal health and its domestic banking system, where stress in one can affect the other.

Sovereign Credit Ratings Assessments of a government's ability and willingness to meet its debt obligations, influencing borrowing costs.

Sovereign Debt Government-issued debt instruments used to finance public spending and development projects.

Sovereign Risk The risk that a government will default on debt or fail to honor other financial commitments.

Strategic Autonomy The ability of a country or firm to act independently in economic or geopolitical matters, particularly in a fragmented global economy.
See also: Geoeconomic Fragmentation, Economic Nationalism.

Strategic Flexibility The ability to adapt strategies and reallocate resources quickly in response to market changes, geopolitical events, or new information.

Supply Chain Resilience The capacity of a supply chain to anticipate, withstand, adapt to, and recover from disruptions.

Sudden Stops Abrupt reversals in capital inflows that can trigger severe economic or financial crises.

Technological Change The adoption of new technologies, including AI, automation, digital infrastructure, and industrial upgrades, driving productivity and growth.
See also: Creative Destruction, Artificial Intelligence.

Total Factor Productivity (TFP) The efficiency with which labor and capital inputs are used to produce output; a key driver of long-term growth.

Transaction Costs The costs incurred in making an economic exchange, including search, negotiation, enforcement, and monitoring costs.

Twin Crises Simultaneous banking and currency crises, often amplifying the economic impact.

Index

R. Marney, P. Waeber, *The Emerging Markets Investor's Guide to Country Risk*,
https://doi.org/10.1007/978-3-032-26824-2

R

S

T

FSC
www.fsc.org
MIX
Papier | Fördert gute Waldnutzung
FSC® C083411

Kolibri 360 GmbH
Ferdinand-Jühlke-Straße 7
99095 Erfurt, Deutschland
produktsicherheit@kolibri360.de